Ecological learning theory

Ecological learning theory

Graham Davey

ROUTLEDGE
London and New York

First published 1989
by Routledge
11 New Fetter Lane, London EC4P 4EE
29 West 35th Street, New York, NY 10001

© 1989 Graham Davey

Typeset by Witwell Ltd, Southport
Printed and bound in Great Britain by
Biddles Ltd, Guildford and King's Lynn

British Library Cataloguing in Publication Data

Davey, Graham
    Ecological learning theory.
    1. Learning by animals
    I. Title
    156′.315

Library of Congress Cataloging in Publication Data
also available

ISBN 0–415–01189–2
        0–415–01190–6 (pbk)

For Bess

Contents

List of illustrations

Preface

If one casts an eye over the animal kingdom in general it is surprising how relatively few species have abandoned fixed behavioral patterns in favor of learning abilities. This tends to surprise us largely because the adaptive benefits of learning seem to be quite obvious: learning affords the animal a means to adapt to changes and fluctuations in the environment and even to exploit new niches when required. Yet there are many hidden costs to evolving learning capacities which make the evolution of such capacities a complex process. These costs include the vulnerability of the organism during the period when it is learning essential biological skills, or the possibility of simply learning the "wrong thing." This competition between the selective costs and benefits of learning abilities has led learning mechanisms to evolve in a rather complex way — a way which is frequently dependent on the nature of the species, the habitat it resides in, and its lifestyle. Understanding these processes, the learning mechanisms that result from them, and the biological function they serve is the essence of ecological learning theory.

In recent years, contemporary learning theory has progressed significantly away from simplistic general process theories. The burgeoning in the "constraints on learning" literature of the 1970s led many writers to believe that an understanding of learning could not occur unless the nature and lifestyle of individual species was somewhere included in the explanatory model. Traditional learning theory, of course, had felt no need to do this, believing that basic laws of learning were common to a wide range of different species. Nevertheless, the initial reaction to the fact that there frequently appeared to be "constraints" or "boundaries" to general laws of learning was confused, and often consisted of no more than a catalog of anomalies with no integrative or predictive value.

However, these theoretical problems gave rise to a renewed interest in returning learning theory back to its biological roots, and in particular they attracted the attention of ethologists and evolutionary biologists. They began to raise questions which, although fundamental, had been overlooked for decades by learning theorists: What is the biological function of learning? How does it contribute to inclusive fitness? What selection pressures bear on the evolution of learning processes? Could generalized learning processes ever be selected for? Have basic learning processes evolved separately in different species? and so on.

Ecological learning theory is an attempt to understand learning not just by analyzing and describing the psychological mechanisms that mediate learned behavior, but also by understanding how these mechanisms might have evolved, what selection pressures might have contributed to this evolution, and what biological function that learning serves. To this extent, learning cannot be fully understood without some knowledge of a range of individual species, their ecological niche and lifestyle — and this is quite different from the concentrated study of single species (such as the laboratory rat) which was practiced by traditional general process theory. Nevertheless, I do not intend to throw out the baby with the bathwater, and there is much of lasting theoretical value in general process theory which I have attempted to integrate as well as possible with the ecological approach of this volume. Overall there were four main goals to the coverage of this book: (1) a comparative analysis of basic learning processes, (2) an analysis of the biological function of various learning processes, (3) a discussion of the way in which evolutionary processes and selection pressures might have shaped different learning capacities, and (4) description of some of the proximal mechanisms (mainly cognitive) that we believe mediate some forms of learning. As always, space restrictions have forced me to omit one or two topics that might easily have been incorporated in a book such as this — obvious omissions include simple nonassociative processes such as habituation and sensitization, and also punishment — but I have, whenever possible, begun discussions from basics so that a reader with only a rudimentary knowledge of learning theory could read the book usefully. I have also included a full reference list in order that the interested student or researcher can follow up any of the topics covered.

Finally, although any inaccuracies in this volume are, of course, my own responsibility, I am indebted to a number of people whose comments on earlier drafts led to important changes and additions. These people include Bob Boakes, Tony Dickinson, Karen Hollis, Alex Kacelnik, and Bill Timberlake. I am also grateful to Bob Boakes, Robert Epstein, Fergus Lowe, Brian McCabe, Dave Oakley, and John Phillips for providing me with prints of certain photographs. Last, but not least, the production of this book would not have been possible without the practical assistance of Cathy Allman, Chris Cromarty, John Phillips, Ruth Newton, Yvonne Hunkin, and my ever-patient publisher, Mary-Ann Kernan. Much of the author's own research reported in this volume was supported by project grants from the Science and Engineering Research Council (GR/A56117 and GR/C/54876). I am indebted to them for their financial support.

Graham Davey
London, March 1989

Chapter one

Ecology, evolution, and learning

A hungry hamster will readily learn to dig, rear, or scrabble to acquire food, yet simply cannot learn to face-wash, scent-mark, or groom to achieve this result. An earthworm has no trouble learning to associate a taste with a hot, dry place, but cannot associate a tactile stimulus with electric shock. Cats eagerly approach and investigate localizable sounds that signal food, but such signals simply do not interest rats. Pigeons learn to peck a lighted key to avoid electric shock only with great difficulty, yet they will quickly learn a wing-flapping response to avoid shock. These examples represent some of the enigmas facing anyone attempting to construct a theory of learning; not only do different species differ in their abilities to cope with different learning tasks, but individual species also frequently exhibit paradoxical irregularities in their learning abilities. Demonstration of a learning ability in one situation (such as the ability to associate behavior with its consequences) is no indication that the animal will be able to learn such a thing in other situations. The theorist appears to be left with a heap of facts and phenomena which show no apparent species or task regularities. So what kind of order, if any, can be imposed on this literature? There are a number of often quite different approaches to this problem, some of which set out to extract general principles of learning from this melee; others take a different conceptual approach by placing emphasis on how learning abilities may have evolved as a form of behavioral adaptation. We shall discuss these different approaches in a moment. However, when setting out on a path to the understanding of learning there are clearly two distinct questions that need raising at the outset. The first asks *what* is learning for? The second asks *how* do animals learn? The first question asks why animals evolved learning abilities at all, in the sense of having to specify what selection pressures were important in the evolution of learning, and it is also concerned with what animals learn in terms of what problems they are faced with in their natural environments.

The second question is concerned with the *mechanisms* of learning: given that an animal has to learn such-and-such in its natural environment, how does it do this? Different species may solve similar problems in completely different ways: evolution only selects for outcomes, not for specific means or processes, and it will select on the basis of the entire functional set of mechanisms available at the time (for example, some species may find Pavlovian associative mechanisms quite adequate for coping with a specific adaptive problem, whereas others may resort to instrumental learning mechanisms to solve the same functional problem).

The questions of *what* and *how* are not as theoretically distinct and separable as they have just been portrayed. In the last forty to fifty years the emphasis in learning theory has been on the question *how*, as exemplified by the attempts of general process theories to extract principles of learning which transcend species and tasks. These theories were addressing the question *how* in the sense that they attempted to specify generalities in basic psychological laws of learning such as principles of association (an instance of this is the assumption that a very wide variety of species possessed the ability to process Pavlovian associations, and the rules by which these associations were learned were relatively universal). Many writers agree that this general learning theory approach has failed, as the list of anomalies at the very beginning of this chapter tends to infer. But what should take its place? Most of the contents of this book reflect a recently expounded alternative to the general learning theory approach: namely, an approach to learning based largely on ecological and evolutionary considerations. Nevertheless, a useful and adaptable ecological learning theory should not attempt to throw out the baby with the bathwater. We should retain some of the conceptualizations of generalized learning theory as being useful to what is basically an ecological approach. This, then, is not a polemical exposition of ecological learning theory but what I hope will be a satisfactory integration of the ecological approach with some of the more durable aspects of generalized learning theory.

Ecology and learning

The tradition in learning theory has always been toward what has been labeled as the "arbitrary general learning theory approach" whose goal was to identify and describe general principles of learning that transcended both species and learning tasks. This approach arguably reached its peak in the theorizing of B. F. Skinner and other neo-behaviorists of the 1950s and 1960s. The pervasive assumption in this approach was that there *were* general principles of learning to be found, and once identified in one species these principles could simply be extrapolated to other — completely unrelated — species. This led to the intensive study of learning in individual species (namely, the laboratory rat and, later, the laboratory pigeon) and also fostered many of the radical behaviorist assumptions about the control and prediction of human behavior (e.g. Skinner, 1953). Examples of the so-called general principles of learning that this approach "discovered" were the principle of instrumental reinforcement (behavior is modified by its consequences), stimulus generalization, the equipotentiality of stimuli (all stimuli are equally capable of becoming Pavlovian conditioned stimuli), and the principle of temporal contiguity (associations between events will only be learned if they occur in close temporal proximity).

Subsequently, during the late 1960s and early 1970s, animal psychologists began to find exceptions to these general principles, particularly when studying species other than the laboratory rat or pigeon, in learning environments different from the Skinner-box and T-maze, and with reinforcers other than food or water. At first, the learning establishment was reluctant to acknowledge such anomalies, as was evidenced by the difficulty of some animal psychologists in getting the studies that reported these anomalies published (cf. Garcia, 1981). Such anomalies were largely considered to be the result of procedural differences or deficiencies in experimental design and control.

Nevertheless, as the catalog of these anomalies began to grow, it became clear that the traditional general laws of learning were no longer sacrosanct. At first the approach to these anomalies was simply to catalog them (e.g. Shettleworth, 1972a; Hinde and Stevenson-Hinde, 1973; Seligman and Hager, 1972), but it soon became clear that a radical rethink was necessary if these so-called "constraints on learning" were to be integrated into any predictive theoretical framework.

1 The biological boundaries approach

The first theoretical attempt to assimilate these learning anomalies alluded in very general terms to *biological constraints* on learning. This approach proposed that certain things could not be learned or were learned in selected ways because the animal's biology determined this. Both ecology and evolution were alluded to in very tangential ways when the notion of "biological constraints" was being unpacked. For instance, it was considered that some kinds of learning were simply not biologically sensible and other forms of adaptation could cope more efficiently with the animal's needs. This

3

type of biological constraint was used in an attempt to explain the great difficulties involved in teaching rats to avoid electric shock by simply pressing a lever. Bolles (1970) suggested that, in the wild, survival is too urgent for an animal to spend time learning to avoid aversive or life-threatening situations, and it therefore had to have a built-in set of defense reactions that it could utilize in response to threatening situations. This gave rise to Bolles's *species-specific defense reactions* (SSDR) theory of avoidance learning (see Chapter 7, pp. 223–4), and provided a rather rough account of how evolutionary pressures might biologically constrain some general learning processes. Some other theorists decided that evolution must make some kinds of learning easier than others and this could go some way to explaining many selective association effects. Seligman (1970) labeled such predispositions *prepared learning*, and he proposed a continuum of *preparedness* onto which all kinds of learning could be graded. For instance, taste aversion learning (TAL) in rats is, for Seligman, an example of prepared learning; when rats are subjected to gastric illness after being fed a particular food, they subsequently associate only the *taste* of the food with the illness and not any other audio-visual properties it possesses (Garcia and Koelling, 1966; see Chapter 6, pp. 183–190). The argument here is that making certain kinds of associations, such as between taste and poisoning, is beneficial to the survival of an omnivorous feeder like the rat and so such learning predispositions are likely to prosper and be selected for during the organism's evolutionary development.

All of these notions related to biological constraints on learning are intuitively sensible even to someone with very little academic knowledge of animal learning. However, although the biological constraints approach has alerted us to the involvement of evolutionary and ecological factors in learning, it has not been an approach capable of fostering a contemporary integrated theory of learning. There are a number of reasons for this. First, the biological constraints view still clings unwittingly to the general processes approach. As Revusky (1977) has pointed out, the use of terms like "boundaries" and "constraints" implies that there is something (such as a general process) which is being constrained. Thus, what biological constraints approaches appear to be doing is, in the way of an addendum, specifying the factors which lead to the list of learning anomalies represented by the constraints on learning literature. Since the general process view was an unproven assumption in the first place, the biological boundaries view must also share many of its increasingly shaky assumptions.

Second, the biological boundaries approaches of the kind originally outlined by Bolles (1970) and Seligman (1970) are basically *post hoc* theories with either little predictive value or potentially circular definitions. For

4

instance, according to Seligman's view of preparedness, an association can only be labeled as "prepared" if it can be shown to be learned more rapidly than other associations. The circularity appears when one then attempts to assert that the association is learned more quickly because it is "prepared." Clearly, to break this circularity one would need some good independent criteria for determining what associations would have been selected for in the animal's evolutionary past. Unfortunately, such criteria are difficult to formulate and it is often very easy to conjure up plausible adaptive scenarios for almost any behavioral characteristic of an organism, making intuitive guesses as to what might or might not be selected for rather unhelpful. There are some useful techniques for attempting to identify the selection pressures involved in the evolution of particular learning abilities, but they require a detailed knowledge of the function that the learning serves and comprehensive cross-species comparisons (cf. Cullen, 1957; Hailman, 1965, 1976). Theories such as preparedness have failed to appreciate the need for such knowledge.

Third, biological constraints explanations have generally been couched in the absence of relevant ethological information on the behavior and lifestyle of the species concerned. For instance, the SSDR hypothesis of avoidance learning proposed by Bolles is loosely based around the "flight-fight-fright" defense reactions of the rat. Yet it is not clear how this hypothesis might apply to other species with clearly different defensive strategies to the rat, nor what defense reactions will be elicited in what situations and whether these reactions exist in a hierarchical or parallel framework. This makes the SSDR hypothesis relatively unpredictive beyond its basic assertion that only SSDRs will be learned as effective avoidance responses — and this is only helpful if one has clear criteria for identifying a behavior as an SSDR (for instance, is shaking with fear an SSDR?). These criteria are not outlined in the hypothesis, and clearly rely on an understanding of the functional interaction between the behavior and the animal's natural environment.

2 *The comparative approach*

When we explore beyond the bounds of simple nonassociative learning, species clearly differ in the relative complexity of their behavior and, presumably, in their abilities to cope with differing adaptive problems. Traditionally, the study of these differences gave rise to the comparative approach to learning which attempted to compare differing species, differing orders (rats, monkeys, dogs, and so on) and differing classes (such as fish, birds, and mammals) according to some arbitrarily defined scale of learning ability or intelligence. Normally, this involved comparing species' performance on a variety of learning tasks of differing complexity and constructing a hypothetical scale of intelligence or learning ability on the basis of the results.

One example of this approach was that employed by Bitterman (1965, 1975). He used the performance of species in a variety of learning paradigms to classify each species as either rat-like or fish-like in its learning abilities. However, while it may seem intuitively reasonable to rank species according to their performance on a number of tasks which require varying degrees of adaptive sophistication, this kind of approach is not particularly helpful theoretically. It fosters misleading beliefs about the evolution of learning and about the adaptive nature of learning. First, Hodos and Campbell (1969) pointed out some time ago that comparative approaches had traditionally been based on fallacious assumptions about evolutionary lineage. In comparative approaches to learning such as that espoused by Bitterman, abilities were compared in species which did not have common ancestor-descendant lines. Classifying pigeons or monkeys as either rat-like or fish-like bears no relation to an understanding of the evolution of intelligence or learning abilities, because fish did not give rise to pigeons, pigeons to rats, or rats to monkeys.

Another obvious problem with this kind of hierarchical approach to the structure of learning abilities is that such programs of study have tended to adopt a human-oriented criterion of intelligence. As a result, associative learning has tended to be regarded as lower on this scale than reversal learning, probability learning, concept formation, or language learning. Intelligence as a notion related to learning and adaptive behavior cannot be adequately assessed outside of its biological function, and how it assists the animal in securing resources in its natural environment. Thus, it cannot easily be defined *a priori* in this context; it needs to be related to the demands that are imposed on a particular species of animal by that species' need to fulfill biological functions (see also Chapter 10, pp. 274–84).

What, then, should a valid comparative approach to animal learning look like, and what, if anything, can it tell us about the structure and evolution of learning? There are at least two alternatives to the rather wholesale traditional approach to comparative studies that took little notice of evolutionary perspectives.

First, we can investigate within taxonomic groups such as mammals, birds, reptiles, and so on to identify principles of learning within these groups. Since animals within such groups share a common ancestry, we may be able to relate adaptive principles to ancestral constraints on possible evolutionary

6

divergence. Similarly, although species within a group share common ancestry, many of them may exploit quite different niches, reflecting environmental pressures which may have selected for quite different adaptive capabilities. If different species within a group do exhibit different learning skills, then examining the lifestyle of these species should help to some extent in differentiating some of the environmental pressures that selected for those learning attributes. This theme will be elaborated in the following section of this chapter.

The second alternative approach within a comparative study of learning is in terms of *anagenesis* or grades of organization. The main theme of anagenesis is that successive species in a lineage often exhibit improvement in structures and functions that can be described as a succession of grades (cf. Demarest, 1983; Gottlieb, 1984, 1985; Rensch, 1959; Yarczower and Hazlett, 1977; Plotkin, 1983). This is distinct from the notion of evolutionary relatedness from a genetic viewpoint as embodied in the notion of *cladogenesis*. Thus, a *clade* is a delimitable, genetically closely related unit resulting from evolutionary diversification, but a *grade* is "a particular level in an ascending series of improvements on any given structural or functional unit of analysis in which the animal groups may or may not be closely related from a genetic standpoint (e.g. brain/body ratio; adaptive behavior; level of problem-solving or learning ability or, more specifically, ability to exhibit various forms of learning)" (Gottlieb, 1984: 449). Thus, different species may be members of a similar grade, but not of a similar clade; that is, they may be classed as having certain adaptive abilities in common but lack any close ancestral — and hence phylogenetic — relationship. This relationship between grades and clades is illustrated in a schematic example in Figure 1.1.

Two problems remain with the anagenetic approach, however, and they are (1) how we objectively define the process of anagenesis, and (2) how we go about identifying different grades. Clearly, unless we are able to do this, we have an approach which differs little in its phylogenetic indiscipline from traditional comparative approaches. In answer to the first problem, Rensch (1959) has listed a number of features considered to be typical of anagenesis. These include (1) increased complexity (differentiation), (2) centralization of structures and functions, (3) special complexity and centralization of the nervous system, (4) increased plasticity of structures and functions, (5) improvements allowing further improvement, and (6) increased independence of the environment and increasing command of environmental factors (increased autonomy, usually the result of improved sensory and nervous systems). Defining anagenesis in these terms — especially in relation to increased autonomy — does have some bearing on the concept of intelligence

7

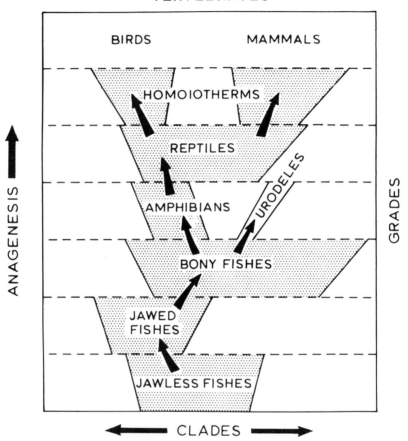

Figure 1.1 Schematic representation of anagenesis, grades, and clades in vertebrate evolution. (From Huxley, 1957, and Gottlieb, 1984).

as that term regularly crops up in learning theories. Gottlieb (1984) suggests that increased autonomy (in terms of ontogenetic plasticity and behavioral versatility) is the "hallmark" of progressive evolution, and species might meaningfully be ranked on a scale of such adaptability measured in terms of their adaptability to experimentally altered ecological conditions. In this sense, anagenesis is not a process which just leads an organism to become better adapted to its niche; it also leads to increased efficiency in that adaptation, and — more importantly from this point of view — allows it to cope with unexpected changes in the ecology of its habitat and to exploit new environments (see Chapter 10, pp. 283-4).

Defining a grade, however, is largely a subjective matter, with a number of difficulties inherent in any definition (cf. Plotkin, 1983). Grades, as they are defined within the concept of anagenesis, can presumably be differentiated on neurophysiological, behavioral, psychological, or even adaptational scales, although none of these scales will be mutually exclusive since, for instance, increased neurophysiological complexity will usually result in concomitant behavioral, psychological, and adaptational modifications. One attempt to base anagenetic analyses on non-behavioral dimensions is that of Jerison (1973). Jerison ranked species according to an encephalization quotient (EQ), which is an objective dimension based on the size of the species' brain relative to its body. There was, for instance, a dramatic increase in the size of the brain at the time when the earliest birds and mammals evolved, and the EQs of mammalian species alone are clearly definable into distinct grades on the basis of EQ. Man and dolphin form one grade whose EQ is greater than the great apes, who form another grade. Horses, dogs, and lemurs form another grade, and rats and mice yet another. Jerison assumes that differences in EQ reflect differences in information-processing abilities, which in turn reflect cognitive and learning differences. On a more specific level this kind of grade classification may reveal other adaptive specializations. For instance, brain size may co-vary with certain ecological and developmental factors such as socialization, long gestation, prolonged postnatal nervous system maturation, and so on (Eisenberg, 1981; Gottlieb, 1984).

An alternative method of defining grades is simply on the basis of the refinement of the strategies adopted by a species to solve a particular adaptational problem. For instance, Holldobler and Wilson (1983) described three progressive grades of nest weaving in some formicine ant species. In each progressive grade the strategy adopted by the ant species had additional adaptive significance with added refinements to that found in the lower grades. What is interesting is that, while these grades can be defined on the basis of their adaptive refinement, these species of ant are not cladistically or phylogenetically related. Each of the species of ant arose independently from different ancestors. The fact that behavioral grades should be based on refinements in the strategies that species use to solve a particular *adaptational* problem they are faced with is quite important, especially if grades are to reflect the evolutionary processes and pressures that determined those grades.

Adaptive processes such as learning cannot be viewed in an evolutionary sense as an abstracted flexibility, but, because evolution selects for *outcomes*, can only be viewed in relation to the function that the learning serves (cf. Plotkin and Odling-Smee, 1982; Plotkin, 1983). This is another reason why it has been biological nonsense to relate phylogenetic development to performance on arbitrarily-defined abstract learning tasks such as serial reversal and probability learning (e.g. Bitterman, 1965, 1975). Since it is not clear that, say, a particular species of fish would ever require such skills to solve a functional problem it is faced with, there is no reason to suppose that such an ability could ever have been selected for. Thus to rank species as either rat-like or fish-like in their abilities to cope with such arbitrary tasks masks an understanding of the environmental pressures that may have selected for those abilities.

Thus, grades can be defined either in neurophysiological terms or in terms of the refinement of behavioral (including psychological) processes with particular functional significance. Once this has been attempted, there are two ways in which useful comparisons can be made. First, we can take representatives of different grades and compare them in terms of a specific attribute, and discover exactly how that attribute changes across grades (possibly in terms of changes in the mechanism which mediates that attribute); or second, we can select different species from a single grade in order to discover how such phylogenetically different organisms have evolved either the same level of organization or similar behavioral strategies.

3 *The ecological approach*

So far throughout this introductory chapter there have been references to the need to understand the functional aspects of learning before we can construct theoretical frameworks in which to understand learning in general. More specifically we need to know what biological function or what adaptational problem the learning is serving. In effect, this is the basis of an ecological approach to learning, and it is based on the assumption that an animal's behavior cannot be described in isolation from its environment (cf. Johnston, 1985). For instance,

> the question of central importance in the ecological approach to learning is: what do animals learn and how do they learn it? The first part of this question (what do animals learn?) reflects a concern with the problems faced by animals in their natural environments: the second part (how do they learn it?), with the way in which experience contributes to the solution

of those problems.... The first of these [questions] takes the form "what are the behavioral problems that this animal must solve in adapting to its environment?" The second question takes a more familiar form: "How does the animal learn to solve those problems?" Not only are questions of the first kind equal in importance to those of the second, they also clearly have logical priority. To draw an analogy, if we were to ask *how* to design a bridge, an engineer's first question, of necessity, would be: "What is it that you wish to bridge?" A question of this kind is a request for a *task description*, and task descriptions play an important and fundamental role in the ecological approach to the study of learning

(Johnston, 1981a: 131–3)

In order to attempt to answer the question of what it is that the animal needs to learn, we have to introduce the notion of *adaptation*. Basically, adaptation to an environment can be defined as the animal's ability to attain certain goals in the environment (these goals will obviously vary with the kinds of species being studied, but generally they relate to such biological functions as searching for and capturing food, finding a mate, building nests, rearing offspring, avoiding predators, and so on). In this sense, adaptation is a relational concept. Whenever a behavioral or learning trait is labeled "adaptive" we imply an environment to which it is adapted, and in most cases that environment will be the animal's own ecological niche (Slobodkin, 1968; Slobodkin and Rapoport, 1974). Thus, adaptation cannot be understood without defining some of the features of the animal's natural environment and how its behavior relates to these features. For instance, the food of some species is patchily distributed across its habitat. A chaffinch, for example, may feed on insects found in dead logs and have to spend time deciding whether to exploit a log it has found or move on to search for another one. Once we understand that this is one of the feeding problems facing the chaffinch (the "why?" question) we can begin to look at how its behavior corresponds to the tasks posed by this problem, and exactly what psychological or learning mechanisms it has evolved to cope with them (the "how?" question).

However, the ecological approach is not one which denies that general principles of learning can be found. It does specify, however, that such general principles (or "global" principles, as they are called by Johnston, 1981a) can only be discovered by first of all formulating a task description (what problems face this organism?) which will allow us then to construct *local* principles of adaptation. General principles of learning may exist, but they only operate for given species if the local principles (based on a task

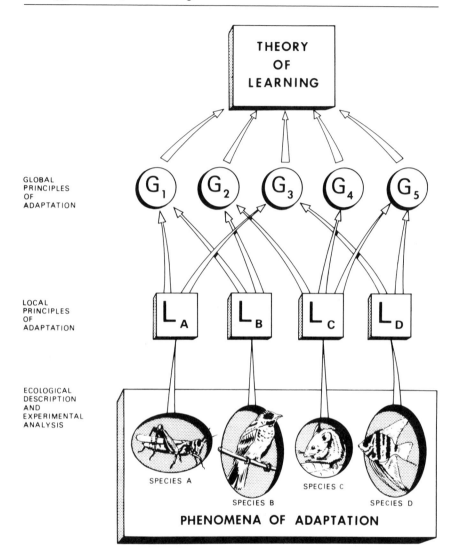

Figure 1.2 The ecological approach to learning. The four phenomena of adaptation represent the study of animals in their natural environments, and description and analysis of adaptation within each of these ecosystems provides the basis for local principles of adaptation (L_A – L_D). Each local principle may then contribute to one or more global (or general) principle of adaptation. Note that not all global principles may apply to all species studied. (Adapted from Johnston, 1981a)

description) operate for that species. For instance, many animals may have learning capabilities which allow them to forage for food in a highly optimal way (see Chapter 8), and many different species exhibit behavior which corresponds to the principles inherent in this optimality. However, such optimally adaptive performance may only exist in animals whose food is distributed throughout their environment in a particular way. Thus, the optimal solution to foraging problems may be quite different for a species whose food is distributed in discrete, physically-separated patches than for a species whose food is much less discretely distributed (such as herbivorous grazers).

Thus *local principles of adaptation* require a task description which

> describes the way in which the animal solves a particular adaptive problem such as feeding, orienting or communicating with conspecifics.... These principles are termed "local" because there is no way to determine, without further analyses of other species, whether they apply to more than the single species in which they are described
>
> (Johnston, 1981a: 135)

General principles of adaptation can be defined when it is clear that different species of animals are faced with similar adaptational problems and appear to solve them in similar ways. These similar adaptational problems may arise because different species share similar habitats or lifestyles, and we might, therefore, find general principles of adaptation which apply, for instance, to migratory species, carnivores, semi-aquatic species, and so on. Figure 1.2 illustrates schematically the relationship between task description, and local and general principles of adaptation.

Finally, it is worth mentioning that an animal may possess adaptive capabilities which are not easily defined in terms of the ecological pressures that might have selected them. For instance, it is clear that certain abilities may have evolved as a result of the need to solve *particular* adaptational problems, but such abilities may be sufficient to enable the animal to solve adaptational problems for which these abilities were not originally selected. In ecological terms these extra functions can be called *ecologically surplus abilities* (Johnston, 1981b, 1985) and must be borne in mind when considering the biological function or adaptational significance of fairly basic associative learning processes such as Pavlovian or instrumental conditioning. It is fairly obvious that a particular learning ability may have evolved in the context of solving a specific adaptive problem (such as identifying food, or recognizing a potential mate), but have sufficient utility to be adapted to other functional needs. This makes identifying the biological function of certain learning

13

processes (for example, Pavlovian conditioning) particularly difficult, especially in the sense of identifying the particular adaptational problems which contributed to the selection of those processes (see Chapter 6 for further discussion of this point). Nevertheless, the apparent versatility of such processes as Pavlovian conditioning does not invalidate an ecological approach in any way. Although a process such as Pavlovian learning may appear relevant to solving a particular adaptational problem, a closer task analysis may reveal that ecological conditions or the animal's lifestyle require that more specific abilities are brought to bear. For instance, parent recognition in young precocial birds, or the learning of the star or solar-compass in birds which migrate early in their first year of life are problems which require very rapid learning, and resistance to modification when learned. Such ecological factors suggest that simple associational learning will not suffice in such conditions (see Chapter 9).

4 *Ecological learning theory*

The next question to ask is how the ecological approach and more traditional learning analyses can interact in supplementary ways which might generate a cohesive learning theory. Most obviously there are two directions in which this interaction can take place. First, traditional analyses of learning lean heavily toward the study of mechanisms (such as the analysis of associative mechanisms in conditioning), and knowledge of these mechanisms in individual species can help to elucidate the selection pressures which determined that learning ability (see below). Second, an ecological approach to learning is essential if we are to understand the "sharp" end of these mechanisms, and in particular the way in which learning is translated into performance. For instance, an understanding of associative processes which operate during conditioning may tell us what an animal learns (in terms of the associations it forms) but it does not tell us how the animal uses this knowledge to solve the kinds of adaptive problems it is faced with. On the other hand, if we do not know how an animal translates knowledge into performance this can in some cases lead us to make spurious inferences about associative mechanisms. We can only infer learning by observing behavior; if we have inadequate knowledge of how learning is utilized in performance then we cannot make accurate inferences about learning.

Learning principles and the selection of adaptive characteristics

Attempting a general understanding of learning mechanisms can, whenever possible, be helpful to an understanding of the evolution of certain adaptive traits. For example, we may be able to use various inferential techniques to detect the associative mechanisms underlying a particular kind of Pavlovian learning in a given species. These associative mechanisms may involve abstracted learning about the relationship between different events in the animal's environment; for example, between a signal (conditioned stimulus) and food (unconditioned stimulus), and thus may represent centralized associative processes available to a wide range of responses and biological functions. Alternatively, the learning may involve associative links between a signal and a particular response system (S–R learning). In this case the response system is an integral component of the associative mechanism, and we might reasonably guess that the learning mechanisms involved in such cases were selected for to deal with specific adaptational problems and are not readily available for other functional problems. An analysis of associative mechanisms in learning can in this way shed some light on the biological functions which the learning serves and, to some extent, help to elucidate the adaptive pressures which led to its selection.

Our existing knowledge of learning processes can also help to understand the evolution of adaptive characteristics which are not directly related to learning. For instance, many insects have evolved very bright and distinctive features which make them fairly easily detectable to potential predators (known as "aposematic coloration"). While many of the insects that have evolved this characteristic are unpalatable to predators, it still begs the questions of (1) why they should still want to make themselves so easily detectable, and (2) why many palatable insect species have copied their distinctive coloration (known as "Batesian mimicry"). The answers appear to lie in the fact that predators can learn to associate this distinctive coloration with the unpalatable consequences of eating such a prey (Pavlovian conditioning), and this learning can occur very rapidly, leading the predator to ignore such colored prey when it subsequently encounters them. The speed with which the predator will learn to avoid a distinctively colored prey is much faster than the speed with which it will learn to avoid a more cryptically decorated prey (cf. Gittleman, Harvey, and Greenwood, 1980; Roper and Wistow, 1986). Thus, an understanding of the Pavlovian principles of stimulus salience and aversive learning lead us to understand why aposematic coloration has been selected for and why potentially palatable species mimic these features (see Chapter 6, pp. 194–5). In this instance, understanding the principles of learning found in one species (the predator) helps us to understand the pressures which have selected for adaptive characteristics in other species (the prey).

From a comparative point of view it is also instructive to discover whether different species from different groups and classes do possess the component abilities necessary to achieve certain kinds of learning. Simply discovering whether an animal can discriminate its own actions or can associate certain environmental stimuli with other kinds of environmental stimuli is not only an endeavor concerned with discovering whether the animal possesses component abilities necessary for certain kinds of learning, but is also important in helping us to describe that species' environmental niche. These descriptions help us to understand the environmental factors which do impinge on an organism and add to the list of environmental variables required to describe an animal's environmental niche (cf. Schleidt, 1985).

Ecological analyses and learning mechanisms

We can now look more closely at the importance of ecological analysis for an understanding of learning mechanisms, and there are a number of ways in which ecological analyses are crucial to our understanding of learning.

First, a study of the mechanisms of learning (especially conditioning) has traditionally been divided into two parts: the study of learning (what cognitive changes occur or what associations are formed?) and performance (how does the animal translate that learning into behavior?). There is a logical priority here. We cannot adequately understand learning until we understand performance, simply because we cannot directly observe learning but have to infer it from performance. Most importantly, recent studies have shown that performance cannot be understood without a knowledge of the biological function that the learning is serving plus an adequate ethological description of the species-typical behaviors that the organism utilizes to satisfy that function (cf. Timberlake, 1983a; Holland, 1984a; see Chapter 5). The performance aspects of learning cannot be understood without a description of the behavior system which serves the biological function involved, and to describe these systems requires a knowledge of the organized nature of an animal's response repertoires and the natural stimuli which release such responses (see pp. 155–69 for a fuller account of behavior systems). This requires an understanding of the factors which activate behavior systems, and a knowledge of the stimuli in an animal's environment which release responses important to fulfilling the function of that biological system. Similarly, this in turn requires a knowledge of the animal's habitat and its lifestyle.

An insightful example of how ecological analysis is important to an understanding of learning mechanisms can be provided by the phenomenon of autoshaping (also known as sign-tracking, see p. 27). When a localizable conditioned stimulus acts as a signal for forthcoming food, many species of animal will eventually "learn" to approach the conditioned stimulus and direct species-specific feeding-related behaviors toward it. There are at least three questions to ask about this phenomenon: (1) what has the animal learned? (2) what determines the kind of behaviors that the animal directs toward the conditioned stimulus? and (3) why should the animal approach the conditioned stimulus at all? Initially, some theorists assumed that the biological significance of autoshaping lay in the fact that signals for food were usually proximal to food (for example, for a cat, the sight of a movement in the undergrowth is likely to be a signal that a small rodent is located there), and in this assumption lay the biological function of autoshaping (Buzsaki, 1982; Wasserman, 1981; Hollis, 1982). However, this clearly fails to take into account the strategies that different species have evolved to enable them to capture prey. While moving toward a signal for food may in many instances be helpful in acquiring that food, it is clearly counterproductive in some situations for some species and in all situations for other species (for example, species that stalk their prey downwind or that attract their prey by remaining immobile and using lure displays). Furthermore, how would this kind of strategy benefit herbivorous browsers or grazers whose food is rarely discretely located?

Subsequent studies of autoshaping have shown that it is *not* a ubiquitous phenomenon, as was first thought following its intensive study in a limited number of species. Its appearance can only be explained by an ecological analysis of the species being studied, its lifestyle and natural feeding habits and the environmental stimuli that release these feeding responses. Autoshaping *is* a learned response, but we can only predict when it might occur and what form it might take by acquiring an extensive knowledge of the life histories and feeding habitats of the species under study. Thus, whether an animal will emit an autoshaped response depends on the ecological significance of the conditioned stimulus for the species concerned and the kinds of feeding strategies the species would normally bring to such a situation. For example, cats will autoshape to a localizable auditory conditioned stimulus signaling food, but rats will not (Grastyan and Vereczkei, 1974; Cleland and Davey, 1983). An ecological analysis will reveal that cats often locate their prey on the basis of auditory cues, but rats rarely do so (Ewer, 1971). Therefore localizable sounds have an ecological significance for a feeding cat but not for a feeding rat.

One further benefit of an ecological analysis to the study of learning is that it clearly helps in the understanding of some traditionally perplexing problems. One such topic is the concept of motivation, which learning theorists have generally tended to treat relatively naïvely. In the traditional approach, motivation has usually been equated with deprivation levels, and learning has been studied in animals that are either food-deprived or water-deprived. Yet this raises a number of difficult conceptual problems. First, how do we conceive of motivation in aversive or defensive learning? There appears to be no obvious physiological deprivation. Second, either in their natural habitat or in closed-economy studies (where animals can obtain all their daily food requirements by operating a response manipulandum in their home cage) animals are rarely under deprivation conditions. Rats responding for food in closed-economies rarely drop below 6–7 per cent of their normal body-weight (Collier, Hirsch, and Kanarek, 1977), and rats tend to drink at set times of the day rather than allow themselves to become thirsty before drinking. Other rodents, such as hamsters, will readily learn to press levers to obtain food even when not food-deprived. The opportunity to pouch and hoard the food is sufficient to maintain such instrumental behavior in hamsters (Charlton, 1984; Launay, 1981).

Here again an analysis of the animal's natural lifestyle is necessary to interpret these findings and to evolve an ecologically-based concept of motivation. The factors which motivate an animal to acquire food are not solely physiological, but reside in the environmental pressures which influence the animal's attempts to acquire these resources. Animals such as the deer and moose which must withstand severe winters when food resources are scarce will normally feed even when replete in the summer months in order to build up adequate adipose layers to withstand the winter deprivation. Such factors which motivate feeding will thus depend on an interaction between the animal's lifestyle and the environmental conditions which determine that lifestyle. A similar analysis can be made for defensive motivation. Here we have to ask about the kinds of things that activate defensive reactions in a particular species in its natural environment. While in many cases these factors might be interspecific (such as loud noises, looming shadows, painful stimuli, and so on), there are many which are likely to be species-specific, such as the sight of an owl for a pied flycatcher, or of hyenas in hunting formation for gazelle (see Chapter 5, pp. 165–8).

The evolution of learning

Why animals have evolved learning abilities is not as simple to answer as we might intuitively expect. There is frequently a temptation to say that learning is a useful means of adapting to a relatively unpredictable environment and an excellent means of gaining and storing information for future use. However, there are two important points that need to be raised here. First, if we assume that animals which possess learning mechanisms can adapt more successfully to their environment than animals which are unable to learn, it is strange that so few species have actually evolved elaborate learning abilities. As Mayr (1974) has pointed out, "Considering this great advantage of learning, it is rather curious in how relatively few phyletic lines genetically fixed behavior patterns have been replaced by the capacity for the storage of individual acquired information" (p. 652). Second, although we are always able to perceive the potential benefits of possessing learning abilities, there are also costs to evolving such abilities, and it is by no means clear that the adaptive benefits outweigh the selective costs (cf. Johnston, 1981b).

Since these two points are interrelated, it is worth discussing them here. For learning to have evolved it must have carried a net selective benefit for the species concerned and not just have possessed some "potential" usefulness. Johnston (1981b) has attempted to catalog some of the selective benefits and selective costs of learning. First, learning is particularly suited to species which have to interact with an environment that does possess properties that vary unpredictably during their own lifetime (e.g. Slobodkin and Rapoport, 1974; Plotkin and Odling-Smee, 1979; Johnston and Turvey, 1980). This may include variability in the nature and distribution of food sources, identifying parents or potential mates, or learning migratory routes or paths to and from the home burrow, nest, or breeding ground. Under such conditions, efficiently exploiting these variable resources is likely to be a primary determinant of reproductive success, and hence to be an important selection factor in the evolution of learning in individual species. Furthermore, the pressures of resource exploitation are less applicable to species the resources of which exhibit relatively invariant characteristics during their lifetime or which have relatively short generation times and which adopt the evolutionary tactic of producing large numbers of offspring in the hope that at least some will survive (called r-selected species by MacArthur and Wilson, 1967). In the case of the latter kinds of species we would be less likely to expect the evolution of learning.

With the evolution of learning abilities to cope with resource variance, what are the selective costs involved to a particular species? Primarily, learning implies that an organism is dependent on individual experience for the development of important behavioral skills necessary to its survival, and in particular this can leave the animal vulnerable until that experience is gained and the necessary skills are acquired. Johnston (1981b) lists a number of potential selective costs in this respect:

1 *delayed reproductive effort and/or success* — if an animal's dependence on learning is high, then the number of offspring it can expect to rear before it

acquires the appropriate competence must be small (cf. Lack, 1966; Ashmole, 1963);

2 *increased juvenile vulnerability* — this will result from inadequate defense against predators and inadequate feeding skills;

3 *increased parental investment in each offspring* — because of the potential vulnerability of offspring that have to acquire behavioral skills through experience, parents will have to invest more time in protecting and rearing their young, which in turn will reduce the number of offspring that any individual can rear at one time and reduce the number of times an individual can breed during its lifetime; it is interesting in this respect to note that those classes of animal in which learning is most obviously displayed are also the classes which exhibit considerable parental investment in their offspring (namely, birds and mammals);

4 *greater complexity of the central nervous system* — learning abilities will clearly involve increased complexity of the nervous system with the high energetic costs of maintaining and serving nerve tissue, and protecting the brain from physiological fluctuation and damage;

5 *developmental fallibility*. If an animal is so dependent on learning skills essential for its survival, it is important that there is some built-in protection against maladaptive learning or simply learning the wrong thing. This protection can be seen in the case of certain kinds of learning such as imprinting and avian song-learning. For example, many species of birds require exposure to the conspecific song for normal song-learning to develop (cf. Marler, 1977; see also Chapter 9). This genetic predisposition insures that the bird learns only the adult conspecific song in an otherwise complex acoustical environment.

As can be seen from the above list of the potential selective costs of possessing learning abilities, it is rather clearer now why many phyla have avoided evolving learning strategies. However, many species have evolved relatively complex learning abilities, and, without having any useful yardstick with which to compare the selective costs and benefits, we can only assume that the selective benefits will outweigh the selective costs for such species.

One final point on the evolution of learning is that it is likely to evolve only when more fundamental processes of information gain (such as phylogenesis) have reached an upper limit to the amount or rate of change that they can cope with. The process of phylogenesis, for instance, allows a species to track the changes in its environment by altering the gene pool of a breeding population. However, there are inevitable problems with this process. First, there will be a time lag between the environmental change and the genetic adaptation which evolves to cope with the change. Second, although phylogenesis is sufficient to enable a breeding species to cope with environmental changes that occur relatively infrequently, it is not sufficient to produce adaptations to changes that occur relatively frequently and, in particular, to environmental invariance that occurs within the lifetime of individual animals (cf. Plotkin and Odling-Smee, 1979; Odling-Smee, 1983). The fact that phylogenesis is a primary means of information gain implies that learning will evolve only in species where this process has reached the upper limits of its ability to track environmental change. The other implication is that species which inhabit relatively invariant and stable environments are considerably less likely to evolve learning abilities than those which inhabit relatively variable and changing environments.

Chapter summary

1 Two questions need to be asked when beginning to study learning. The first asks *what* is learning for? The second asks *how* do animals learn? The first is concerned with understanding what things animals have to learn about in their natural environment; the second is concerned with the mechanism the animal possesses in order to be able to learn.

2 Traditionally, learning theorists have addressed the *how* question by attempting to specify general principles of learning. Most people are agreed that this approach has been unsuccessful because there were always anomalies to be found which violated the general principles that were "discovered."

3 The first attempt to account for the learning anomalies was by adopting a *biological boundaries approach*: i.e., evolutionary pressures might have constrained some general learning processes such that animals adapted to urgent situations with built-in reactions rather than through learning (e.g., Bolles's species-specific defense reaction hypothesis).

4 The *comparative approach* to learning involves comparing the performance of different species on a variety of learning tasks and constructing a hypothetical scale of intelligence or learning ability on the basis of the results (e.g., Bitterman, 1965, 1975).

5 Both the biological boundaries and comparative approaches possess theoretical and conceptual problems which make them inadequate as an overall framework for understanding learning.

6 One alternative comparative approach to learning is in terms of *anagenesis*, or grades of organization (e.g., Jerison, 1973).

7 Although there are some problems involved in defining some of the feature of anagenesis, it is an important approach in that is stresses that adaptive processes such as learning must be viewed in relation to the biological

function that the learning serves (e.g., feeding, defense, reproduction).

8 The *ecological approach* to learning stresses the need to understand the functional aspects of learning before we can construct theoretical frameworks in which to understand learning in general. We need to know what biological function or what adaptational problem the learning is serving.

9 An animal's behavior cannot be described in isolation from its environment and the biological function served by the learning. This involves questions about what the animal needs to learn about to survive and live in its own environmental niche.

10 *Adaptation* to an environment is defined as the animal's ability to attain certain goals in that environment (e.g. searching for and capturing food). Whenever a behavioral or learning trait is labeled "adaptive," we imply an environment to which it is adapted.

11 Thus we cannot understand learning without a knowledge of the biological needs of the species concerned and how the environment creates the problems that need to be solved in satisfying these needs.

12 Because of its functional approach, ecological learning theory requires two types of principles. *Local principles of adaptation* describe the way in which an individual species solves a particular adaptive problem. *General principles of adaptation* can be defined when it is clear that different species of animals are faced with similar adaptational problems and appear to solve them in similar ways.

13 A traditional approach to learning can still be beneficial when integrated with the ecological approach. The former approach can help to pinpoint some of the selection pressures which have led to the evolution of certain learning abilities, while the latter can help to elucidate the characteristics of learning mechanisms themselves.

14 The ecological approach has the benefit of aiding an analysis of the performance aspects of learning (i.e., predicting the kind of adaptive behavior the animal will perform in the learning situation) and in clarifying some traditionally perplexing learning problems such as an understanding of the notions of motivation.

15 Learning has replaced genetically fixed behavior patterns in relatively few phyletic lines, largely because, in order to have evolved, it must have possessed a net selective benefit for the species concerned. Although learning abilities do possess some "potential" usefulness, they also frequently possess hidden costs which may frequently preclude their evolutionary selection.

16 Learning will evolve only when more fundamental processes of information gain (such as phylogenesis) have reached an upper limit to the amount or rate of change they can cope with.

Chapter two

Comparative aspects of conditioning: Pavlovian learning

In the early part of the twentieth century conditioning had been considered to consist solely of the kind discovered and espoused by Pavlov, and it was not until the 1920s and 1930s that theorists began to consider that there might be two fundamentally different types of basic associative learning. The dichotomy between Pavlovian and instrumental responding was arguably first discussed by Konorski and Miller (1937) and then later popularized by Skinner (1938) in his classic book *Behavior of Organisms*. Skinner's position on the differences between Pavlovian and instrumental conditioning was particularly radical: not only were they different learning procedures, but they also possessed different biological and adaptive functions and thus, by implication, were manifestations of different underlying learning mechanisms. Skinner's view was that Pavlovian conditioning represented the adaptive mechanism by which the more reflexive, autonomic components of behavior were modified, whereas instrumental conditioning was the process by which the more integrated, skeletally-mediated and "voluntary" behaviors of an organism were learned. This dichotomy persisted until well into the 1960s, when it began to become clear that integrated skeletally-based responses could be acquired and modified by Pavlovian contingencies (for example, autoshaping, see p. 27), and that certain autonomic and visceral reponses were directly susceptible to instrumental contingencies (cf. Miller, 1969).

Contemporary views of the relationship between instrumental and Pavlovian conditioning are complex, but it is generally considered that neither type of learning is restricted to particular types of responses. Both types of conditioning represent the acquisition of information about relationships existing in the animal's world, and in both types of learning the animal acts on this information in rather complex ways (see Chapters 5 and 7). Both types of learning also serve rather generalized biological functions and provide the animal with capacities valuable for survival and successful reproduction (see Chapters 6 and 7).

This and the following chapter will attempt to explore some of the comparative aspects of Pavlovian and instrumental conditioning, first, by describing some of the basic phenomena associated with these two types of learning and, second, by assessing if different species utilize them.

Pavlovian conditioning

In Pavlovian conditioning a conditioned stimulus (CS) is paired in close temporal contiguity with an unconditioned stimulus (UCS), such that, after a number of CS–UCS pairings, the CS itself comes to elicit a conditioned response (CR) relevant in some way to the UCS (see Figure 2.1). The UCS is usually some biologically important event which itself evokes an unlearned, reflexive type of reaction known as the unconditioned response (UCR). In Pavlov's prototypical conditioning experiment a hungry dog was presented with pairings of a bell or metronome (the CS) with a bowl of food (the UCS); after a number of pairings of CS followed by UCS, the dog began to salivate during the CS. The learned response that occurred during the CS was salivation (the CR).

UCSs normally adopted in Pavlovian conditioning studies include food for a hungry animal and aversive UCSs such as electric shocks or loud noises, but a much wider range of UCSs than this have been utilized in the study of Pavlovian learning processes (see pp. 153–4). CSs used are normally innocuous audio-visual stimuli, but recently a wider range of species-relevant CSs have been used which have helped to cast light on the mechanisms underlying Pavlovian conditioning. These have included conspecifics (Timberlake, 1983a; Timberlake and Grant, 1975), toy hedgehogs (Keith-Lucas and Guttman, 1975), and live cats as CSs for rat subjects (Blanchard and Blanchard, 1969b), and so on. Ecologically neutral CSs are useful for helping us to understand the mechanisms of Pavlovian *learning* (for example, what associations the animal learns), but ecologically relevant CSs give important insights into how that learning is translated into suitably adaptive behavior for individual species (see Chapter 5).

1 Basic phenomena of Pavlovian conditioning

Response type

Theoretically it should be possible to use any biologically significant event, or any stimulus that evokes a UCR, as a UCS to produce Pavlovian

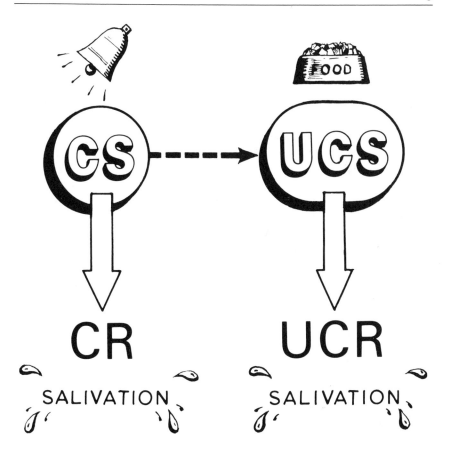

Figure 2.1 Schematic representation of the typical Pavlovian conditioning procedure. Pairing a conditioned stimulus, CS (e.g. a bell), with an unconditioned stimulus, UCS (e.g. food), eventually evokes the conditioned response, CR to the CS (in this case salivation).

conditioning. In fact, animals can even learn to associate two correlated stimuli which have no apparent biological significance (for example, sensory preconditioning, see p. 114). However, the kinds of Pavlovian preparation that have been utilized have been chosen largely because of their traditionality (such as salivation) or because of the ease of presentation of stimuli and measurement of responses. It is worth briefly describing some of the more common Pavlovian preparations here.

(a) *The conditioned eye blink* is obtained by pairing a brief stimulus (CS) such as a tone (usually of < 1 sec in duration) with either a puff of air to the cornea or a mild electric shock to the paraorbital region of the eye (UCS). This results in a conditioned eye blink during the CS (e.g. Vardaris and Fitzgerald, 1969), or in the case of animals such as rabbits — which have a third eyelid — a *nictitating membrane response* (NMR) (Gormezano, 1966).

(b) *Conditioned salivation* is the traditional Pavlovian conditioned response which can be obtained in dogs by using either food (e.g. Wagner, Siegal, Thomas, and Ellison, 1964) or a weak acid solution (e.g. Fitzgerald, 1963) as the UCS.

(c) *Heart-rate conditioning* generally involves using an aversive UCS such as electric shock or loud noise. The conditioned response is most frequently heart-rate deceleration (bradycardia) during the CS (e.g. Fitzgerald, Vardaris, and Brown, 1966; de Toledo and Black, 1966).

(d) *Conditioned activity* is one of the more common preparations used primarily with rats and pigeons. When an appetitive UCS such as food is paired with a CS, the CR that develops is an increase in generalized motor activity usually measured via a stabilometer attached to the floor of the conditioning chamber (e.g. Sheffield and Campbell, 1954; Zamble, 1967, 1969).

(e) *Conditioned suppression* is an aversive conditioning preparation which involves superimposing a CS paired with an aversive UCS such as electric shock onto a baseline of ongoing instrumental responding. For instance, the subject (such as a rat) would be trained to make an instrumental response (such as to press a lever) to obtain food on an intermittent schedule of reinforcement. When a steady and reliable rate of responding has been established, the subject is given pairings of a CS followed by electric shock (e.g. Estes and Skinner, 1941; Rescorla, 1967a, 1968). This kind of "fear" conditioning eventually produces a suppression of instrumental responding during the CS. This is usually measured in terms of a suppression ratio (SR) calculated according to the following formula

$$SR = \frac{A}{A + B} \qquad (2.1)$$

where A is the rate of instrumental responding during the CS, and B is the rate of instrumental responding during an equivalent period of time immediately prior to CS onset. Thus, an SR of 0.5 would mean there was no change in response rate during the CS compared with the rate which existed immediately prior to CS presentation — and hence no "fear" conditioning. An SR of zero would mean total suppression of responding during the CS, and hence a substantial amount of "fear" conditioning (cf. Annau and Kamin, 1961; Blackman, 1972; Millenson and de Villiers, 1972).

(f) *Autoshaping* is a more recently developed procedure which was first described in pigeons by Brown and Jenkins (1968). In their procedure, they presented the subject with pairings of an 8-sec illumination of a pecking key located on the wall of the conditioning chamber (CS) followed by response-independent food (UCS). They found that this training eventually resulted in the pigeon approaching and pecking the CS when it was illuminated and called the procedure "autoshaping" because they considered that its value lay in being a more efficient method of "shaping" animals to respond in instrumental conditioning experiments. However, autoshaping has acquired much greater theoretical importance than this, and represents a general tendency of animals to approach and contact localizable CSs which predict appetitive UCSs. Because of this, it has also been known as *sign-tracking* or *signal-directed behavior* (cf. Hearst and Jenkins, 1974), and it has been demonstrated in a very wide variety of species (Schwartz and Gamzu, 1977; Locurto, Terrace, and Gibbon, 1981; Hollis, 1982). This tendency of animals to approach and contact localizable CSs which predict appetitive UCSs such as food had largely gone undetected because of the traditional practice of physically restraining experimental subjects. However, even Pavlov had informally noted that one of his dogs, when released from its harness, actually approached and licked the metronome that was being used as the CS. Apart from approaching appetitive CSs there is also some evidence that animals will approach CSs which predict the *absence* of an aversive UCS such as an electric shock (Leclerc, 1985; Leclerc and Reberg, 1980) and *withdraw* from localizable CSs which predict the *absence* of appetitive UCSs such as food (Hearst and Franklin, 1977; Wasserman, Franklin, and Hearst, 1974). Autoshaping is a valuable Pavlovian preparation for a number of reasons: it tells us something about how unrestrained animals might react to Pavlovian contingencies in their natural habitat, which in turn helps us to understand the biological significance of Pavlovian conditioning. Second, it is a fairly easy Pavlovian procedure to arrange and produce an easily detectable and measurable CR (for example, rate of contact with the CS). The significance of autoshaping and signal-directed behavior in general is described in detail in Chapter 5 (pp. 150–69).

(g) *Conditioned taste aversion learning* is also a relatively recently developed Pavlovian procedure. When rats experience a distinctively-tasting food immediately followed by induced gastric illness (usually produced either by intraperitoneal injections of lithium chloride (LiCl) or rapid rotation in a centrifuge) they subsequently avoid consuming foods which possess that particular taste. In this procedure, taste is the CS, gastric poisoning is the UCS, and the resultant aversiveness of the taste is measured by the subsequent avoidance of foods possessing that distinctive taste. This procedure was originally described by Garcia and Koelling (1966) and has subsequently been replicated and extended many times. There has been a great deal of theoretical speculation about the nature of taste aversion learning which it is not necessary to detail here (see Chapter 6). However, it is increasingly being used as a Pavlovian conditioning preparation largely because reliable conditioning can be achieved after as few as only one pairing of CS (taste) and UCS (gastric illness). This can be useful for elaborating details of the associative substructure which underlies Pavlovian conditioning (cf. Rescorla, 1980a; Chapter 4).

Traditionally, the concept of what should be considered as a legitimate Pavlovian CR was very restricted. It was generally considered that a legitimate CR was one which resembled or mimicked the UCR, and an objective criterion for defining a CR was obtained "by requiring that the responses to the CS appear in the same effector system as the UCR" (Gormezano and Kehoe, 1976: 149). Clearly, the CR is not always a facsimile of the UCR. For instance, the UCR to electric shock in rats is jumping and prancing accompanied by a heart-rate increase; the CR in such circumstances is usually immobility and freezing accompanied by heart-rate deceleration (de Toledo and Black, 1966). More recently, as investigators have begun studying Pavlovian conditioning in unrestrained subjects, measures of learning have become more diverse and indirect. This is because our conception of Pavlovian conditioning has moved away from the view that pairing a CS with a UCS invokes a reflexive or mechanistic process which elicits a rather limited adaptive response. Currently, Pavlovian conditioning is seen as the acquisition of information about stimulus relationships in the environment, and the animal may act on this information in a variety of ways — not just by emitting an anticipatory facsimile of the UCR during the CS. This contemporary conception of Pavlovian learning has meant that learning theorists now study CRs other than those which are members of the same effector system as the UCR (e.g. Holland, 1977, 1979a, 1980a; Wasserman, Hunter, Gutowski, and Bader, 1975; see above) and they often measure conditioning indirectly by assessing the effect of a CS on the frequency of some independent ongoing behavior (for example, in conditioned suppression studies). In other circumstances it is clear that the animal may have learned something about the relationship between the CS and UCS but that this is not being translated into any observable change in behavior. This is known as "behaviorally silent" learning (cf. Dickinson, 1980), which has to be detected inferentially and can be done in a number of ways, some of which are described in the following chapters (see pp. 114 and 116). Nevertheless, the point to be emphasized here is that Pavlovian conditioning can be detected in a number of different ways and can also be manifested in a variety of adaptive guises in order to suit the animal's immediate needs. The complexity, variety and significance of Pavlovian learning is discussed in detail in chapters 5 and 6.

Control procedures

In order to begin to understand what an animal learns during a Pavlovian conditioning episode it is necessary to devise control procedures which guarantee that the observed changes in behavior are the result of associative learning and not of other unrelated factors. Clearly, there are other nonassociative learning processes, such as habituation and sensitization, which could produce spurious behavior changes in a Pavlovian procedure. Another process which has to be ruled out is *pseudo-conditioning*. This is where the CS comes to elicit a CR relevant to the UCS but not as a result of the animal learning about the CS–UCS relationship. For example, Grether (1938) first made monkeys fearful by presenting a number of powder flashes. Following this, the monkeys were given a series of presentations of a bell, all of which elicited reliable fright reactions which they had not done prior to the powder flashes. In this example the powder flash is a UCS and the bell a CS, yet a CR has been established without any pairing between CS and UCS, and presumably no associative learning between CS and UCS.

Because the important manipulation in Pavlovian conditioning is the arrangement of the CS and UCS in a consistent temporal relationship, any Pavlovian conditioning experiment should possess controls which retain all the features of the conditioning procedure *except* the predictive relationship between CS and UCS. The most appropriate control procedure is known as the *truly random control* (Rescorla, 1967b). In this procedure, control subjects are given a similar number of CS and UCS presentations to experimental subjects, but CS and UCS are programed independently of each other. Thus, control subjects receive exactly the same number of CS and UCS presentations, but not the predictive relationships between them. So, if control subjects exhibit similar behavior changes to experimental subjects, those changes must be due to nonassociative factors and so cannot be attributed to Pavlovian conditioning.

Predictiveness of the CS

Traditionally it had been assumed that the important feature of Pavlovian

29

conditioning which generated conditioned responding was the simple pairing of CS and UCS. That is, the number of pairings of a CS with a temporally contiguous UCS was the prime determinant of the strength of the CR (e.g. Kimble, 1961). Nevertheless, while temporal contiguity is an important contributor to learning, it is not necessarily the number of CS–UCS pairings that is important, but the predictive significance of the CS as measured by the correlation between CS and UCS. Normally, the correlation between CS and UCS in a simple Pavlovian experiment is 1.00. However, this correlation can be reduced in at least two ways: (1) by failing to present the UCS after some of the CS presentations (a partial reinforcement schedule), or (2) by presenting surplus UCSs unsignaled by the CS. Both of these procedures can reduce the strength of the CR to the CS.

When a partial reinforcement (PR) schedule rather than a continuous reinforcement schedule is used, acquisition of the CR is usually retarded, and this effect has been demonstrated in dogs (Vardaris and Fitzgerald, 1969; Fitzgerald, 1963; Wagner, Siegel, Thomas, and Ellison, 1964; Fitzgerald, Vardaris, and Teyler, 1966), rabbits (Thomas and Wagner, 1964; Gormezano and Coleman, 1975; Leonard and Theios, 1967), rats (Scheuer, 1969), fish (Berger, Yarczower, and Bitterman, 1965; Gonzalez, Milstein, and Bitterman, 1962) and humans (Prokasy and Kumpfer, 1969; Froseth and Grant, 1961; Ross and Hartman, 1965); and with a variety of responses such as the eyeblink CR, salivation, heart-rate changes, conditioned activity, and conditioned suppression of instrumental responding. Studies which have used appetitive preparations (such as salivation in dogs) also demonstrate that asymptotic CR strength in continuously reinforced subjects is greater than in subjects which receive only 50 per cent reinforcement (e.g. Fitzgerald, 1963; Wagner, Siegel, Thomas, and Ellison, 1964; Brogden, 1939a; Sadler, 1968). However, in a majority of studies which have used an aversive UCS, eventual CR strength in partially reinforced subjects does not differ from that obtained in continuously reinforced animals (e.g. Gormezano and Coleman, 1975; Thomas and Wagner, 1964; Fitzgerald, 1966; Fitzgerald, Vardaris, and Teyler, 1966; Brimer and Dockrill, 1966; Hilton, 1969; Scheuer, 1969; Wagner, Siegel, and Fein, 1967; Willis, 1969; Gonzales, Milstein, and Bitterman, 1962). However, there is one particular preparation in which PR produces a higher asymptotic level of conditioning. This is in autoshaping procedures where the CR is measured as behavior which is directed toward the CS, and studies using both rats and pigeons demonstrate greater CS-directed behavior in partially reinforced subjects (50 per cent reinforcement) than in continuously reinforced subjects (100 per cent reinforcement) (e.g. Gonzalez, 1974; Poling and Thompson, 1977; Davey and Cleland, 1982). However, this phenomenon appears to represent a performance feature of the orienting reaction characteristics of autoshaping rather than reflecting any particular oddity in the animal's processing of the predictive relationship between CS and UCS (cf. Collins, Young, Davies, and Pearce, 1983).

Other studies have attempted to manipulate directly the correlation between CS and UCS by the addition of surplus unsignaled UCSs during inter-trial intervals: the greater the number of unsignaled UCSs, the weaker the correlation between CS and UCS. These studies have been unanimous in demonstrating that the strength of the CR at asymptote is a function of the correlation between CS and UCS (Rescorla, 1967b, 1968) and that the CR is acquired more rapidly the higher the correlation between CS and UCS (Gibbon, 1981; Gibbon and Balsam, 1981; Jenkins, Barnes, and Barrera, 1981).

What partial reinforcement and CS–UCS correlation studies tell us is that Pavlovian conditioning will occur only if the probability of the UCS following the CS is greater than the probability of the UCS occurring without the CS [i.e. $p(UCS/CS) > p(UCS/no\ CS)$]. In effect, many animals possess the abilities to detect the correlation between CS and UCS, and it is this predictive significance of the CS which mediates the strength of the conditioned response. The only real exception to this simple proviso is the fact that in aversive conditioning studies, partial reinforcement generally produces asymptotic levels of responding which are similar to the levels produced with continuous reinforcement. It is not clear why this anomaly should exist, but it may reflect the greater urgency required in the learning of relations involving potentially dangerous or lethal outcomes. For example, if one stimulus is a reliable predictor of a predator and another stimulus predicts a predator only 50 per cent of the time, the animal needs to be equally alert in both cases. The reason for this is that the outcome of encountering the predator is possible death, and so even if a stimulus signals a predator on only a percentage basis the animal must have its defensive reactions primed just as much as it would if the stimulus reliably signals the predator.

Inhibitory conditioning

The majority of Pavlovian conditioning emphasizes that certain events such as CSs signal that something important is about to happen and that this generates anticipatory responses during CS presentation. However, animals also have the capacity to learn *negative* relationships between events; that is, they can learn that a particular stimulus predicts the *absence* of a UCS. This is known as *inhibitory conditioning* and can be demonstrated in a number of ways.

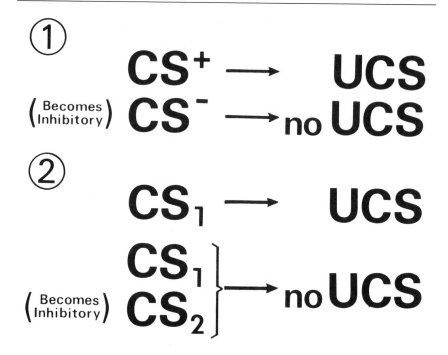

Figure 2.2 Two procedures for producing inhibitory conditioning to a CS. In procedure (1) CS⁻ is simply paired with the omission of the UCS. In procedure (2) CS₂ becomes inhibitory because the UCS is omitted on occasions when CS₂ is presented in compound with CS₁ (see text for further explanation).

In the previous section we described how learning takes place only if there is a positive correlation between the CS and UCS. It is also possible to generate situations in which there is a negative correlation between the CS and UCS: that is, the CS predicts the absence of the UCS. For instance, the presentation of the CS may signal that the UCS is some considerable time away (e.g. Rescorla, 1969). Alternatively, a stimulus may be presented simultaneously with a CS that has previously been paired with a UCS, but the compound signals the omission of the UCS on that trial (e.g. Marchant, Mis, and Moore, 1972; Rescorla, 1975, 1979) (see Figure 2.2). In both of these situations the CS acquires inhibitory properties; that is, it acquires the ability to inhibit excitatory conditioning. This inhibition, of course, has to be measured indirectly, and there are a number of ways of doing this.

First, there is what is known as the compound stimulus or summation test. This is where the inhibitory stimulus (usually known as a CS⁻) is presented in compound with an already established excitatory CS (known as a CS⁺). If the CS– has acquired inhibitory properties, the strength of the CR to CS⁺ will be reduced or eliminated completely on trials when CS⁺ and CS⁻ are presented together (cf. Reberg and Black, 1969; Miller and Speare, 1985). Second, it is possible to test the inhibitory properties of a CS⁻ by subsequently attempting to condition it as a CS⁺. If the CS⁻ has acquired inhibitory properties it should take relatively longer to develop excitatory conditioning to such a stimulus (e.g. Hammond, 1968; Rescorla, 1969). Nevertheless, this retardation-of-acquisition test is fraught with problems because there are many factors which might retard the acquisition of excitatory conditioning and not just the fact that the CS has previously been used in inhibitory training (e.g. Baker and Baker, 1985). Because of this it is currently more acceptable to adopt the summation test as a measure of the inhibitory properties of a CS– (Miller and Spear, 1985).

So animals do not just ignore a stimulus which is not paired with a UCS. They extract what information they can from its relationship to the UCS. If it reliably predicts the absence or omission of the UCS, then that information is acquired by the animal and translated into the inhibition of UCS-relevant behaviors when the stimulus occurs. This presumably has the benefit of preventing the animal from wasting its time on anticipatory reactions when no UCS is imminent.

Overshadowing and blocking

Pavlov (1927) observed that when two stimuli are presented simultaneously as a compound CS, conditioning frequently occurs to only the most salient of the two stimulus elements. That is, when the two CS elements are subsequently presented on their own after conditioning, only the more salient or intense of the two elements will elicit a CR. This is known as *overshadowing*, and can occur between stimuli from the same or from different modalities (Mackintosh, 1971; Sutherland and Mackintosh, 1971). This phenomenon presumably reflects some aspect of the animal's selective attention; that is, it learns about only one element of the compound and it is this element that becomes associated with the UCS.

A similar related phenomenon is called *blocking*. The blocking paradigm contains three stages: (1) a CS (call it A) is paired with a UCS until conditioning to A has been established; (2) the subject then receives further training with a compound CS consisting of A and a new element B; (3) after training in the second stage the added element B is tested to see if it evokes a

CR. Normally what happens in this procedure is that pretraining with element A "blocks" conditioning to the added element B and element B on its own fails to evoke a CR (cf. Kamin, 1969). Once again this phenomenon appears to reflect the animal's ability to process useful information. Since the UCS is reliably predicted by element A, the new added element B is redundant information, so the animal effectively ignores it. Blocking is an important theoretical phenomenon in Pavlovian conditioning because it tells us something about the mechanisms which lead an animal to associate CS and UCS. (These are discussed further on pp. 129–31).

Higher-order conditioning

Once a CS has been associated with a UCS and is capable of eliciting a reliable CR, that CS can then be used to reinforce other potential CSs. For instance, second-order conditioning can be demonstrated using the following procedure:

1   CS_1 (e.g. a light) is paired with a UCS (e.g. food); then
2   CS_2 (e.g. a tone) is paired with CS_1 (light). This will usually result in a CR relevant to food being evoked by CS_2, even though CS_2 has never been directly paired with food (cf. Rescorla, 1980a: 1–8; Rizley and Rescorla, 1972).

Second-order conditioning of this kind is a fairly robust phenomenon, although care must be taken during the second stage of the procedure when CS_2 is being paired with a CS_1. If too many CS_2–CS_1 pairings are presented without "refresher" trials relating CS_1 and UCS, CS_2 could acquire inhibitory properties because it effectively signals an occurrence of CS_1 without the UCS. Higher-order conditioning is theoretically important for the learning theorist largely as a procedure which permits the experimenter to analyze the nature of individual associations (see pp. 117–20).

2   Comparative aspects of Pavlovian conditioning

Ever since the time of Pavlov, it has been widely agreed that Pavlovian conditioning is a simple but important means by which animals learn about the basic relationships between events in their environment. As such it is possibly the most basic form of information acquisition. But how prevalent is Pavlovian conditioning among members of the animal kingdom? Most studies of Pavlovian conditioning have been carried out on a very limited number of species, primarily mammals such as dogs or laboratory rats, or birds such as pigeons. But do organisms with simple nervous systems possess

Pavlovian learning abilities? At the other extreme, is Pavlovian conditioning too simple a learning process to be useful to behaviorally complex organisms such as humans? At least some writers once thought so (e.g. Brewer, 1974). It is not difficult to conceive of the kinds of advantages that possessing Pavlovian learning abilities might bestow on an animal (see Chapter 6), and clearly, being able to anticipate biologically important events by learning about the stimuli that signal them must be a selective benefit to most, if not all, species of animals. The following section attempts to deal with two broad aspects of Pavlovian learning in several different groups of animals.

First, what range of species is actually able to learn in Pavlovian conditioning procedures? And second, what kinds of things can they learn? This latter question addresses the problem of whether some species can only be conditioned within certain responses systems (this might be especially true of invertebrates), and also whether they can only learn certain kinds of associations. For instance, it is fairly clear that both birds and mammals can learn about the relationships between environmental stimuli (such as between a CS and UCS). However, some theorists (e.g. Amiro and Bitterman, 1980) have claimed that other groups of species — such as fish — are only capable of learning S–R associations (that is, associations between stimuli and particular responses). Some of the evidence relating to these questions is set out below.

Pavlovian conditioning in invertebrates

There is a very wide variety of invertebrate species which vary dramatically not only in their neural complexity but also in their habitats and lifestyles. However, because the study of Pavlovian conditioning has traditionally been concentrated on vertebrate species, it is not until just recently that experimenters have turned their attention to the possibility of associative learning in invertebrates.

There are four issues which are important in the study of Pavlovian conditioning in invertebrates. First, can invertebrates be shown to exhibit simple Pavlovian conditioning when suitable controls are used to eliminate nonassociative factors such as habituation, sensitization, and pseudo-conditioning? Second, when Pavlovian learning has been demonstrated, do such species exhibit other phenomena associated with Pavlovian learning such as conditioned inhibition, overshadowing, blocking, or higher-order conditioning? Demonstration of such phenomena would indicate relatively sophisticated capacities for processing the relationship between CS and UCS. Third, are invertebrates constrained by the variety of stimuli that can be used as CSs and UCSs in Pavlovian conditioning? Because of their relative neural simplicity they may have developed the capacity to form Pavlovian associations only within a limited number of response systems. Fourth, because of their neural unsophistication, many invertebrates provide a useful medium for studying the cellular mechanisms that underlie associative learning, and much recent research has illuminated some of the intracellular and synaptic mechanisms responsible for simple associative learning (e.g. Hawkins and Kandel, 1984; Quinn, 1984).

In order to demonstrate Pavlovian conditioning it is necessary to compare subjects which have received pairings of CS and UCS with subjects which have received only random presentations of CS and UCS (see p. 29). In studies which have been adequately controlled in this way, Pavlovian conditioning has been demonstrated in a range of invertebrates. These include protoza such as *Paramecium caudatum* and the planarian flatworm (Applewhite and Morowitz, 1966; Jacobson, Fried, and Horowitz, 1967; Huber, Rucker, and McDiarmid, 1974; Hennessey, Rucker, and McDiarmid, 1979), numerous species of mollusks including the sea slug aplysia (Alkon, 1974; Carew, Hawkins, and Kandel, 1983; Croll and Chase, 1980; Crow and Alkon, 1978; Davis and Gillette, 1978; Gelperin, 1975; Mpitsos, Collins, and McClellan, 1978; Sahley, Gelperin, and Rudy, 1981; Walters, Carew, and Kandel, 1981a, b), bees (Bitterman, Menzel, Feitz, and Schafer, 1983; Couvillon and Bitterman, 1980; cf. Heinrich, 1985), the fruit fly drosophila (Booker and Quinn, 1981; Quinn, Harris, and Benzer, 1974; Tempel, Bonini, Dawson, and Quinn, 1982), crabs and crayfish (Mikhailoff, 1923; Cowles, 1908), leeches (Henderson and Strong, 1972), starfish (Landenberger, 1966), and octopuses (Wells and Young, 1968). However, coelenterates (such as jellyfish and sea anemones), which control their movements largely via nerve nets, have not yet been shown unambiguously to exhibit associative learning (Haralson and Groff, 1975; Ross, 1965).

At this stage it is probably valuable to describe the details of an individual study on invertebrate Pavlovian learning to familiarize the reader with the kinds of procedures involved. A study by Carew, Hawkins, and Kandel (1983) demonstrated differential classical conditioning of a defensive withdrawal reflex in the sea slug *Aplysia california*. The response conditioned was a simple one, the gill and siphon withdrawal reflex which is mediated by a well-delineated neural circuit. The UCS which elicits this withdrawal response is a strong electric shock to the tail. In this differential study they used two different CSs, a light tactile stimulus to the siphon and a weak electric shock to the mantle shelf. One of these stimuli was paired with the UCS and thus became a CS+, the other stimulus was specifically unpaired (a CS−). Subjects showed significantly greater CRs to the CS+ than to the CS− (see Figure 2.3).

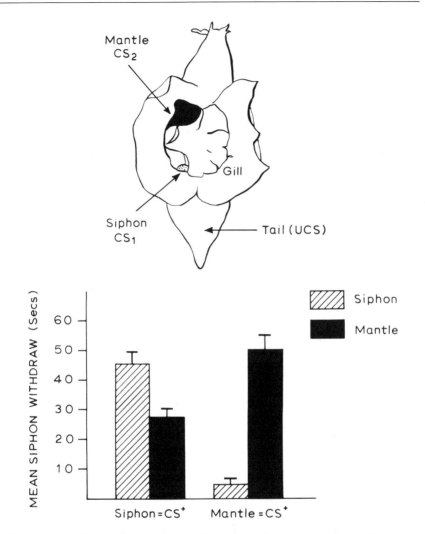

Figure 2.3 A dorsal view of aplysia illustrating the siphon and mantle shelves which were used as sites for CS presentation. The UCS was an electric shock to the tail. The bottom half of the figure shows the results of a differential conditioning procedure. On the left, the group that had CS⁺ presented to the siphon (siphon = CS⁺) showed significantly more CRs to the siphon CS than the mantle CS (the latter of which was not paired with the UCS). On the right, the group which had CS⁺ presented to the mantle (mantle = CS⁺) showed more CRs to the mantle CS than to the siphon CS. (From Carew, Hawkins, and Kandel, 1983)

(i) *Predictive significance of the CS* A number of studies have indicated that some invertebrates may respond to the predictive significance of the CS in some of the ways that vertebrate species do. For instance, Carew, Hawkins, and Kandel (1983) found that conditioned responding in aplysia was dependent on temporal contiguity between CS and UCS. The optimal CS–UCS interval was found to be 0.5 sec, and CR strength declined dramatically with a CS–UCS interval greater than 2 sec. The predictive significance of the CS has also been found to be important in determining CR strength in other studies using mollusks (Sahley, Rudy, and Gelperin, 1981; Farley and Alkon, 1983). However, in studies which have investigated evidence of blocking and overshadowing (see p. 33) the results have been less consistent with those from vertebrate experiments. For instance, Couvillon, Klosterhalfen, and Bitterman (1983) found no evidence of blocking effects in honeybees, and the existence of blocking would have indicated some sophistication in the processing of CS–UCS information. However, Couvillon and Bitterman (1980) and Couvillon *et al.* (1983) did demonstrate overshadowing effects in honeybees, but these particular results were not easy to interpret in attentional terms (cf. Sahley, 1984).

(ii) *Inhibitory conditioning* Bitterman, Menzel, Feitz, and Schafer (1983) found that honeybees that had experienced explicitly unpaired presentations of an odor CS and a food UCS would actually extend their proboscises when the CS– odor was not present and retract them when the CS⁻ odor was present. Honeybees trained in the standard Pavlovian manner with normal CS–UCS pairings exhibited the opposite tendency — they extended their proboscises only when the CS⁺ odor was present. Similarly, when a compound stimulus or summation test is used to measure conditioned inhibition (see p. 33), honeybees showed a significant resistance to conditioning. Both experiments from the Bitterman *et al.* (1983) study clearly demonstrate the existence of conditioned inhibition.

(iii) *Higher-order conditioning* Second-order conditioning has been obtained on a number of occasions in invertebrate subjects such as honeybees and mollusks (Menzel, 1983; Mikhailoff, 1923; Sahley, Rudy, and Gelperin, 1981). Sahley *et al.* (1981) exposed slugs (*Limax maximus*) first to pairings of a carrot odor (CS$_1$) and quinidine (UCS), then they received simultaneous presentations of a potato odor (CS$_2$) and the carrot odor (CS$_1$). In comparison with appropriate controls, subjects that underwent this second-order conditioning procedure exhibited a differential second-order CR to CS$_2$. Perhaps what is more interesting is that inferential techniques were then used to analyze the associations that had been formed during such second-order conditioning (see pp. 116–17). Using these inferential techniques, Sahley *et al.* (1981) were able to show that when CS_2 and CS_1 were presented *simultaneously* during second-order conditioning, the response to CS_2 was dependent on an association being formed between CS_2 and CS_1. However, when CS_2 and CS_1 were presented *sequentially*, destroying the association between CS_2 and CS_1 by extinguishing the response to CS_1 did not affect CR_2. This suggests that the slug had associated CS_2 with some component of its response to CS_1 (an S–R association) in much the same way that vertebrate species have been shown to (see pp. 116–17 for a summary of the techniques and results on vertebrate subjects).

(iv) *Constraints on Pavlovian conditioning in invertebrates*   While it is clear that invetebrates do exhibit many of the Pavlovian phenomena also exhibited by vertebrates, they also appear to learn certain kinds of things more efficiently than others. For instance, honeybees will learn to associate certain kinds of colors and scents with food more readily than others. They will learn to associate the color violet (CS) with sugar (UCS) with an 85 per cent reliability after only one pairing; however, it takes four pairings to achieve the same learning if the CS is green; furthermore, they will learn to forage from blue flowers only after 50 rewards, from white flowers only after 250 rewards (Menzel, Erber, and Masuhr, 1974; Heinrich, Mudge, and Deringis, 1977). Presumably, such selective learning is based on the extent to which these colors are reliable food indicators in the wild (Heinrich, 1985). Similarly, in proboscis reflex conditioning bees can readily associate an odor CS with sucrose solution, but have great difficulty in associating a visual CS with food. Even when odors are used as the CS, honeybees learn more quickly when the CS odor is one which is 'flower-like' (Menzel, 1983).

Another example of such associative constraints in invertebrates is provided by the earthworm. Although an earthworm will respond to and habituate to a vibrational stimulus, it cannot associate such a tactile CS with an electric shock UCS. However, if the CS is a taste or odor signaling a hot, dry place (an aversive UCS for earthworms), the organism can form this kind of association quite readily and subsequently avoids the taste CS (Mayr, 1974; Eisenstein, 1967).

(v) *Summary*   All of these studies of Pavlovian conditioning in invertebrates demonstrate a number of facts. First, Pavlovian associative learning is possible in the most neurologically uncomplex of organisms such as protozoa and planaria. Second, some of the organisms reviewed here demonstrate attributes of Pavlovian conditioning which reflect a certain capacity for information acquisition and selective attention (such as detecting contiguity between CS and UCS, conditioned inhibition, and higher-order conditioning). However, this information is sketchy, and there is no evidence that invertebrates exhibit blocking, or that CR strength is a function of the correlation between CS and UCS. Demonstrating these phenomena in invertebrates would suggest rather sophisticated processing of the relationship between CS and UCS. Third, some invertebrate organisms do appear to exhibit Pavlovian conditioning in some response systems but not others (for instance, the earthworm). This may either reflect the specialized evolution of such learning for the needs of specific response systems, or it may reflect the distinct possibility that neurologically simple organisms do not possess an associative mechanism which is independent of individual response systems. Nevertheless, we must be cautious in our interpretation of negative results, since — being at the relatively early stage that we are in the study of invertebrate learning — we may still need to discover the stimulus parameters which may indeed reveal Pavlovian associative learning where we had previously failed to observe it.

Pavlovian conditioning in fish

When appropriate controls for nonassociative factors have been used (the truly random control, see p. 29). Pavlovian conditioning has been demonstrated in fish on a number of occasions using a variety of different CSs, UCSs, and response measures. It has been demonstrated in sharks (Gruber and Schneiderman, 1975), goldfish (e.g. Bitterman, 1964; Overmier and Curnow, 1969; Brandon and Bitterman, 1979), Siamese fighting fish (*Betta splendens*) (Thompson and Sturm, 1965), the blue gourami (*Trichogaster trichopterus*) (Hollis, 1984b), and the archer fish (*Toxotes chatarens*) (Waxman and McCleave, 1978), to name a few. Just one report by Wickelgren (cited by Rovainen, 1979) failed to find Pavlovian conditioning in lampreys when experimental subjects were compared with random control subjects. UCSs used have included food, electric shock, exposure of a mirror to Siamese fighting fish (which elicits an aggressive display), and conspecific males which elicit threat display and fighting in blue gouramis (cf. Macphail, 1982: 58–64; Hollis, 1984b).

Autoshaping has been demonstrated in fish on a number of occasions. For instance, when a response key (CS) is illuminated for a brief period prior to delivery of food (UCS), goldfish will approach and 'nose' the CS when it is illuminated (Brandon and Bitterman, 1979; Bottjer, Scobie, and Wallace, 1977; Woodard and Bitterman, 1974). Squier (1969) has shown that a number of teleost species will direct species-specific feeding responses toward an appetitive CS (the Oscar, *Astronotus oscellatus*; mouthbreeders, *Tilapia mossambica*; and mullets, *Mugil cephalus*). Similarly, archer fish will squirt water at a red light (CS) that signals delivery of a fruit fly (UCS) (Waxman and McCleave, 1978). Although squirting water is not a behavior the fish utilizes in consuming the fly, it is a food-procuring response which is directed at insects above the water level, causing them to fall to the water's surface.

There is also some evidence that the acquisition of CRs in some species of fish is dependent on the relationship between CS and UCS. Subjects that are given continuous reinforcement tend to exhibit higher asymptotic levels of responding and superior rates of acquisition than partially reinforced subjects. This has been found in goldfish (Berger, Yarczower, and Bitterman, 1965; Gonzalez, Longo, and Bitterman, 1961; Gonzalez, Milstein, and Bitterman, 1962), and in African mouthbreeders (*Tilapia macrocephala*) (Gonzalez, Eskin, and Bitterman, 1962). The possibility that teleosts do process the predictive significance of the CS in ways similar to birds and mammals is suggested by preliminary studies which have obtained both overshadowing and blocking in goldfish (Wolach, Breuning, Roccaforte, and Solhkhan, 1977).

However, although it is possible to produce successful second-order conditioning in goldfish (Amiro and Bitterman, 1980), attempts so far to produce sensory preconditioning have failed (Amiro and Bitterman, 1980; Sergeyev, cited by Razran, 1971). Sensory preconditioning is a higher-order conditioning procedure in which pairings of two neutral stimuli (CS_1 and CS_2) are given *before* CS_2 is eventually paired with the UCS (see p. 114 for a fuller report of the procedure). In birds and mammals, this procedure produces a CR to subsequent presentations of CS_1 indicating that, although pairings of CS_1 and CS_2 in the first stage of the experiment evoked no observable changes in behavior, the animal did actually learn the relationship between them (e.g. Rizley and Rescorla, 1972). The failure to obtain sensory preconditioning in goldfish, along with a number of other related results, has led Brandon and Bitterman (1979) to suggest that goldfish cannot learn about relationships between external stimulus events (S–S learning) but only between an external stimulus and their own behavior (S–R learning). Thus, they imply that Pavlovian conditioning in teleosts is a result of the subject learning to associate the CS with its response to the paired UCS (that is, the UCR) rather than with the UCS itself. The fact that goldfish do not appear to be able to learn to associate two neutral stimuli in the sensory preconditioning procedure lends support to this. Thus, there are two implications of goldfish being S–R learners: (1) they should be unable to learn about the relationship between two stimuli unless the latter of the two stimuli evokes a response; and (2) the CRs that are learned in the Pavlovian conditioning situation should only be of the same kind that are normally evoked by the UCS or appear in the same effector system as the UCR. There is certainly no evidence available at present which is obviously inconsistent with these two implications. However, as we have mentioned before, negative evidence has to be interpreted cautiously. For instance, studies may have failed to observe sensory preconditioning in teleosts as much from inadequate parametric considerations as from the animal lacking the necessary associative mechanisms. Nevertheless, there is another important implication of Brandon and Bitterman's (1979) assertion that goldfish are S–R learners. If teleosts do acquire Pavlovian CRs through S–R learning, then the CR should be independent of any postconditioning manipulation of the UCS. Such manipulations in birds and mammals do suggest that the CR is sensitive to post-conditioning revaluation of the UCS (see p. 116) and that these animals learn S–S rather than S–R associations. Until comparable postconditioning UCS revaluation studies are carried out on fish, we must be cautious in assuming that teleosts are S–R learners.

In summary, then, fish do show reliable Pavlovian conditioning, both in a variety of species and response systems. They also show some sensitivity to the predictive relationship between CS and UCS, and exhibit overshadowing, blocking, autoshaping, and higher-order conditioning. Although all of this shows *prima facie* equivalence with Pavlovian performance in most nonhuman mammals, it does not, of course, imply that the cognitive mechanisms underlying this learning are identical in fish and nonhuman mammals.

Pavlovian conditioning in reptiles and amphibia

There have been relatively few Pavlovian studies on reptiles and amphibia, and what studies are available have usually been less than optimally controlled. Nevertheless, they do appear to indicate that Pavlovian conditioning exists in such groups.

For instance, Davidson and Richardson (1970) found that pairing auditory and visual CSs with a shock UCS produced reliable heart-rate CRs in collared lizards (*Crotaphytus collaris*), although they did not use the necessary random control procedure to rule out nonassociative effects such as sensitization or pseudo-conditioning. Czaplicki, Porter, and Wilcoxon (1975) successfully demonstrated conditioned taste aversion learning in garter snakes (*Thamnophis sirtalis*) by pairing pieces of minnows or worms (CS) with gastric poisoning (UCS). Subjects undergoing this procedure showed significantly greater aversion to the CS foods than did control subjects which were not poisoned after exposure to the food. An experiment by Loop (1976) also appears to demonstrate autoshaping in the Bengal monitor lizard (*Varanus bengalensis*). Loop paired 15-sec presentations of an illuminated response key with food and found that the subjects developed "biting-like" CRs directed at the CS key. A final study by Farris and Breuning (1977) has some implications for the associative processes underlying Pavlovian conditioning in reptiles. They used a visual CS paired with a hammer-tap UCS which produced a CR of head withdrawal in red-eared turtles (*Chrysemys scripta elegans*). However, following conditioning they subjected the animal to postconditioning habituation of the UCS (that is, the UCS was presented alone on a number of occasions and elicited a weaker and weaker UCR). On subsequent presentations of the CS they found that extinction proceeded more quickly in those subjects which had received UCS habituation training than those which had not. This is very similar to a technique devised by Rescorla (1973) to discover whether the CR is mediated by associations between the CS and UCS (see p. 116). If the CR is mediated by an association between the CS and UCS, then any technique which produces a revaluation of the UCS (such as habituation) should influence the strength of the CR. This is exactly what Farris and Breuning found, suggesting that the red-eared turtle had in fact learned an association between CS and UCS (S–S learning).

Amphibia have traditionally had the reputation of being behaviorally inflexible and difficult to train (e.g. Thorpe, 1963; Hodos and Campbell, 1969). However, there are a couple of studies which suggest that Pavlovian conditioning can be obtained in this group of species. Goldstein, Spies, and Sepinwall (1964) found that they were able to produce nictitating membrane CRs in leopard frogs (*Rana p. pipiens*) using a touch to the nostril as the CS and a touch to the cornea as the UCS. Yaremko, Boice, and Thompson (1969) ran a similar nictitating membrane response study with toads (*Bufo americanus*). The CS was a touch to the cephalic region and the UCS a touch on the cornea. They found that subjects which received pairings of CS and UCS developed increases in the probability of the CR which were significantly greater than in subjects which had CS and UCS explicitly unpaired. The fact that Yaremko *et al.* (1969) used a random control group and that Goldstein *et al.* (1964) used a group designed specifically to control for the effects of sensitization strongly suggests that the amphibian subjects used in these studies were exhibiting Pavlovian conditioning.

Pavlovian conditioning in birds

There is no doubt that birds exhibit Pavlovian conditioning, and one species of bird, the pigeon, is probably the most utilized subject in such studies after the laboratory rat.

Pavlovian conditioning has been demonstrated in "fear" conditioning preparations using aversive UCSs (e.g. Davis and Coates, 1978), in heart-rate and respiration studies (e.g. Cohen and Durkovic, 1966), in food aversion learning studies (e.g. Wilcoxon, Dragoin, and Kral, 1971), in eyeblink conditioning studies (e.g. Davis and Coates, 1978) and, most prominently, in autoshaping studies (e.g. Brown and Jenkins, 1968; Hearst and Jenkins, 1974; Schwartz and Gamzu, 1977; Locurto, Terrace, and Gibbon, 1981). Pavlovian conditioning has been demonstrated not just with food or electric shock UCSs, but also with water (Jenkins and Moore, 1973; Woodruff and Williams, 1976), heat (Wasserman, 1973; Wasserman, Hunter, Gutowski, and Bader, 1975) and conspecific mates (Farris, 1967; Rackham, 1971) as UCSs.

Apart from pigeons as the most widely studied bird in Pavlovian procedures, conditioning has been demonstrated in a variety of other species. For instance, chicks will readily approach and contact an illuminated pecking key (CS) that predicts heat reinforcement in a cold environment (UCS) (Wasserman, 1973; Wasserman, Hunter, Gutowski, and Bader, 1975). Chicks that are given only random pairings of CS and UCS in this procedure fail to show CS-directed responses. In an aversive conditioning study, Shettleworth (1972b) found that chicks would run around, jump, and shrill call when an auditory CS was paired with unavoidable food shock (UCS). However, there were much less dramatic changes in behavior when the CS was a visual stimulus. Woodruff and Starr (1978) conducted appetitive Pavlovian conditioning in chicks that had never been allowed to eat or drink naturally from hatching (they were force-fed food, water, or sand during rearing). The chicks were subsequently exposed to pairing of a lit key (CS) and either food, water, or sand (UCS). Woodruff and Starr found that chicks given the food UCS directed pecking and scratching movements toward the key-light CS, chicks given water directed "drinking-like" movements toward the CS, but the chicks who had the CS paired with sand did not direct any CRs toward the CS. Thus, even though the sand had elicited swallowing, when force-fed during rearing it did not produce any CRs. This study produced CRs very similar to the topogrophy of CS-directed behavior in pigeons using food and water UCSs (Jenkins and Moore, 1973).

Sexual UCSs also produce CS-directed behaviors to localizable CSs in birds. Rackham (1971) exposed male pigeons to repeated pairings of a stimulus lamp (CS) and a conspecific mate. The male and female were housed in adjacent compartments of a chamber separated by a dividing door. The stimulus lamp was illuminated once a day immediately prior to the opening of the door between the compartments. Within 5–10 trials the male subjects were approaching the CS lamp and exhibiting courtship responses toward it such as nodding, bowing, cooing, strutting, and pirouetting. Similar results to this have been found using conspecific mate UCSs with Japanese quail (*Coturnix coturnix japonica*) (Farris, 1967).

Autoshaping studies using food reinforcement have revealed a considerable amount about the nature of Pavlovian conditioning in birds. For instance, the strength of signal-directed CRs in pigeons is a function of the predictive significance of the CS. If there is no correlation between CS and UCS presentation, autoshaping fails to occur (Gamzu and Williams, 1971, 1973). Similarly, if the predictive significance of the CS is reduced by making the CS duration *longer* than the inter-trial interval, then autoshaping is minimal (Ricci, 1973; Terrace, Gibbon, Farrell, and Baldock, 1975). Pigeons readily exhibit blocking and overshadowing (cf. Rescorla and Durlach, 1981), and second-order conditioning of autoshaped responding is also easily obtained using pigeons exposed to higher-order conditioning procedures (e.g. Rashotte, Griffin, and Sisk, 1977; Nairne and Rescorla, 1981), and some progress has been made in understanding the associations that the birds form during such higher-order conditioning (see pp. 119–20).

One criticism of authoshaping studies, however, has been that the CS-directed behavior found in such studies may not necessarily be the result of Pavlovian conditioning. For instance, because the UCS immediately follows presentation of the CS, then any CS-directed pecking that occurs may be the result of superstitious instrumental reinforcement (see p. 62); that is, on all occasions when the CS is contacted, this behavior will be closely followed by UCS delivery. One way of controlling for this possibility is with the use of an *omission contingency* (but see p. 103). An omission contingency specifies that on all of those trials when the CS is contacted, the UCS will be withheld: thus, there can be no superstitious associations between CS contact and the UCS. If, under these circumstances, CS contact does still persist, one can be fairly sure that the behavior is being generated by Pavlovian rather than superstitious instrumental contingencies. Studies which have imposed omission contingencies on autoshaped key-pecking in pigeons have had fairly clear results. For instance, Williams and Williams (1969) found that when an omission contingency was in operation, autoshaped key-pecking was still maintained at quite high levels for a substantial number of trials. Even when autoshaped responding is reduced by an omission contingency it has frequently been found that the subjects are still directing pecks toward the key-light CS but these pecks either fail to reach and operate the key (Lucas, 1975) or hit the wall of the conditioning chamber in the close vicinity of the key (Barrera, 1974). When omission contingencies are imposed on pre-key pecking or on actual approach behaviors to the key, then these behaviors are significantly resistant to suppression, suggesting that they are being generated by Pavlovian contingencies (e.g. Lucas, 1975; Peden, Browne, and Hearst, 1977).

While these results imply that autoshaped responding is truly Pavlovian, we must be quite sure what the results of omission studies mean. If a CR fails to be suppressed by an omission contingency or emerges even when an omission contingency is in operation from the outset of training (cf. Locurto, 1981), that is good evidence that the response is Pavlovian. If, however, the CR *is* suppressed or eliminated by the omission contingency, that can imply either that the CR was generated by superstitious instrumental contingencies in the first place, *or* that it was generated by Pavlovian conditioning *but is sensitive to instrumental contingencies.* So suppression or modification of a CR by instrumental contingencies does not necessarily imply that the CR was *not* generated by Pavlovian conditioning.

One other set of studies which indicates that autoshaping results from the bird learning about the association between CS and UCS, is where the responses either to the CS or UCS are blocked during training. For instance, in situations in which the subject is physically restrained either from pecking the key-light CS or from eating the grain UCS, pecking occurs almost immediately when the physical restraints are removed (Browne, 1974; Kirby, 1968). This suggests that perception of the relationship between CS and UCS was sufficient for the bird to form an association between these two events which immediately became manifest when the behavioral restraints were removed.

Although other species of bird, such as the bobwhite quail, have been shown to autoshape using a food UCS (Gardner, 1969), some other species of bird do fail to exhibit autoshaped key pecking in such circumstances. For instance, Powell, Kelly, and Santisteban (1975) and Wilson (1978) have reported repeated failures to obtain autoshaped key pecking in crows or other corvids such as rooks, jackdaws, and European jays. However, there is no evidence available as to whether these species actually directed their behavior toward the CS but simply failed to operate the response key. Other interpretations of this failure to obtain autoshaping rest on species differences in feeding behavior (see pp. 150-1).

Finally, two other aspects of Pavlovian conditioning in birds will be mentioned in passing here, but are covered in more detail elsewhere in this volume. First, when mammals such as rats are given pairings of a novel-tasting food with gastric poisoning (taste aversion learning), they normally learn only to associate the taste of the food with illness and ignore any audio-visual features the food may possess (see pp. 183–93). However, most birds are quite different. Birds such as chickens (Martin and Bellingham, 1979) will show a predisposition to associate visual attributes of the food (such as its color) with poisoning. This learning can occur after only one trial (Wilcoxon, Dragoin, and Kral, 1971) and appears to reflect the tendency of most birds to forage for food visually rather than olfactorially as the rat does (but see Lett, 1979, for a fuller discussion of this phenomenon).

An associated predisposition is also shown in the tendency of pigeons to associate visual CSs with food and auditory CSs with aversive UCSs, such as electric shock. If pigeons are given pairings of a compound audio-visual CS with food, only the visual component will come to elicit appetitive CRs. However, if the audio-visual CS is paired with electric shock, only the auditory component comes to elicit "fear" CRs (Lolordo, 1979).

In summary, this section suggests that a variety of bird species do exhibit genuine Pavlovian conditioning, and are sensitive to the predictive significance of the CS in such studies.

Pavlovian conditioning in nonhuman mammals

There is no disputing that Pavlovian conditioning can occur in nonhuman mammals; Pavlov's prototypical salivating dog is a testament to this. What is perhaps more at question here is how large a role it plays in mammalian adaptive behavior.

A variety of mammalian species can be shown to demonstrate a range of Pavlovian CRs. "Fear" conditioning is readily found, as measured either by conditioned suppression (Blackman, 1972; Millenson and de Villiers, 1972) or heart-rate changes (de Toledo and Black, 1966). Eyeblink conditioning (nictitating membrane response) is reliably found in rabbits (e.g. Gormezano, 1966) or dogs (Vardaris and Fitzgerald, 1969). Rodents such as rats show increased activity and a variety of different behavioral CRs to CSs paired with food (e.g. Holland, 1977; Zamble, 1967). Conditioned sexual arousal is found in male rats who have CSs paired with access to a female in oestrus (Zamble, Hadad, Mitchell, and Cutmore, 1985). Autoshaping is also reliably found in a variety of nonhuman mammalian species, including rats (Peterson, 1975; Davey, Oakley, and Cleland, 1981), guinea pigs (Poling and Poling, 1978), hamsters (Phillips and Davey, 1986), dogs (Jenkins, Barrera, Ireland, and Woodside, 1978), cats (Grastyan and Vereczkei, 1974), rhesus monkeys

(Likely, 1974; Sidman and Fletcher, 1968), and squirrel monkeys (Gamzu and Schwam, 1974). Conditioned taste aversion can be acquired in rats after a single CS (food) – UCS (illness) pairing (cf. Revusky, 1971; Rozin and Kalat, 1971), and suitable controls have suggested that this is a Pavlovian rather than instrumental conditioning phenomenon (cf. Domjan and Wilson, 1972; Domjan, 1983; see pp. 183–93). Taste aversion learning has also been demonstrated in bats (Terk and Green, 1980), cows (Zahorik and Houpt, 1977), guinea pigs (Kalat, 1975), coyotes (Gustavson, 1977; Gustavson, Garcia, Hankins, and Rusiniak, 1974), and squirrel monkeys (Gorry and Ober, 1970).

The strength of the CR in rats is dependent on the predictive significance of the CS or the correlation between CS and UCS (Rescorla, 1968). Rodents such as rats also exhibit overshadowing and blocking (cf. Mackintosh, 1974) and can also acquire second-order conditioning and sensory preconditioning (Rizley and Rescorla, 1972; Holland and Rescorla, 1975).

However, whether nonhuman mammals display Pavlovian conditioning and exhibit phenomena which indicate that elaborate processing of the relationship between CS and UCS is not essentially in doubt. What is more at issue with mammalian Pavlovian conditioning is how flexible it is, and how far it is relegated to a subsidiary role by different learning processes such as, for instance, instrumental learning.

The first way in which we can look at this is to see how susceptible Pavlovian CRs in mammals are to antagonistic instrumental contingencies. Some evidence suggests that a number of Pavlovian CRs can either be significantly suppressed or modified in form by an instrumental contingency. For instance, an omission contingency is effective in reducing the frequency of leg-flexion CRs in dogs and rats (Schlosberg, 1936; Wahlsten and Cole, 1972), conditioned running in guinea-pigs (Brogden, Lipman, and Culler, 1938), certain kinds of appetitive CRs to food in rats (Holland, 1979b), and autoshaped CS contact in rats (Locurto, Terrace, and Gibbon, 1976; Atnip, 1977). More sensitive instrumental contingencies can actually change the form of the CR from one topography to another (e.g. Davey, Oakley, and Cleland, 1981; Timberlake, Wahl, and King, 1982). However, there are still a sizable number of studies which have failed to demonstrate any significant effect of omission contingencies on the strength or frequency of the CR. These include conditioned salivation in dogs (Sheffield, 1965), conditioned licking of a water-tube in rats (Patten and Rudy, 1967), conditioned jaw-movement in rabbits (Gormezano and Hiller, 1972), and conditioned orienting responses to appetitive CSs in rats (Holland, 1979b). The most one can probably say about this mixed bag of evidence is that some Pavlovian

CRs in mammals are susceptible to modification by instrumental contingencies, others are not. The reason why those which are not sensitive should be so remains unclear, as do any criteria for predicting which CRs these are likely to be. What is clear, however, is that some behaviors which are generated by Pavlovian contingencies can be subtly modified by the demands of instrumental contingencies. Nevertheless, this does not appear to be an adaptive attribute possessed solely by mammals, since instances of this have been recorded in birds (e.g. Schwartz and Williams, 1972a; Barrera, 1974; Wasserman, Hunter, Gutowski, and Bader, 1975), and goldfish (Brandon and Bitterman, 1979).

From another point of view, the brain structure which most strikingly differentiates mammals from nonmammals is the neocortex, and this is the most dominant type of cortex throughout mammals (see Figure 2.4). This has led some experimenters and writers to speculate about the role of brain structure in conditioning, and, because of the apparent ubiquity of Pavlovian conditioning across phyla and species, to suggest that the brain mechanisms responsible for Pavlovian conditioning may reside subcortically. Studies which have investigated Pavlovian conditioning in surgically neodecorticated mammals such as rabbits and rats have presented rather striking results: Pavlovian conditioning, it seems, is more efficient in mammals when the neocortex is removed than when it is present (cf. Oakley, 1979a). For instance, acquisition of a simple nictitating membrane CR is very rapid in rabbits that have had all neocortex surgically removed (Oakley and Russell, 1972), and neodecorticated rats and rabbits show better CS^+/CS^- discrimination learning and more rapid reversal learning (when the predictive significance of CS^+ and CS^- are reversed) than intact control animals (DiCara, Braun, and Pappas, 1970; Oakley and Russell, 1974, 1975, 1976). Furthermore, Oakley, Eames, Jacobs, Davey, and Cleland (1981) found that surgically neodecorticated rats would still exhibit autoshaped responses to a localizable CS paired with food. This tendency to autoshape was stronger than in normal control animals and, interestingly enough, showed a significant sensitivity to omission contingencies. That is, when food omission was the consequence for contacting the CS, all neodecorticate subjects showed a significant decrease in this response compared with yoked control subjects.

What these results on surgically neodecorticated subjects suggest is that neocortex is clearly not necessary for Pavlovian conditioning in mammals. This does not, of course, imply that Pavlovian conditioning in intact mammals occurs at the subcortical level — it may be, for instance, that while the neocortex was evolving in mammals, mechanisms designed to mediate

49

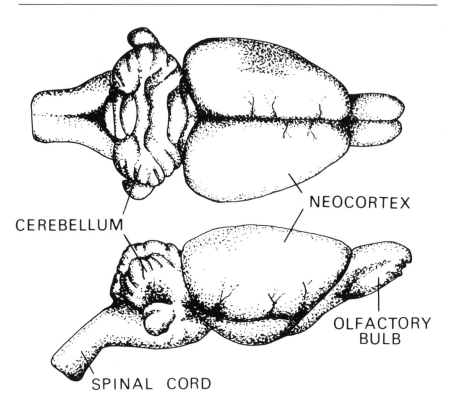

Figure 2.4 Lateral and dorsal views of the rat brain showing the location and extent of the neocortex.

Pavlovian conditioning were duplicated and perhaps refined at the cortical level (cf. Oakley, 1979a).

In summary, nonhuman mammals clearly exhibit Pavlovian conditioning. In some cases this learning is rigid enough to be insensitive to modification by instrumental contingencies, and lesion studies have demonstrated that the brain structure which best identifies mammals — the necortex — is not necessary for Pavlovian conditioning to occur.

Pavlovian conditioning in humans

Pavlovian learning in humans is distinguished from that in all other animals by two important features. First, the strength of the CR can be radically modified simply by the presentation of verbal information about the contingencies or the stimuli in the conditioning situation. For instance, simply informing subjects of the CS–UCS contingency can generate a CR prior to any actual pairings of the CS and UCS (e.g. Dawson and Grings, 1968; Katz, Webb, and Stotland, 1971; McComb, 1969; Wilson, 1968); informing the subject of extinction can also produce an immediate dramatic drop in CR strength (Colgan, 1970; Koenig and Castillo, 1969; Davey and McKenna, 1983); even when subjects are given false information about the CS–UCS relationship, they will respond in accordance with the false information rather than the actual contingencies they experience (e.g. Deane, 1969; Epstein and Clarke, 1970; Spence and Goldstein, 1961). Second, human subjects appear to develop a CR only when it is clear that they have become "consciously aware" of the contingency relationship between CS and UCS (Dawson and Furedy, 1976; Dawson and Schell, 1987). For instance, only subjects who can verbalize the correct CS–UCS relationship in post-experimental interviews exhibit conditioning (Baer and Fuhrer, 1968, 1970); when awareness of contingencies is measured on a trial-by-trial basis, differential CRs appear only after the appearance of contingency awareness (Dawson and Biferno, 1973; Biferno and Dawson, 1977; Fuhrer and Baer, 1980); and in studies which have deliberately attempted to "mask" the relationship between CS and UCS by employing a distractor task, subjects regularly fail to acquire conditioned responding (Dawson, 1973; Grings and Dawson, 1973; Ross, Ferreira and Ross, 1974; Dawson, Catania, Schell, and Grings, 1979).

Most human Pavlovian conditioning studies have been carried out either in the electrodermal conditioning paradigm — that is, using an aversive UCS such as an electric shock or loud noise and measuring changes in skin conductance levels (SCLs) as the CR to the CS (cf. Siddle, 1983) — or by using the eyeblink preparation in which the UCS is usually a puff of air to the cornea (cf. Martin and Levey, 1969). Both of these preparations reveal the "sensitivity to instructions" and the "conditioning with awareness" phenomena (cf. Dawson and Schell, 1987).

In a partial attempt to incorporate these uniquely human effects with other animal Pavlovian phenomena, a number of writers proposed what has come to be known as a *dual-level theory* of human Pavlovian conditioning (Razran, 1955, 1971; Baer and Fuhrer, 1973; Grings, 1965; Mandel and Bridger, 1967). This view suggests that Pavlovian learning in humans can occur at any one of two levels: (1) "true" primitive conditioning in which learning occurs at an autonomic, noncognitive level, and (2) "cognitive relational learning", which involves the subjects' higher cognitive processes and "can be usefully conceptualized as a complex and active information processing task with the autonomic indices of conditioning reflecting in large part the sequence of central cognitive processes" (Dawson, Catania, Schell, and Grings, 1979: 38). Thus, because of its sensitivity to instructions and awareness factors, the majority of human Pavlovian conditioning observed in the laboratory is considered to reflect cognitive relational learning, rather than true or primitive conditioning. The only real problem with the dichotomy between levels of conditioning is its distinct lack of predictive value. "True" conditioning only appears to be identifiable by exclusion: that is, when results of a human conditioning experiment do not fit the criteria for "conscious relational learning" they are labeled as "true" conditioning (cf. Davey, 1983). More recently, it has become clear that failures to observe "conscious relational learning" may result more from inadequate methods of monitoring such factors as contingency awareness than from the tapping of any hypothetical "true" conditioning mechanism (cf. Dawson and Schell, 1985, 1987). Whether any true or primitive Pavlovian conditioning process does exist in humans still has to be proven by independent criteria.

Before we continue to consider how "conscious relational learning" in humans fits in with Pavlovian conditioning in other animals, let us consider just one or two more phenomena associated with human Pavlovian conditioning.

A number of Pavlovian conditioning phenomena common in nonhuman mammals can also be demonstrated in humans. For instance, human subjects exhibit blocking (Dickinson, Shanks, and Evenden, 1984) and latent inhibition (Siddle, Remington, and Churchill, 1985; Siddle and Remington, 1986). Higher-order conditioning can be demonstrated in humans (Davey and McKenna, 1983; Davey and Arulampalam, 1981, 1982), and CR strength in humans can be shown to be a function of the predictive significance of the CS as measured by the correlation between CS and UCS (Alloy and Tabachnik, 1984; Prokasy and Williams, 1979; Prokasy and Kumpfer, 1969). Human subjects also appear to exhibit certain kinds of selective associations. For instance, Öhman, Fredrikson, and Hugdahl, (1978), Öhman, Fredrikson, Hugdahl, and Rimmo (1976), and Öhman, Eriksson, and Olofsson (1975) have shown that when slides of snakes and spiders are used as the CS for predicting an aversive electric shock UCS, CR acquisition is more rapid and more resistant to extinction than when more innocuous slides of flowers or houses are used as the CS. Öhman (1979) has interpreted results such as this as suggesting that humans have a *preparedness* to associate stimuli such as snakes or spiders with aversive UCSs because it has been beneficial for humans to have such a predisposition in their evolutionary past. As we have frequently encountered during this discussion of Pavlovian conditioning, learning about aversive consequences is more urgent than most, since survival often depends on rapid learning in such circumstances. Because snakes and spiders frequently have lethal poisonous effects it may be that our ancestors evolved predispositions to learn rapidly about events relating to these kinds of animals. Nevertheless, while this associative predisposition appears to exist we must be careful about interpreting its origins. All we have as evidence is what we observe in human conditioning studies today, and it can be argued that the "preparedness" phenomena observed by Öhman and colleagues may as likely reflect current cultural and social influences as the effects of evolutionary pressures (cf. Delprato, 1980).

Nevertheless, despite the fact that human subjects can exhibit typically Pavlovian phenomena such as blocking, latent inhibition, higher-order conditioning, and selective associations, how can those features of conditioning which appear to be uniquely human (for instance, the roles of verbal instructions and conscious awareness of contingencies) be reconciled with the rest of the animal literature?

First, it must be stressed that we do not know whether verbal instructions or conscious awareness of contingencies do influence nonhuman animal conditioning because we have not yet developed techniques suitable for investigating them. The Pavlovian performance of many nonhuman animals can be influenced by them observing a conspecific performing on a similar task (observational learning) (e.g. Davey, 1981: 267–75), so it at least appears that information about contingencies provided in the form of a demonstration can affect the rate of their Pavlovian learning.

However, perhaps a more suitable method of reconciling human and nonhuman Pavlovian learning is by attempting to understand the associations that are learned by humans during a Pavlovian conditioning episode. Here, we can use the same inferential techniques on humans as have been used on other animals (see Chapter 4, pp. 115–17). For instance, Davey and McKenna (1983) found that a second-order aversive CR in humans was mediated by associations between CS_2 and the aversive UCS. That is, any manipulation which produced a favorable revaluation of the UCS abolished the second-order CR. This revaluation could be done experimentally, by habituating subjects to the UCS, or instructionally, simply by informing subjects that they would receive no more presentations of the aversive UCS. Both manipulations eliminated the CR to CS_2, suggesting that it was cognitions related to the UCS which played an important role in mediating this response. This is similar to the *postconditioning stimulus revaluation* technique used with other animals to identify the associations formed during conditioning (see pp. 115–20). However, whereas nonhuman animal subjects have stimuli revalued via experiential means (that is, they have to have certain experiences with the UCS for it to be revalued), stimulus revaluation can occur in humans through information which might lead them to revalue their knowledge about the UCS. Thus, if a CR in human subjects is mediated via associations between the CS and UCS, then any manipulation which leads the subject to revalue or reassess the UCS (even the provision of verbal information) will directly affect the strength of the CR (cf. Davey, 1983, 1987b). Unfortunately, very little direct research has been carried out on the associations formed during human Pavlovian conditioning, but the indications are that it would not necessarily reveal any findings radically different from those found in other mammals. What does make human conditioning unique, however, are (1) the methods by which we can provide information about the various stimuli in the situation and the relationships between them, and (2) the fact that we can directly monitor such things as "conscious awareness" of contingencies. At present this makes Pavlovian conditioning in humans different from that in other animals only to the extent of the sophistication of the independent and dependent variables used in human studies — not in any obvious differences in the mechanisms which underlie Pavlovian conditioning.

Summary

This selective review of Pavlovian conditioning in animals provides evidence for the existence of Pavlovian mechanisms in the widest possble range of organisms from protozoa to humans. There may be limits to this kind of learning in invertebrates and possibly in some species of fish. These limitations take three forms: (1) the ability to learn Pavlovian associations in some response systems but not others; (2) the inability to exhibit Pavlovian phenomena which indicate sophisticated processing of the relationship between CS and UCS; and (3) selective learning of associations which have a natural significance for the organism. Both birds and nonhuman mammals exhibit flexibility in some Pavlovian CRs but not others: that is, some Pavlovian CRs can be significantly suppressed or modified by consequential contingencies. Although Pavlovian conditioning in humans is characterized by the sophisticated ways in which information about contingencies and stimuli can be transmitted to the subject, and the way in which certain cognitive correlates of conditioning can be monitored, there is no obvious evidence that Pavlovian associative mechanisms in humans are any different from those in either birds or nonhuman mammals. Human subjects still exhibit most of the basic Pavlovian phenomena found in both birds and other mammals.

Finally, this kind of comparative analysis is not complete, however, from a truly ecological point of view for at least two reasons. First, the majority of the available studies on Pavlovian associative learning have failed to take into account the adaptive problems faced by the species concerned and, consequently, whether Pavlovian learning might serve any adaptive function for these species. If there are no suitable problems for the animal to solve in its natural habitat using Pavlovian learning, then such a trait could never have been selected for. Second, this analysis has been concerned with Pavlovian *learning* and not Pavlovian *performance*. If a learning process is to have selective benefits then it depends crucially for those benefits on how the learning is utilized behaviorally. Pavlovian learning cannot be viewed as truly adaptive in the absence of the way in which the animal utilizes that learning (in relation to Pavlovian learning in birds and mammals this question is considered more fully in chapters 5 and 6). Nevertheless, there are some general insights to be gained from this kind of analysis. First, the limitations on Pavlovian learning in invertebrates described above does suggest that this group of species lacks centralized associative mechanisms that are response-independent. Where Pavlovian learning has been detected it is largely specific to certain types of responses (for example, earthworms can associate tastes with avoidance of hot, dry places but cannot associate a tactile CS with shock) or to specific kinds of stimuli which are integral to the solution of certain functional problems such as feeding or defense. Presumably, further ecologically-based studies will be able to demonstrate the kinds of functional problems to which individual invertebrate species might bring a Pavlovian learning ability and — equally importantly — what alternative adaptive strategies to learning they can bring to bear on these problems.

As one last point we might consider human Pavlovian learning in relation to the social and cultural environment inhabited by this species. Clearly, there are many adaptive problems that humans need to solve using associative processes, and — as implied above — there may indeed be no qualitative difference in basic associative mechanisms between humans and other mammals (as suggested by the similarity in the range of Pavlovian associative phenomena exhibited by humans and other mammals). Nevertheless, humans' ability to transmit information by linguistic means is a social adaptation to their complex environmental niche, and while associative mechanisms may play an important role in assimilating and storing information transmitted in this way, it is an adaptation that renders much experiential Pavlovian learning unnecessary (that is, we do not learn that certain textures or colors of snow and ice are associated with dangerously thin ice, we simply learn to avoid signs that say "Danger — Thin Ice"), and this appears to be an adaptive specialization uniquely possessed by the human species.

Chapter summary

1 In Pavlovian conditioning a conditioned stimulus (CS) is paired in close temporal contiguity with an unconditioned stimulus (UCS) such that the CS eventually elicits a conditioned response (CR) which is in some way relevant to the UCS.

2 The most commonly used Pavlovian response paradigms are the conditioned eyeblink, conditioned salivation, heart-rate conditioning, conditioned activity, conditioned suppression, autoshaping, and conditioned taste aversion.

3 Pavlovian conditioning is characterized by the organism learning to associate the CS with the UCS. To be sure that changes in behavior are not the result of *pseudo-conditioning* or *sensitization* rather than associative learning, certain control procedures need to be used. The most important of these control procedures is the *truly random control* where animals receive presentations of the CS and UCS which are unpaired.

4 The strength of the learned CR is normally a function of the predictive significance of the CS as measured by the correlation between CS and UCS presentations.

5 If there is a *negative* correlation between CS and UCS, then the CS may acquire *inhibitory* properties which prevent the relevant CR from being exhibited.

6 The phenomena of *overshadowing* and *blocking* occur when different stimuli are presented in a compound CS. In such circumstances some elements of the compound fail to become associated with the UCS and thus fail to elicit a CR.

7 When a CS has been associated with a UCS, it too can be used to reinforce other potential CSs. This is known as *higher-order conditioning.*

8 Pavlovian associative learning does appear to occur in invertebrates, such as protozoa, planaria, mollusks, bees, and fruit flies. Evidence also exists that they demonstrate attributes of Pavlovian conditioning which reflect a certain capacity for information acquisition and selective attention. However, Pavlovian conditioning in some invertebrates is restricted to some response systems and not others (e.g. the earthworm).

9 A wide variety of fish species show reliable Pavlovian conditioning and exhibit sensitivity to the predictive relationship between CS and UCS, overshadowing, blocking, autoshaping, and higher-order conditioning.

10 There are few properly controlled studies on Pavlovian conditioning in reptiles and amphibia, but what studies do exist appear to indicate that Pavlovian learning can be found in such groups.

11 A variety of bird species do exhibit genuine Pavlovian conditioning and are sensitive to the predictive significance of the CS. Furthermore, some use has been made of the autoshaping paradigm, which has revealed a considerable amount about the nature of Pavlovian conditioning in this group.

12 Nonhuman mammals clearly exhibit Pavlovian conditioning, as testified by Pavlov's prototypical salivating dogs. In some cases this learning is rigid enough to be insensitive to modification by instrumental contingencies, and lesion studies have shown that the brain structure that best identifies mammals — the neocortex — is not necessary for Pavlovian conditioning to occur.

13 Pavlovian conditioning in humans is distinguished from that in other animals by two important features: (1) the CR can be modified by verbal information about the CS–UCS contingency; and (2) human subjects appear to develop a differential CR only when it is clear that they have become "consciously aware" of the CS–UCS contingency. However, humans exhibit many Pavlovian phenomena also exhibited by other animals (e.g. blocking, latent inhibition, higher-order conditioning, CR strength being a function of the CS–UCS correlation, and selective associations) and what appears to make human Pavlovian conditioning different is not necessarily any fundamental difference in the underlying conditioning mechanism but (1) the methods by which we can provide information about CS–UCS contingencies to the subject, and (2) the fact that, in humans, we can directly monitor such things as their conscious awareness of contingencies.

Chapter three

Comparative aspects of conditioning: instrumental learning

Whereas Pavlovian conditioning involves a contingency relationship between two environmental stimuli (the CS and UCS), instrumental conditioning involves a contingency between some aspect of the organism's behavior and some aspect of the environment, such that the organism's behavior modifies its environment in some way. Whereas Pavlovian conditioning involves stimulus–stimulus (CS–UCS) contingencies, instrumental conditioning involves response–stimulus contingencies. Instrumental conditioning acts to alter the frequency of the response involved in the contingency relationship in a predictable way, depending on the nature of the consequence of that response.

In most instrumental conditioning studies the outcome of the response is in some way biologically important for the organism; in the experimental situation the response may procure food for a hungry animal, or it may help to avoid a noxious stimulus such as an electric shock. Those consequences which increase the future probability of the response are known as *reinforcers*, and those which decrease the future probability of the response are known as *punishers*. A common example of a reinforcer is food for a hungry animal, and a frequently used punisher in experimental studies of instrumental conditioning is mild electric shock. Generally speaking, reinforcers and punishers are defined only in terms of their effect on the frequency of responding, and it is possible to get certain stimuli (such as electric shock) to act as punishers in one situation and reinforcers in another (e.g. McKearney, 1969, 1972). Reinforcers and punishers can be either positive or negative, depending on the kind of change the response exerts on the environment. Positive means that the response adds something to the situation (for example, it delivers a food pellet or an electric shock), and negative means that the response removes or avoids some environmental consequence (for instance, it terminates or avoids an electric shock). Thus,

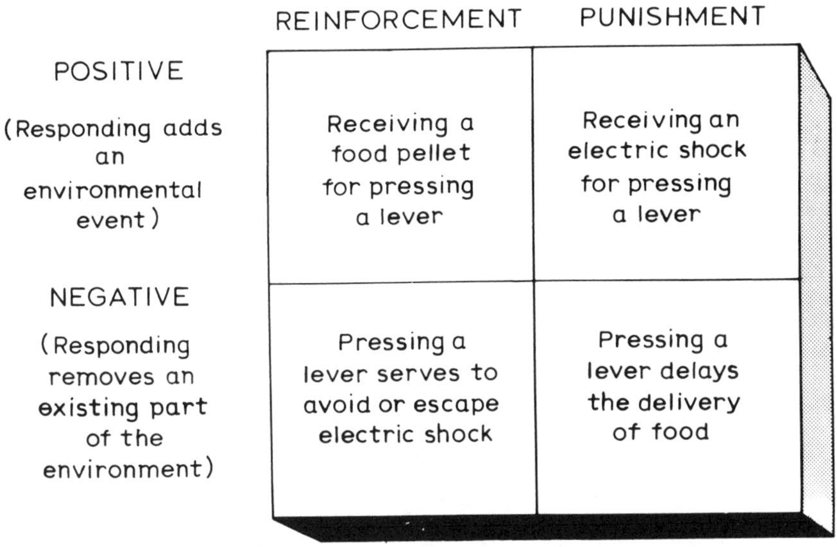

	REINFORCEMENT	PUNISHMENT
POSITIVE (Responding adds an environmental event)	Receiving a food pellet for pressing a lever	Receiving an electric shock for pressing a lever
NEGATIVE (Responding removes an existing part of the environment)	Pressing a lever serves to avoid or escape electric shock	Pressing a lever delays the delivery of food

Figure 3.1 Reinforcement and punishment as procedures in instrumental conditioning. Each cell contains an example of positive and negative reinforcement and punishment. See text for a fuller explanation.

reinforcer/punisher refers to the effect of the consequence on the *frequency* of the response, and the adjective positive/negative refers to the nature of the response consequence. This terminology is illustrated in Figure 3.1.

It must be stressed at this point that although instrumental conditioning involves contingencies between the animal's behavior and some outcome of that behavior, there is no reason to suppose that this is what the animal learns. There are a number of ways in which apparently successful instrumental conditioning can result without the animal learning to associate its own behavior with some environmental consequence. A discussion of the possible mechanisms underlying instrumental conditioning can be found in Chapter 7.

In the laboratory, the rat and pigeon have traditionally been the species used to investigate the characteristics of instrumental conditioning, and to this end very stylized conditioning apparatuses have been designed for use with each. The *Skinner-box* is probably the best-known. Designed by B. F. Skinner to study instrumental learning in the rat, it comprises a small

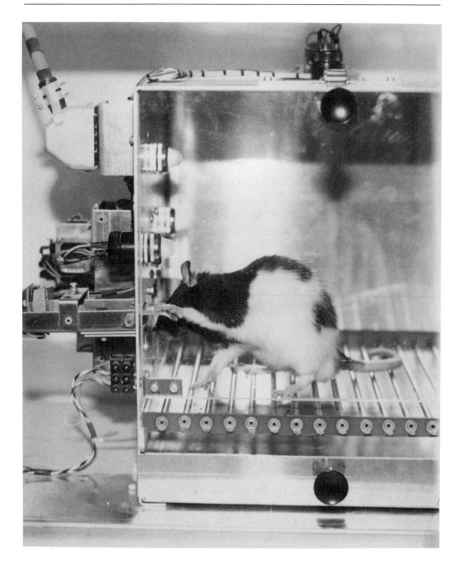

Figure 3.2 A rat conditioning chamber or Skinner-box. The lever acts as the response manipulandum and the rat can receive food pellets delivered to a small aperture next to the lever. The lamps on the front wall can be programed as discriminative stimuli.

Figure 3.3 A pigeon conditioning chamber. Pecking keys used as response manipulanda are mounted at head height and can be illuminated with colored lights or patterns. The aperture below the key is where the pigeon receives limited access to grain.

enclosed chamber containing a response lever which the rat can press to produce environmental consequences. These consequences may be either food (for example, in the form of a 45-mg food pellet or a sucrose solution) or electric shock to the feet delivered through the bars of the grid floor. Various lamps and loudspeakers are also situated in the chamber to provide extra stimuli when required (see Figure 3.2). In the pigeon conditioning chamber (Figure 3.3), a number of small illuminable disks are mounted at head height on one of the walls to act as keys at which the pigeon can peck in order to deliver reinforcers or punishers. Food can be presented to the pigeon in the form of limited-access time to grain delivered from a hopper. Visual stimuli can be projected onto the pecking keys for use as extra stimuli.

Rats and pigeons have traditionally been used in such studies primarily because they are cheap and easy to keep, and both emit responses (lever pressing and key pecking) which are easy to record and can be maintained for long periods without fatigue. The wisdom of using such a limited number of species for the study of learning phenomena is questionable if only because it tends to lead to a belief (either rightly or wrongly) that generalized laws of learning exist which are common to most if not all species of animals. However, intense study of individual species can be useful for examining particular aspects of learning in detail (such as the nature of associative mechanisms) (cf. Mackintosh, 1974).

Basic phenomena associated with instrumental conditioning

1 *Superstitious reinforcement*

Instrumental conditioning is defined in part by the contingency that exists between a response and a subsequent reinforcer or punisher. However, it is unclear what aspect of this relationship between response and reinforcer is important in modifying the frequency of the response. It could be the *causal* relationship between response and reinforcer or merely the temporal *contiguity* between the two. Skinner (1948) argued that animals are sensitive to the contiguity between response and reinforcer in such a way that mere accidental correlation between response and reinforcer will result in the animal learning about that relationship and modifying its behavior accordingly. Skinner (1948) delivered response-independent food to pigeons periodically every 15 sec. After a number of food presentations two observers were asked to describe the behaviors being exhibited by the pigeons, and all agreed that 6 out of 8 subjects displayed regular stereotyped behaviors in the interval between reinforcers. Some birds circled the chamber regularly, another thrust its head into the corner of the chamber, and a third appeared to indulge in "head-bobbing." Skinner claimed that these behaviors had been strengthened by a process of *superstitious reinforcement.* That is, on occasions when food was delivered the behavior being indulged in by the pigeon at that time would be "accidentally" reinforced and thus be more likely to occur in the future. Because it would be more likely to occur in the future it would be more likely to be accidentally correlated with future food deliveries and thus reinforced even more. Thus, even though there is no *causal* contingency between the animal's behavior and food, the organism behaves as though there is, and some stereotyped or "superstitious" behavior emerges.

Although it is clear to anyone who has carried out instrumental conditioning experiments that superstitious reinforcement of arbitrary behavior patterns does occur (e.g. Blackman, 1974: 17–29), it is doubtful whether it is a particularly robust conditioning phenomenon. First, from an adaptive point of view it seems very curious that animals should have evolved learning mechanisms which react to *accidental* correlations between behavior and its consequences. In an environment where it is important to distinguish between causal and noncausal relationships between events, superstitious reinforcement would be something of a disadvantage. Second, extended and more detailed replications of Skinner's original experiment suggest that while superstitious behaviors can be distinguished in the initial stages of noncontingent food reinforcement, the eventual stereotyped behaviors that develop are not just arbitrary responses — as would be predicted by superstitious reinforcement — but are all species-specific food-related responses (Staddon and Simmelhag, 1971; Timberlake and Lucas, 1985). Timberlake and Lucas (1985) argue that periodic delivery of response-independent food eventually acts to release species-typical behaviors characteristic of feeding. At the times when food is imminent to the pigeon, these behaviors resemble consummatory-type responses such as mandibu-lating objects or pecking. At times early in the inter-food interval these behaviors appear to resemble searching or foraging for food, such as circling or brushing and poking at the ground to expose new search areas. When reinterpreted in this way many of the stereotyped behaviors reported by Skinner in his original experiment can be seen to be species-typical feeding behaviors rather than mere arbitrary actions.

Finally, superstitious reinforcement has acquired an important status in conditioning theory over the last thirty years or so — but not necessarily because of its robustness as a behavioral phenomenon. As we shall see during the course of this volume, many theorists have used superstitious reinforcement as a convenient explanation or counter-explanation for certain phenomena. But the popularity of its evocation in theoretical matters is in stark contrast to its lack of resilience as a behavioral process, and readers should be alert to this fact. What clearly appears to be the case is the periodic response-independent reinforcement may initially evoke superstitious behavior, but this very quickly gives way to stereotyped patterns of species-typical behavior.

2 Discrimination-generalization

Responses generated by instrumental reinforcement can be brought under what is known as *discriminative control*. In a discrimination learning experiment the responses of the animal will be reinforced only in the presence of a distinctive stimulus cue such as a light or sound. Eventually, this training will produce responses only in the presence of the distinctive cue. A stimulus in the presence of which responses are reinforced is generally called a *discriminative stimulus* (S^D or S^+ for short). A stimulus in the presence of which responses are *not* reinforced is known simply as an S^Δ (pronounced "ess delta") or S^- ("ess minus"). The degree of discrimination learning can be measured in a number of ways. One simple way is to calculate a *discrimination ratio* from response rates during the S^D and S^Δ. This is done simply by dividing the response rate during the S^D by the total response rate during S^D and S^Δ.

i.e.
$$\frac{S^D}{S^D + S^\Delta} = DR \text{ (discrimination ratio)} \tag{3.1}$$

A more widely used means of discovering the extent of an animal's discrimination of an S^D is to construct a *generalization gradient* by presenting the animal with a number of different stimuli which approximate to the S^D. Figure 3.4 shows a generalization curve obtained by Guttman and Kalish (1956). In this experiment, pigeons were trained to peck the key for food when the key was illuminated by light whose wavelength was 580 nm. Subsequently illuminating the key with light of different wavelengths produced a reduction in response rate as a function of the difference in wavelength between the test light and the original S^D light. This experiment demonstrates that the pigeons had associated the key light color with the response-food contingency, providing evidence of stimulus discrimination.

The degree of discrimination learning frequently depends on the type of training given to the animal. Figure 3.5 shows the generalization gradients obtained under three different procedures: (1) when only an S^D was presented

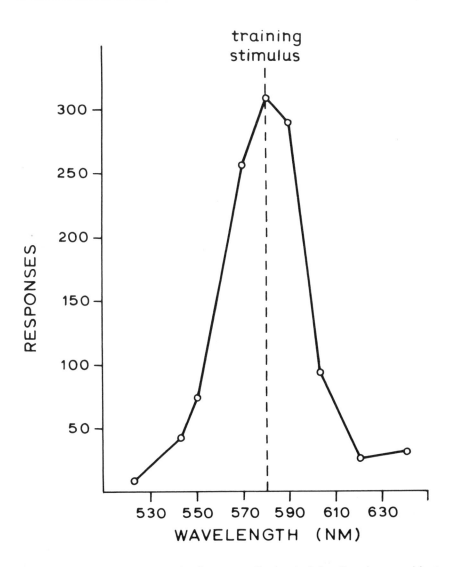

Figure 3.4 A stimulus generalization curve. During training the pigeon subject is initially reinforced for pecking in the presence of a colored light of 580 nm wavelength. During testing the pecking key is periodically illuminated with light of different wavelengths. The number of responses in the presence of each test stimulus is inversely related to its distance from the original training stimulus on the wavelength continuum. (After Guttman and Kalish, 1956)

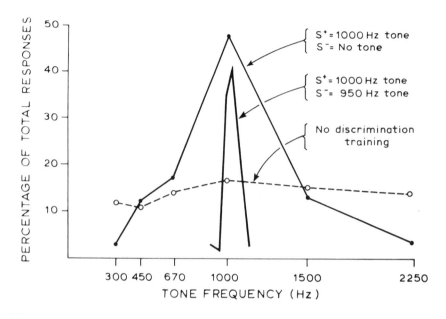

Figure 3.5 Stimulus generalization curves to tones of different frequencies after different kinds of training. See text for further explanation. (After Jenkins and Harrison, 1960, 1962)

and no discrimination training was given (a control group), (2) when the S^D was a tone and the S^Δ was the absence of the tone, and (3) when the S^D was a tone of 1000 Hz and the S^Δ was a tone of 950 Hz. From this comparison it can be seen that the discrimination of the S^D stimulus is finer when it is contrasted with an S^Δ, and when that S^Δ stimulus is similar to the S^D.

During discrimination training not all aspects of the S^D stimulus come to control responding. This was demonstrated in an experiment by Reynolds (1961b). Using pigeons as subjects. Reynolds used a white triangle on a red background as a compound S^D signaling reinforced responding, and a white circle on a green background as an S^Δ signaling reinforcement. After training, the pigeons were presented with the individual elements of these compounds, that is, red, green, triangle, and circle. Reynolds found that one bird had learned to respond only to red and not to triangle, while another had learned to respond only to triangle but not to red (see also Eckerman, 1967; Keehn, 1969). What this suggests is that animals select out only particular features of discriminative stimuli to associate with reinforcement. This may reflect aspects of selective attention in the animal, in that it cannot process all features of a stimulus simultaneously and must therefore selectively process only certain features of the stimulus. Or it may reflect the tendency of certain species to attend selectively to features of the S^D which have some ecological or biological relevance to them. For instance, pigeons tend to associate only the visual features of a compound visual-auditory S^D with responding for food (Lolordo, 1979), and this appears to reflect the fact that they are predominantly visual feeders in the wild.

As well as excitatory generalization gradients which can be obtained from an S^D, one can also construct *inhibitory* generalization gradients by giving test presentations of stimuli which resemble the S^Δ. Figure 3.6 shows both excitatory and inhibitory generalization gradients obtained by giving test presentations of stimuli which resemble S^D and S^Δ. The interesting finding here is that animals do not appear simply to ignore an S^Δ; they appear to learn that it is associated with nonreinforcement. This is demonstrated by the fact that stimuli that resemble the S^Δ stimulus evoke more responding than the S^Δ stimulus itself. What this implies is not exactly clear. It may imply that an S^Δ stimulus acts at a cognitive level to inhibit the reinforced instrumental response (e.g. Spence, 1937; Mackintosh, 1983), or it may imply, as other theorists have suggested, that the S^Δ stimulus elicits behaviors which *compete* with the reinforced response. Staddon (1983) has suggested that S^Δ stimuli come to elicit behaviors which are unrelated to either the reinforcer or the reinforced response. We know, for instance, that on a food-reinforcement schedule, periods when food is unavailable are characterized by a variety of stereotyped behaviors which are unrelated to feeding. These have variously been called adjunctive behaviors (Falk, 1971), interim responses (Staddon and Simmelhag, 1971) or schedule-induced responses (see pp. 83–91, this chapter), and appear to be manifestations of behaviors which are representative of motivational systems other than feeding (cf. Staddon, 1977; but see Timberlake and Lucas, 1985). The fact that these adjunctive behaviors are elicited by stimuli which signal nonreinforcement may be important in this context, since the inhibitory generalization gradients obtained from S^Δs may reflect the suppression of instrumental responding by competing adjunctive behaviors elicited by the S^Δ as a signal for nonreinforcement.

Studies of discrimination and generalization tell us quite a number of things about learning. First, they suggest that external stimuli can come to control the emission of instrumental responses. In such circumstances the animal may learn to associate the S^D with reinforcement (e.g. Trapold and Overmier, 1972) or to associate the S^D with the fact that responses emitted

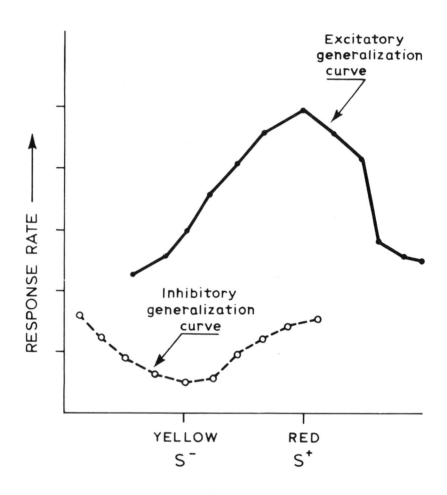

Figure 3.6 Examples of excitatory and inhibitory generalization curves. During training subjects were reinforced for responding in the presence of red light, but never reinforced for responding in the presence of yellow light.

during its presentation will be reinforced (e.g. Mackintosh, 1983). Second, animals frequently learn only about certain features of the S^D, implicating mechanisms of selective attention which may either reflect information processing limitations of species-specific discriminative tendencies. Third, S^Δ stimuli also control behavior by inhibiting the instrumental response or generating behaviors which compete with the instrumental response. Finally, discrimination learning also tells us something about the perceptual capabilities of animals by allowing us to test what kinds and ranges of stimuli the animal can actually detect. This kind of procedure allows us to investigate such factors as the range of color vision in animals, the limits of sound frequencies and intensities they can detect, and so on (e.g. Blough, 1958; Sutherland, 1957; D'Amato and Salmon, 1982; Terman, 1970).

3 Conditioned reinforcement

Traditionally, it was fashionable to make the division between what were known as primary and secondary reinforcers. Primary reinforcers are those stimuli which were considered to have intrinsic and immediate biological importance, such as food for a hungry animal. Secondary reinforcers, however, are those stimuli whose reinforcing properties are established by conditioning — usually by pairing with a primary reinforcer. If, for instance, a rat is trained to press a lever to obtain food, and food delivery is accompanied by a brief tone stimulus, that tone stimulus is likely to acquire conditioned reinforcing properties. This can be demonstrated by showing that rats that have received such training will continue to press the lever in extinction merely to present the tone, and also the tone can frequently be used to reinforce a completely new response. Using conditioned reinforcers, particularly long chains of behavior can be established which are reinforced with food only at their termination (e.g. Pierrel and Sherman, 1963).

However, the distinction between primary and secondary or conditioned reinforcers has not been particularly helpful. The distinction is a difficult one for a number of reasons. First, there is no obvious taxonomy of primary reinforcers. Food, water, and sexual partners were traditionally cited as examples of such stimuli, but it is clear that many other kinds of stimuli have intrinsic response-reinforcing properties, and these stimuli depend very much for these properties on the nature of the species and its natural history (see Chapter 7). Second, the effect that certain so-called "primary reinforcers" exert on behavior can differ radically depending on the animal's previous experience with that reinforcer. For instance, electric shock can act both as a punisher and, in some cases, as a reinforcer (McKearney, 1969, 1972; Fowler, 1971).

Although the primary–secondary reinforcement dichotomy is a difficult one to uphold, it is clear, however, that an animal's experience with environmental stimuli will modulate the stimulus's response reinforcing properties. Stimuli of no apparent biological value may acquire reinforcing

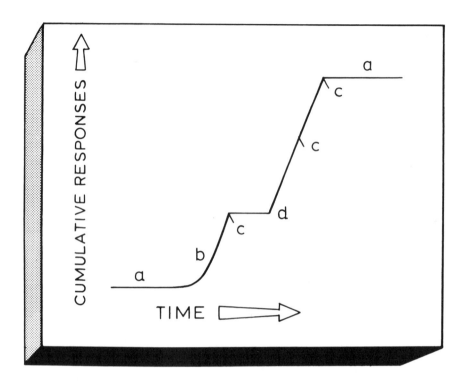

Figure 3.7 An example of a cumulative recording. The record moves from left to right recording responses in a cumulative fashion. At points marked *a* the record is flat indicating no responding. Point *b* represents a steady rate of responding leading up to the hatch mark *c*, which indicates the delivery of the reinforcer. Point *d* represents an abrupt transition from a period of no responding to a period of steady, constant responding.

properties (such as saccharin-flavored water) and stimuli of obvious biological value may have their reinforcing or punishing properties altered by individual experiences (that is, some animals may be trained to deliver electric shocks to themselves).

4 *Schedules of reinforcement*

One of the important features of instrumental conditioning is that not every response (for instance, not every lever press) is necessarily reinforced.

Intermittent reinforcement of this kind can be programed on what are known as *schedules of reinforcement*, and these schedules are important because the way in which reinforcement is scheduled normally determines the temporal patterning and rate of responding. The way in which responding is measured and described on a schedule of reinforcement is normally via a *cumulative recording*. A cumulative recorder is a modified polygraph recorder which gives a minute-to-minute indication of the rate of responding by plotting cumulative responses against time. This allows the experimenter to assess at a glance both local and overall rates of responding. Each response the subject makes steps the pen of the cumulative recorder by one unit while the paper is being fed out of the recorder at a standard rate (this represents the time axis). If the subject reponds frequently, the slope of the resulting graph will be steeper than if it responds only occasionally (see Figure 3.7 for an explanatory example of a cumulative record). The cumulative record thus allows the experimenter to examine local response rates during an experimental session and to investigate how animals adapt their responding in circumstances where not every response results in reinforcement. There are two basic methods of selecting responses to be reinforced: (1) on the basis of time (interval schedules); and (2) on the basis of number (ratio schedules), and this gives rise to four basic schedules of reinforcement.

Fixed-interval schedules

A fixed-interval (FI) schedule is one which reinforces the first response to occur after a specified period of time. For instance, an FI 60 sec schedule would reinforce only the first response (for example, lever press) to occur 60 sec after the preceding reinforcer had been obtained. This type of schedule usually generates a characteristic pattern of responding which eventually reflects a temporal discrimination on the part of the animal. Figure 3.8 shows a typical cumulative record from an animal that has been trained on an FI schedule. This is characterized by a pause after reinforcement (the post-reinforcement pause, PRP) followed by an accelerating rate of responding up to the time of availability of the next reinforcer. This characteristic cumulative record is known as the FI "scallop" and is a fairly robust phenomenon occurring even with FI values of up to 27 hours (Dews, 1965)!

There are a number of features of the FI scallop which suggest that it does indeed reflect a temporal discrimination on the part of the animal. First, the length of the PRP varies proportionally with the value of the FI schedule. The average point at which the pause is terminated has been found to be approximately two-thirds of the FI value (Schneider, 1969). Indeed, even after the PRP has been terminated, rats exhibit local rates of responding

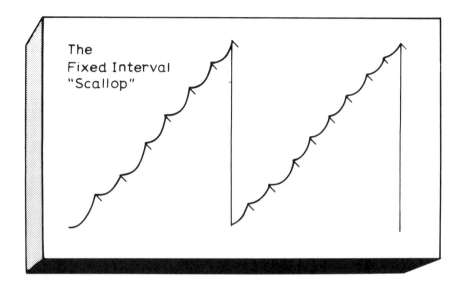

Figure 3.8 A stylized example of fixed-interval responding where the rate of responding is positively accelerated between each reinforcer.

during the interval which are a function of the amount of time that has elapsed since the previous reinforcer (Lowe and Harzem, 1977). Second, animals that have been given prior training on a response-independent fixed-time (FT) 60 sec schedule (a schedule which delivers food to the animal periodically without any response contingency) show very rapid development of scalloping when the reinforcer is subsequently made response-contingent on an FI 60 sec schedule (Trapold, Carlson, and Myers, 1965; Zamble, 1969). This implies that the FI scallop reflects some learning about the temporal parameters of reinforcer delivery on the previous FT schedule. Third, even when the FI scallop is disrupted in some way by interrupting the animal's responding during an interval, subjects will recommence responding at a rate which is a function of the time into the interval when responding resumes (e.g. Dews, 1962, 1965, 1966; Wall, 1965). This suggests that the FI scallop does not represent a rigid "chain" of responses which reflects the learning of a superstitious pattern of responding, but actually represents responding which is directly controlled by temporal variables.

One question that remains about FI responding is why animals always resume responding some time before the next reinforcer is available. For instance, why, on an FI 60 sec schedule, do they resume responding after around 40 sec and not wait until the 60 sec has elapsed? We know that many animals can space their responses very accurately up to inter-response intervals of 2–3 min (Ferraro, Schoenfeld, and Snapper, 1965; Richardson and Loughead, 1974b), so a lack of timing ability is not the answer. Presumably, two factors might account for this. First, if the animal is responding fairly rapidly at the moment when the interval elapses and reinforcement becomes available, then this will minimize any delay in acquiring food and maximize the number of food deliveries that can be obtained in a given period of time. Second, the Skinner-box is not exactly a true analog of the animal's natural feeding habitat. If, in the wild, a particular food source did deliver food periodically, then at times when the food was unavailable from this source, animals would presumably leave and search elsewhere — returning only at the time when food was due to become available again. However, the Skinner-box does not provide alternative food sources, nor does it permit the animal to leave to investigate alternative food prospects elsewhere. While animals do appear to exhibit some generalized foraging responses during periods of nonreinforcement in Skinner-boxes and the like (e.g. Timberlake and Lucas, 1985), these do not appear strong enough to prevent the animal from exhibiting responses anticipating the scheduled food delivery some time before it is due (see Skinner and Morse, 1958, as an example of how temporal discrimination on FI schedules can be sharpened by providing alternative activities to lever pressing).

Fixed-ratio schedules

A fixed-ratio (FR) schedule is one which reinforces every *n*th response — for instance, on an FR20 schedule only every 20th response is reinforced. After some training on this type of schedule a characteristic pattern of responding develops which is known as *break-and-run*. After each reinforcement there is a brief pause followed by an abrupt transition to a relatively high and stable rate of responding which persists up to the delivery of the next reinforcer (see Figure 3.9).

Fixed-ratio performance has a couple of interesting characteristics. First, in some cases typical break-and-run performance can be maintained on FR schedules as high as FR900 (Ferster and Skinner, 1957), but usually, high-ratio values result in *ratio strain*, where normal responding is interrupted by long periods of pausing and inactivity. Second, FR schedules — like FI schedules — generate a post-reinforcement pause (PRP), the length of which is a direct function of the FR value (e.g. Felton and Lyon, 1966). Adaptively, this is clearly odd. On an FR schedule, the rate at which the animal will

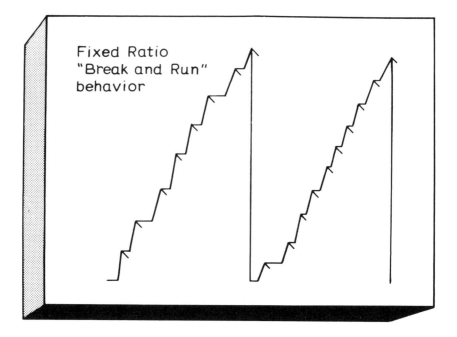

Fixed Ratio
"Break and Run"
behavior

Figure 3.9 A stylized example of typical "break-and-run" behavior found on fixed-ratio schedules. Receipt of each reinforcer is followed by a brief pause with no responding leading to an abrupt transition to a relatively high rate of responding which is maintained up to the next reinforcer delivery.

acquire reinforcers is directly dependent on the rate at which the animal can respond; any pauses will therefore delay acquisition of the next reinforcer. In order to maximize reinforcer procurement animals should recommence responding as soon as possible after the delivery of the last reinforcer. Yet the greater the number of responses they have to make to acquire each reinforcement the longer they pause after reinforcer delivery. However, this apparent maladaptiveness appears to reflect the animal's sensitivity to the temporal parameters that are generated as a consequence of FR responding. Animals can only respond at a particular finite rate, such that it requires t sec for the animal to make n responses. This means that there will always be an interval between reinforcer deliveries, and the more responses the animal has to make (the greater the FR value), the longer this interval will be. Thus, the period after each food delivery is in effect a period of nonreinforcement, and this period of nonreinforcement increases with the number of responses the animal has to execute to obtain food. So, the animal learns to discriminate this period of nonreinforcement and ceases to respond during it. Studies which have artificially manipulated the inter-reinforcement interval without altering the number of responses required to obtain the reinforcer, have shown that the PRP is a function of the inter-reinforcement interval duration and not directly a function of the FR value (e.g. Killeen, 1969; Neuringer and Schneider, 1968; Lowe, Davey, and Harzem, 1974). The apparent maladaptiveness of pausing on FR schedules demonstrates a number of things. First, it shows that animals will readily discriminate periods when responding is not reinforced, and consequently cease to respond during these periods. Second, it again demonstrates the difficulty of extrapolating from simple schedule performance to what an animal might do in such circumstances in its natural environment. The Skinner-box provides only one source of food; an animal's natural environment usually has many. Thus, Skinner-box schedules which either directly or indirectly program for reinforcement intermittently generally prohibit the animal from investigating other sources of food during periods of nonreinforcement, and thus may well give false impressions of how a free-ranging animal might act in such circumstances (see Chapter 8).

Variable-interval and variable-ratio schedules

Variable-interval (VI) and variable-ratio (VR) schedules are the variable counterparts of FI and FR. A VI schedule reinforces the first response that occurs after a specified period of time has elapsed since the previous reinforcer. However, the time between reinforcers varies from interval to interval. For instance, on a VI 60 sec schedule the *average* time between reinforcers is 60 sec, although each successive interval duration may be different. Thus, on a VI schedule the animal has no real means of predicting exactly when the next reinforcer is to become available. On a VR schedule an animal has to emit a particular number of responses to acquire each reinforcer, but this number varies with each successive reinforcer. On a VR 20 schedule the animal will have to emit an average of 20 responses to acquire each reinforcer, but this number can vary from as few as, say, 5 or as many as, say, 60. As on a VI schedule, the animal has no means of predicting how many responses will be required to obtain the next reinforcer.

VI and VR schedules of reinforcement normally generate steady and stable rates of responding with few, if any, pauses (see Figure 3.10). The overall rate of responding is usually a direct function of the rate of reinforcement on these

75

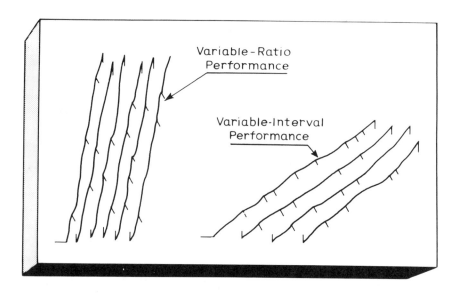

Figure 3.10 Stylized examples of typical variable-ratio and variable-interval performance. Both schedules maintain fairly constant rates of responding, with variable-ratio schedules generating higher overall response rates.

schedules (Catania and Reynolds, 1968; Ferster and Skinner, 1957). However, because of its response requirement when reinforcer rate is equated, a VR schedule will generally maintain overall response rates that are higher than an equivalent VI schedule (Thomas and Switalski, 1966; Peele, Casey, and Silberberg, 1984). In fact, rate of responding on VR schedules can often be so high that the energy that the animal expends in earning the reinforcer is not compensated for by the calorific value of that reinforcer (Skinner, 1957a)!

What VI and VR schedules suggest is that when reinforcement is unpredictable, animals will sustain responding for long periods. However, animals do appear to be sensitive to local changes in reinforcement frequency on these variable schedules. The length of the post-reinforcement pausing that does occur on VI schedules is usually a function of the *shortest* programed inter-reinforcement interval. Similarly, local rates of responding do fluctuate in accordance with the local rate of reinforcement (cf. Catania and Reynolds, 1968). This suggests that on these variable schedules animals are constantly sensitive to the frequency of reinforcement and their responding is adjusted accordingly (but see Shimp, 1967).

Differential reinforcement of low rate

One final schedule of reinforcement that has acquired some importance over the years is the differential reinforcement of low rate (DRL) schedule. A DRL schedule is a temporally-based schedule which specifies that a minimum amount of time must elapse between two responses before the latter of these two responses is reinforced. For example, on a DRL 20 sec schedule, having made a response, the animal must wait at least 20 sec before making the next response in order for it to be reinforced. If the animal responds before this period of time has elapsed, that response goes unreinforced and the timer is reset to zero. Typically, this schedule produces a very low rate of responding, with the modal inter-response time (IRT) closely approximating the DRL value.

DRL schedules generate a number of interesting phenomena. First, they demonstrate that many animals have very precise timing abilities. Rats can very accurately space their responses apart on DRL schedules with values up to 2–3 min (Ferraro, Schoenfeld, and Snapper, 1965; Richardson and Loughead, 1974b). Second, animals performing on DRL schedules very frequently exhibit stereotyped patterns of behavior which appear to help them to bridge the time gap between responses (e.g. Laties, Weiss, Clark, and Reynolds, 1965; Wilson and Keller, 1953; Bruner and Revusky, 1961). These response chains are called *collateral* or *mediating* behaviors and appear to be superstitiously reinforced (cf. Davey, 1981: 83). There is quite some evidence that these stereotyped response chains do help the animal in mediating the time interval between responses. For instance, disruption of any ongoing collateral behavior usually disrupts efficient DRL performance (Laties, Weiss, and Weiss, 1969); providing the animal with the opportunity to indulge in collateral behaviors increases the efficiency of DRL performance (Laties, Weiss, and Weiss, 1969; Schwartz and Williams, 1971; Zuriff, 1969), and using physically restricting conditions which are not conducive to the development of overt mediating responses reduces DRL efficiency (Frank and Staddon, 1974; Richardson and Loughead, 1974a). Nevertheless, while collateral behaviors may aid efficient DRL performance, they are not essential for it. For example, there are many instances where efficient DRL performance does not appear to be accompanied by overt stereotyped collateral behavior (Kelleher, Fry, and Cook, 1959). Furthermore, while collateral chains of responding may aid discrimination of the interval to be judged by the animal, they cannot substitute for temporal discrimination. Presumably, even if the animal is emitting a chain of behavior which fills a specific time interval, in order to do this accurately and consistently the animal must make some discrimination of the temporal duration of each element in the response chain (cf. Nevin and Berryman, 1963).

Summary

Finally, there is one important point to be made about the performance of animals on schedules of reinforcement, and in particular the fact that the characteristic performances generated by different schedules appear to be similar in many different species. Many writers have used this cross-species similarity to argue for general laws of learning which encompass a wide range of species (e.g. Skinner, 1953; Morse, 1966). However, such topographically similar performances should not be taken as an indication of similar underlying mechanisms — these performances tell us very little about the developmental history of learning mechanisms in different species. For instance, White, Juhasz, and Wilson (1973) argue that the similar FI performances found in different species do not necessarily reflect interspecies similarity in the mechanisms which mediate this performance, nor necessarily any phylogenetic relatedness between these species. What this similarity reflects is the similarity across species of the environmental constraints which produce this performance. Just as the wings of birds and bats evolved as independent adaptations to a similar environment, so animals may have independently evolved different underlying learning mechanisms to cope with similar environmental problems.

5 *Concurrent schedules and choice behavior*

Unlike the situation in simple schedules of reinforcement, animals in their natural environment usually have to make a choice about what responses to make for which reinforcers. That is, their behavior is determined by a number of different sources of reinforcement, each of which is in competition with the others. Instrumental studies of choice behavior are most frequently carried out using *concurrent schedules of reinforcement*. On such schedules, the subject is faced with two manipulanda and the frequency or schedule of reward on each manipulandum can be varied. For instance, a pigeon may be confronted with two pecking keys: on the left-hand key pecks are reinforced on, say, a VI 1-min schedule, and on the right-hand key pecks are reinforced on, say, a VI 5-min schedule. This is known as a concurrent VI:VI schedule and we can assess the proportion of responses that are made on the two keys as a function of the frequency of reinforcers which are either programed or obtained on the two keys.

The way in which choice behavior on concurrent schedules is usually measured is in terms of the relative rate of responding to the two alternatives. The relative rate of responding to one key (key A) is calculated thus:

$$\frac{R_A}{R_A + R_B} \qquad\qquad (3.2)$$

where R_A is the rate of responding to alternative A, and R_B is the rate of responding to alternative B. If the animal shows no preference in responding to A and B the ratio derived from equation 3.2 will be 0.5.

The matching law

In concurrent choice experiments using VI schedules, an empirical law appears to hold between the relative rates of responding on the two alternatives and their relative rates of reinforcement. Figure 3.11 shows the data from a series of concurrent schedule experiments carried out by Herrnstein (1961). He found that the relative rate of responding to one of the two alternatives closely *matched* the relative rate of reinforcement on that alternative. This can be expressed in the form of the following equation:

$$\frac{R_A}{R_A + R_B} = \frac{r_A}{r_A + r_B} \qquad\qquad (3.3)$$

where R_A and R_B are the rates of responding to the two alternatives and r_A and r_B are the rates of reinforcement earned on each alternative. This relationship is known as the *matching law*, and appears to hold over a wide range of schedules and parameter values (Herrnstein, 1970; Baum, 1981).

As such, the matching law is an important empirical law in that it *describes* the relationship between responding and reinforcement in simple two or even three choice situations (e.g. Pliskoff and Brown, 1976). However, the matching law only appears to hold under a limited set of conditions. In some situations, animals will tend to choose the more profitable alternative more frequently than is predicted by the matching law. This is known as *overmatching*. In other situations they will tend to respond to the more profitable alternative less frequently than is predicted by the matching law. This is known as *undermatching* (cf. Wearden and Burgess, 1982, for examples of such deviations from the matching law). Studies which demonstrate overmatching and undermatching are important in that they help to specify the conditions which are necessary for matching to occur.

For instance, first, matching often fails to occur when sequences of switching from one alternative to the other are superstitiously reinforced. This can be overcome by introducing a *change-over delay* (COD) which specifies that the animal cannot obtain a reinforcer for a brief period after a switch. Second, matching frequently fails to occur when the magnitude of reward on the two alternatives is different (Catania, 1966; Neuringer, 1967),

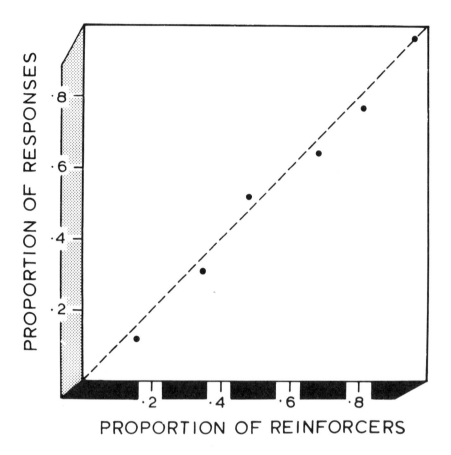

Figure 3.11 The relative frequency of responding to one alternative in a two-choice concurrent VI:VI schedule of reinforcement as a function of the relative frequency of programed reinforcers on the two alternatives. Data are taken from Herrnstein (1961).

although the matching effect can be redressed by taking into account relative reinforcer magnitude in equation 3.3. Third, the matching law also fails to apply if the effort required to transfer from one alternative to the other is increased, either by increasing the value of a COD or by increasing the travel time required between the two alternatives (see pp. 245–8). Finally, the matching law applies only if the responses to the two alternatives share the same topography. Quite clearly, different responses may require differing amounts of effort and will also require different means of measurement, either of which could contribute to deviations from the matching law (cf. Williams, 1986).

However, how does this fit in with what we know about the adaptive predispositions of animals and the possible mechanisms which might underlie choice behavior?

Matching and maximizing

Optimization appears to be an important factor in determining many of the adaptive tendencies in animals. Those individuals which evolve the most efficient means of executing biological functions such as feeding, finding a mate, reproducing, and so on, are likely to be the ones whose genes will survive and proliferate in future generations. So, to what extent does the matching law reflect an optimal feeding strategy, given a choice of alternative food sources? Certainly, in many cases matching is consistent with the animal behaving so as to *maximize* the number of reinforcers obtained over a particular time period. For instance, on a concurrent FR:FR schedule, in order to maximize the number of reinforcers obtained in a session the animal should respond exclusively on the FR alternative with the lower ratio value. In practice this is usually what happens (e.g. Herrnstein, 1958) and is consistent with the matching law (the only way that matching can be achieved on a concurrent FR:FR schedule is by responding exclusively on one of the alternatives). Quite clearly, then, maximizing might be considered as the *goal* of matching or performance on concurrent schedules (cf. Hinson and Staddon, 1983; Staddon and Hinson, 1983), and in most cases matching is consistent with maximization. But how does the animal manage to achieve this?

Mechanisms of matching

One explanation of matching is simply to suggest that animals sample the relative density of reinforcers on the alternatives over specific periods of time and adjust their behavior so as to maximize the receipt of these rewards (e.g. Rachlin, Battalio, Kagel, and Green, 1981). This is what can be called a *molar* account of matching, since it assumes that the animal is monitoring the characteristics of the alternative reward schedules over a period of time. However appealing this type of account might sound, it does have a number of difficulties. First, as it is stated above, it is little more than a restatement of the fact that animals tend to maximize and that generally matching is consistent with maximization. There is little evidence provided by this account about how animals might go about calculating the relative richness of the alternatives, nor of the memorial or information-processing mechanisms required to achieve it. Second, although maximizing might be an important goal for an animal, there are some conditions in which matching is not necessary for maximization, yet nevertheless, matching still occurs (cf. Heyman, 1983). Since matching frequently results in maximizing anyway, we might suggest that the animals possess a mechanism which, over a period of time, matches response output to reinforcer density — even though maximizing is the important biological goal that this mechanism is indirectly designed to achieve. Even so, there is still no independent evidence that such a mechanism exists, and there is some empirical evidence that outcomes other than matching can be achieved given schedules in which the alternatives have different response requirements (such as concurrent VR:VI schedules – Prelec, 1982).

An alternative approach to explaining the mechanism underlying matching is at a *molecular* level. Some theorists have suggested that matching can be achieved if the animal is sensitive to the moment-to-moment probabilities of reinforcement on the two alternatives (e.g. Shimp, 1966, 1969; Mackintosh, 1974: 194). Thus, the matching relationship could be a function of the animal switching from one alternative to the other as the probabilities of reinforcement on each schedule alter with time. At a *prima facie* level this idea is attractive, because it is consistent with matching on simple concurrent schedules and also incorporates much of the evidence from discrete-trial probability learning (Mackintosh, 1969, 1970). Similarly, there is some empirical evidence that animals can track the momentary probability of reinforcement when it is manipulated experimentally (Fantino and Duncan, 1972; Shimp, 1966). Nevertheless, the evidence bearing on molecular maximizing also contains some instances where matching has been achieved in the absence of animals being sensitive to the moment-to-moment changes in reinforcer probability (e.g. Nevin, 1979), and so we must await further evidence before assessing this account.

Finally, some theorists have recently suggested that matching might be accounted for by a process of *melioration* (e.g. Herrnstein and Vaughan, 1980). That is, animals may adjust their behavior between the two alternatives in the short term in an attempt to improve the current local rate of reinforcement they are receiving, and in an attempt to equate the rate of reinforcement across the alternatives. For instance, Vaughan (1981) and Herrnstein and Vaughan (1980) have demonstrated mathematically that if animals distribute their responses so as to achieve the same local rates of reinforcement across the alternatives, this also achieves maximizing. Thus, molar matching according to this theory is the result of a mechanism which tends the animal toward equating the local rates of reinforcement from the alternative reinforcer sources. It is, therefore, a slightly modified version of molecular maximizing in that instead of adjusting behavior according to momentary probabilities of reinforcement, the animal adjusts its behavior according to local rates of reinforcement, but not in such a global way as implied by molar accounts of matching.

In summary, while there is still much debate about the nature of the mechanism which underlies matching, it is important to distinguish between mechanism and function when understanding such a phenomenon. For instance, molar matching as embodied in the matching law may be the end result of mechanisms which act at the molecular level. Similarly, while matching is the empirical outcome of such processes, the *function* of these processes may be to optimize interaction with the alternatives. That is, the biological function or goal of the mechanisms underlying matching may be to maximize the rate of reinforcement acquired from the alternative reinforcer sources. The function, such as maximization, is a factor or pressure that is specified by the constraints imposed on the organism by the need to perform efficiently in its environment in order to survive; the actual mechanism which evolves to serve this function need not, of course, be infallible in producing this outcome. This is why under certain conditions we may sometimes observe matching without maximization.

6 *Schedule-induced behavior*

Figure 3.12 shows the kinds of behaviors exhibited by two pigeons on an FT 12 sec schedule of food reinforcement conducted by Staddon and Simmelhag (1971). The various behaviors exhibited by these pigeons could be divided into two broad categories: (1) those behaviors that increased in probability as the inter-food interval progressed; and (2) those behaviors whose probability resembled an inverted U-shaped function with a peak near the beginning of the inter-food interval. The former set of behaviors generally resembled feeding responses (such as pecking and orienting toward the food hopper) and were called *terminal behaviors*; the latter were unrelated to feeding and were called *interim behaviors*; (Staddon and Simmelhag, 1971).

These two kinds of behaviors with their different dynamic properties have since been observed on response-independent schedules of both food and water reinforcement (Innis, Simmelhag-Grant, and Staddon, 1983; Reberg, Innis, Mann, and Eizenga, 1978; Reberg, Mann, and Innis, 1977; Innis, Reberg, Mann, Jacobson, and Turton, 1983; Timberlake and Lucas, 1985). What was theoretically interesting about *interim* behaviors in particular was

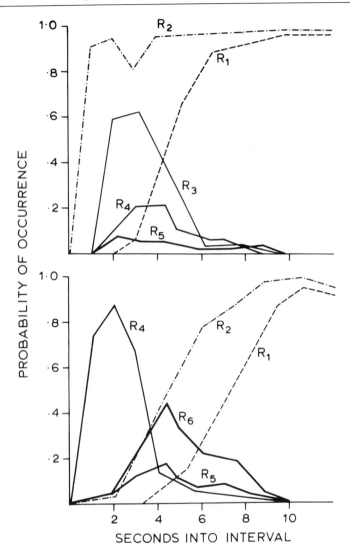

Figure 3.12 The probability of different behaviors as a function of post-food time for two pigeons on a response-independent FT 12 sec schedule. R_1 = pecking at the magazine wall, R_2 = orientation toward the magazine wall, R_3 = side-stepping along the magazine wall, R_4 = turning $\frac{1}{4}$ circles, R_5 =pecking at the floor, R_6 = holding head in the food magazine. The broken lines are examples of terminal behaviors and the solid lines examples of interim behaviors. (After Staddon and Simmelhag, 1971)

that they were only induced on schedules of reinforcement, became excessively stereotyped, occurred only in the immediate post-reinforcer period, and were not behaviors obviously related to the reinforcer (but see Timberlake and Lucas, 1985). To this extent they were dynamically very similar to what are known as schedule-induced *adjunctive behaviors*. Adjunctive behaviors are responses apparently induced by schedules of reinforcement, which occur only in the immediate post-food period, are not obviously related to the same motivational system as the reinforcer, and are frequently excessive or stereotyped.

Thus, interim or adjunctive behaviors appear to reflect a unified class of behaviors which represent a fairly robust behavioral phenomenon. However, why do these schedule-induced behaviors occur? They are not obviously related to feeding on schedules of food reinforcement, so what is their function? Before we discuss these questions it is worth looking at some of the responses that have been identified as adjunctive behaviors.

Polydipsia

Falk (1961, 1964, 1969) reported that when rats are reinforced with food for lever pressing on either a VI or FI schedule of reinforcement, they will eventually exhibit excessive drinking from an available water bottle in the period immediately following reinforcer delivery. This has come to be known as *polydipsia* and has been demonstrated not just in rats but also in monkeys (Schuster and Woods, 1966) and pigeons (Shanab and Peterson, 1969).

Polydipsia exhibits a number of characteristics: (1) it is generally excessive, as rats will often drink one-half their weight in water in a few hours; (2) it is not obviously related either to a state of water deprivation or to the need for post-prandial fluid (Falk, 1969; Stein, 1964; Stricher and Adair, 1966); (3) it occurs only on a schedule of reinforcement. If the rat is given a "session's worth" of food in one meal, this will evoke nothing like the same amount of drinking as if the food is intermittently presented on a schedule (Falk, 1969, 1971; Reynierse, 1966); (4) the amount of polydipsic drinking induced depends on the mean inter-reinforcement time specified by the schedule. Inter-food times of less than 4–5 sec do not induce drinking, whereas for rats at approximately 80 per cent of their free-feeding body weight, polydipsic drinking is an increasing function of mean inter-food time up to values of 2–3 min, at which point polydipsia falls to progressively lower levels (see Figure 3.13) (Falk, 1966); (5) polydipsic drinking occurs primarily in the post-reinforcer period, although it will occur in the interval if access to the water bottle is restricted in the immediate post-food period (Flory and O'Boyle, 1972).

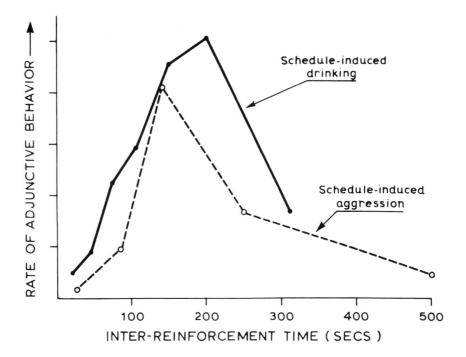

Figure 3.13 Rate of adjunctive drinking and aggression as a function of the inter-reinforcement interval. (Drinking data adapted from Falk, 1972; aggression data from Flory, 1969)

Aggression

Aggression, like drinking, can be induced in the period immediately following food delivery on a schedule of reinforcement (Gentry, 1968; Hutchinson, Azrin, and Hunt, 1968; Richards and Rilling, 1972; Knutson and Kleinknecht, 1970; Flory, 1969; Looney and Cohen, 1982). This is usually induced by providing an appropriate target such as a restrained conspecific, a taxidermically prepared model, or presentation of a mirror for pigeon subjects (Azrin, Hutchinson, and Hake, 1966; Cohen and Looney, 1973; Flory and Ellis, 1973), a rubber hose for squirrel monkeys to bite (Hutchinson, Azrin, and Hunt, 1968), or a conspecific for a rat subject (Gentry and Schaeffer, 1969; Thompson and Bloom, 1966). Schedule-induced aggression is a function of the average inter-food interval with an optimum value of 2–3 min (Cherek, Thompson, and Heistad, 1973; Cohen and Looney, 1973) (see Figure 3.13). It is also excessive in that pigeons will often badly bruise and pull out the feathers of live conspecific targets (Azrin, Hutchinson, and Hake, 1966) and quickly destroy taxidermically prepared model targets (Flory, 1969).

Pica

When either blocks of wood or wood shavings are made available in the conditioning chamber, both rats and monkeys exhibit stereotyped chewing and ingesting of the wood during inter-reinforcement periods on schedules of reinforcement (Villarreal, 1967; Roper, Edwards, and Crossland, 1983). This is known as schedule-induced *pica*.

Air-licking

When a continuous stream of air is delivered from a drinking tube, rats will exhibit licking of the tube during the post-food period on schedules of reinforcement (Mendelson and Chilliag, 1970). Increasing the level of food deprivation also increases the level of this schedule-induced air-licking (Chilliag and Mendelson, 1971).

Explanations of adjunctive behavior

There is no doubt from the foregoing descriptions that schedule-induced drinking, aggression, pica, and air-licking all share similar dynamic characteristics and thus appear to represent a functionally distinct class of schedule-induced behaviors (Falk, 1971). But this still leaves the question of why such behaviors should develop and what apparent function they serve. Let us discuss the possibilities.

Superstitious reinforcement It may be that adjunctive behaviors become accidentally correlated with the delivery of reinforcement; this might especially be so on response-independent schedules of reinforcement. There are numerous reasons why this is unlikely.

1 Some studies have superimposed a minimum delay between the occurrence of an induced behavior and food delivery such that the behavior can never become accidentally correlated with reinforcement. In such circumstances adjunctive behaviors are still developed and maintained (Falk, 1964; Flory, 1969; Cherek, Thompson, and Heistad, 1973).
2 If adjunctive behaviors are superstitiously reinforced, they should primarily occur in the period immediately *prior* to food delivery, not just after it (Stein, 1964).

3 If superstitious reinforcement were responsible for schedule-induced behaviors it is not at all clear why two different types of response should develop (interim and terminal responses) and why they should possess different dynamic characteristics. Certainly, most adjunctive behaviors are not obviously related to feeding, and one would intuitively expect that if any responses were going to be superstitiously reinforced they would be feeding-related ones.

4 Finally, the induction of adjunctive behaviors is a fairly robust phenomenon. It seems very unlikely that a transitory process like superstitious reinforcement could generate behaviors which include excessiveness among their characteristics.

Elicitation by reinforcement Since adjunctive behaviors normally occur in the immediate post-reinforcer period it is possible that they are responses which are a result of unconditioned elicitation by the reinforcer. For instance, rats normally drink after meals (Kissileff, 1969) and it may be that polydipsia is an exaggerated form of this post-prandial reinforcer-elicited drinking. Although this is intuitively appealing, it certainly cannot provide a full explanation of adjunctive behavior. First, adjunctive behaviors take time to develop and do not occur spontaneously as would an unconditioned reaction. Second, adjunctive behaviors do not occur on either continuous reinforcement schedules or schedules with very brief inter-reinforcement intervals (Falk, 1966), as might be expected if their relation to the reinforcer were unconditioned. Third, adjunctive behaviors can be found following stimuli which are presented in lieu of the reinforcer and which have never been paired with the reinforcer (Corfield-Sumner, Blackman, and Stainer 1977; Rozenblith, 1970); similarly, adjunctive behaviors develop in the period following unreinforced responses on DRL schedules (Knutson and Kleinknecht, 1970; Segal and Holloway, 1963). In both these cases, stimuli in lieu of reinforcement and nonreinforced responses on DRL schedules possess the same *predictive significance* as the reinforcer (that is, they tell the animal roughly when the next reinforcer delivery can be expected), but they do not possess the physical characteristics which might be expected to generate adjunctive behaviors if such behaviors were elicited by reinforcement.

Induction by periods of nonreinforcement One theoretically important feature of adjunctive behaviors is that they all appear to occur at times when reinforcement is unavailable. They occur immediately after reinforcement on periodic schedules of reinforcement (cf. Falk, 1971), they occur following stimuli which predict a period of nonreinforcement (e.g. Corfield-Sumner,

Blackman, and Stainer, 1977; Rozenblith, 1970; Knutson and Kleinknecht, 1970; Segal and Holloway, 1963), and they can also be observed during stimuli signaling extinction on multiple schedules of reinforcement (Panksepp, Toates, and Oatley, 1972; Azrin, Hutchinson, and Hake, 1966; Hutchinson, Azrin, and Hunt, 1968). This has led some theorists to suggest that discriminated nonreinforcement is the important causal factor which induces adjunctive behaviors.

Staddon (1977) proposed a categorization scheme which consisted of three categories of behavior which could be observed on periodic schedules:

1 *interim or adjunctive behaviors* are behaviors which occur in the presence of stimuli correlated with a *low* probability of reinforcement (that is, they normally occur early in the inter-reinforcement interval);
2 *facultative activities* are behaviors which are not actually schedule-induced, which show an inverse relation to reinforcer frequency (e.g. Riley, Wetherington, Delamater, Peele, and Dacanay, 1985), occur during the middle of inter-reinforcement intervals, and immediately follow interim or adjunctive behaviors. Wheel-running has been defined by some people more as a facultative rather than as an adjunctive behavior (Roper, 1981), in the sense that it is probably a behavior that the animal would indulge in regardless of whether food was delivered on an intermittent schedule or not; and
3 *terminal activities* are the third category of behaviors which normally occur in the presence of stimuli *highly* correlated with reinforcement, and hence normally occur immediately prior to reinforcer delivery on periodic schedules.

However, having suggested that stimuli correlated with nonreinforcement are important factors inducing adjunctive behaviors, this still begs a number of questions. For instance, what mechanism mediates this relationship between nonreinforcement and adjunctive behavior? And second, what, if anything, might be its adaptive function?

Staddon (1977) has suggested that stimuli which signal nonreinforcement on intermittent schedules of reinforcement may come to induce motivational states different from that which is relevant to the reinforcer. The adjunctive behavior that actually appears and the alternative motivational state that will be induced will depend on what releasing stimuli are present in the situation. The presence of a drinking tube, for instance, appears to induce or release drinking, while a conspecific target induces or releases aggression. In this sense, adjunctive behaviors are very similar dynamically and functionally to what have been known in the ethological literature as *displacement activities*.

Displacement activities are seemingly inappropriate behaviors that occur when sequences of highly-motivated behaviors are either interrupted or thwarted (Tinbergen, 1952, 1964). For instance, birds show displacement feeding and preening during intervals in intraspecific fighting or mating, and sticklebacks have been shown to exhibit displacement nest digging and fanning when successful courtship with a female is foiled (e.g. Tinbergen, 1952; Tinbergen and Van Iersel, 1947). Displacement activities also show other dynamic similarities to adjunctive behaviors. For instance, the particular type of displacement activity that is engaged in can be determined by the presence of external stimuli relevant to releasing or supporting that behavior (Van Iersel and Bol, 1958; Sevenster, 1961; Rowell, 1961), and Armstrong (1950) has observed that displacement activities can also occur when a goal has just been achieved (that is, it can occur in the immediate period following a reward). Thus, it is quite possible that the same mechanisms underlie adjunctive behavior as also underlie displacement activities. The variables controlling the two kinds of behaviors appear similar, but we must await further inferential evidence regarding the similarity of underlying mechanisms.

The adaptive function of adjunctive behavior

One of the puzzles surrounding both displacement activities and adjunctive behaviors is why animals should invest such time and energy indulging in activities which are clearly excessive in their intensity and stereotypy, and which appear to have no immediate utility. However, although displacement activities may not topographically or motivationally appear to be relevant to the immediate goal in hand, it has been proposed that they do have indirect adaptive benefits. For instance, displacement activities have actually been shown to facilitate the transition from one motivational state to another (such as from aggression to courtship), and, to be a necessary factor in, for instance, courtship in some species (e.g. Wilz, 1970; Tinbergen, 1952). The ritualization of displacement activities induced by motivational thwarting has been credited with producing relatively complex and important adaptive behavior patterns in some species. It has been suggested as responsible for the evolution of many courtship and threat displays which provide a communicative function (e.g. Huxley, 1966). Behaviors such as nest building may have evolved directly from displacement movements (Armstrong, 1950), and subsequent nest-material-gathering displacement during thwarted feeding may have led to certain species of birds evolving the use of twigs or straws as tools to dislodge insect prey from otherwise inaccessible locations (cf. Alcock, 1972). What this all implies is that the adaptive function of a particular behavioral phenomenon may not be specific to the circumstances which induce it. The phenomenon of displacement, for instance, may provide a means of generating behaviors which — depending on the particular circumstances — may subsequently prove useful to the solution of a more general adaptive problem.

In relation to adjunctive behavior as it is observed on intermittent schedules, Falk (1977) has proposed one possible general function for schedule-induced behavior. He suggests that adjunctive behavior is "a stabilizing activity maintaining the organism's engagement with a situation containing escape components" (Falk, 1977: 332). That is, when species are highly mobile feeders which exploit a wide feeding-range by moving between areas of patchily distributed food, indulging in adjunctive behaviors insures that they remain in the vicinity of food when it is found intermittently in one particular location. There are two implications of this account. First, species that hunt by lying hidden and ambushing their prey but have a relatively large foraging environment would benefit most from induced adjunctive activities (Falk quotes the constant tail twitching of felines as they stalk their prey as a probable example of this). Second, species that stay within one relatively small area to capture prey (such as through lure displays), or which exploit relatively small, densely-supplied home ranges (such as herbivorous grazers and browsers), should benefit less from developing adjunctive activities. These two implications are presumably experimentally testable but remain to be explored.

Nevertheless, we must still consider that in the reinforcement contexts in which we observe them, adjunctive behaviors such as polydipsia and schedule-induced aggression may play no particular adaptive roles. They may simply be particular manifestations of displacement activities whose general utility is to provide behavioral variation in situations where a functional goal is being thwarted. Some variations generated by this mechanism may prove useful and subsequently become incorporated into the organism's behavioral repertoire.

Comparative aspects of instrumental conditioning

One obvious question to ask at this stage is what range of species possesses the ability to learn via instrumental conditioning? However, there are many reasons why this is not a particularly easy question to answer, and it is certainly less straightforward than posing the same query about Pavlovian conditioning. The first problem is that there is currently no general consensus about the mechanisms which underlie learning in instrumental conditioning (see Chapter 7). Indeed, some theorists have proposed that instrumental conditioning can be adequately reduced to principles of Pavlovian conditioning (e.g. Moore, 1973; Bindra, 1972, 1974; see pp. 204–9). If this were so, then those species that possessed Pavlovian learning abilities should also be able to perform adequately on instrumental tasks. The second problem is that many species possess rather limited behavioral repertoires that make the interpretation of any learning difficult. If instrumental conditioning is a learning process which does not necessarily rely on Pavlovian abilities, then one of the main criteria for demonstrating its existence in a particular species is to show that the frequency of completely arbitrarily-defined responses can be manipulated by reinforcement contingencies. The limited behavioral repertoires of some species (such as invertebrates) makes it very difficult to define and isolate completely arbitrary responses for use as operants. For instance, successfully reinforcing a fruit fly for choosing one of the alternatives in a two-choice learning situation need not necessarily reflect instrumental learning of a particular response sequence. It could equally well reflect a predetermined tendency to approach stimuli which have been paired with reinforcement (such as autoshaping). Since much of what passes as instrumental learning can also be explained quite adequately in Pavlovian terms we must be quite precise about what criteria we are to use as evidence for instrumental learning.

In this context, I intend to adopt rather strict criteria for instrumental learning. First, any instrumental response which is directed toward some aspect of the animal's environment (for example, maze or alleyway performance or operating a manipulandum) could result from Pavlovian processes such as autoshaping (see p. 27 and pp. 144–69) and are not therefore unequivocal evidence of instrumental learning. Second, learning about responses appears to be an important feature of instrumental conditioning — regardless of whether this involves either learning to associate responses with antecedent stimuli (such as Thorndikian S–R learning) or with consequential stimuli such as reinforcers (such as R–S learning). This implies that the organism is in some way able to isolate the important features of the contingent behavior and, when required, reproduce the actions which constitute the behavior. Third, instrumental conditioning should be capable of generating completely novel arbitrary behavior sequences which are not species-typical and which the animal may never have exhibited before. No existing performance model of Pavlovian conditioning could adequately cope with this eventuality (see Chapter 7). Fourth, omission contingencies which are effective in suppressing responses which have been generated by other means (for instance, by Pavlovian contingencies) are not necessarily evidence of response–consequence learning. In circumstances where a behavior is directed at some aspect of the environment (such as in instrumental lever pressing in rats or in autoshaped responding), the omission contingency may merely redirect the animal's attention to some other aspect of the environment which then becomes established as a CS^+. For instance, when an omission contingency is imposed on autoshaped key pecking in the pigeon, food only follows those trials on which the piegon has *not* pecked the key. If the pigeon is attending to some other aspect of the environment when this happens it may establish this new aspect as a CS^+. Thus, suppression of key pecking by the omission contingency may not result from response–consequence learning but from the fact that the bird is now approaching and contacting some other aspect of the conditioning chamber which has inadvertently become established as a CS^+.

Thus, the following sections should be read with these points borne in mind, and with no preconception that unequivocal detection of instrumental learning is easy!

1 Instrumental conditioning in invertebrates

Figure 3.14 shows the kind of maze apparatus used to investigate instrumental discrimination learning in the fruit fly *Drosophila* by Platt, Holliday, and Drudge (1980). The negative geotaxic tendency of the flies used in this study means they must learn the correct route upward in order to escape the maze. The correct path at each choice-point is signaled by a distinctive substrate (for example, sandpaper). Platt, Holliday, and Drudge (1980) found that individual drosophila increased their avoidance of culs-de-sac over trials and more frequently chose the correct horizontal alley. When substrate cues were inconsistent, such learning did not occur. Is this sufficient evidence to conclude that instrumental learning can occur in drosophila? Certainly, there is considerable confusion about whether this type of learning does exist in such a species. First, using aversive or disruptive stimuli with drosophila usually produces escape tendencies which disrupt performance and mask any learning that might exist (e.g. Quinn, Harris, and Benzer, 1974), and many studies that have claimed to have observed instrumental learning in drosophila have failed to use adequate controls for nonassociative learning, have adopted very loose criteria for instrumental learning, or have failed to observe this learning in individual organisms (Hay, 1975; Murphey, 1967, 1969; Spatz, Emanns, and Reichert, 1974; Threlkeld, Bentley, Yeung, and Henriksen, 1976). Indeed, there are many published studies which have failed to observe learning under instrumental contingencies in drosophila (e.g.

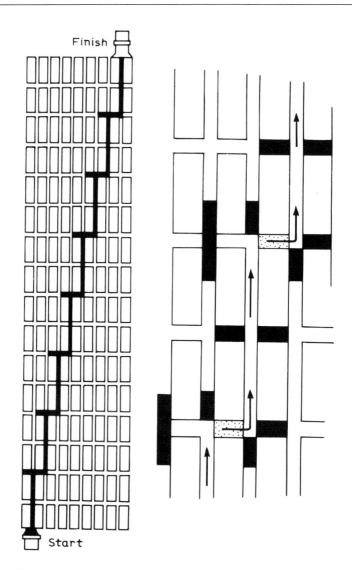

Figure 3.14 Maze apparatus for studying instrumental learning in individual *Drosophila melanogaster*. On the left is a diagramatic representation of the maze with its 7 choice-point learning path. On the right is an enlarged section displaying the sandpaper substrate indicating the correct choice (stippled areas) and the rubber plugs used to delineate culs-de-sac. (Adapted from Platt, Holliday, and Drudge, 1980)

Bicker and Spatz, 1976; McGuire and Hirsch, 1977; Murphey, 1973; Pluthero and Threlkeld, 1979; Yeatman and Hirsch, 1971), although, as we mentioned in the previous chapter, we must be cautious in our interpretation of such negative evidence.

Clearly, the example study of Platt, Holliday, and Drudge (1980) does not satisfy the stringent criteria for instrumental learning outlined earlier. Successful learning could have occurred as a result of the discriminative sandpaper substrate becoming a CS^+ toward which the fly is directed as a result of autoshaping. In this case the fly would be learning the Pavlovian association between sandpaper (CS) and the subsequent opportunity to indulge in negative geotaxis (UCS) rather than any association between its own behavior and the consequences of that behavior.

Some other studies have attempted to adopt procedures which use nondirected responses. For instance, if an individual drosophila is shocked whenever it extends one of its legs, it very quickly comes to maintain that leg in a flexed position (Booker and Quinn, 1981). Other studies in the cockroach and the locust suggest that this learning is encoded in a motor neurone involved in leg flexion (Eisenstein and Cohen, 1965; Tosney and Hoyle, 1977), but the failure to adopt adequate noncontingent control conditions makes it unclear whether these behavior changes represent response–consequence learning.

Some other writers have used the behavioral variability of some invertebrate species as evidence for instrumental learning. For instance, Heinrich (1985) points out that honeybees rely on many different kinds of flowers for their nectar, and different flowers frequently require different and novel motor patterns to facilitate successful nectar collection. In order to collect pollen from blue bindweed (*Solanum dulcamara*), bumblebees usually grasp the flowers with their mandibles and collect the pollen by shaking the flowers. To collect pollen from wild rose flowers, however, they grasp groups of anthers between the thorax and abdomen and release the pollen this way. In other cases they crawl over the flowers of the wild carrot and loosen the pollen by body friction. Such variability may be partially "hard-wired" but presumably some aspects may be open to environmental manipulation due to their success in collecting pollen. Certainly, in circumstances where the pollen is hidden and in uncommon arrangements, the bee's performance improves with experience (Heinrich, 1976; Laverty, 1980). While there is no direct evidence that the learning of these idiosyncratic foraging behaviors are mediated by instrumental conditioning, instrumental learning would provide a useful means of modifying inherited skills to produce novel behavior patterns suited to individual foraging instances.

Thus, while there are many examples of how invertebrates can adapt to instrumental contingencies, there is no evidence that they possess a learning ability evolved specifically to cope with learning about such contingencies. Of course, an invertebrate may frequently encounter instrumental contingencies which can be successfully negotiated with the use of Pavlovian associative mechanisms, and this may be sufficient to have prevented the evolution of an instrumental learning mechanism in such a group.

2 Instrumental conditioning in fish

Macphail (1982: 64–9) has reviewed a number of studies on instrumental learning in fish, and concludes that fish (in particular, teleosts) (1) are capable of learning about responses under instrumental contingencies, (2) can do this when responses are contingent upon either appetitive reinforcers or the avoidance of an aversive UCS such as electric shock, and (3) show acquisition of instrumental performance which does not differ in any significant respect from that in either birds or nonhuman mammals.

Successful appetitive reinforcers used have included food (e.g. Clark, 1959), visual exposure to a conspecific (Bols, 1977), opportunity to regulate water temperature or obtain oxygenated water (Rozin and Mayer, 1961; Van Sommers, 1962) or access to a model of a symbiotic cleaner fish (Losey and Margules, 1974). Many studies have observed discriminated shock-avoidance responding (e.g. Behrend and Bitterman, 1962; Rakover, 1979; Bintz, 1971) as well as successful Sidman or nondiscriminated avoidance learning (Behrend and Bitterman, 1963; Pinckney, 1968). Appetitive instrumental conditioning has been claimed in lemon sharks and nurse sharks (*Ginglymostoma cirratum*) (Clark, 1959), and successful avoidance responding found in goldfish, Siamese fighting fish, guppies, and Beau gregory (*Bomacentrus leucostictus*) (e.g. Otis and Cerf, 1963; Werboff and Lloyd, 1963; Wodinsky, Behrend, and Bitterman, 1962).

Two particular studies suggest that fish are capable of learning in instrumental situations without this learning being easily attributed to accidental Pavlovian conditioning. In a discrimination procedure, Van Sommers (1962) trained goldfish to swim down a tube in the presence of a red light in order to obtain oxygenated water. However, when a green light was presented these subjects were given oxygenated water only when at least 20 sec had passed without a tube-swimming response (a differential reinforcement of other-behavior, DRO, schedule). All subjects learned to respond at a much higher rate during the red light than during the green light and thus obtained rewards during both components of the discrimination. As

Macphail (1982) points out, this cannot be explained easily in Pavlovian terms because both red and green stimuli will be paired with reinforcement, yet only the red stimulus elicits swimming down the tube. In such circumstances it seems most likely that the fish learned that individual responses were associated with the two stimuli. Such a discrimination is often difficult for mammals such as rats to acquire — especially when the two responses required of the discrimination produce identical reinforcers (e.g. Trapold, 1970; Overmier, Bull, and Trapold, 1971).

Mandriota, Thompson, and Bennett (1968) studied avoidance responding in mormyrid fish (*Gnathonemus*) using an elevation in rate of electric organ discharge as the avoidance response. This response is a nondirected one, and so successful learning cannot be attributed to the fish simply directing its behavior toward environmental stimuli that come to be associated with the offset of shock, or directing its behavior away from stimuli that become accidentally paired with shock. They compared the performance of fish whose responses avoided the electric shock (instrumental group) with yoked partners which received the same number of shocks as the instrumental subjects but whose behavior had no effect on the presentation of shock. The instrumental group showed significantly more responding than the yoked control group, suggesting that the instrumental subjects had in fact learned about the response-avoidance contingency.

In some cases the nature of the reinforcer can severely affect instrumental learning in fish. For instance, Sevenster (1968) reinforced male sticklebacks for either rod-biting or swimming through a ring with the opportunity to court a female. He found that swimming through a ring was acquired more readily with this sexual reinforcer than was rod-biting. In fact, rod-biting was more frequent during periods of extinction than during periods of reinforcement. Sevenster explains this discrepancy by suggesting that rod-biting as an instrumental response is incompatible with the stickleback's natural courtship behaviors that were elicited by the sexual reinforcer. Similarly, Hogan (1967) and Hogan, Kleist, and Hutchings (1970) reinforced male fighting fish (*Betta splendens*) on a fixed-ratio (FR) schedule with either food or the opportunity to display in a mirror as the reinforcer. The response in both cases was swimming through an alley. While the rate of response acquisition was identical with the two reinforcers, when the fish were exposed to increasing FR values, only response rate for the food reinforcer increased in order to maintain a constant rate of reinforcement. Far from suggesting that fish cannot learn about instrumental contingencies in certain situations, these constraints on instrumental learning in fish resemble the interference between reinforcer-elicited behaviors and the instrumental response which has been observed in a wide variety of animals, including both birds and nonhuman mammals (e.g. Shettleworth, 1972a; Davey, 1981; see pp. 202–4).

3 *Instrumental conditioning in amphibia and reptiles*

There is certainly a good deal of evidence that both amphibia and reptiles can acquire responses in instrumental procedures, but little or no evidence that this learning proceeds as a result of these groups of animals possessing an instrumental learning mechanism.

Hershkowitz and Samuel (1973) found that both larval and adult crested newts (*Triturus cristatus*) would learn to make a snapping response at either a black circle or a black triangle when these stimuli were used as discriminative stimuli setting the occasion for the snapping response to be reinforced with a piece of worm. Other studies using amphibian subjects have demonstrated successful Y-maze learning. Frankhauser, Vernon, Frank, and Slack (1955) found efficient Y-maze learning in both salamanders and larval newts (*Triturus viridescens*). Boice (1970) found successful active avoidance learning in Woodhouse's toad (*Bufo woodhousei*) when compared with yoked controls. However, he failed to find any evidence of active avoidance responding in spadefood toads (*Scaphiopus hammondi*) and leopard frogs. These latter two species are generally inactive in their natural habitat, and this passive tendency may have played some role in their failure to condition. If this were so, then presumably they would learn a passive avoidance response much more readily, which would suggest that Boice's failures with leopard frogs and spadefoot toads do not stem from an associative deficit in these species.

Instrumental studies in reptiles have utilized both maze-learning and response manipulandum procedures. For instance, Van Sommers (1963) successfully conditioned red-eared turtles to press a submerged lever for a period of access to air. Kleinginna (1970) trained indigo snakes (*Drymarchon corais*) to press an illuminated key for water rewards. Gossette and Hombach (1969) also report successfully training alligators and crocodiles to press a lever for food reward. Kemp (1969) successfully trained desert iguanas to press a black disk to produce ambient temperature reductions in an environment which was constantly becoming hotter.

Successful T-maze discrimination performance has been obtained in tuataras and caimans (Northcutt and Heath, 1971, 1973) where the reward was access to the home pen, and Krekorian, Vance, and Richardson (1968) successfully reinforced maze running in desert iguanas (*Dipsosaurus dorsalis*) for reinforcing temperature increases.

In aversive procedures, successful avoidance responding has been reported in alligators (Davidson, 1966) and rat snakes (Crawford and Holmes, 1966), but a number of authors report that, although escape learning is found in reptiles, actual avoidance responding is much more difficult to establish (Powell and Mantor, 1969; Bicknell and Richardson, 1973). One possible reason for this is the problem of response initiation. Although a number of species do not appear to be incapable of associative learning in avoidance situations, they do appear to have problems initiating the response (e.g. McGill, 1960; Yori, 1978), and in a number of cases this may be because it is a response which is orthogonal to their natural species-typical activities in such circumstances (cf. Macphail, 1982: 156-8).

When the avoidance response is a natural defensive reaction, some reptiles do appear to learn the response very quickly. For instance, Granda, Matsumiya, and Stirling (1965) found rapid avoidance learning in red-eared turtles when the avoidance response was head withdrawal.

Clearly, this evidence suggests that amphibia and reptiles can learn responses in instrumental procedures, but there is little or no evidence that this is *not* the result of Pavlovian processes. Most studies use directed operants such as maze running or manipulandum operation which may result from Pavlovian autoshaping, and few studies have used either omission procedures or noncontingent controls. All of this evidence does not allow us to make a conclusion about the existence of instrumental learning mechanisms in amphibia and reptiles. Nevertheless, what the studies quoted in this section do show is that many reptiles and amphibia can adapt very rapidly and efficiently to instrumental contingencies whether this is mediated by an instrumental mechanism or not.

4 *Instrumental conditioning in birds*

One species of bird, the pigeon, is probably the most researched animal in instrumental learning procedures after the laboratory rat, and this species was studied intensively during the pioneering period of work on schedules of reinforcement (Ferster and Skinner, 1957). Nevertheless, there is surprisingly still a great deal of debate about whether birds such as the pigeon do possess learning mechanisms devoted to learning instrumental contingencies (cf. Macphail, 1982; Moore, 1973). One of the major problems of interpretation has concerned the nature of the key pecking response so frequently utilized in instrumental studies with pigeons, and there is certainly a good deal of evidence that this response does have reflexive components to it which are insensitive to consequential contingencies. Moore (1973) has put forward a well-argued case that most, if not all, of the evidence of instrument key pecking in the pigeon can be explained by Pavlovian — and, in particular, autoshaping — principles (see pp. 206-8). Although we may argue later that this assertion is perhaps a little extreme, there is certainly good evidence that the pigeon's key peck is not as sensitive to instrumental contingencies as the whole-hearted instrumental theorist would like.

For instance, Schwartz (1977a, b) and Schwartz and Williams (1972b) have argued that there are two types of pigeon key peck: a relatively long-duration peck (40–100 msec) which is sensitive to instrumental contingencies, and a short-duration peck (< 20 msec) which is insensitive to these contingencies. For instance, when autoshaped key pecking was subjected to an omission contingency, long-duration pecks did decrease in frequency, but short-duration pecks were completely unaffected by this contingency (but see Ziriax and Silberberg, 1978, for an alternative explanation of this). Similar evidence relates to studies which have attempted to reinforce key pecks of particular duration or particular force; such studies have generally failed in their attempts, and suggest that such properties of the key peck are not easily amenable to control by instrumental contingencies (e.g. Schwartz, 1971).

Another oddity concerning the pigeon's key peck has been reported by Lowe and Harzem (1977). They reinforced lever pressing in rats and key pecking in pigeons on fixed-interval (FI) schedules of reinforcement. Following this, the subjects were immediately transferred to a response-independent fixed-time (FT) schedule of the same value. Whereas rats quickly ceased responding on transfer from FI to FT, the pigeons, in general, continued to key peck as though they had failed to detect that the schedule had changed to a response-independent one. Here again, key pecking seemed insensitive to the change in contingencies. Pigeons are also notoriously inaccurate on differential reinforcement of low-rate (DRL) schedules of reinforcement, where food is obtained for spacing responses according to a minimum inter-response time requirement (see p. 77). Although we have good evidence that pigeons can accurately discriminate quite lengthy intervals (e.g. Reynolds, 1966), the key peck behavior of pigeons being trained on DRL schedules breaks down at DRL values beyond 15–20 sec (Staddon, 1965). In these cases the birds emit too many key pecks before the DRL criterion has elapsed. However, when treadle hopping rather than key pecking is used as the response, pigeons can achieve accurate performances on DRL schedules that compare favorably with those of rats (Hemmes, 1975), suggesting that it is the key peck response itself which is insensitive to the DRL temporal contingency.

Finally, reflexive components of the pigeon's key peck can also be found in

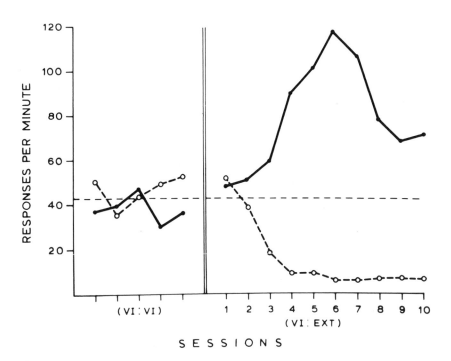

Figure 3.15 Response rates of a pigeon during the last 5 sessions of nondifferential training (a multiple VI:VI schedule) and the first 10 sessions of discrimination training between the VI component (closed circles) and the extinction component (open circles). Although response rate declines during the extinction component, response rate during the unchanged VI component actually increases, producing "behavioral contrast." (After Halliday and Boakes, 1971)

certain discrimination procedures which involve multiple schedules of reinforcement (a multiple schedule is where reinforcement is programed according to two schedules which alternate randomly and are each signaled by distinctive stimuli). When a multiple VI:VI schedule is changed to multiple VI:extinction (EXT), not only does the rate of response in the extinction component decrease, but the rate of responding in the unchanged VI component actually *increases* (see Figure 3.15). This is known as *behavioral contrast*, and has been widely observed, primarily in pigeons key pecking for food reinforcement (Reynolds, 1961a; Terrace, 1966; Halliday and Boakes, 1972, 1974). Various manipulations have since suggested that the increase in responding to the unchanged VI component is a result of the addition of Pavlovian key pecks to the key pecks already generated by the instrumental contingency (e.g. Keller, 1974; Morris, 1976; Hearst and Gormley, 1976; cf. Schwartz and Gamzu, 1977). That is, when the schedule is changed from VI:VI to VI:EXT, the stimulus associated with the unchanged VI component becomes a Pavlovian CS^+ which differentially predicts food, and this Pavlovian signaling function appears to elicit more key pecks on top of those already maintained by the instrumental VI schedule. What this suggests is that, even in explicitly instrumental procedures, some key pecking can be the result of accidental Pavlovian contingencies. That this phenomenon again appears to be specific to the key peck response is demonstrated by the fact that behavioral contrast does not appear when the instrumental response is treadle hopping (Hemmes, 1973; Westbrook, 1973).

Even in aversive conditioning studies, key pecking also exhibits a distinct insensitivity to instrumental contingencies. There are a number of studies which have failed to produce efficient avoidance learning in pigeons using key pecking as the avoidance response (Azrin, 1959; Hineline and Rachlin, 1969; Hoffman and Fleshler, 1959; Rachlin, 1969; Rachlin and Hineline, 1967), and Schwartz and Coulter (1973) have shown that even when key pecking has been established by prior training on a VI schedule for food reward, it does not efficiently transfer to avoiding shock. This latter study suggests that the poor control of key pecking by instrumental avoidance contingencies is not just a result of any difficulty in establishing the response in the first place. Nor do these failures represent an inability of the pigeon to learn avoidance responses. When behaviors such as locomotion (Macphail, 1968), wing flapping (Rachlin, 1969) and flying (Bedford and Anger, 1968) are used as avoidance responses, efficient performance is achieved fairly rapidly.

It has been worth spending some time discussing these idiosyncrasies of the pigeon's key peck because that response is a cornerstone of the instrumental literature. Yet it regularly demonstrates either its insensitivity to instrumental contingencies or its tendency to come under the control of other factors, such as Pavlovian contingencies, implicit in the instrumental procedure. What does this lead us to conclude about instrumental learning in the pigeon? First, in appetitive schedules of reinforcement the key peck response is problematic because even on noncontingent schedules of food delivery, pecking is readily induced (cf. Staddon and Simmelhag, 1971; pp. 83–4). Pecking appears to be induced either by contextual stimuli that come to signal food delivery or by temporal factors signaling the imminent availability of food. All of the insensitivities of the key peck response to appetitive instrumental contingencies listed above can be explained in terms of this induction. The failure of key pecking to act as an effective avoidance response appears to reflect the fact that pecking is not a prominent species-specific defensive behavior, and to this extent this phenomenon is not specific to pigeons but common to a very wide range of species (see pp. 222–5). Using an avoidance response which is more readily compatible with a natural defense reaction (such as wing flapping or flying) does result in successful avoidance learning.

How does all this relate to Moore's (1973) assertion that all pigeon behavior on instrumental schedules is the result of Pavlovian processes? Certainly, pecking appears to be readily induced by any stimulus (temporal or contextual) which differentially indicates food, but there is no reason to suppose that this is the sole determinant of the pecking response in instrumental studies. A more parsimonious suggestion is that the constraints on instrumental key pecking noted above result from competition between instrumental and Pavlovian contingencies. In order to lend support to this proposition it is necessary to demonstrate that examples of instrumental responding in pigeons exist where the implication of Pavlovian processes can be more or less ruled out.

Early evidence that the pigeon's key peck might be sensitive to instrumental contingencies was supplied by the study of Schwartz and Williams (1972a). They imposed an omission contingency on key pecking generated by an autoshaping procedure. Pigeons were presented periodically with one of two different key colors: red trials were associated with an omission contingency, while on white trials food delivery was unrelated to responding, but the reinforcement frequency on these trials was yoked to the obtained reinforcement frequency on red trials. Both key colors were paired with identical numbers of food deliveries, but only the red key had negative consequences for pecking. Schwartz and Williams (1972a) found that subjects pecked significantly more on the white key than on the red key. They claim that this difference could not have resulted from any Pavlovian process, because the two keys had identical numbers of CS–UCS pairings, and that reduced responding to the red key must have resulted from the sensitivity of the key peck response to the omission contingency operating on red key trials. Nevertheless, these results are partially confounded by the fact that during red key trials some other aspect of the environment may have become associated with food, and the reduced responding on the red key may simply have been a result of the subjects directing their pecking at this new stimuli (see pp. 92–3). Unfortunately, because pecking is a directed response, it may prove impossible to determine its sensitivity to instrumental contingencies by ruling out implicit Pavlovian processes. However, there are instances of pigeons successfully learning instrumental responses which are not obviously directed at any part of the environment. For instance, Jenkins (1977) successfully reinforced "head bobbing" and was able to bring this response under discriminative control. Similarly, Rudolph and Van Houten (1977) were able to maintain key pecking by pigeons for food reinforcement in total darkness. It is very difficult to conceive of pecking being directed toward some contextual CS in this latter situation. Finally, Boakes (1977) demonstrated that pigeons were able to learn a ring-pulling response which required complex manipulation of the operandum over and above simple behavior directed toward the ring. This again provides some evidence for direct instrumental reinforcement of arbitrary operants in pigeons.

Nevertheless, reliance on the pigeon's key peck in instrumental studies has left us with less independent evidence that birds do possess an instrumental learning mechanism that we would like. The kind of evidence required in this respect is the kind that shows that pigeons can discriminate sequences of their own behavior that they then might be able to reproduce as instrumental responses, and that nondirected responses (such as leg flexion or individual wing flexion) are sensitive to instrumental contingencies. Such evidence toward these goals is provided by Jenkins (1977), Rudolph and Van Houten (1977), and Boakes (1977).

5 *Instrumental conditioning in nonhuman mammals*

Like the pigeon, the laboratory rat is one of the prototypical species utilized in studies of instrumental learning, and there is clearly no doubt that a wide range of mammalian species can adapt rapidly and effectively to instrumental contingencies. Whether mammals do learn response-reinforcer (R–S) associations, however, is still a hotly debated topic (see Chapter 7), but there are clearly some indications that mammals possess some of the attributes necessary for this kind of learning. For instance, rats can discriminate discrete aspects of their own behavior (Beninger, Kendall, and Vanderwolf, 1974; Morgan and Nicholas, 1979) — a useful if not indispensable ability if they are to reproduce an arbitrary instrumental response. A number of mammals are also capable of learning nondirected instrumental responses where mediation by Pavlovian contingencies is minimized. These include wheelrunning in rats (Bernheim and Williams, 1967; Bolles, Stokes, and Younger, 1966; Mackintosh and Dickinson, 1979), and leg flexion in dogs (Konorski, 1948; Wahlsten and Cole, 1972). Similarly, subtle aspects of rats' behavior can be altered by an omission contingency without the general directedness of the behavior being changed (e.g. Davey, Oakley, and Cleland, 1981; Atnip, 1977), suggesting that instrumental contingencies can influence response topographies without affecting the aspect of the environment to which they are directed. All evidence of this kind suggests that mammals such as rats do not simply negotiate instrumental contingencies using Pavlovian processes.

However, there are some occasions when instrumental contingencies do fail to have the predicted effect. For instance, rats find it very difficult to learn to press a lever to avoid electric shock (D'Amato and Schiff, 1964; Meyer, Cho, and Weseman, 1960; Smith, McFarland, and Taylor, 1961; Weissman, 1962; see pp. 222–5). Rats and hamsters also find it very difficult to learn to groom to acquire food (Shettleworth, 1975; Charlton, 1983; Morgan and Nicholas, 1979; Annable and Wearden, 1979). And hamsters usually fail to learn to face-wash, scratch, or scent-mark in order to acquire food (Shettleworth, 1973 1975). There are many such other examples of certain responses in mammals appearing to be relatively insensitive to instrumental contingencies (cf. Shettleworth, 1972a; Davey, 1981; Hogan and Roper, 1978), but rather than suggesting inadequacies in underlying associative abilities, these examples appear to represent some kind of incompatibility or competition between the target response (the operant) and patterns of behavior elicited either directly or indirectly by the reinforcer (see pp. 202–4).

One interesting aspect of the debate on the existence of specialized instrumental learning mechanisms in mammals is that some writers have suggested that the mammalian neocortex is essential for instrumental learning (e.g. Russell, 1966), and early studies supported this belief by failing to establish instrumental conditioning in surgically neocorticated rats and rabbits (e.g. DiCara, Braun, and Pappas, 1970). The argument here is that qualitative changes in intelligence and the ability to process complex contingencies as we progress from fish to mammals is a result of the development of neocortex (e.g. Bitterman, 1975). Thus, according to this argument, mammals would represent the only class of animals truly capable of processing response-reinforcer contingencies. However, more recent studies on decorticate mammals suggest that they can learn in instrumental tasks. Early failures appeared to result from the use of aversive reinforcers in avoidance procedures and the disruption of responding by hyperemotionality elicited by these reinforcers (Oakley, 1979b, 1983). When decorticate animals are given training in appetitive instrumental situations with sufficient remedial training to focus their attention on the response manipulandum, the response is acquired relatively efficiently (Oakley, 1979c, 1980) and even relatively normal "break-and-run" performance can be achieved on simple fixed-ratio (FR) schedules (Oakley and Russell, 1978; Oakley, 1979c). Nevertheless, we know that decorticated mammals can process Pavlovian contingencies fairly efficiently, so the instrumental performance we observe in these animals could in fact be mediated by Pavlovian processes. Certainly, all of the responses so far learned by decorticates involve directed behavior or manipulandum operation, and this does not rule out these aspects of the environment being established as Pavlovian CSs toward which the decorticate simply directs its behavior (cf. Oakley, Eames, Jacobs, Davey, and Cleland, 1981). Clearly, more controlled studies are necessary to establish the validity of arguments which assert that instrumental learning abilities reside in the neocortex.

6 *Instrumental conditioning in humans*

It may seem facetious to ask whether humans are capable of learning instrumental contingencies — especially since we devised the concept! There is certainly plenty of evidence that humans do learn about the relationship between their behavior and its consequences, both in simple instrumental learning procedures (Dickinson, Shanks, and Evenden, 1984) and more generally (cf. Alloy and Tabachnik, 1984). However, the variables that influence human instrumental performance appear to be much more involved than those already implicated in the performance of nonhuman animals. This leads to some important anomalies in human and animal instrumental behavior which often characterize human performance as rigid and insensitive to the scheduled contingencies. For instance, some experimenters have encountered great difficulty in extinguishing a simple learned operant in human subjects under experimental conditions (e.g. Buchwald, 1959; Bijou and Baer, 1966). Others have reported that human responding on schedules of reinforcement frequently entails erratic rates often interspered with long and unpredictable pauses (Barrett and Lindsley, 1962; Lindsley, 1960; Orlando and Bijou, 1960; Sidman, 1962; Spradlin and Girardeau, 1966; Weiner, 1969; Lowe, 1979).

Particularly illuminating in this respect is the phenomenon of human subjects on simple fixed-interval (FI) schedules. Whereas nonhuman animals exhibit a slowly accelerating response gradient throughout the interval (the FI "scallop"), human subjects tend to emit either a very high, constant rate of responding without pauses, or a very low response rate consisting of just one or two responses at the end of the inter-reinforcement interval (cf. Lowe, 1979, 1983; Davey, 1981) (see Figure 3.16). The former of these two response patterns appears to be completely insensitive to the temporal parameters of the schedule, and frequently results in a completely exhausted subject at the end of the experimental session! Furthermore, human subjects will rarely show the flexibility in performance demonstrated by nonhuman animals

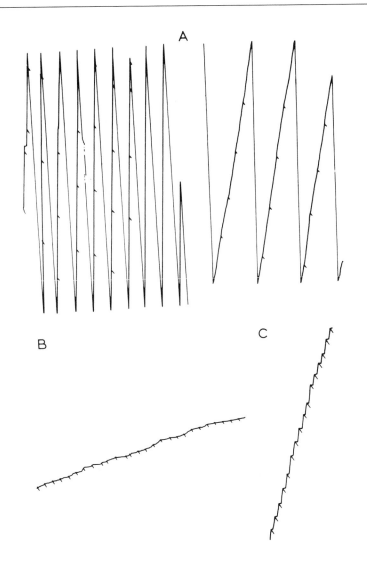

Figure 3.16 Typical cumulative recordings from human subjects on fixed-interval schedules. *A* represents typical high-rate performance frequently found with human subjects; *B* represents low-rate performance; and *C* illustrates how human FI performance often resembles "break-and-run" behavior when it does come under the control of the schedule contingencies.

when transferred from one schedule to another. Human subjects often carry over the response patterning acquired on a previous schedule to the performance on a completely different subsequent schedule (e.g. Weiner, 1969, 1972).

These apparently maladaptive aspects of human instrumental performance can to a large extent be explained by the difference between what Skinner (1966) called instruction-controlled vs. contingency-controlled behavior. In cases where high-rate FI performance is observed, subjects frequently adopt an inappropriate response strategy based on some rule they have formulated; in such circumstances subjects usually report that they believe that reinforcement was contingent in some way on the *number* of responses they made (e.g. Leander, Lippman, and Meyer, 1968; Lippman and Meyer, 1967). The kind of rule that subjects formulate to control their responding also appears to be affected crucially by the nature of the instructions given to subjects at the outset of the experiment. High-rate FI performance appears to result when information is given about the *response* requirement, while low-rate FI performance results from information in the instructions concerning the temporal pattern of reinforcement (Kaufman, Baron, and Kopp, 1966). Inappropriate performance can be maintained for long periods when misleading instructions are given, but more detailed instructions about reinforcement contingencies typically produce response rates approximating the requirement of the schedule (Dews and Morse, 1958; Kaufman, Baron, and Kopp, 1966; Weiner, 1962; Baron, Kaufman, and Stauber, 1969). Lippman and Meyer (1967) have suggested that instructions which simply tell the subject that "they will receive reinforcers for pressing the response button" are like the "setting operation for a vigilance task"; that is, they prime the subject to adopt response-based rather than temporally-based strategies.

What all this evidence suggests is that much human instrumental performance is rule-governed rather than contingency-governed. These rules are formulated by the subject during the course of performance, may be influenced by the nature of the instructions given prior to the experiment, and often produce behavior which is inappropriate to the scheduled contingencies. There are at least two questions to ask at this point. First, if rule-governed performance can be prevented, does human schedule behavior then show any similarity to that of nonhuman animals? Second, why should human instrumental performance be so susceptible to control by self-generated rules when animal performance is quite clearly contingency-controlled?

A number of approaches can be devised to investigate the first question. A few studies have attempted to limit the biasing effects of instructions by eliminating them and shaping up the appropriate response by reinforcing successive approximations to the required behavior. In such circumstances, the resulting performance is favorably comparable to that found in animals (Shimoff, Catania, and Matthews, 1981; Matthews, Shimoff, Catania, and Sagvolden, 1977). A further method of eliminating self-produced rules is to provide the subject with a concurrent task of some kind. Laties and Weiss (1963) found that when subjects were given a relatively simple problem-solving task at the same time as responding on a telegraph key for rewards on an FI schedule, typical FI scalloping was rapidly established and maintained. A third method of eradicating self-produced rules is to attempt to externalize them in some way. If the experimenter is aware of the nature of such rules (such as counting on temporally-based schedules) then the effect of these can be attenuated by providing comparable external cues. For example, Lowe, Harzem, and Hughes (1978) and Lowe, Harzem, and Bagshaw (1978) were able to replace covert counting on FI schedules by instituting a second response which briefly illuminated a digital clock. They found that responding to produce the digital clock exhibited the familiar "scalloped" pattern similar to that found in other animals on FI schedules. Clearly, then, these results do suggest that the contingency-controlled performance of human subjects is formalistically very similar to that of nonhuman animals when rule-governed behavior is minimized.

But why does so much human instrumental performance become rule-governed rather than contingency-governed? Lowe (1983) has suggested that the answer to this anomaly may lie in the unique linguistic abilities possessed by humans. He suggests that "It is the human subjects' capacity to formulate their own descriptions of reinforcement contingencies, to 'self-tact' [Skinner, 1957b: 138], and to use these descriptions to formulate rules to govern their behavior which results in human operant behavior being so different from that of lower animals" (Lowe, 1983: 77). In order to test this hypothesis, Lowe suggested that contingency-governed performance should be found readily in the schedule behavior of humans who have not developed language sufficiently well to be able to describe their own behavior and its consequences. In support of this hypothesis Bentall and Lowe (1982) and Lowe, Beasty, and Bentall (1983) compared the performance of young infants on FI schedules with that of older children of different ages and language ability. The performance of children in age ranges 5–6½ years and 7½–9 years resembled that of adults and was similar to the performances shown in Figure 3.16. The performance of young infants (2½–4 years), however, was more typical of nonhuman animals and showed obvious signs of contingency control (see Figure 3.17). Although evidence such as this is consistent with

Figure 3.17 A simple apparatus used for studying schedule performance in pre-lingual children. Responses are produced by the child simply contacting the drum. (Photograph courtesy of C. F. Lowe)

Lowe's (1983) suggestion that linguistic and verbal abilities may underlie rule-governed schedule performance in humans, these results provide only correlational evidence. It may be, for instance, that some other unique cognitive ability underlies both the development of linguistic abilities and rule-governed performance. We must await further evidence to clarify these possibilities.

What the evidence reviewed in this section indicates is that while humans are clearly able to learn about the relationship between their behavior and its consequences (that is, they can learn directly about instrumental contingencies), the factors which translate this learning into performance are very complex, and frequently involve processes not obviously observed in nonhuman animal performance.

7 Conclusion

This comparative review of instrumental conditioning demonstrates that learning in instrumental procedures has been investigated in a very wide range of species. However, there are numerous difficulties inherent in interpreting the results of these investigations. There is no unambiguous evidence that instrumental learning abilities exist in invertebrates, reptiles, amphibia, and only incomplete evidence that response-consequence learning exists in fish or even birds. Nevertheless, there are some studies in both birds and nonhuman mammals which suggest that these groups do possess some of the attributes essential to instrumental learning (namely, they can learn nondirected operants, are sensitive to omission contingencies on nondirected action patterns or show the ability to discriminate discrete aspects of their own behavior). Certainly, in neurologically less complex organisms such as invertebrates and possibly fish, reptiles, and amphibia, it is clearly possible for these animals to negotiate many instrumental contingencies using Pavlovian processes, and this may be sufficient reason for them to lack independent instrumental learning facilities. The problem lies not directly in showing that a particular animal can process response-reinforcer relationships, but in ruling out alternative interpretations. The skeptical scientist may be tempted to adopt Lloyd Morgan's canon in such circumstances and in no case "interpret an action as the outcome of the exercise of a higher psychical faculty if it can be interpreted as the exercise of one which stands lower in the psychological scale" (Morgan, 1894). However, in this instance, this would seem to me rather harsh and unjustified. The current problem of identifying instrumental learning mechanisms is more one of experimental technique than philosophical judgment, and even where we suspect that the neurological capacities of an organism may be insufficient to cope with the various abilities required to process and utilize response-reinforcer contingencies, we should still keep an open mind until more definitive evidence surfaces.

Chapter summary

1 Instrumental conditioning involves response-consequence contingencies in which a consequence which increases the future probability of a response is

known as a *reinforcer* and one which decreases that probability is known as a *punisher*.

2 The accidental correlation between a behavior and food will often produce an increase in the probability of that behavior. This is known as *superstitious reinforcement*. However, this is not a robust phenomenon and superstitiously reinforced behavior will often be replaced by species-specific feeding-related responses.

3 A stimulus in the presence of which responses are reinforced is generally called *a discriminative stimulus*. Presentation of a discriminative stimulus comes to control the emission of the response, but in some cases this control may be exerted only by specific features of the discriminative stimulus.

4 Stimuli which signal nonreinforcement of a response often acquire *inhibitory* properties. That is, their presentation will reduce the probability of the response recurring.

5 Stimuli can acquire reinforcing properties by being paired with an already effective reinforcer. These stimuli are known as *conditioned reinforcers*.

6 Reinforcers can be delivered on what are known as *schedules*. There are two basic methods for selecting responses to be reinforced: (1) on the basis of time, (2) on the basis of number. This gives rise to four basic schedules of reinforcement known as fixed-interval (FI), fixed-ratio (FR), variable-interval (VI), and variable-ratio (VR). Each schedule generates its own characteristic pattern of responding.

7 More than one source of reinforcement may be available at once, such that the animal has to make a choice about which reinforcer to respond for. Such schedules are known as *concurrent schedules of reinforcement*.

8 Choice behavior on a concurrent schedule follows a basic empirical rule known as the *matching law*.

9 When food is presented periodically on a schedule of reinforcement, stereotyped behaviors often develop which fill the time when reinforcement is unavailable. These are known as *schedule-induced* or *adjunctive* behaviors. The most common adjunctive behaviors are polydipsia and schedule-induced aggression.

10 Explanations of why schedule-induced behaviors develop normally relate them to *displacement* activities which are elicited by events which signal nonreinforcement.

11 Deciding what species can learn by associating responses with their consequences is not an easy matter. This is because (1) there is no general consensus about the kind of mechanism which allows animals to associate responses with reinforcing consequences, and (2) many species possess limited behavioral repertoires, which make interpretation of the underlying learning difficult.

12 In order to be able to say that an animal has learned to associate a response with its consequences, (1) we would need to rule out the involvement of any implicit Pavlovian processes; (2) we would need to show that the animal is able to isolate and discriminate the important features of the contingent response; and (3) we would want to show that instrumental reinforcement would generate completely novel arbitrary behavior sequences.

13 While invertebrates such as the fruit fly *Drosophila* can learn under instrumental contingencies, it is by no means clear that they do this by learning to associate the response with its consequences.

14 Studies of instrumental learning in fish show that they can learn under both appetitive and aversive learning contingencies — even when the response is a nondirected one (ruling out autoshaping responses generated by Pavlovian conditioning).

15 There is good evidence that amphibia and reptiles can learn under instrumental contingencies, but in no case has implicit Pavlovian conditioning been ruled out as the cause of this learning.

16 The pigeon is one of the most highly-researched species in instrumental conditioning, and there is ample evidence that it can learn under such contingencies. However, the response normally used in such studies — the key peck — is often strongly influenced by Pavlovian contingencies, and thus it is difficult to conclude that instrumental learning using the key peck response is the result of direct response-consequence learning. Nevertheless, there is some evidence using responses other than key pecking that the pigeon may be able to learn under instrumental contingencies without this learning being complicated by implicit Pavlovian conditioning.

17 There is good evidence that nonhuman mammals, such as the rat, do not simply negotiate instrumental contingencies using Pavlovian processes.

18 Even surgically neodecorticate rats and rabbits can negotiate instrumental contingencies and exhibit standard performance on schedules of reinforcement. It is still not clear, however, whether this learning is due to Pavlovian processes, and neocortex may still be necessary for true response-consequence learning.

19 The performance of human subjects on schedules of reinforcement is often maladaptive, insensitive to changes in the contingencies and frequently dissimilar to the performance found in nonhuman animals. These apparently maladaptive aspects of human instrumental performance can be explained by the fact that responding appears to become controlled by self-generated rules rather than by the schedule contingencies. When control by these rules is eliminated, human schedule performance resembles that found in nonhuman animals.

Chapter four

Cognitive aspects of conditioning: associations, representations, and memories

The behavioral changes that are observed during conditioning procedures are mediated by underlying psychological mechanisms which cannot be directly observed but have to be inferred from the results of experimental manipulations. Because these underlying mechanisms are not open to direct observation, many learning theorists have been content to understand learning at the level of controlling variables: that is, they were willing simply to catalog the regularities between environmental input into the organism and the subsequent behavioral output (e.g. Skinner, 1950, 1953). This approach was typical of the behavior analysts of the 1960s and early 1970s and gave rise to the intense period of research on, for instance, schedules of instrumental reinforcement during these years. Nevertheless, although analyses of learning in terms of controlling relationships are quite valid, the inquiring scientist should still be curious as to the psychological mechanisms that mediate these relationships.

As objective experimenters, we can only observe an animal's performance — but how can this tell us what it has learned? Intuitively it is quite easy to conceive of circumstances where the animal may have learned something but, for the time being, this learning is not manifest in changes of behavior. An example is the phenomenon of *sensory preconditioning*. If an animal is exposed to pairings of two neutral stimuli such as a brief light (CS_1) followed by a brief tone (CS_2), there appear to be no obvious behavioral changes. However, if the animal is then given pairings of CS_2 with a UCS, subsequent presentation of CS_1 alone will elicit CRs appropriate to the UCS (Brogden, 1939b; Rizley and Rescorla, 1972). Thus, it is only subsequent tests that reveal that learning did occur in the initial phase of the sensory preconditioning procedure. Such learning is generally known as *behaviorally silent* learning (Dickinson, 1980), and can only be detected either inferentially or by conducting further manipulations subsequent to the original training.

So, learning clearly is something that is distinct from observed changes in behavior. But, what then is the nature of learning and how can we acquire the knowledge necessary to describe the mechanisms which mediate learning? A good deal of the necessary knowledge can be achieved by developing appropriate inferential techniques which will throw some light on these underlying processes.

Associations

Consider the example of Pavlov's prototypical dog learning to salivate in the presence of a bell that has been paired with food. We can ask very generally what kinds of things the dog *might* have learned which led it to salivate during the bell. From the point of view of the conditioning theorist there are two obvious candidates. The dog may have learned that the bell predicts food: that is, after some pairings of the bell with food, the bell comes to elicit a "memory" or internal representation of the food that is to follow, and it is this evoked representation that stimulates salivation. Alternatively, the dog may be much less "cognitive" in its learning. Instead of becoming associated with food, the bell may have become associated with the act of salivation which is also associated with food. Thus, a direct link may have been formed between centers representing the bell and the reflex arc which controls salivation. The first example implies that the CR of salivation is mediated by representations of the food UCS; the second example implies that what is learned is much more reflexive and is not mediated by representations of the food UCS. The former is known as S–S (stimulus–stimulus) learning and the latter as S–R (stimulus–response) learning. Having established what the basic associative possibilities might be, the next task is to develop experimental techniques which can help differentiate between these possibilities. Remember, simply because an experimenter sets up a contingency between two stimuli (for example, between a bell and food delivery) does not mean that that is what the animal learns.

1 *First-order Pavlovian conditioning*

Initial attempts to determine the kinds of associative learning underlying Pavlovian conditioning were confined to either proving or disproving the S–R point of view which had originally been expounded by authors such as Guthrie (1935) and Hull (1943). Evidence for basic S–R learning from these studies was, however, sparse. One of the basic procedures to test the S–R hypothesis is to block the occurrence of the UCR during training: such a manipulation should prevent the animal associating the CS with the response to the UCS. Solomon and Turner (1962) found that when dogs were paralysed with the drug curare and then given pairings of a CS with electric shock to the leg (UCS), subsequent testing after the drug had worn off showed that the dogs exhibited an immediate leg-flexion CR to the CS. Similarly, when salivation is blocked by administration of the drug atropine, and dogs are given pairings of a CS with food, subsequent testing in the absence of the drug showed that the dogs had acquired conditioned salivation to the CS (Crisler, 1930; Finch, 1938). Although these results did not augur well for an S–R interpretation of Pavlovian learning, it was still quite possible that in the absence of *overt* UCRs the CS may have become associated with covert neural correlates of the UCR.

However, it was not until the 1970s that animal learning theorists attempted to tackle the problem of what is learned by investigating the possibility that Pavlovian conditioning was mediated by S–S rather than S–R learning. The logic of the inferential techniques used runs thus: if the CR is mediated by internal representations of the UCS and by associative connections established between CS and UCS centers, then any manipulation which leads the animal to revalue the UCS should also influence the strength of the CR. The procedures which utilize this logic are commonly known as *postconditioning revaluation techniques*, and the stages in the experimental procedure are the following: (1) animals are given simple Pavlovian training by pairing a CS with a UCS; (2) the animal is then given some treatment which leads it to revalue the UCS; and (3) test presentations of the CS are given to assess any change in the strength of the CR.

Rescorla (1973, 1974) was the first to use these techniques with aversive Pavlovian conditioning in rats using a conditioned suppression procedure. A tone CS was paired with electric shock (UCS) until fear CRs were elicited by the CS. Subsequently, without the CS being presented, the electric shock UCS was revalued in two ways. First, some subjects were given a series of unavoidable shock presentations which eventually resulted in an habituation of the defensive reactions to the shock. Second, in other cases rats were given independent unavoidable presentations of an electric shock which was of a greater intensity than the shock used during original training. So, in the first case, the shock UCS was revalued so as to seem less aversive, and in the second case it was revalued to appear more aversive. Subsequent test presentations of the original CS showed that the first manipulation had produced a *reduction* in CR strength, while the second manipulation resulted in an *increase* in CR strength. Results such as these strongly indicate that the strength of the CR can be manipulated by independently manipulating the subject's evaluation of the UCS. The inference from this is that the CR was being mediated by UCS representations evoked by CS–UCS associations formed during training; that is, the CR was being mediated by S–S associations.

Further studies have indicated that in nearly all first-order Pavlovian studies, associations between CS and UCS appear to be formed, and the CR is thus mediated by the animal's evaluation of the UCS. In appetitive Pavlovian conditioning, for instance, once training has established an appetitive CR, a food UCS can be devalued by pairing it with gastric illness (see pp. 183–4). Devaluation of the food UCS in this way either abolishes or substantially reduces the strength of the CR to subsequent CS presentations (e.g. Holland and Straub, 1979; Colby and Smith, 1977; Cleland and Davey, 1982). All of these results imply that first-order Pavlovian conditioning in both appetitive and aversive preparations establishes CS–UCS associations.

2 *Higher-order Pavlovian conditioning*

The rationale of the post-conditioning revaluation technique can be extended to a study of the associations formed in higher-order Pavlovian conditioning, with some interesting results. Second-order conditioning is established in the following way: (1) a CS_1 (for example, a light) is paired with a UCS; (2) a new CS_2 (such as a tone) is then paired with CS_1; and (3) CS_2 is tested to see if it elicits a second-order CR appropriate to the original UCS. Such second-order Pavlovian learning can be readily established (e.g. Rizley and Rescorla, 1972; Holland and Rescorla, 1975; Konorski, 1948; cf. Rescorla, 1980a: 1–10), but there are a number of possible associative routes by which the CR_2 may be learned (see Figure 4.1). For example, (1) the animal may learn two different associations, CS_1–UCS and CS_2–CS_1 and interpret these two associations as the logical syllogism A then B, B then C, therefore A then C; (2) the animal may learn a direct associative link between CS_2 and the UCS representation (e.g. Konorski, 1948): this may arise because during the second-order CS_2–CS_1 conditioning phase, CS_2 may be followed not only by the presentation of CS_1 but also by the internal representation of the UCS evoked by CS_1. Thus, instead of learning an association between CS_2 and CS_1 during this phase, the animal learns an association between CS_2 and the representation of the UCS evoked by CS_1; (3) during the second-order conditioning phase the animal may learn to associate CS_2 with its reaction to CS_1, thus forming a CS_2–CR_1 (S–R) association.

The post-conditioning revaluation technique can be used to differentiate among all three of these possibilities. For instance, if possibility (3) is the case,

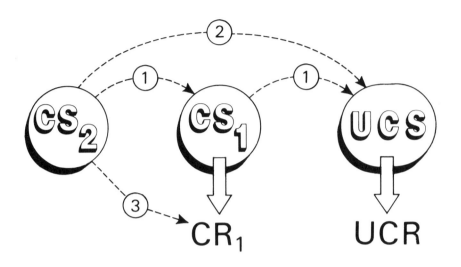

Figure 4.1 Schematic representations of the possible associations that might be formed during second-order Pavlovian conditioning. Responding to CS_2 may result from (1) the subject integrating two associations (CS_1–UCS and CS_2–CS_1); (2) the subject forming an association directly between CS_2 and the UCS; or (3) by associating CS_2 with the response to CS_1. See text for further explanation.

then postconditioning revaluation of either the UCS or CS_1 should not affect the response to CS_2 (because it is controlled by direct S–R associations). If possibility (2) is the case, then the response to CS_2 should be affected by UCS devaluation but not by CS_1 revaluation. If possibility (1) is the case, then the response to CS_2 should be affected by revaluation of *both* the UCS and CS_1.

Initial analyses of second-order learning suggested that the second-order response (CR_2) was much more resistant to revaluation of the UCS than was the response in first-order Pavlovian conditioning. For instance, Holland and Rescorla (1975) found that second-order conditioned activity in rats was not affected by postconditioning devaluation of the original food UCS. Similarly, Rescorla (1973) also found that a second-order CR established through aversive conditioning was not affected by postconditioning devaluation of the electric shock UCS. Other studies attempted to assess the effect on CR_2 of postconditioning devaluation of CS_1. Devaluation of CS_1 is achieved simply by exposing the animal to unpaired presentations of CS_1 after conditioning so that the CR to CS_1 extinguishes. Once again this manipulation failed to have any substantial effect on the ability of CS_2 to evoke a conditioned response (Holland and Rescorla, 1975; Rizley and Rescorla, 1972). The fact that CR_2 was unaffected by subsequent devaluation of both the UCS and CS_1 suggested that second-order conditioning was mediated by S–R associations formed between CS_2 and the animal's reaction to CS_1. What is more, these S–R associations need not be associations between CS_2 and specific actions elicited by CS_1, but can also be between CS_2 and some more general affective state elicited by CS_1. For instance, even when CR_1 is a different behavior (for example, increases in general activity levels) to CR_2 (such as key pecking), CR_2 can still be unaffected by devaluation of CS_1, suggesting that CR_2 is in fact a manifestation of learning between CS_2 and the motivational state elicited by CS_1 (Nairne and Rescorla, 1981). These initial findings from second-order Pavlovian studies raised an important question. Is second-order conditioning mediated by associative mechanisms independent of, and qualitatively different from, those which mediate simple first-order conditioning?

Some studies which indicated that second-order learning probably was not independent of and qualitatively different from first-order learning came from second-order conditioning studies of autoshaping in pigeons. In these studies (Rashotte, Griffin, and Sisk, 1977; Leyland, 1977) CS_1 is a colored key light paired with a food UCS, and CS_2 is a different colored key light which is paired with CS_1. After second-order conditioning had established conditioned pecking at CS_2, these studies then extinguished key pecking to CS_1. Both studies found that this manipulation also abolished key pecking to CS_2, suggesting that, unlike the earlier studies, second-order responding was mediated in some way via CS_2–CS_1 associations. This had a number of possible implications for second-order learning: (1) it may have reflected a species difference in that pigeons may learn second-order responses differently from rats; (2) it could be that autoshaped responding is learned differently trom other responses; or (3) there may have been something special about the procedures in the Rashotte, Griffin, and Sisk (1977) and Leyland (1977) studies which promoted second-order S–S rather than S–R learning.

However, a study by Nairne and Rescorla (1981) does throw some light on the processes involved here. Using pigeons in a second-order conditioning paradigm similar to Rashotte *et al.* (1977) and Leyland (1977), they contrasted the use of a diffuse auditory stimulus with a localizable key light as the CS_1. When both CS_2 and CS_1 were colored key lights, extinction of responding to CS_1 also abolished responding to CS_2. However, when CS_2 was a colored key light and CS_1 was a diffuse tone, extinction of CS_1 had no effect on second-order pecking at CS_2. This suggests that the nature of the association formed during second-order conditioning can be manipulated by altering procedural details. For instance, animals may form a CS_2–CS_1 association only when CS_2 and CS_1 are similar kinds of stimuli (such as colored pecking keys) or when the CR to these two stimuli is similar (that is, key pecking). When CS_2 and CS_1 are stimuli presented to different modalities it is conceivable that animals are more prepared to associate CS_2 with their *reactions* to CS_1.

An alternative explanation of these results can be couched in terms of stimulus saliency. Forming associations is clearly an information-processing task, and animals have a limited capacity for processing simultaneous information from different channels. Thus, instead of learning all possible associations between events, they only process associations between those events which are the most salient. When CS_1 is a colored pecking key it is difficult for the pigeon to ignore the stimulus because autoshaped key pecking insures that it is closely attended to, hence the sensory features of the stimulus are particularly salient for the animal. However, it is well known that pigeons prefer to associate visual rather than auditory stimuli with food, and they process auditory stimuli less quickly than visual stimuli in such circumstances (cf. Lolordo, 1979). Now, there are at least three obvious and distinguishable events which immediately follow CS_2 presentation. These are: (1) the sensory features of CS_1, (2) any representations of the UCS evoked by CS_1, and (3) the animal's own reaction to CS_1. Presumably only the most salient of these events will be attended to and enter into association with CS_2. When CS_1 is a colored pecking key which the pigeon approaches and pecks, it may be the features of this which become associated with CS_2. When CS_1 is a diffuse auditory stimulus this may be less physically salient and as a result the pigeon may associate CS_2 with its reaction to CS_1, hence the findings of Nairne and Rescorla (1981).

A similar view based on stimulus saliency can be used to account for the results of Davey and McKenna (1983) on second-order electrodermal conditioning in humans. They found that extinction of CS_1 did not affect responding to CS_2, but devaluing the UCS *did* abolish responding to CS_2 (see also Davey and Arulampalam, 1982; Davey, 1983). This implies that CR_2 was mediated directly by internal UCS representations (condition 2 in Figure 4.1). Davey (1983) argues that in the human conditioning procedure CS_2 becomes associated with the UCS representation elicited by CS_1 because neither the response to CS_1 (a weak and poorly discriminable electrodermal reaction) nor CS_1 itself (in this case a simple geometric shape) are salient enough to overshadow the subject's memories of the aversive UCS; thus it is the UCS which becomes associated with CS_2.

3 *Within-event associations*

We have so far discussed the types of inter-stimulus associations that are learned during conditioning and also some of the processes which might lead to these associations being formed. However, we have talked about associations between events and even between different internal representations, but what is the nature of such representations? Does, for instance, the animal represent a reinforcer as a bundle of inter-associated features, or does it form a representation of that event as a unit? Some insights into this problem can be gained from a study of the associations formed between the elements of compound stimuli.

Rescorla and Cunningham (1978) presented rats with simultaneous compounds of either sucrose and hydrochloric acid (SH) or salt and quinine (NQ). Following this, half the sets of animals received presentations of H followed by induced gastric illness and nonreinforced presentations of Q. Other subjects received poisoned presentations of Q but not H. Next, all animals were given a choice between S and N. They found that consumption of S was significantly less in those subjects that had received H followed by toxicosis, and consumption of N was significantly less in those subjects that had Q followed by toxicosis. Thus, rat subjects had clearly formed within-compound associations between S and H, and N and Q during the first stage of the experiment. Similar within-event associations have been found using visual compound stimuli in an autoshaping procedure with pigeons (cf. Rescorla, 1980b).

There are a number of implications of this within-event learning for various conditioning phenomena. For instance, in some cases the addition of a second element to a CS actually potentiates conditioning to the original element, and this is particularly true when an odor–taste compound is used during conditioned taste aversion learning (Clarke, Westbrook, and Irwin, 1979; Rusiniak, Hankins, Garcia, and Brett, 1979). Addition of the taste element potentiates the subsequent learned aversion to the odor. Rescorla and Durlach (1981) interpret this as the result of within-event learning. The odor might be more aversive when compounded with the taste not because the odor itself has stronger associations with the poisoning UCS, but because it has an additional association with taste that is also aversive because of its pairing with poisoning.

One curiosity associated with potentiation is that it is found almost exclusively in taste-aversion learning (Palmeriono, Rusiniak, and Garcia, 1980; but see pp. 189–90). When compound CSs are used in more standard Pavlovian conditioning paradigms the result is usually *overshadowing*. That is, the added element will actually suppress the degree of learning to the original element (Mackintosh, 1971; Pavlov, 1927; see pp. 33–4). Rescorla and Durlach (1981) explain this discrepancy in terms of the animal's limited ability to process both within-stimulus associations *and* between-stimulus associations when the UCS or reinforcer immediately follows presentation of the compound CS. If the presentation of the UCS is delayed slightly following CS presentation, then the animal will have time to process associations between different features of the CS before processing the association between CS and UCS. Thus, potentiation should be more likely to occur when the UCS is delayed (as it is in taste-aversion learning). This explanation appears to fit the available facts (cf. Rescorla and Durlach, 1981; Palmerino, Rusiniak, and Garcia, 1980).

Within-event learning has also been used to explain a phenomenon known as "unblocking." When a stimulus (A) is paired with a UCS, and then subsequently A is compounded with a new element (B), and further CS–UCS pairings are carried out, very little conditioning accrues to the new element B (see also pp. 33–4). This is known as *blocking* (Kamin, 1969). However, even when blocking occurs it can be demonstrated that the subject has learned to associate the two elements of the new AB compound, and the strength of this within-compound association is frequently utilized as an attempt to explain those situations where blocking fails to occur (cf. Rescorla and Colwill, 1983). That is, although element B has not become well associated with the UCS, it does exhibit a CR through its associative link with the conditioned element A. Procedures that facilitate this within-compound learning will obviously facilitate unblocking (but see Holland, 1984b).

Finally, two facts about within-event learning are odd, and perhaps help to cast light on the nature of the underlying representations formed during conditioning. First, sequential presentation of two stimulus elements promotes much less associative learning between the two elements than does simultaneous presentation of these elements (Rescorla, 1980b). Second, when the association between two elements is extinguished by presenting them independently, subsequent retraining with the two elements again in compound apparently fails to re-establish the association (Rescorla and Freberg, 1978; cf. Rescorla and Durlach, 1981). Rescorla and Durlach (1981) and Rescorla (1981) have suggested that these two facts are consistent with the notion that when an animal processes a complex event, it forms an integrated representation of that event as a unit and *not* as a series of inter-associated features, and new events are evaluated according to their similarity to established representations. If they are similar to existing memories, these new events activate them; if they are different, they result in the formation of a new representation. According to this interpretation, *sequential* presentation of stimulus elements would generate separate representations, and thus subsequent presentation of one element would not activate the other. However, *simultaneous* presentation should result in a unitary representation which either element (through their partial similarity to the compound representation) could activate. Similarly, when within-event associations are extinguished by individual presentation of the elements, these individual element presentations will result in separate memory representations of each element. When the two elements are retrained as a compound, subsequent presentation of the elements will still activate only their own element representations formed during extinction and hence will not reveal any relearning of within-compound associations.

4 *Learning about the context of conditioning*

There is a good deal of evidence to suggest that animals not only learn associations between the various stimulus elements relevant to the conditioning procedure (that is, CS and UCS), but they also associate this learning with the particular context in which it is carried out. For instance, when conditioning is conducted in one context (a distinctively decorated conditioned chamber), performance is reduced when the CS is tested in another, different context (Balaz, Capra, Hartl, and Miller, 1981). Similarly, extinction also appears to be context-specific. If an animal is given training in one context and then extinction trials in another, it will respond more readily to the CS when tested in the original training context than in the extinction context (Bouton and Bolles, 1979).

Animals also appear to associate specific elements of the conditioning paradigm with the context. For instance, pigeons will readily associate a CS with the context in which it is presented, and this learning can enhance the performance to other CSs presented in that context (Rescorla, 1984). Similarly, when a subject is pre-exposed to unpaired presentations of the CS, subsequent conditioning of that CS with a UCS is more difficult than if pre-exposure had not occurred. This is generally known as *latent inhibition* (see also pp. 173–4). However, latent inhibition is context-specific, and subjects who are pre-exposed to the CS in one context and then conditioned in another do not exhibit latent inhibition (Bouton and Bolles, 1979; Channell and Hall, 1981; Hall and Minor, 1984; Lubow, Rifkin, and Alek, 1976). This does suggest that during pre-exposure the CS becomes associated with the context, and this learning retards subsequent acquisition of CS–UCS associations (cf. Wagner, 1978).

Other studies have suggested that the UCS can also become associated with the context in which it is presented, and that this learning will also interfere with the subsequent acquisition of associations between CS and UCS if the subject has been pre-exposed to UCS-alone presentations (e.g. Randich, 1981; Randich and Lolordo, 1979). However, once a context–UCS association has been formed it can facilitate performance of existing CS–UCS learning (Grau and Rescorla, 1984; Durlach, 1983; Durlach and Grau, 1984), presumably because both context and CS contribution to response strength via their shared association with the UCS.

5 *Representation-mediated learning*

So far in this chapter we have discussed both the nature of associations and the nature of representations formed during Pavlovian conditioning. The evidence implies that external pairing of a CS and UCS will frequently result in an association between CS and UCS, such that performance of the CR results from the CS activating an internal representation of the UCS. Further evidence suggests that associative learning can also occur as a result of stimuli being paired with CS-evoked representations of the UCS; that is, CS-evoked representations of events can substitute for those events themselves in the acquisition of new associations. For instance, Holland (1981) paired an auditory CS with one food substance and a visual CS with a different food substance. The rats then received pairing of one of the CSs with gastric illness. Subsequent tests revealed that the rats had acquired an aversion to the food that was associated with the CS paired with illness. Both Holland and Forbes (1983) and Holland and Ross (1981) have noted that a CS-evoked representation of a food can also substitute for the food itself during the extinction of either a food aversion or within-compound associations. For example, if a CS is paired with a particular food flavor and then the rat is made averse to that flavor by pairing it with illness, this aversion can be alleviated simply by repeated presentations of the CS alone. The assumption here is that the CS evokes memories of the flavor which then fail to be followed by illness, and that this continued process eliminates the original learned aversion. Other representation-mediated conditioning phenomena such as overshadowing and potentiation have also been demonstrated (cf. Holland, 1983).

Apart from demonstrating the ubiquity of associative learning, procedures such as CS-evoked representation learning also give us an insight into the mind of the nonhuman animal. If learning can eventually be demonstrated between a CS-evoked stimulus representation and a CS-evoked UCS representation, then we begin to have good inferential evidence of image-based thinking processes in animals.

6 *Selective associations*

So far this discussion has proceeded as though all animals in conditioning studies possess identical associative mechanisms which do not discriminate between qualitatively different stimulus events. There are a number of reasons why one might believe this generalization to be false. First, there is the obvious fact that different species possess central nervous systems of differing complexities and of differing structures. Intuitively, we might well believe that the associative mechanisms possessed by the sea slug *Aplysia* would differ in both detail and function from the associative mechanisms possessed by a small mammal such as the rat or primates such as humans.

There are two points to be raised tangentially on this matter (but see Chapter 6 for a fuller discussion of this issue). First, different species may independently have evolved different associative mechanisms to cope with similar adaptive problems. Much of the preceding discussion on associations is based on learning by rats and pigeons, and suggests that the Pavlovian mechanism involved in first-order conditioning promotes the learning of the relation between CS and UCS. When we begin to use these inferential techniques on a wide range of species it may well become apparent that some species have evolved more reflexive and less centralized methods of associating two stimuli (for example, S–R learning). Second, an animal's ecological niche and its natural lifestyle will determine that learning about some associations is more urgent than others. For instance, learning to associate signals with aversive consequences (such as attack by predators) is paramount for the survival of most species, so one might expect that such animals have evolved the capacity to carry out this learning rapidly and efficiently. So, as we study the nature of aversive Pavlovian conditioning in more detail it is possible that we may discover that such learning proceeds through more direct associative links between the CS and the response centers mediating the defensive reaction rather than via a representation of the UCS (that is, via S–R rather than S–S learning, e.g. Moore, 1979). Even rapid backward conditioning (that is, UCS–CS pairings result in a CR to the CS) can be demonstrated in aversive conditioning procedures (cf. Spetch, Wilkie, and Pinel, 1981; see Chapter 7, p. 218), implying that animals are ready to learn rapidly about the features of an aversive UCS even when those features occur *after* experiencing the traumas of the UCS. This would seem sensible if one were to consider that many animals are likely to experience the trauma of attack by a hidden predator before they detect the stimulus features of the predator itself. If an animal escapes such an attack, it is adaptive and wise to avoid future encounters with those predator features.

A slightly different way in which an animal's ecology may determine the nature of the associations it learns is not by selecting for the evolution of specific associative mechanisms, but selecting for attention to specific features of stimulus events which — because of the processing priority given to these features — become associated with their consequences. One example of this selectivity is conditioned taste aversion learning (Garcia and Koelling, 1966; see Chapter 6, pp. 183–90). Omnivorous foragers such as rats appear to learn only to associate the taste characteristics of food with subsequent toxic illness, and they only rarely associate auditory or visual cues with this illness. Alternatively, visual feeders such as pigeons readily associate visual characteristics of food with subsequent poisoning (e.g. Capretta, 1961; Wilcoxon, Dragoin, and Kral, 1971). Although some have argued that this learning specificity may represent specialized associative mechanisms serving gastric learning (e.g. Garcia, Hawkins, and Rusiniak, 1974), much of the evidence suggests that the actual associative processes underlying conditioned taste aversion learning do not differ from those found in other Pavlovian preparations; the differences arise merely on the basis of the stimulus cue selected for associative processing (see pp. 188–90).

Another example of selective cue utilization is in the predisposition of birds to associate visual or auditory cues with either appetitive or aversive consequences. Both pigeons and chicks seem predisposed to associate the visual but not the auditory component of a visual-auditory compound CS with a food UCS, and associate the auditory but not the visual component with an aversive UCS (Shettleworth, 1972a, b; Foree and Lolordo, 1973, 1975; Lolordo, 1979). One might superficially be prepared to say that this is not surprising, since both pigeons and chicks are visual feeders and may thus be primed to attend to visual rather than auditory cues in such circumstances. Similarly, defensive reactions are quite likely to be associated in nature with auditory cues signaling, for instance, approaching predators. However, the story is not quite as simple as this, since pigeons will learn about the *visual* component of a compound audio-visual signal for shock if they are concurrently key pecking to obtain food (Foree and Lolordo, 1975). That is, if food is somewhere involved in the procedure, this is a sufficient condition for the animal to learn about the visual element of a compound CS regardless of whether the consequence of the CS is appetitive or aversive. This certainly indicates that there are unlikely to be pre-wired associative links which determine that auditory CSs become associated with aversive UCSs and visual CSs with appetitive UCSs. However, it does suggest that the actual associations formed between a CS and UCS during conditioning can be radically influenced by attentional predispositions.

Models of associative strength

Associations do not appear to be all-or-none in their nature, as can be implied from any Pavlovian acquisition curve. Figure 4.2 gives a representative example of a CR acquisition curve which is typically negatively accelerated. CR acquisition occurs rapidly over initial pairings of CS and UCS, and then tails off to an asymptotic, steady level of conditioning. There are a number of things implied by this learning curve. First, it presumably represents in some way the animal's processing of the relationship between CS and UCS, and is an indication of the extent to which CS presentation will evoke representations of the UCS during various stages of the learning process. Second, it is clear that more learning occurs during CS–UCS pairings early in training than during subsequent CS–UCS pairings given later in training, and this has traditionally been taken to imply that repeated CS–UCS pairings produce successively smaller increments in associative strength.

What is important to animal learning theorists is how this process can be formally characterized and what it tells us about the mechanisms which mediate association formation. That is, what are the important characteristics of this process that we can integrate into a formal model of the learning process which allows us to predict the rate and strength of conditioned responding in a variety of Pavlovian procedures?

1 *The Rescorla–Wagner model*

Traditionally, the negatively accelerated Pavlovian acquisition curve had been assumed to represent a kind of "saturation" process in which the associative strength of the CS became less and less as conditioning progressed (e.g. Hull, 1943). However, Wagner and Rescorla (1972) and Rescorla and Wagner (1972) characterized this process differently. They assumed that increments in learning became less and less due to the changing status of the UCS and not the CS. They suggested that "repeated CS–UCS pairings produce smaller and smaller increments, not because the associative strength of the CS is becoming less and less capable of being incremented, but because the UCS is becoming less and less effective as it is announced by a cue with increasingly greater associative strength" (Wagner and Rescorla, 1972: 303). That is, the amount of associative strength that a UCS can bestow on a preceding CS

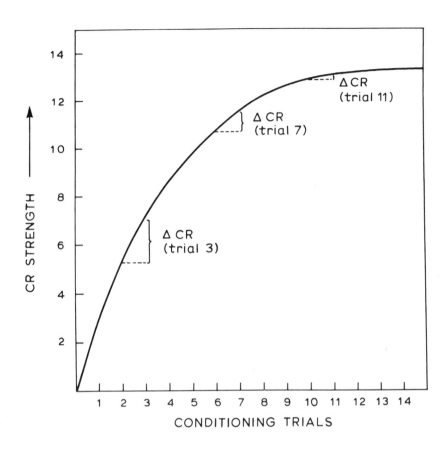

Figure 4.2 An idealized negatively accelerated Pavlovian learning curve. The amount of increment in response strength is greater on earlier trials than on later trials, as illustrated by the decreasing increments on trials 3, 7, and 11 respectively.

depends on how "surprising" it is. Or alternatively, its ability to promote conditioning is inversely related to how well it is already predicted by preceding stimuli. These ideas can be formulated more precisely in an equation of the following kind:

$$\Delta V_A = \alpha\beta \, (\lambda - V_\Sigma) \qquad (4.1)$$

where

ΔV_A = the increment in associative strength to a CS, A, on trial n.

λ = the asymptotic level of associative strength that the UCS will support.

V_{Σ} = the aggregate associative strength that has already accrued to stimuli predicting the UCS.

α and β are learning-rate parameters reflecting the saliency or intensity of the CS_A and UCS respectively.

By simply examining equation 4.1 it becomes clear that as the value of V_{Σ} approaches λ the amount of associative strength that can accrue to a CS becomes less and less. At the outset of conditioning, when the difference between λ and V_{Σ} is very large, increments in associative strength to the CS will be relatively large. Hence, this equation predicts the typical negatively accelerated Pavlovian acquisition curve.

This model not only predicts the nature of the acquisition curve, but also a number of other Pavlovian phenomena. First, if an animal is given pairings of a CS, A, with a UCS until an asymptotic level of conditioning is obtained, and following this the UCS is subsequently paired with a compound CS consisting of the original element A (such as a light) plus a new element X (for example, a tone), subsequent testing usually reveals that the added element X elicits little or no CR. This is known as *blocking* (Kamin, 1969; see also pp. 33-4). The Rescorla–Wagner model explains this by predicting that the UCS has already granted most of its available associative strength to component A; when X is added, the increments in response strength that might accrue to X (determined by $\lambda - V_{\Sigma}$) are so small as not to be detectable.

The Rescorla–Wagner model also predicts a couple of other phenomena. First, it predicts that if a CS is paired with the *absence* of the UCS it will acquire inhibitory properties. That is, ΔV_A can become negative. Presumably, the asymptotic level of associative strength supported by the absence of a UCS will be zero, therefore any increments in associative strength to the CS would be negative. Indeed, CSs that are correlated with the absence of the UCS do become inhibitory in the sense that they will reduce the strength of the CR to an already conditioned CS (cf. Miller and Spear, 1985), and they will take longer to be transferred into excitatory CSs (by subsequent pairing with a UCS) than stimuli that have not previously been paired with the absence of the UCS (e.g. Rescorla, 1969). Second, the Rescorla–Wagner model predicts that if a CS and UCS are presented randomly in relation to each other (normally a truly random control procedure, cf. Rescorla, 1967b) then during early training the CS may acquire some associative strength. This is because an accidental association between CS and UCS in early training will increment more associative strength to the CS than will an accidental association much later in training (cf. Wagner and Rescorla, 1972).

One of the questions raised by this model is how the UCS comes to lose its effectiveness as conditioning proceeds. Does the animal attend less to the UCS as it becomes more and more predicted by the CS? Or does the conditioned response itself diminish the saliency of the UCS? This latter possibility has been explored by a number of theorists when considering the possible processes that underlie the dynamics of the Rescorla–Wagner model. For instance, it is well known that a CS comes to control a variety of CRs, one of which is a physiological reaction which involves physiological changes which are *opposite* to those normally elicited by the UCS. This effect is known as the *opponent-process theory* of motivation, because one of the effects of the CS is to produce conditioned physiological changes which *compensate* for the physiological effect of the UCS (cf. Solomon and Corbit, 1974; Schull, 1979). Clearly, if as conditioning progresses the CS comes to elicit a stronger and stronger compensatory CR, this will diminish the effective physiological strength of the UCS. Such a process may well underlie many of the circumstances where the effectiveness of the UCS diminishes with conditioning (cf. Wagner, 1981; Wagner and Larew, 1985).

Nevertheless, despite its utility in generating valuable research during the ten years or so following 1972, the Rescorla–Wagner model cannot accommodate a number of important facts about Pavlovian conditioning. More recently, this has led theorists to suggest that changes in the effectiveness of the CS may be equally important as, if not more important than, changes in the effectiveness of the UCS during conditioning.

2 The Pearce–Hall model

Two particular experimental results provided difficulties for the Rescorla–Wagner model. First, Dickinson, Hall, and Mackintosh (1976) found that blocking could be alleviated if the nature of the UCS was changed in some way when compound conditioning was introduced. That is, the added component (X) did acquire associative strength when the UCS was changed. The Rescorla–Wagner model predicts that "unblocking" such as that found in the Dickinson *et al.* study should only occur when λ is increased or V_Σ is reduced on the compound trials. If all of the associative strength has been granted to component A, changing the UCS (by *reducing* its intensity in the Dickinson *et al.* case) should not affect blocking. Second, using a blocking paradigm, Mackintosh (1975b) found that if only *one* compound trial was given and conditioning was then stopped, some associative strength did accrue to the added element X. Furthermore, the amount of conditioning that accrued to X on this one trial was equal to the amount that would accrue to that element on a compound trial that had *not* been preceded by pretraining with element A alone. That is, normal conditioning proceeds on the first compound trial of a blocking procedure but then ceases on subsequent trials. This, again, is not predicted by the Rescorla–Wagner model.

Mackintosh (1975a) interpreted these findings to suggest that it was not changes in the effectiveness of the UCS which determined the incrementation of response strength on each trial — it was changes in the associability of the CS. Specifically, he suggested that the associability of a stimulus (denoted as α in equation 4.1) will increase or decrease as a direct function of how accurately that stimulus predicts the UCS. Thus, unblocking results in the experiment of Dickinson *et al.* (1976) because the new, added element X is a better predictor of the change in the nature of the UCS than is the original element A. This predictiveness increases the associability of element X (see also Mackintosh, Bygrave, and Picton, 1977; Dickinson and Mackintosh, 1979).

Nevertheless, useful though Mackintosh's account is in explaining excitatory conditioning, Pearce and Hall (1980) point out its limitations when applied to some other conditioning phenomena such as latent inhibition. They proposed quite the opposite to Mackintosh, in effect that 'a stimulus (CS) is likely to be processed to the extent that it is *not* an accurate predictor of its consequences' (Pearce and Hall, 1980: 538, my italics). Thus, the negatively accelerated acquisition curve in Pavlovian conditioning is, according to this model, a result of the fact that the CS gradually loses associability as it becomes a better predictor of the UCS. This model accounts for most of the facts assimilated by the Mackintosh model *plus* those few instances where conditioning is *retarded* by pretraining which has already granted some associative strength to the CS (e.g. Hall and Pearce, 1979).

Pearce and Hall (1980) also attempt to account for inhibitory conditioning effects not by suggesting that V_Σ becomes negative as the Rescorla–Wagner model predicts, but because a CS can independently become associated with a representation of reinforcer absence or omission ($\overline{\text{UCS}}$). This learning proceeds in much the same way as excitatory learning is dealt with in this model, except that a $\overline{\text{UCS}}$ representation is activated when an *expected* UCS is omitted. This helps to explain many of the phenomena associated with extinction and conditioned inhibition.

3 *Summary*

Formalized models of associative learning such as those proposed by Rescorla and Wagner (1972), Mackintosh (1975a), and Pearce and Hall (1980) tell us something not just about the associative mechanisms of animals but also about their information-processing capacities. Learning to associate two stimuli together is an information-processing task that requires the involvement of mechanisms of attention and memory, as well as association. It is still not entirely clear whether models of associative acquisition must exclusively take into account variations in processing of either the UCS or the CS, or variations in the processing of both of these events (e.g. Wagner, 1981), but such formalized models provide a useful guide to research relevant to an understanding of associative capacities in animals.

Working memory

Learning, by implication, involves processes of memory: learning cannot occur without some kind of memory of past events being retained. Thus, memory processes must be involved in some way during conditioning, and in recent years conditioning theorists have come to recognize that characteristics of associative learning might well be understood better by also considering the memory processes which underlie them (e.g. Wagner 1981; Terry and Wagner, 1975). The memory processes involved in learning about simple conditioning episodes are known as *working memory*. Working memory is basically synonymous with the traditional notion of short-term memory (STM) and is characterized by the retention of information only sufficiently long enough to complete a given task. So, for instance, working memory will operate where "different stimuli govern the criterion response on different trials, so that the cue that the animal must remember varies from trial to trial" (Honig, 1978: 213). It is also assumed to operate in simple Pavlovian conditioning procedures where an association between the CS and UCS must involve the rehearsal of these two stimuli in some short-term, limited-capacity processor (Wagner, 1981; Grant, 1984).

Apart from recent studies of working memory in Pavlovian conditioning, it has traditionally been studied in a simple procedure known as delayed matching-to-sample (DMTS). In the DMTS procedure the animal is first shown a sample stimulus, which is then followed by a delay interval, after which the animal is presented with a set of choice stimuli. A response to the choice stimulus which matches the original sample stimulus is a correct response and will be reinforced (see Figure 4.3). This kind of procedure is

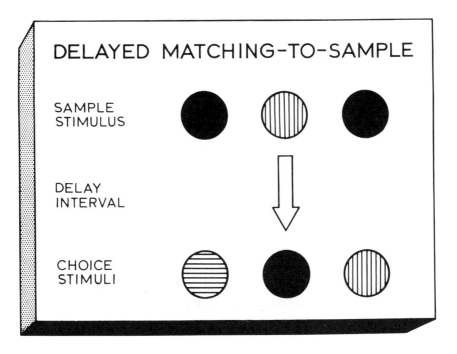

Figure 4.3 The delayed-matching-to-sample procedure for pigeons. At the beginning of a trial the center key is illuminated with the sample stimulus. After a while this is removed and all keys are blank during the delay interval. At the end of the delay interval the choice stimuli are projected onto the two side keys. Pecking at the choice stimulus which matched the original sample stimulus is reinforced.

useful for studying the features of working memory because the experimenter can manipulate a wide variety of variables ranging from sample size, delay interval, choice size, and delay-interval interference (cf. Roberts and Grant, 1976; D'Amato, 1973; Grant, 1981b, 1984; Maki, 1984). DMTS has been used successfully to study working memory in a wide variety of species, including pigeons (Grant and Roberts, 1973; Shimp and Moffitt, 1974; Grant, 1984; Roberts and Grant, 1976), rats (Roberts, 1972, 1974; Wallace Steinert, Scobie, and Spear, 1980), monkeys (D'Amato, 1973; Jarvik, Goldfarb, and Carley, 1969; Moise, 1970; Jarrard and Moise, 1970), dolphins (Herman, 1975; Herman and Thompson, 1982), and goldfish (Steinert, Fallon, and

Wallace, 1976). Basic parametric studies of DMTS in the pigeon (the most widely adopted species for this procedure) suggest that accuracy is an inverse function of delay interval duration and a direct function of the duration of the sample stimulus. When the sample stimulus is presented for 4, 8, or 14 sec, pigeons perform at a better than chance level with a delay interval of up to 60 sec (Grant, 1976). DMTS recall in capuchin monkeys, however, can be highly efficient, with delay intervals up to two minutes (D'Amato and O'Neill, 1971). Nevertheless, this kind of procedure is not particularly appropriate for making comparative judgments about the memorial abilities of different species, since how a particular species performs on a memory task appears to depend on what kinds of problems that species has to solve in its natural habitat. Thus, what is considered to be an arbitrary memory task for one species may not be so for another, and experimenters need to take into account ecological considerations before designing their learning procedures (cf. Kamil and Yoerg, 1982; Legg, 1983). What DMTS does provide, however, is a procedure for studying the features of working memory itself rather than the memorial capacities of different species.

So, given that a wide range of animals can perform relatively accurately on the delayed learning procedure provided by DMTS, what have we learned about the characteristics of working memory?

1 *Trace decay*

Figure 4.4 shows the declining performance of pigeons on a DMTS task as the delay interval is successively increased. The function in Figure 4.4 is clearly consistent with a simple trace decay hypothesis of working memory: initial processing of the sample stimulus activitates a simple memory trace which gradually decays with time. Further assumptions would also be consistent with trace decay: increased sample duration would simply allow a stronger trace to be laid down before decay began (see Figure 4.4); and memory is better when the delay interval is spent in darkness rather than in an illuminated chamber (e.g. Maki, 1979a; Grant and Roberts, 1973; Maki, Moe, and Bierley, 1977; Roberts and Grant, 1978; D'Amato and O'Neill, 1971), suggesting that darkness would be less likely to disrupt any decaying trace — especially if the trace were a kind of visual after-image.

However, not all of the facts fit a simple trace decay model of working memory, and many lines of inquiry suggest that it is a much more active process than trace decay would suggest. First, performance on a DMTS task improves over time or experience on the task: a simple trace decay model would presuppose that since each trial is a new learning task, the memory

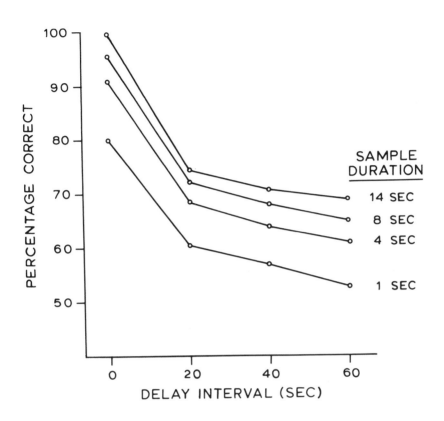

Figure 4.4 Performance of pigeons on a delayed-matching-to-sample task as a function of sample duration and delay interval. (After Grant, 1976)

trace formed on each trial should be roughly of the same strength (e.g. D'Amato, 1973; Zentall, Hogan, and Edwards, 1984; Grant, 1976). Even when a *different* sample stimulus is used on each trial (a trials-unique procedure), subjects still improve their performance over trials (Overman, McLain, Ormsby, and Brooks, 1983). Second, some kinds of events are remembered much more accurately than others. In particular, if a sample stimulus is made "surprising" in some way, it is much more likely to be remembered than one that was not "surprising" (Maki, 1979b; see also Terry and Wagner, 1975). Finally, while correct performance on DMTS is an inverse function of delay interval, this performance can be disrupted by presentation of "pre-choice" stimulus which proactively interferes with recall of the sample. However, there is no interaction between delay interval duration and the frequency of interfering "pre-choice" stimulus as might be expected if the "pre-choice" interference stimulus was interfering in a pragmatic way with a simple memory trace (cf. Roitblat, 1984).

2 *Maintenance rehearsal*

Instead of depending on a decaying memory trace for working memory, a number of writers have suggested that animals *rehearse* the sample stimulus during the retention interval (Grant, 1981a, 1984; Maki, 1981). This type of account has two particular features. (1) this rehearsal is for the temporary maintenance of information only (that is, only within trial), and (2) the animal becomes more efficient at executing this rehearsal procedure during the learning of the DMTS task. To the extent that the animal has to learn the rehearsal capability, it is thus an active process which is under the control of the organism.

There are a number of facts which are consistent with this notion. First, as we have already noted, DMTS performance improves with training (D'Amato, 1973; Zentall, Hogan, and Edwards, 1984; Grant, 1976). This is consistent with the animal acquiring the necessary rehearsal skills over trials. Second, the rehearsal process does appear to be under the control of the organism to the extent that it can be "switched on" or "switched off" by appropriate cues. Pigeons, for instance, can be taught not to rehearse in what are known as *directed forgetting* procedures. In such a procedure, either "remember" or "forget" cues are presented during the delay interval. On "remember"-cued trials the animal is subsequently given the choice test at the end of the delay interval. On "forget"-cued trials the delay interval terminates without the choice test. After sufficient training on this procedure, memory for the sample on "forget"-cued trials can be tested by unexpectedly presenting the choice stimulus on selected probe trials. Typically, performance on these probe trials is not significantly above the chance level, suggesting that the "forget"-cue did indeed terminate a rehearsal process (e.g. Grant, 1981b; Kendrick, Rilling and Stonebraker, 1981; Maki and Hegvik, 1980; Maki, Olsen, and Rego, 1981; Stonebraker and Rilling, 1981).

3 *Associative rehearsal*

Wagner (1981) has also proposed a rehearsal model of working memory which is specifically designed to explain the formation of associations during Pavlovian conditioning. Wagner suggests that (1) a UCS will provoke rehearsal of its representation in working memory to the extent that it is surprising, and (2) post-trial rehearsal is necessary for an association between CS and UCS to occur. Like the Rescorla–Wagner and Pearce–Hall models of associative strength discussed earlier (see pp. 127–32), Wagner's account also explains the negatively accelerated Pavlovian acquisition curve (see Figure 4.2). As conditioning progresses and the UCS becomes more and more reliably predicted by the CS, then the UCS is less and less "surprising" and hence is not rehearsed in working memory. Thus, the increments in associative learning get smaller and smaller as training progresses, simply because the UCS is not being rehearsed in association with the preceding CS.

However, this account rests crucially on the assumption that stimuli which are "surprising" or which are made "surprising" by various experimental manipulations will be rehearsed more readily and so remembered better. What evidence is available suggests that surprising events are more memorable than expected events in both DMTS tasks (e.g. Grant, Brewster, and Stierhoff, 1983) and Pavlovian conditioning tasks (e.g. Terry and Wagner, 1975).

4 Conclusion

This brief discussion of working memory does suggest that active rehearsal takes place in working memory when the animal is processing the important events in a learning task. This is a process that the animal can initiate or terminate when cued to do so, but certain features of the events to be remembered (such as their surprisingness) also determine the extent to which they will gain access to the limited capacity processors necessary for rehearsal.

Chapter summary

1 Because the processes and mechanisms that underlie conditioning and learning cannot be directly observed, they must be inferred from the results of experimental manipulations.

2 Learning is not always manifest in changes in behavior. The process of *sensory preconditioning* shows that an animal can learn an association between two events without this being immediately manifest in behavior.

3 Using a number of inferential techniques (such as *postconditioning revaluation* techniques), studies have shown that the majority of first-order Pavlovian conditioning is mediated by associations learned between the CS and UCS (S–S learning).

4 In higher-order Pavlovian conditioning there is some evidence that animals learn S–R rather than S–S associations. The reasons for this are not clear, although it may be more to do with the saliency of the different events in higher-order conditioning.

5 Animals can also form within-event associations, such as between the elements of a compound stimulus. This type of within-event learning helps to explain the phenomena of *potentiation* and "*unblocking.*"

6 Animals also learn associations between the important stimuli in the learning situation (such as the CS and UCS) with the context in which that learning occurs. This helps to explain phenomena such as *latent inhibition.*

7 Associative learning can also occur as a result of stimuli being paired with CS-evoked representations of the UCS — i.e., CS-evoked representations of the UCS can substitute for those events themselves in the acquisition of new associations.

8 Animals frequently exhibit a predisposition to associate certain features of stimuli with accompanying reinforcers. This is known as *selective associations*, and it appears to reflect the fact that animals need to learn some things more urgently than others, and as a consequence they have evolved methods of insuring that this selective learning occurs efficiently and rapidly.

9 The aquisition of associations does not appear to be all-or-none in its nature, and models can be constructed which attempt to describe the rate at which the strength of an association develops.

10 The first of these types of models was the *Rescorla–Wagner* model, which assumed that increments in associative strength between CS and UCS become less and less due to the less "surprising" status of the UCS as conditioning proceeds. This gives rise to the characteristic negatively accelerated Pavlovian conditioning curve.

11 By formulating these ideas into an equation, Rescorla and Wagner were able to explain such phenomena as blocking, inhibitory conditioning, and the acquisition of a weak CR even when CS and UCS are presented randomly.

12 A more recent model of associative strength is the *Pearce–Hall* model. This model claims that the decreasing increment in associative strength with conditioning trials is a result in the changing status of the CS and not the UCS. This model appears able to account for slightly more conditioning phenomena than the Rescorla–Wagner model.

13 Learning cannot occur without invoking processes of memory, and conditioning theorists have come to believe that conditioning processes might be better understood by considering the memory processes that underlie them.

14 *Working memory* is the term given to the memory processes involved in

learning about simple conditioning episodes. This is synonymous with the traditional notion of short-term memory, and is characterized by the retention of information only sufficiently long enough to complete a given task.

15 Delayed matching-to-sample (DMTS) is a traditional method of studying working memory in animals, and has been used successfully to study working memory in a wide variety of species.

16 Most animals show a declining performance on a DMTS task as the retention interval is increased. This function has been explained by a number of theories, which include *trace decay, maintenance rehearsal,* and *associative rehearsal.*

Chapter five

Performance models of Pavlovian conditioning

One of the more neglected aspects of conditioned responding concerns its structure and its function, and this can be divided into two more or less specific questions. The first question asks about the origins of the behavior which is established as a result of conditioning: that is, what are the rules by which learning is transformed into the behavior we observe in the conditioning situation? The second question concerns the *biological function* of conditioning. Given that conditioning is so pervasive as a learning phenomenon, what is its function from a biological point of view and what advantages does it bestow on an animal? We will deal with the latter of these two questions in the next chapter, but for the moment let us consider the questions surrounding the origins of conditioned behavior.

We can now say with some certainty that Pavlov's prototypical salivating dog probably learned an association between the CS and the UCS (see Chapter 4). This, from the point of view of the cognitive animal psychologist, is what was learned in the situation. However, just because we might know the nature of the associations learned by Pavlov's dog, this still does not tell us why his dog salivated. We might tritely say that the dog salivated because it "anticipated" the forthcoming food, but that neither constitutes a theoretical explanation nor helps us to predict what other organisms are going to do in other Pavlovian situations.

Consider a more insightful example. An experiment quoted by Hearst and Jenkins (1974) describes an autoshaping study on pigeons carried out in a "long box." That is, the CS — a periodically illuminated pecking key — was situated some distance from the site of food delivery. Even so, when key illumination reliably preceded food delivery, the pigeon would consistently traverse the long alley and peck the key even though this behavior was independent of the delivery of food and frequency resulted in the subject missing the subsequent limited access to food. The procedure is Pavlovian, and we have established with some certainty that in autoshaping studies subjects learn CS–UCS associations (cf. Hearst and Jenkins, 1974; Locurto, 1981; Wasserman, 1981). Yet the CR "in anticipation" of the UCS is to move away from the UCS site and peck a relatively distal CS. How is the learning of the CS–UCS association in this case translated into behavior which might well be termed maladaptive for this particular situation?

These questions relate specifically to performance models of conditioning and attempt to inquire about the processes and structures which translate the learned associations into observable CRs. Sadly, until a few years ago, little effort had been expended on attempts to construct truly general performance models of conditioning, with perhaps only Pavlov (1927) and Konorski (1967) providing integrated associative-performance models that bear any resemblance to a unified account of Pavlovian conditioning. Performance accounts of instrumental conditioning are also, as we shall see later, still very much in their infancy stages.

Another couple of factors have to be considered when discussing performance models. First, the nature of these models has understandably changed as we have come to discover the diversity of Pavlovian CRs. At one time a legitimate CR had to be a response selected from among those effector systems elicited as UCRs by the UCS (Konorski, 1967; Gormezano and Kehoe, 1976: 149). Now the category has expanded to include behaviors which are considered to reflect conditioning of motivational states (Mowrer, 1960; Rescorla and Solomon, 1967), behaviors which represent preparation to receive the UCS (Konorski, 1967; Zener, 1937), and behaviors which are directed toward or away from the CS (Brown and Jenkins, 1968; Hearst and Jenkins, 1974; Hearst, 1979; Schwartz and Gamzu, 1977; Wasserman, 1981; Williams, 1981). Indeed, a CR need in no way mimic the UCR, and may often represent a response in the opposite direction to that of the UCR. An example of the latter is the conditioning of heart-rate changes using aversive UCSs. The UCR in such conditions is usually an *increase* in heart-rate, but the CR is frequently a *decrease* in heart rate (bradycardia) (de Toledo and Black, 1966; Parrish, 1967; Yehle, Dauth, and Schneiderman, 1967). Finally, specific CRs may be conditioned in situations where the UCS elicits little or no UCR, such as with intracranial stimulation as the UCS (Peterson, 1975; Wilkie and McDonald, 1978) or with thermal reinforcement (Wasserman, 1973; Wasserman, Hunter, Gutowski, and Bader, 1975; Davey, Phillips, and Witty, 1989). These kinds of examples have very specific consequences for very many traditional and simplistic performance models, as we shall see later.

The second consideration to bear in mind when discussing performance models is that we can no longer ignore the biological function of conditioned responding when analyzing performance factors. Presumably, when we have a fuller description of the performance mechanisms which generate conditioned responsing, this description will shed light on the function and evolutionary benefit of this kind of learning — both generally, in terms of the reasons why learning evolved, and more specifically, in terms of how conditioned behavior benefits individual organisms in specific situations. However, this relationship between performance models and biological function works both ways. Attempting to consider how conditioned responding in a particular situation might help an organism — either from the point of view of its own survival or in terms of its inclusive fitness — should help to shed light on the origins of conditioned responding and the structures that mediate it.

These, then, are the general factors that the reader should take into consideration during the following sections. These sections attempt to review the various performance models of Pavlovian conditioning.

An analysis of performance models in Pavlovian conditioning

1 *Instrumental reinforcement*

One historically popular way of attempting to account for the nature of the CR in Pavlovian conditioning has been to try to subsume it under the auspices of instrumental conditioning. This has variously been called "preparatory responding" (Perkins, 1968), "response shaping" (Gormezano, 1972) or "pseudo-contingent reinforcement" (Davey, 1981), and appeared to have the advantage of accounting for the many examples where the CR was dissimilar to the UCR (cf. Holland, 1984a). There are two variations on this type of explanation. First, because behavior occurring during the CS is emitted in close temporal proximity to the delivery of the UCS, this behavior could be instrumentally "adventitiously" reinforced if the UCS is appetitive. There are a number of serious problems with this kind of account that we can list very briefly: (1) it would apply only to appetitive conditioning, and some other kind of process would have to be postulated to account for the appearance of the CR during aversive Pavlovian conditioning; (2) adventitious reinforcement is not a particularly robust phenomenon (cf. Staddon and Simmelhag, 1971) and is thus unlikely to account for the strength and persistence of Pavlovian CRs; and (3) adventitious reinforcement accounts would suggest that CRs should transfer with little modification in their form across different appetitive UCSs. However, this kind of transfer is very difficult to establish (Brogden, 1939c; Konorski and Szwejkowska, 1956).

The second variation on the instrumental reinforcement account is one originally labeled "parasitic reinforcement" by Konorski (1967) which suggests that the CR has a direct modifying effect on the UCS, making receipt of the UCS more effective in the case of appetitive UCSs and reducing the intensity of aversive UCSs. Although it might seem intuitively sensible to suggest that a leg flexion CR in dogs might reduce the perceived severity of the electric shock UCS, or that an eyeblink CR might protect the cornea from an air-puff or a mild para-orbital electric shock, there is much evidence to suggest that this process cannot account for many aspects of the Pavlovian CR. Nevertheless, having said this, it is quite clear that many Pavlovian CRs can be *influenced* in some way by the nature of their consequences and this has been demonstrated particularly with the use of *omission procedures*. An omission contingency is one whereby the subjects are presented with the UCS only if they *refrain* from emitting the CR in appetitive conditioning, or alternatively, they avoid an aversive UCS only if they *refrain* from emitting the CR in aversive conditioning. Using this procedure, many CRs established through the Pavlovian procedure have been shown to be sensitive to their consequences. These include conditioned running in guinea pigs (Brogden, Lipman, and Culler, 1938), conditioned leg flexion in dogs and rats (Schlosberg, 1936; Wahlsten and Cole, 1972), conditioned key pecking in pigeons (Barrera, 1974; Schwartz and Williams, 1972a; Lucas, 1975), and conditioned lever contact in rats (Atnip, 1977; Davey, Oakley, and Cleland, 1981). Nevertheless, despite this consistency with a "parasitic" or "pseudo-contingent" instrumental account, there is an equivalent body of evidence which suggests that certain other Pavlovian CRs *cannot* be influenced by omission contingencies. These CRs include conditioned salivation in the dog (Sheffield, 1965), conditioned licking of water tubes by rats (Patten and Rudy, 1967), conditioned jaw movement in rabbits (Gormezano and Hiller, 1972), and conditioned eyeblink in both humans (Logan, 1951) and rabbits (Gormezano and Coleman, 1973). In all of the above cases, subjects found it difficult, if not impossible, to refrain from emitting the CR even though this had detrimental consequences on UCS receipt.

Finally, two other studies suggest that the role of adventitious instrumental reinforcement in determining the nature and strength of the CR may only be a secondary one. First, Soltysik and Jaworska (1962) presented electric shock to the forepaws of dogs (UCS) preceded by a buzzer CS, and during the course of conditioning introduced a number of test trials on which the UCS was deliberately omitted. They argued that if the paw-flexion CR was a product of it being instrumentally reinforced because it helped to reduce the intensity of the shock UCS, then CR strength on trials immediately following test trials (where the UCS was omitted) should be *stronger* than on the test trial itself. The assumption here is that if the CR was established because it reduced the intensity of shock, then actually omitting the shock altogether should result in even greater instrumental reinforcement of the CR. However, what they found is that CR strength was actually *weaker* on trials following UCS-omission test trials. This is quite contrary to a "parasitic reinforcement" interpretation and is consistent with the alternative suggestion that CR strength is a function of the contingency between CS and UCS.

Second, Holland (1977) also reports data which do not fit comfortably into an instrumental account of Pavlovian conditioning. He found that rats emitted differential CRs to the individual auditory and visual elements of a compound CS which had previously been paired with a food UCS, and that these differential CR patterns were similar to those emitted by subjects which had received separate conditioning with just the auditory and visual components. Because both sets of CRs occurred during compound conditioning, an adventitious account would predict that both types of CRs should occur during either the auditory or visual elements alone (cf. Holland, 1984a: 140). Although this result does not mesh comfortably with an instrumental account of Pavlovian CRs, it does have other more important implications, as we shall see later.

The conclusions from this brief summary seem fairly clear. In very many cases, the form of the CR *can* be modified in some way by its consequences: of this there is no doubt. But instrumental reinforcement is inadequate in accounting for the acquisition, the form, and the persistence of most Pavlovian CRs. For more fundamental determinants of the nature of the Pavlovian CR we must look elsewhere.

2 *Reflex transfer and stimulus substitution*

The most traditional approach to performance phenomena in Pavlovian conditioning can be traced back to the physiologists of the late nineteenth century and subsequently to Pavlov himself. This approach assumes that continued pairing of a CS and a UCS leads to a cortical link between the CS and the reflex arc subserving the UCS: thus, in effect, the reflex or UCR normally elicited by the UCS is transferred to the CS. This has been characterized as simple "reflex transfer" (Holland, 1984a), or as a kind of "false start" of the reflex system adapted to cope with receipt of the UCS (Hollis, 1982). As we will argue later in this chapter, to characterize the CR as a "false start" makes no sense from an adaptive evolutionary viewpoint; one might consider it to be an "anticipatory" reaction resulting in more efficient handling of the UCS — but even then one has to consider how this anticipation bestows an advantage on the animal (Hollis, 1982, 1984a; Shettleworth, 1984).

The operation of reflex transfer is more obvious in organisms which are neurologically relatively uncomplicated (cf. Carew, Walters, and Kandel, 1981; Hawkins and Kandel, 1984; Quinn, 1984), and as a consequence relatively behaviorally unsophisticated. Furthermore, if we suppose that a conditioning situation results in the learning of S–R associations (as some preparations appear to — see Chapter 4), then reflex transfer is often a logical consequence of this learning. However, reflex transfer is by no means an adequate account of the majority of Pavlovian conditioning. In the first place, the evidence available mitigates against reflex transfer: CRs frequently include behaviors which are not part of the UCR complex. Furthermore, even a CR as prototypical and traditional as the salivary CR in dogs differs from the UCR in its enzymatic content and pH (Bykov, 1959). Second, from an adaptive viewpoint, it would seem that in order to benefit from learning about the CS–UCS relationship the animal would often need to do something other than merely replicate the UCR during the CS. For example, while for many species the defensive reaction to an actual predator (UCS) would be to flee (UCR), a more adaptive reaction to the signals (CSs) of an approaching predator (for example, auditory, visual, or olfactory cues) might be to freeze and to remain immobile in the hope of avoiding detection.

Before examining all the evidence on this point let us just outline a variation on reflex transfer which has been known as *stimulus substitution theory*. This account claims that the CS not only comes to elicit those behaviors normally elicited by the UCS, but that the CS comes to act as a "substitute" or "surrogate" for the UCS such that behaviors normally elicited by the UCS are directed at and supported by the CS (Pavlov, 1927; cf. Dickinson and Mackintosh, 1978; Hearst, 1979). Thus, behaviors normally functioning to consume an appetitive UCS become centered upon and directed toward the CS (given that the CS is localizable and has the physical characteristics capable of supporting these behaviors). There is much evidence which is consistent with this explanation. For example pigeons will direct eating and drinking responses toward a lighted pecking key CS depending on whether it is paired with food or water (Jenkins and Moore, 1973); rats will bite retractable lever CSs paired with solid food, but sniff and lick the same CS when it is paired with a liquid food such as sucrose (Davey and Cleland, 1982; Davey, Phillips, and Cleland, 1981); various species of fish will direct species-specific food-procuring and eating behaviors at CSs paired with food UCSs (Brandon and Bitterman, 1979; Waxman and McCleave,

1978; Squier, 1969); dogs have been observed licking CSs paired with food (Pavlov, 1934; Jenkins, Barrera, Ireland, and Woodside, 1978); and male quail and pigeons have exhibited species-specific courting behaviors to localizable CSs paired with access to a female conspecific (Farris, 1967; Rackham, 1971). All of these results support a stimulus substitution account, and, in and of themselves, ask questions about a simple "reflex transfer" account of the Pavlovian CR — a simple reflex transfer model does not explain why the CR should be directed toward or centered upon the CS, stimulus substitution does try to answer this question.

However, it might be argued that the evidence given above in support of stimulus substitution could merely reflect the conditioning of species-specific UCS-related behaviors characteristic of an individual motivational system such as feeding, and need not represent transfer of consummatory behavior from one stimulus to another. This is not necessarily the case, since Davey and Cleland (1982) found that different CS-directed behaviors were observed in hungry rats depending on whether the food UCS was either solid or liquid. This suggests that at least some components of the CR are determined by the nature of the specific UCS rather than by more general factors such as the nature of the motivational system involved. In this instance, the CRs resembled the behavior required to consume the different UCSs (biting and licking, respectively) even though in both cases the motivational system involved was feeding.

Now, although the evidence presented above looks fairly compelling, there is still a substantial amount of evidence which is inconsistent with stimulus substitution theory.

First, animals have been found to approach and contact appetitive CSs even when such behavior is absent to the UCS. Woodruff and Williams (1976) obtained "drink-like" pecking of a key-light CS even when the water UCS was injected directly into the mandibles; Wasserman (1973) and Wasserman, Hunter, Gutowski, and Bader (1975) found that chicks would peck a lighted key CS predicting a thermal UCS in a cool environment even though the UCR was quite different — in this case, wing flapping and "tweeting." In a similar thermal conditioning study using rats, Davey, Phillips, and Witty (1989) found that rats would contact and investigate a "furry" CS when the UCR to the heat UCS was a "basking"-type rearing response. Jenkins, Barrera, Ireland, and Woodside (1978) observed CS-directed species-specific hunting and food-soliciting behaviors in dogs — behaviors which were never directed toward the food UCS itself. Timberlake and Grant (1975) found that when rats were presented with pairings of a conspecific rat CS and food, subject rats directed social feeding behaviors to the conspecific CS rather than

Figure 5.1 The use of a conspecific CS in an appetitive autoshaping procedure using rats. The restrained conspecific CS is inserted into the chamber immediately prior to food deliveries. Instead of directing consummatory-type feeding behaviors toward the conspecific CS, the subject rat indulges in social behaviors such as mouth sniffing and anogenital sniffing. (Photograph courtesy of W. Timberlake)

the food consummatory behaviors predicted by stimulus substitution theory (see Figure 5.1). Finally, UCSs such as intracranial stimulation (ICS), which produce no obvious external UCRs, conditions CS-directed investigatory responses in rats when a retractable lever is used as the CS (Wilkie and McDonald, 1978; Peterson, 1975).

Other facts which are clearly in contrast with stimulus substitution and reflex transfer accounts are those where the response to the CS is in the opposite direction to that to the UCS. The best-documented example of this is in aversive conditioning where the CR in rodents to a CS predicting shock is freezing with accompanying heart-rate deceleration (bradycardia), while the UCR is fleeing or prancing and squealing with associated heart-rate acceleration (tachycardia) (Blanchard and Blanchard, 1969a; de Toledo and Black, 1966; de Toledo, 1968). Other examples include conditioned compensatory responses when drugs or toxins are used as the UCSs (cf. Siegel, 1979), an example being hypothermia and hyperalgesia as the CRs to a CS predicting morphine injection in rats, where the UCR to morphine is hyperthermia and hyperalgesia (Siegel, 1977).

One final line of evidence which does not comfortably comply with predictions from stimulus substitution accounts is that the nature of the CR frequently appears to be determined — at least in part — by the nature of the CS. Clearly, one way in which the nature of the CS might interfere with the process of stimulus substitution was if it did not possess the physical characteristics required to support the appropriate consummatory responses, but the evidence suggests that the nature of the CS plays a more direct role in determining the nature of the CR. This can be illustrated at this point with just one example. Holland (1977) found that diffuse auditory and visual CSs paired with food UCSs for rats produced quite different CRs: the auditory CSs resulted in startle behavior (a rapid movement or jump resulting in a change in position) and head jerk (short, rapid, horizontal or vertical movements of the head); the visual CSs resulted in rearing behavior (standing on hind legs) and food-magazine-directed behavior (standing motionless with head in the food magazine). In a subsequent study, Holland (1979a) compared the CRs to auditory and visual CSs when they were paired with quite different UCSs: food or electric shock. Here, Holland found that the behavior in the latter part of the CS–UCS interval was determined by the nature of the reinforcer (food or electric shock), but the behavior in the early part of the CS–UCS interval was determined by the nature of the CS (auditory or visual), regardless of whether it was followed by food or shock. Such evidence suggests that certain components of the CR are generated independently of the nature of the UCS, and in all probability are determined by the nature of the CS — we shall come back to this point in more detail later in this chapter. Suffice it to say here that Holland's results are not predicted even by a "liberal" interpretation of stimulus substitution theory.

Finally, before stimulus substitution theory is laid to rest prematurely, it may be that this model cannot account for all aspects of the CR, but it may well, in a modified form, account for certain components of the CR. The nature of the UCS clearly does determine certain aspects of the CR (cf. Davey and Cleland, 1982; Davey, Phillips and Cleland, 1981); what needs to be specified in more detail is how this is mediated, and what features of the conditioning situation enhance or diminish it.

3 *The nature of the CS*

This discussion is clearly coming round to a position where it might be seen that the apparent diversity in the form of Pavlovian CRs could better be understood by a closer consideration of the role of the CS during conditioning. The CS and the associated CS–UCS interval do have important influences on the strength and nature of the CR. We have already mentioned the studies of Holland (1977, 1979a) (see p. 148) which indicate that the nature of an appetitive CR in rats is determined by whether the CS is a diffuse auditory or visual stimulus. In other studies, the form of the CR varies with the intensity of the CS (Gray, 1965), and with the length of the CS–UCS interval in both nonhuman subjects and human subjects (cf. Dawson and Schell, 1987). Localizable CSs frequently invoke CS-approach responses (Hearst and Jenkins, 1974; Jenkins, Barrera, Ireland, and Woodside, 1978; Grastyan and Vereczkei, 1974), whereas difuse or nonlocalizable CSs do not (e.g. Holland, 1980b; Bilbrey and Winokur, 1973).

There are various ways in which the nature of the CS might exert these differential effects on CR form. It is pertinent to discuss two of them here.

CSs and UCSs as multifeatured events

Both Estes (1969) and Holland (1984a) have suggested that variation in CR form with the nature of the CS may result from the possibility that only certain features of the UCS or UCR become associated with individual features of the CS. In this case, the nature of the CS might determine which features of the CS are attended to and similarly might determine which features of the UCS are attended to, resulting in individual features of the CS being selectively associated with individual features of the UCS. For instance, "swallowing might not be transferred to a CS signaling food in salivary conditioning because that component of the complex of behaviors evoked by food delivery occurs too distant temporally from the CS" (Holland, 1984a: 141–2).

This type of explanation could clearly account for results which show that the nature of the CR depends on the length of the CS–UCS interval, since the different temporal features of the CS may come into contiguous relationship with only certain UCS features. However, the main reason for doubting this account as an important influence on CR form is that CSs which control quite different CRs can be shown to be associated with similar features of the UCS. For instance, Holland (1977) found that conditioning rats to associate a diffuse auditory CS with food subsequently resulted in that CS blocking conditioning to a diffuse light CS when the auditory and light CSs were reinforced in compound. Pretraining with the diffuse auditory CS blocked the acquisition of "rear" and "magazine-directed" responses during the light CS — even though the auditory CS had never controlled these behaviors during pretraining.

Similar and related results have been obtained in other studies (Blanchard and Honig, 1976; Tomie, 1981; Nairne and Rescorla, 1981). What this implies is that CSs can be associated with similar features of a UCS, yet evoke quite different CRs. A further implication is that while a CS may reliably be associated with a particular UCS, how that learning is to be translated into performance will depend to a large extent on the nature of the CS.

The ecological relevance of the CS

One of the more interesting facts from a study of the effects of CS-type on CR form is that a particular type of CS does not have a uniform effect across species.

Consider the example of the use of a localizable auditory stimulus as a CS for food. In the rat, such a CS results in CRs which are primarily directed at the food magazine (Harrison, 1979; Cleland and Davey, 1983), or at best reflect a discrete head-turning orienting response in the direction of the CS. However, when such a CS is used with cats, the CR is primarily CS-directed. Grastyan and Vereczkei (1974) found very strong signal-directed behavior to a localizable appetitive auditory CS in cats. Even when the CS was spatially discontiguous with the food site, a hungry cat would still approach the CS even when this resulted in the loss of food. Similarly, although many experimenters have found that pairing an illuminated pecking key with food for pigeons readily results in conditioned key pecking (e.g. Brown and Jenkins, 1968; Schwartz and Gamzu, 1977), members of the crow family (*Corvus brachyrhynchos*) do not autoshape in this way even though they will readily peck the key when this behavior is an instrumental response (Powell, Kelly, and Santisteban, 1975). As a final example, we have already mentioned that rats will approach and direct social feeding behaviors toward a conspecific rat that predicts food (Timberlake and Grant, 1975; Timberlake, 1983a). However, when hamsters are used as both the experimental subject and the CS, the subject hamster actually exhibits a *decrease* in social contact with the conspecific CS (Timberlake, 1983a).

The differing effects that these CSs have on different species can perhaps be understood better by examining the ecological relevance of each CS type to the species concerned. The majority of experiments studying Pavlovian conditioning in unrestrained subjects using a localizable CS (autoshaping) have used hungry pigeons or hungry rats as subjects with, respectively, illuminated pecking keys or retractable or illuminated levers as the CS for food. These studies invariably produced signal-directed behaviors which, *prima facie*, resemble the behaviors required to consume the reinforcer (e.g. Jenkins and Moore, 1973; Peterson, Ackil, Frommer, and Hearst, 1972; Davey and Cleland, 1982). However, Timberlake (1983a) has suggested that the nature of the CS plays an important role as a *natural releaser* for appetitive activities, and he proposed that the *ecological relevance* of the CS will determine the strength and nature of the Pavlovian CR. Thus, in standard autoshaping studies, pigeons learn to peck the illuminated pecking key CS because pigeons normally peck at small punctate objects when foraging for food (Murton, Isaacson and Westwood, 1963; Murton, 1971).

Hungry rats, on the other hand, generally exhibit investigative foraging responses that include sniffing and manipulating any small objects in the immediate environment — whether they be food or not (Barnett, 1956; Ewer, 1971), and the retractable and illuminable levers normally used as CSs in autoshaping studies with rats are tailor-made to release and support these manipulative responses.

Now, how does the notion of ecological relevance and the idea that CSs may act as natural releasers for appetitive CRs help explain the aforementioned interspecies anomalies? First of all, rats are mainly omnivorous foragers, which, even when preying, rarely detect food on the basis of auditory signals (cf. Ewer, 1971), and so an auditory CS — even if it is localizable — possesses neither an ecological relevance for the rat (in that rats do not normally detect food through auditory cues) nor the physical properties necessary for supporting species-specific manipulative–investigative appetitive reactions. The cat, on the other hand, is primarily a carnivorous predator whose repertoire of appetitive behaviors includes phylogenetically pre-organized predatory responses. Because the prey of cats is often located on the basis of auditory signals, it seems reasonable that such signals will release stalking and aggressive responses related to prey killing. Consistent with this is the observation of Grastyan and Vereczkei that their subjects "approached the CS and performed a thorough investigation around it — sniffing and searching. Some of the animals also used their paws and teeth, and exploration often assumed a definitely aggressive manner" (1974: 126). The differing results from rats and cats appear to reflect a species difference based on natural feeding habits.

The same can be applied to the difference in the autoshaping performance of pigeons and crows. Unlike the pigeon, the crow is an opportunistic, omnivorous feeder which spends most of its time searching for larger food items than would a pigeon. Therefore, for crows, a relatively small illuminated pecking key would not possess the natural characteristics capable of releasing appetitive CS-directed activities.

The conspecific CS studies of Timberlake (1983a) and Timberlake and Grant (1975) also comply with the notion of ecological relevance. Rats are social feeders and possess a social component to their feeding repertoires (Ewer, 1971; Stimbert, Schaeffer, and Grimsley, 1966), and using a conspecific CS should release social feeding activities. In subsequent studies using conspecific CSs, Timberlake (1983a) found that the strength of the approach CR to a conspecific CS was inversely dependent on the age of the subject rat: pup subjects would approach an adult conspecific CS more readily than would an adult subject. This can be explained by the fact that rat pups have a strong tendency to approach older rats that are feeding (Barnett, 1956; Galef and Clark, 1972). Finally, hamsters are by nature solitary feeders, which suggests that they lack social components to their feeding repertoire, and thus a conspecific CS for such a species would lack the ecological relevance to release appetitive social activities.

The ecological relevance of the CS can also be observed in aversive conditioning studies, where the nature of the CS will often determine the form of the defensive CR. For instance, a static CS produces freezing behavior in rats (Blanchard and Blanchard, 1969a) while a CS which is moving toward the subject produces avoidance and fleeing behavior (Blanchard and Blanchard, 1969b). Clearly, in the wild, such animals would best be advised to flee from signs of an approaching predator, while remaining immobile to avoid detection in other circumstances. Indeed, Karpicke, Christoph, Peterson, and Hearst (1977) found that rats typically turned and faced an aversive CS which elicited an immobile freezing response. Such a response is similar to "flash behavior" (Edmunds, 1974) observed in rodents and rabbits, where the pursued animal will run some distance and then stop and turn to face the predator while remaining motionless (cf. Hollis, 1982).

This body of evidence demonstrates that not all appetitive CSs elicit approach-and-investigate behaviors. When autoshaping or signal-directed behavior was first reported, it led many theorists to suggest that Pavlovian conditioning might be viewed as a "learned taxic response" (Hollis, 1982: 8). That is, that approach towards a stimulus was an invariable result of establishing that stimulus as a localizable, appetitive Pavlovian CS. However, the anomalies cited above (Timberlake, 1983a; Cleland and Davey, 1983; Harrison, 1979; Powell, Kelly, and Santisteban, 1975) suggest that whether an autotaxic response is elicited by a CS depends on the nature of the CS, the nature of the species involved, and its repertoire of appetitive behaviors. As a consequence, accounts of signal-directed behavior which appeal to the evolutionary benefits of approaching stimuli which signal appetitive UCSs, such as food (e.g. Buzsaki, 1982; Wasserman, 1981; Hollis, 1982), are incomplete, in that animals do not appear to possess an innate appetitive tracking reaction to food signals *per se*, but specific stimuli appear to have particular relevance to particular species.

However, although it is appealing to suggest that the form of the CR is determined primarily by the nature of the CS, this is clearly not the whole story. One important contradiction here is the fact that you can generate different CRs to a single CS-type merely by manipulating the nature of the reinforcer. For instance, Davey and Cleland (1982) found that CRs directed toward a retractable-lever CS by rats could be altered in form by changing the food reinforcer from a solid to a liquid (see also Jenkins and Moore, 1973). Similarly, Boakes, Poli, Lockwood, and Goodall (1978), and Timberlake (1983b) have found that the form of the CR to a rolling ball-bearing CS in rats was affected by whether the UCS was solid or liquid — rats contacted the CS less and tended to lick it more when the UCS was liquid. In other circumstances it is clear that a single UCS-type will produce the same kind of CR to a very wide variety of CS: for instance, Pavlov's dog would salivate whether the CS was a bell, a buzzer, a metronome, a flashing light, or a tactile CS. On the face of it, it would seem a little difficult to explain this fact in terms of the ecological relevance of these stimuli.

4 *The role of the reinforcer and the underlying motivational system*

Obviously, a very wide range of reinforcers have been used in Pavlovian studies of unrestrained vertebrate subjects. These include grain for hungry pigeons (e.g. Brown and Jenkins, 1968; Gamzu and Williams, 1973; Jenkins and Moore, 1973), water for thirsty pigeons (Jenkins and Moore, 1973; Woodruff and Williams, 1976), female conspecifics for male pigeons, quail, and rats (Rackham, 1971; Farris, 1967; Zamble, Hadad, Mitchell, and Cutmore, 1985), food for hungry dogs (Jenkins, Barrera, Ireland, and Woodside, 1978), radiant heat for cold chicks and rats (Wasserman, 1973; Wasserman, Hunter, Gutowski, and Bader, 1975; Davey, Phillips, and Witty, 1989), water for thirsty rats (Timberlake, 1983a, b; Davey and Cleland, 1982), reinforcing brain stimulation for rats (Peterson, 1975; Wilkie and McDonald, 1978), food for various species of fish (Brandon and Bitterman, 1978; Squier, 1969; Waxman and McCleave, 1978), solid and liquid foods for rats (Davey and Cleland, 1982; Davey, Cleland, and Phillips, 1981), male rivals or the opportunity to mirror display in blue gouramis (*Tricogaster triopterus*) and *Betta splendens* (Hollis, 1984b; Thompson and

Sturm, 1965). Specifically aversive UCSs have included electric shock for rats (e.g. Blanchard and Blanchard, 1969a; Rescorla, 1967a; Black, 1971), and approaching cats for rat subjects (Blanchard and Blanchard, 1969b). As a general rule the nature of the CRs in these unrestrained animals resemble species-specific activities which are normally supported or elicited by the motivational system related to the reinforcer (namely either feeding, defense, or sex, and so on) — but they are not restricted to the sub-set of behaviors elicited solely by that particular reinforcer.

Initial disillusionment with reflex transfer and stimulus substitution explanations of Pavlovian performance spawned a number of what came to be known as *learned release* views of Pavlovian conditioning. According to these views the CS did not act as a substitute for the UCS, but became a "learned releaser" which released phylogenetically preorganized species-specific appetitive reactions (e.g. Woodruff and Williams, 1976). This approach was extended by Jenkins, Barrera, Ireland, and Woodside (1978), who suggested that the CS, rather than acting as a substitute for the UCS, came to act as substitute for the "natural precursors" of the UCS. They wrote that

> The artificially arranged signal of food . . . imitates the natural precursor or prefeeding object encountered by [animals] in their environmental niches; it does not stand for food itself. The response to natural food precursors is the product of evolutionary specialization and previous food-signaling encounters, and it is these behavior patterns that occur as signal-centered actions in the Pavlovian food signaling experiment. We propose that the artificial signal substitutes for a natural signal, not for the object being signaled as in the Pavlovian concept of substitution.

(1978: 292)

These kinds of "learned release" approaches appear to have superficial validity in that they can cope with the fact that CRs usually consist of a wider range of behaviors than those which constitute the UCR; and CRs are considered to reflect natural species-specific foraging behaviors. The one serious problem with them is that they lack any structural framework which allows firm predictions to be made about what reinforcers and what CSs will elicit what CRs in which species. Presumably, any model of this kind which is predictive must specify in some detail the range of species-specific activities and the kinds of stimuli — internal and external — that will release them. We will discuss this approach in more detail in the following section.

However, these kinds of approaches still raise the question of whether the origins of Pavlovian CRs rest in the functional and biological attributes of the motivational system involved or in the full range of reactions to the specific UCS. The answer appears to be both. For instance, the topography of signal-centered behavior cannot be explained simply by recourse to the principle of stimulus substitution, yet even when the motivational state is held constant and the nature of the specific reinforcer is varied, concomitant changes occur in the nature of certain Pavlovian CRs. Davey and Cleland (1982) found that hungry rats would tend to bite, sniff, and paw a retractable-lever CS paired with a 45-mg solid food-pellet UCS, but lick, sniff, and paw a retractable-lever CS paired with a liquid sucrose UCS. Such a result cannot easily be explained by recourse to a generalized set of appetitive reactions which are determined by the underlying motivational state alone: appetitive responses to the specific UCS also appear to become directed toward the CS. The picture if further complicated by the fact that while hungry rats will readily lick a CS that predicts sucrose, this behavior occurs only very rarely to a CS paired with sucrose or water when the rat is thirsty (Davey and Cleland, 1982). This latter fact reflects a general difficulty in obtaining reliable CS-directed behaviors in water-deprived animals (e.g. Davey and Cleland, 1982; Jenkins and Moore, 1973), unless deprivation level is particularly severe (Davey and Cleland, 1982, Experiment 2; Jenkins and Moore, 1973). In studies using a water UCS, the most common CR appears to be remaining in the immediate vicinity of the water dipper.

What these results suggest is that the form of the CR and in particular the tendency of the CS to produce an autotaxic response depend in some as yet unspecified way on both the nature of the underlying motivational state and the nature of the specific reinforcer. These two factors, plus the nature of the CR itself, appear to be the primary determinants of the form of the CR. The next section looks at the way in which these factors might interact.

The functional organization of behavior: behavior systems and their releasers

At this stage in the discussion of Pavlovian performance models, two questions need to be raised. First, how can so-called "learned release" models be firmed up to make them serious predictive models? And second, what is the best way to go about understanding how the nature of the UCS, the nature of the CS, and the type of motivational system involved interact to determine the form of the CR? A number of writers have suggested that a *behavior systems* approach might prove to be the most valuable here (Timberlake, 1983a, b; Holland, 1984a; Davey and Cleland, 1984).

A behavior system is a theoretical means of relating together three specific

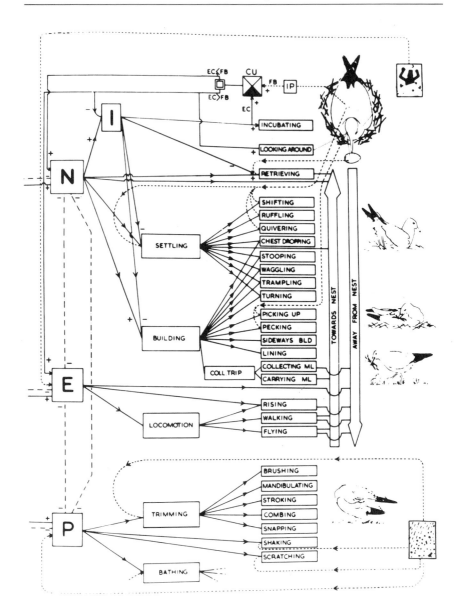

Figure 5.2 Representation of the functional organization of the behavior of the herring gull during incubation. See text for further explanation. (From Baerends, 1976. Reprinted by permission)

aspects of an animal's behavior: (1) phylogenetically-preorganized responses, (2) internal, motivational states (such as a deprivation state like hunger), and (3) external stimuli which may act to release responses relevant to that motivational state. Animals possess a number of different behavior systems, each of which serves specific biological functions (such as feeding, defense, sex, and so on) (cf. Baerends, 1975, 1976). For instance, Figure 5.2 illustrates a behavior system proposed by Baerends (1976) to underlie egg incubation in the herring gull. In this system, incubation-related behaviors (I) are the phylo-genetically-predetermined responses which can be triggered by a combination of internal motivational cues and external releasing stimuli. These incubation-related behaviors in turn trigger sub-systems related to settling and nest building. Similarly, incubation can be interrupted by cues which release preening (P) and escape from the nest (E).

The best way to describe how behavior systems help our understanding of performance in Pavlovian conditioning is to discuss a specific example. In this case there is enough evidence to make some propositions about the organization of the feeding behavior system in the rat, and how this may help to explain the kinds of appetitive CRs that rats emit in a Pavlovian conditioning situation which uses food as the UCS.

1 The feeding behavior system of the rat

Figure 5.3 represents a picture of the feeding behavior system of the rat constructed from the data on feeding activities of laboratory and feral rats (compiled from Ewer, 1971; Barnett, 1956, 1975; Timberlake, 1983a; Steiniger, 1950; Galef and Clark, 1972; Davey and Cleland, 1982). This diagram represents aspects of the functional organization of the behavior system governing feeding in the rat, and should enable us to predict some of the CRs to emerge following appetitive Pavlovian conditioning in this species.

This behavior system consists of sub-systems, each of which represents some characteristic aspect of the animal's natural method of feeding. In this case, the rat feeds by preying, by feeding socially with other rats, by preparing food ready to eat, by hoarding, by systematically investigating its immediate environment for food, by gnawing materials, and, when appropriate, by drinking. Each of these sub-systems can be broken down into integrated patterns of sequences of behavior (here called "modules" or "fixed action patterns"), which attempt to fulfill the specific function of the sub-system. Furthermore, each sub-system is related to a specific external cue that activates or releases it. These cues are called "external releasers," and when

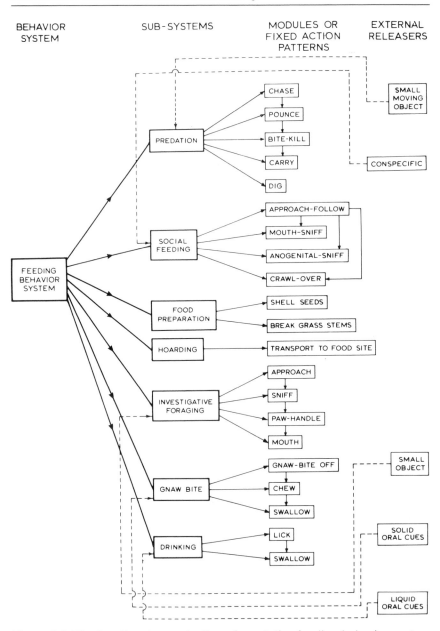

Figure 5.3 The functional organization of a putative feeding behavior system for the rat. See text for further explanation.

detected by the animal, will activate the sequence of activities controlled by its related sub-system. For example, when the rat is hungry and it detects a conspecific, this will activate the social feeding sub-system, which in turn will lead the animal to approach or follow the conspecific, and in some cases direct social behaviors toward it, such as anogenital sniffing and crawling over.

Clearly, these sequences of interactions between external releasers and sub-systems will occur only when the feeding behavior system as a whole is activated. That is, rats do not feed all of the time, so there will be occasions when the feeding behavior system is inactive. So one final aspect of the behavior system that needs to be specified is the kinds of events or stimuli which will activate or prime the behavior system as a whole. One obvious factor which would activate the feeding behavior system in the rat is a state of hunger or food deprivation. Nevertheless, deprivation states are not the only factors involved here, and to obtain a full understanding of the factors which will activate an animal's feeding behavior system we need to have a good understanding of its feeding ecology. For instance, many animals do not just eat when they are hungry; they eat *in anticipation* of their food requirements — especially if they have high metabolisms (such as shrews or chickens), their food is seasonal or requires stocking (such as hibernators or migrators), or they live in a "boom-or-bust economy" where food procurement is sporadic and unpredictable (such as some carnivorous predators) (cf. Collier and Rovee-Collier, 1983).

What these facts imply is that hunger is not the sole variable that activates a feeding behavior system, and the other factors that will act as system activators will depend on the nature of the species, its natural history, its metabolic requirements, and its feeding habits. Such factors might include time of day, seasonal or climatic factors, or even something as simple as a hoarding species recalling that its home food stockpile is badly depleted (see Figure 5.4).

2 *Behavior systems and appetitive conditioning*

The details of the feeding behavior system outlined in Figure 5.3 now allow us to make some predictions and deductions about the kinds of appetitive CRs that a rat will emit in an appetitive Pavlovian conditioning situation. As we saw earlier, the nature of many appetitive CRs appears to be dependent on the nature of the CS that is used, and the reason for this becomes more apparent when the external releasing function of these different CSs is considered. For instance, when the CS is a small, manipulable object (such as

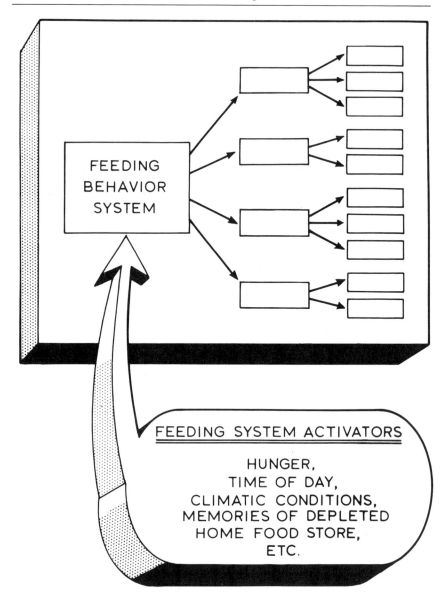

Figure 5.4 Examples of the kinds of factors which might act as feeding system activators in a range of species. Once activated, the system is primed to generate appetitive behaviors depending on the kinds of external releasers the animal encounters (see Figure 5.3).

a retractable or illuminable lever) the CRs tend to resemble the investigative foraging behaviors released by this kind of stimulus (namely approaching, sniffing, pawing, mouthing, and so on) (Davey, Oakley, and Cleland, 1981; Davey and Cleland, 1982); when the CS is a small, moving object (such as a rolling ball bearing), and CRs resemble predatory responses such as chasing, pouncing, carrying (Boakes, Poli, Lockwood, and Goodall, 1978; Timberlake, Wahl, and King, 1982); and when the CS is a rat conspecific the CRs resemble social feeding behaviors such as approaching, following, mouth sniffing, and anogenital sniffing (Timberlake and Grant, 1975; Timberlake, 1983a). In all of these cases, the CS is not only acting to signal food, but it also possesses sensory properties which act to release some specific sub-system of the rat's feeding behavior system.

Nevertheless, there are some CRs observed during appetitive Pavlovian conditioning in the rat which cannot simply be attributed to the releasing properties of the CS. For instance, Davey and Cleland (1982) found that the nature of the rat's CR was partially dependent on the nature of the UCS: if the food was solid the rats tended to bite the retractable-lever CS, if it was liquid they tended to lick the CS. Clearly, in both cases the characteristics of the CS are the same, so what is acting differentially to release biting and drinking sub-systems, because the releasers for these two sub-systems (solid oral cues or liquid oral cues) are not physically present during CS presentation? However, there is a good deal of converging evidence that suggests that biting and licking can be activated by CS-evoked representations of the releasers for these sub-systems. For instance, there is evidence to show that Pavlovian CSs evoke quite detailed and specific internal representations of the UCS they are paired with (cf. Dickinson, 1980; Rescorla, 1980a; see Chapter 4), and these CS-evoked representations of the UCS may be salient enough to release biting and drinking sub-systems during CS presentation itself. Two pieces of evidence provide support for this. First, small, localizable CSs often provide appropriate physical support for these types of behaviors, but they can occur in the absence of any physical support at all (Kierylowicz, Soltysik, and Divac, 1968; Debold, Miller, and Jensen, 1965; Gormezano, 1972), or at the food site rather than the CS site (Reberg, Mann, and Innis, 1977; Poling and Poling, 1978; Timberlake, Wahl, and King, 1982). Second, Cleland and Davey (1982) found that postconditioning devaluation of a liquid food reinforcer through pairing with lithium chloride (LiCl) subsequently suppressed the rate of CS-directed sniffing and licking in rats. Both of these responses would be behaviors released by the oral and olfactory characteristics of the UCS, and their suppression following devaluation of the UCS representation would appear to be consistent with a disruption of the UCS representation's ability to release the appropriate sub-systems.

Finally, it must be understood that stimuli which predict food (such as a Pavlovian CS^+ not only have a releasing function which determines the nature of the CR, they also appear to have an important role in modulating the overall activation of the behavior system itself. For instance, when an animal has learned to discriminate a CS^+ from a CS^-, the CS^- will no longer evoke appetitive CRs even though it may be a natural releaser for a feeding sub-system and the animal is still hungry (that is, the feeding behavior system itself should still be primed and active). Indeed, hungry animals will often actively withdraw from a stimulus that has been established as a CS^-, even if it possesses characteristics which would normally release feeding activities (Hearst, 1975; Hearst and Franklin, 1977; Wasserman, Franklin, and Hearst, 1974). Clearly, learning that in certain conditions food is unavailable appears to inhibit activation of the feeding system. However, as yet we have little knowledge of how this inhibition is mediated.

So, to summarize so far:

1 In order to understand and predict what appetitive CRs will appear in a conditioning situation we must initially have a clear picture of the feeding behavior system of the species concerned, and how this system relates phylogenetically-predetermined feeding behaviors to external releasing stimuli and to conditions which activate the overall system. In order to do this we need a good deal of ethological evidence on the natural feeding tendencies of the individual species concerned;

2 When a feeding behavior system has been constructed, the nature of the CR can frequently be traced to releasing properties possessed either by the CS or the UCS representation that is elicited by the CS;

3 CS-directed behavior (autoshaping) will not be observed if the CS releases a sub-system that does not contain an autotaxic "approach" module, or has no releasing properties at all for that species; and

4 learned discrimination between a CS^+ and CS^- also modulates the effects of the behavior system such as a CS^+ will facilitate the activation of the system and a CS^- will inhibit it (Davey and Cleland, 1984).

3 Behavior systems in drinking, thermoregulation, and defense

So far we have discussed the role of behavior systems in determining the nature of the Pavlovian CR primarily in relation to feeding — simply because most experimental and ethological evidence is available on this system.

However, there are some preliminary observations that can be made on the behavior systems approach to other motivational systems.

Drinking

When water is used as the UCS for thirsty animals, the resultant CRs tend to be activities directed toward the UCS-site rather than the CS (Davey and Cleland, 1982b, Experiment 1; Reberg, Innis, Mann, and Eizenga, 1978; Reberg, Mann, and Innis, 1977), unless water deprivation is particularly severe when more CS-directed behavior seems apparent (Davey and Cleland, 1982b, Experiment 2; cf. Jenkins and Moore 1973). Nevertheless, CS-directed CRs are considerably less frequent with a water UCS than with a food UCS (Davey and Cleland, 1982b; Timberlake, 1983b; Boakes, Poli, Lockwood, and Goodall, 1978). To explain this difference between feeding and drinking CRs within the behavior system framework, one would have to look at the natural feeding and drinking activities of the species involved to discover (1) how they might forage differently for food and water, and (2) what factors might differentially potentiate the feeding and drinking behavior systems.

The answers to these points are perhaps a little difficult to discern, since, in a species like the rat, there is an overlap between feeding and drinking systems. Rats obtain both nourishment and fluid from live prey and most vegetable matter, so we might expect those activities that function to forage for food also to satisfy fluid needs, hence perhaps we might have expected CRs to water UCSs to resemble those to food UCSs, which to some extent they do (cf. Timberlake, 1983b). However, in the rat, there are some interesting differences between drinking and feeding. First, rats rarely drink under "emergency" conditions: that is, free-living rats are seldom in a state of fluid deprivation. Second, rats tend to imbibe water either at set times during the day or post-prandially (e.g. Kissileff, 1969). These two facts suggest that a physiological state of water deprivation may not be the most important factor that activates the drinking behavior system — a more important activator of the drinking behavior system may be time of day or diurnal rhythms. Thus, water deprivation may be less powerful than food deprivation in activating the respective behavior system, and what we may be observing in most water UCS studies with rats are instrumentally-maintained UCS-directed activities. Nevertheless, the problem of the origins of water-reinforced CRs is difficult to unravel in species where food and fluid intake are so interrelated, and where we have very little ethological evidence as to how a species such as the rat "forages" for fluids.

Thermoregulation

Wasserman, Hunter, Gutowski, and Bader (1975) found that presenting chicks with a 4 sec burst of radiant heat from a 250-w heat lamp (UCS) in a cold environment produced pecking of a small key-light (CS) which was illuminated for 8 sec prior to the heat reinforcement. At first sight it is difficult to determine how this CR might fit into a behavior systems account (it was quite unlike the UCR, which was a "basking" response where chicks "stopped scurrying about, extended their wings, and often emitted twittering sounds" (Wasserman, 1973: 876)). However, Hogan (1974) has suggested that the CS-directed pecking was very similar to the warmth-soliciting behaviors that young chicks would direct toward the hen — pecking the hen's wings makes the hen ruffle her feathers so that the chick can snuggle. Indeed, the topography of this behavior eventually came to resemble "snuggling," whereby the chicks would nudge their beaks along the wall surface next to the key occasioning rather inefficient manipulation of the key. Nevertheless, although the chick's behavior can be seen to be one which is species-specifically relevant to thermoregulation, a behavior systems account implies that the CS should possess some of the features necessary for releasing these warmth-soliciting and snuggling CRs. In chicks it is difficult to confirm this implication because we lack knowledge of the features of a hen which would release warmth-seeking activities in the chick.

However, there do exist some studies from other species which have isolated the cues which release thermoregulatory responses., In an extensive series of investigations, Alberts (1978a, b), and Alberts and Brunjes (1978) found that those cues which elicit huddling in rat pups include immobile conspecifics, a loop of warm tubing, nonthermal cues such as a dead, ambient-temperature conspecific, olfactory cues, tactile stimuli such as vertical contours, furry "comfort" cues, and photic responses. In a thermal conditioning study, Davey, Phillips, and Witty (1989) found signal-directed CRs in rats when the CS was a retractable lever covered in synthetic fur, but not when the CS was a normal aluminium retractable lever. The CRs directed toward the "furry" lever included investigatory sniffing, "head-under" responses typical of rats joining a "huddle," and simple body contact with the lever. These behaviors were not observed when the "furry" lever was presented randomly in conjunction with the heat UCS. Clearly, it seems that CRs conditioned using a heat UCS depend on the availability of suitable natural releasers for behaviors relevant to thermoregulation — a finding consistent with predictions from a behavior systems analysis of conditioned thermoregulation.

Defense

How can the behavior systems approach be utilized to help predict the origins of Pavlovian CRs in aversive or defensive conditioning? As before, two questions must be asked. (1) What natural factors activate the defensive behavior system of a species? And (2) what is that species' repertoire of defensive reactions and what internal and external stimuli release these reactions?

The range of aversive UCSs that can be used in defensive conditioning is obviously very broad — arguably much broader than the range of possible UCSs in appetitive conditioning, since survival against predators in a potentially hostile environment is an urgent business. Although an organism might survive for some time without food, failure to detect a predator is likely to have fatal consequences with no second chance to learn about the relevant cues (cf. Bolles, 1970; Hollis, 1982). Hence, the range of antipredator defense strategies that different species have evolved is extremely varied (cf. Edmunds, 1974), but these strategies can — for the purpose of integrating them into a behavior systems analysis — be divided into two categories: (1) the detection of those stimuli which activate the defensive behavior system (which we will call *defensive activators*), and (2) the repertoire of evolved defensive reactions and the stimuli that release them (*natural defensive releasers*). The first category of stimuli can be used as Pavlovian UCSs and transfer their behavior system activating qualities to the CS with which they are paired. The second category of stimuli determine the nature of the eventual defensive CR.

1 *Defensive activators* Most species of animal require both inter- and intra-specific defense capabilities. That is, they need to defend against natural predators and against conspecific intruders. Nevertheless, there are some stimuli which act as defensive activators for most organisms. The obvious ones, which are most commonly used as aversive UCSs in Pavlovian studies, include direct physical abuse such as electric shock or loud noises which result in pain. Movement features also elicit defensive arousal in many species. Moving rather than immobile cats elicit escape in rats (Blanchard, Mast, and Blanchard, 1975; Bronstein and Hirsch, 1976), and moving rather than stationary predator hawks or owls elicit defensive reactions in small birds (Nice and Ter Pelkwyk, 1941; Curio, 1975). Movement "toward" is particularly capable of inducing defensive reactions in many species (Schiff, Caviness, and Gibson, 1962; Ball and Tronick, 1971), as is a looming shadow indicating an approaching object (Schiff, 1965; Hayes and Saiff, 1967). Suddenness and jerkiness are also features of movement which elicit defensive

arousal (Landis and Hunt, 1939; Bronson, 1968; Scarr and Salapatek, 1970).

Most prey species have evolved natural defensive reactions to specific features of their predators. Specific visual features appear to be involved in the elicitation of defensive reactions in birds such as turkeys, geese, and ducks to aerial predators such as hawks (Lorenz, 1939; Tinbergen, 1951) and in the mobbing reactions of pied flycatchers to owls and shrikes (Curio, 1975). Many predators fixate their prey before pouncing, which results in some prey species evolving defensive reactions to the detection of eyes as an isolated feature (Blest, 1957; Scaife, 1976a, b; Gagliardi, Gallup, and Boren, 1976). Olfactory cues associated with predators can induce defensive arousal (Dieterlen, 1959; Brett and MacKinnon, 1954; Sieck, Baumbach, Gordon, and Turner, 1974), as can predator-associated auditory cues (Miller, 1952; Russell, 1979), and conspecific fear or alarm calls (Walther, 1969; Marler, 1956; Washburn and DeVore, 1961).

All of these stimuli appear to act as defensive activators which lead to defensive arousal and priming of the organism's defensive behavior system. The effects that these stimuli have may be pre-wired or learned very rapidly during the early development of individual animals. The actual defensive reaction that the organism emits will depend on the availability and detection of releasers for components of that defensive behavior system.

2 *Natural defensive releasers* It is common knowledge that many organisms, including the rat, have a defensive strategy based on "fright, flight, or fight": that is, they will either remain immobile and freeze, or flee, or respond aggressively to the predator or intruder. What is less obvious is predicting which of this triad of reactions the animal will engage in when defensively aroused. However, the form of the defensive reaction does appear to be determined by features of the proximal environment. For instance, rats will normally flee when provided with an escape route or when simply given the opportunity to run (Masterson, 1970; Theios, 1963; Bolles, Stokes, and Younger, 1966; Bolles and Grossen, 1970; Anisman and Wahlsten, 1974). Laboratory rats exposed to a cat attempt to escape if the environment is novel but freeze if it is familiar (Blanchard, Fukunaga, and Blanchard, 1976), and in conditioning studies rats normally freeze in an enclosed, inescapable chamber (Blanchard and Blanchard, 1969a; Shettleworth, 1978).

What seems to be happening here is that the environment offers cues which release modules of defensive activity when the defensive behavior system has been activated. In the rat, for instance, detection of an escape route appears to be a releaser for fleeing, while aspects of inescapable enclosure release freezing and bradycardia (heart-rate deceleration). In other circumstances, features of

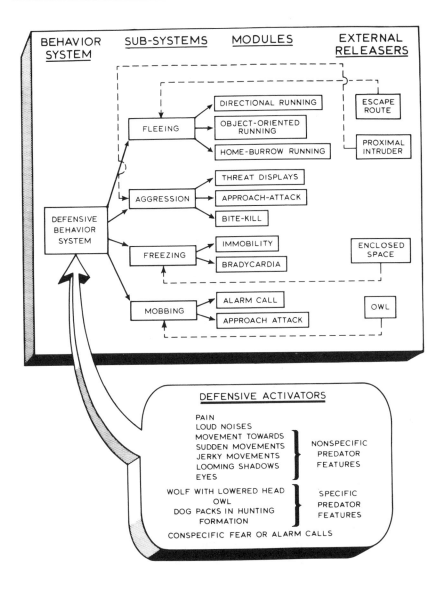

Figure 5.5 A putative defensive behavior system for a hypothetical hybrid organism illustrating the kinds of events that could serve to activate the behavior system and the functional organization of defensive reactions and their external releasers.

a proximal predator or intruder may not only serve as a stimulus to activate the defensive behavior system, but also act as releasers for modules of defensive behavior such as threat displays and approach attack (e.g. Hollis, 1984a; Azrin, Hutchinson, and Hake, 1963; Ulrich and Azrin, 1962) or species-specific defense reactions like mobbing in small birds (Curio, 1975; Kruuk, 1976). In the latter case, the detection of an owl by pied flycatchers not only acts as a defensive activator but also as an apparent natural releaser for mobbing behavior (Curio, 1975).

Figure 5.5 gives a schematic summary of how defensive activators and natural defensive releasers interact within a behavior systems view. This kind of formalization allows us to make predictions about the nature of the CR in aversive Pavlovian conditioning studies, given that we have a knowledge of the organism's defensive behavior repertoire and the stimuli that activate the system and release particular defensive activities. The aversive UCS in such Pavlovian studies will be what we have described here as a *defensive activator*, and through its pairing with the aversive UCS, the CS comes to acquire the defensive activating properties of the UCS, thus allowing the animal "rapid mobilization of energy reserves [which] is imperative in all anti-predator strategies" (Hollis, 1982: 28). The resultant CR will be determined by the availability of appropriate *defensive releasers* in the conditioning environment. Often the effective releaser may be the CS itself (e.g. Blanchard and Blanchard, 1969a, b), but more frequently it is some other feature of the immediate surroundings such as the availability or unavailability of an escape route. The fact that in defensive conditioning it is more likely to be some neutral aspect of the conditioning situation rather than the CS itself that determines the form of the CR emphasizes that, although the CS may act as both a defensive activator and releaser in some situations, these roles are functionally independent.

Conclusion

This chapter has dealt largely with constructing a detailed and predictive performance model of Pavlovian conditioning that can be applied across species. This model is known as the *behavior systems* approach to conditioned responding, and requires that any understanding of the origins of conditioned responding lies in an understanding of the particular species' natural repertoire of behaviors in relation to the motivational system being conditioned. The behavior systems approach offers a framework for understanding how these behaviors and internal and external releasing stimuli interact, and also provides a suitable approach to the construction of a taxonomy of Pavlovian CRs.

However, there are two aspects to the understanding of Pavlovian CRs —just as there are to any biological problem. This chapter has investigated the mechanisms underlying Pavlovian performance and hence asked the "How?" question posed by process biology. The next chapter investigates the "Why?" question posed by evolutionary biology: what is the biological function and evolutionary benefit of Pavlovian conditioning?

Chapter summary

1 Just because we might know that an animal has learned to associate a CS with a UCS does not tell us what CR it will perform. We therefore need some set of rules (*performance rules*) which allow us to predict what CR an animal will make in a particular Pavlovian conditioning situation.

2 Some theorists have attempted to suggest that Pavlovian CRs result from a form of *instrumental reinforcement*. That is, the UCS acts to reinforce instrumentally certain types of CRs. The balance of evidence does not favor these theories as complete accounts of Pavlovian performance.

3 Some accounts of Pavlovian performance assume that the reflex or UCR normally elicited by the UCS is transferred to the CS. These are known as *reflex transfer* accounts. However, contrary to reflex transfer accounts, there is considerable evidence that Pavlovian CRs cover a wider range of responses than those elicited by the UCS.

4 One variation of reflex transfer theory is *stimulus substitution theory*, which claims that the CS not only comes to elicit those behaviors normally elicited by the UCS, but that they become directed toward the CS as if it were a substitute for the UCS. This account, however, suffers the same criticisms as all reflex transfer accounts (see 3).

5 The nature of a Pavlovian CR is often determined in part by the nature of the CS itself.

6 In particular, the CR will be affected by the *ecological relevance* of the CS for the species being conditioned and whether it is a *natural releaser* for species-specific behaviors.

7 If all other things are held constant, the nature of the CR is also affected by the physical nature of the UCS itself.

8 In order to account for the fact that CRs often cover a wider range of responses than those elicited by the UCS, some theorists have proposed what are known as *learned release* views of Pavlovian conditioning. These accounts suggest that the CS does not become a substitute for the UCS, but is a

"learned releaser" which releases a range of phylogenetically preorganized species-specific reactions.

9 Learned release accounts of Pavlovian performance can be made more predictive by integrating them into a *behavior systems* approach to responding.

10 A behavior system is a theoretical means of relating together phylogenetically-preorganized responses, internal motivational states (e.g. hunger), and external stimuli which may act to release responses relevant to that motivational state.

11 Constructing behavior systems describing different biological functions requires considerable ethological knowledge of the natural lifestyles of individual species. Nevertheless, where it has been possible to do this (e.g. in the case of the feeding behavior system of the rat), a behavior systems approach provides a relatively successful predictive model of Pavlovian performance.

Chapter six

The biological function of Pavlovian conditioning

Pavlovian conditioning is found in as wide a range of species as one cares to mention: from neurologically uncomplicated organisms such as planaria (Thompson and McConnell, 1955) and headless insects (Horridge, 1962), to marine mollusks (Carew, Walters, and Kandel, 1981), drosophila (Tompkins, Siegel, Gailey, and Hall, 1983), honeybees (Bitterman, Menzel, Feitz, and Schafer, 1983), nonmammalian vertebrates such as fish (Brandon and Bitterman, 1979; Waxman and McCleave, 1978), amphibia (Goldstein, Spies, and Sepinwall, 1964) and birds (cf. Macphail, 1982: 192–3), as well as in nonhuman mammals (cf. Marler and Terrace, 1984: 419ff) and, of course, humans (cf. Davey, 1987a). Clearly, if such a range of living organisms possesses the ability to learn about the relationship between two environmental stimuli, then it seems reasonable to assume that this ability serves an important biological function. If this is so, then either this ability appeared very early in the evolution of living organisms and serves a generalized biological purpose across the whole gamut of existing species, or it evolved independently in different species or in different biological functions as a means of coping with the different kinds of evolutionary pressures which afflict different species in their own ecological niche. To express some extremes of these possibilities, we might suggest that (1) Pavlovian conditioning evolved because it allows animals to reduce the unpredictability of their environment, or allows them to optimize interaction with a forthcoming biologically important event regardless of what that biologically important event might be (Hollis, 1982); or (2) different species have evolved the capacity of Pavlovian learning to cope with very specific adaptive problems.

Examples of the latter might include the recognition of toxic foods in animals which are basically omnivorous in their feeding habits (taste aversion learning). Because omnivorous foragers sample a large range of foods they need to be particularly sensitive to potentially poisonous foodstuffs and recognize them quickly. Pavlovian conditioning permits this. Another example is when Pavlovian conditioning facilitates the milk-ejection reflex in mammalian mothers (cf. Hollis, 1982). Stimuli which regularly precede infant nursing, such as a crying infant, come to elicit the same milk ejection reflex as suckling itself. Such a process in organisms which suckle their young would have obvious beneficial effects on the survival of the offspring. There is a third possibility which must also be considered. Maybe Pavlovian conditioning serves no biological function but is just an accidental concatenation of other, more basic biological functions producing a behavioral "false start." This is certainly a less theoretically exciting possibility but must be considered seriously.

Generalized biological function

There are two important ways in which the general biological function of Pavlovian conditioning can be examined. The first is to determine whether Pavlovian conditioning provides the organism with useful information about its environment, and the second is to consider how the behaviors learned through Pavlovian conditioning might influence an organism's inclusive fitness. The first considers how Pavlovian *learning* might bestow an adaptive advantage on the animal, the second considers how Pavlovian *performance* might contribute to inclusive fitness.

1 *The optimal time allocation hypothesis: information value of the CS*

The Pavlovian CS is frequently referred to as a "signal" that warns the animal of a forthcoming biologically important event. In an unpredictable world such information has obvious biological value by allowing the organism to allocate its time successfully to different biological functions. However, such a mechanism for information gathering would have to be fairly highly tuned in order to avoid attributing signaling functions to spurious environmental correlations — a mechanism for learning about the causal relationships that exist in the environment would lose all its advantages if it also promoted spurious learning that resulted in the animal wasting time and effort on false premises. It must also protect against learning about redundant information. In a world where optimal utilization of information processing capacities is essential, spending time and energy learning more than once about the same thing should be avoided at all costs.

Traditionally it was assumed that the contiguous pairing of a CS with a

UCS was sufficient to generate Pavlovian conditioning (Kimble, 1961). This has since been demonstrated on numerous occasions to be incorrect. What is important is the *correlation* between CS and UCS: the greater the correlation between CS and UCS, the greater the strength of the Pavlovian CR (Rescorla, 1967a, 1968). If surplus unsignaled UCSs are presented during the inter-trial intervals, conditioned responding is weakened (cf. Gibbon, 1981; Gamzu and Williams, 1971, 1973). If surplus CS-alone trials are presented during the inter-trial intervals, conditioned responding is again weakened (e.g. Jenkins, Barnes, and Barrera, 1981). Unlike intermittent reinforcement in instrumental conditioning, which strengthens the conditioned response, intermittent reinforcement in Pavlovian conditioning generally weakens it. Thus, the important feature of the CS which promotes conditioning is its *predictive value*, not simply the fact that it has been contiguously paired with a UCS. This "predictive" feature of the CS is one which has been a central characteristic of recent models of Pavlovian response strength (cf. Rescorla and Wagner, 1972; Mackintosh, 1975a; Pearce and Hall, 1980), and all of these models conceive of the Pavlovian learning process as an optimal information-processing exercise. Clearly, this safeguards the animal from acquiring false or unreliable information about the contingencies in its environment.

Further safeguards appear to be available to discourage unnecessary learning. When a CS is presented alone on a number of occasions prior to conditioning, it subsequently takes longer to generate conditioned responding to that CS than when no pre-exposure has taken place. This phenomenon is known as *latent inhibition* and has been widely demonstrated in a variety of Pavlovian preparations (Lubow, Markman, and Allen, 1968; Carlton and Vogel, 1967; Siegel, 1969; Chacto and Lubow, 1967). As latent inhibition is studied in the laboratory it may at first glance appear to be a counter-productive process because it hinders the learning about a subsequent CS–UCS relationship. But in most nonlaboratory situations its adaptive value is fairly obvious — if a stimulus possesses no information value, it is best to learn that fact as soon as possible so that subsequent processing time is not wasted on it. But are animals learning to ignore a biologically irrelevant stimulus or are they learning that it signals nothing of importance? For instance, latent inhibition may result from a simple process of stimulus habituation. If a stimulus is repeatedly presented without reinforcement, the response elicited by that stimulus gradually declines (e.g. Groves and Thompson, 1970). However, there is evidence to suggest that latent inhibition is a more active learning process than this. For instance, pre-exposure to a CS appears to retard subsequent conditioning regardless of whether conditioning is commenced immediately after pre-exposure or not until a week later

(Siegel, 1970; Crowell and Anderson, 1972). This suggests a process more permanent than nonassociative habituation (cf. Mackintosh, 1974: 39). What is apparent from the phenomenon of latent inhibition is that something specific does appear to be learned about the pre-exposed CS: that is, it does become associated with something, either the context in which it is presented (Wagner, 1978) or the fact that it is followed by nonreinforcement (Pearce and Hall, 1980). For instance, latent inhibition is reduced (1) if animals are re-exposed to the conditioning "context" alone between pre-exposure and conditioning (Wagner, 1978); (2) if subsequent conditioning takes place in a context different from that in which pre-exposure occurred (e.g. Lubow, Rifkin, and Alek, 1976); (3) if, during pre-exposure, the CS predicts a second, different CS (Szakmary, 1977; Doré, 1980); and (4) if animals are pre-exposed not just to the CS, but to uncorrelated presentations of the CS and UCS (Baker and Mackintosh, 1977).

All of this evidence mitigates against a simple interpretation of latent inhibition in terms of habituation — either of preparatory CRs or attention to the CS. Clearly, from this animals appear to learn *about* the pre-exposed CS, but whether they learn about its nonsignificance in a particular context or whether they associate it with subsequent nonreinforcement is still far from clear (cf. Siddle and Remington, 1987). However, from an adaptive point of view it would make sense for the animal to learn that the stimulus predicted nothing of any significance. If so, it would either reduce the apparent correlation between CS and UCS, thus slowing down conditioning (Baker and Mercier, 1982), or reduce the saliency or associability of the CS resulting in associative strength accruing to the CS more slowly than without pre-exposure (e.g. Mackintosh, 1975a; Pearce and Hall, 1980).

Thus, latent inhibition appears to be a useful safeguard against the processing of irrelevant stimuli, and serves to protect the organism from designating a stimulus as significant if, after being sampled alone, it is subsequently *accidentally* correlated with a biologically important event. However, for this process to be of truly biological significance we would have to demonstrate that, in an animal's natural environment, only very rarely do stimuli which the animal initially samples as having no predictive significance subsequently come to acquire predictive significance. It would be of dire consequences for an animal if a stimulus which the animal had learned to consider as irrelevant subsequently came to signal, for example, a predator.

A further safeguard which protects the animal from acquiring redundant information and optimizes the learning process is known as *blocking*. If a UCS is already reliably predicted by a CS, A, then subsequently signaling that UCS with a compound CS consisting of the original CS, A, plus a new component, CS, B, results in little or no learning about the new component, B (Kamin, 1968, 1969). In terms of processing efficiency, this implies that animals do not learn about a CS–UCS relationship if that UCS is already reliably predicted by another CS. This is further evidence that mere contiguous association between a CS and a UCS is not sufficient for Pavlovian conditioning to occur, since, if this were so, then the element B should acquire associative strength. However, blocking can be prevented by subtly changing the nature of the UCS between pretraining and subsequent compound training: blocking occurs only when the UCS is unchanged between pretraining and compound training. For instance, if an electric shock UCS is changed in intensity between pretraining and compound training, or if a brief unexpected shock is added shortly after each compound trial, then blocking is attenuated (Gray and Appignanesi, 1973; Dickinson, Hall, and Mackintosh, 1976; Dickinson and Mackintosh, 1979). It appears that conditioning to the new element, B, in the AB compound can be enhanced by the occurrence of a surprising or unpredicted event shortly after each compound trial — whether this be an unexpected change in the value or nature of the UCS or some other unexpected event shortly after compound conditioning trials. Thus, if the signaling value of a CS or element of a CS is redundant it is not learned about. If, however, the situation changes to one which is new or surprising, then the formerly redundant element is processed. A phenomenon such as blocking provides efficient processing of environmental contingencies without loss of information if something new or unpredicted occurs.

One other process which should be mentioned in this context is extinction. If, after conditioning, a CS is subsequently presented alone, the strength of the CR to that CS declines over trials until the CS no longer elicits a CR. Theoretically, this might be conceived of in a number of ways: (1) simply as the habituation of a CR that is no longer reinforced; (2) the weakening of previously established associations (e.g. Rescorla and Wagner, 1972); or (3) the learning of a new CS–no UCS association (e.g. Pearce and Hall, 1980). There is some evidence to suggest that the third interpretation might be valid. First, presenting a novel stimulus during extinction usually re-establishes the CR on the following or subsequent trials (disinhibition, Pavlov, 1927: 61–2). Similarly, introducing a long interval between the last extinction trial and re-presentation of the CS results in the reappearance of the CR (known as spontaneous recovery, e.g. Wagner, Siegel, Thomas, and Ellison, 1964; Schneiderman, Fuentes, and Gormezano, 1962). Neither of these effects can be explained adequately in terms of extinction representing the loss of previously established associations, since, if this was the case, only relearning of those associations should cause the CR to reappear.

While disinhibition and spontaneous recovery are phenomena that are also associated with habituation processes (cf. Thompson and Spencer, 1966; Groves and Thompson, 1970), further evidence suggests that extinction might represent a more active associative process. For instance, Pearce and Hall (1980: 546) report an experiment which suggests that extinction can be enhanced by facilitating the associability of the CS immediately prior to extinction. In an aversive conditioning study, rats that were given an unexpectedly more intense UCS on the final conditioning trial prior to extinction actually extinguished more quickly than rats that did not receive this manipulation. They argue that altering the UCS parameters on the last trial of acquisition should restore the associability of the CS and allow rapid CS–no UCS learning to take place on immediately succeeding trials. Thus, extinction appears to be not just a simple dissipation of response strength in the absence of reinforcement, but an active learning process undertaken by the organism. Clearly, it makes sense that an animal should learn as quickly as possible that a CS no longer predicts anything of any biological importance.

To learn that a CS predicts no UCS is similar to latent inhibition — it safeguards the animal from inferring incorrect contingencies from subsequent spurious environmental correlations. It also has other beneficial effects. For instance, if a signaled food source or patch has been depleted it is as well to learn this fact since a revisit will not be profitable. A revisit would certainly not be deterred if extinction were simply due to the unlearning of CS–UCS associations or habituation of the CR. There is evidence in the ethological literature that this kind of CS–no UCS learning occurs: animals appear to *learn* not to return to food sources that they have recently depleted (Kamil, 1978; Shettleworth and Krebs, 1982).

What the evidence presented in this section implies is that Pavlovian conditioning is the end product of an efficient and optimizing information-gathering process. This process attempts to ensure that learning does not occur to spurious environmental contingencies nor when information is redundant. It also involves an active learning about situations where the CS becomes associated with nonreinforcement, such as in latent inhibition or extinction. This learning of CS–no UCS relationships appears to have greater benefit than "unlearning" of CS–UCS relationships or simply ignoring the CS. It is frequently as important to know that a CS signals no UCS as it is to know that a CS signals reinforcement: especially in terms of optimizing behavioral resources. We discuss in Chapter 8 that evolutionary pressures will probably have selected for optimal performance in most biological systems, and that also appears to be the case with Pavlovian associative learning: the animal only spends time learning about the barest essentials and rejects uninformativeness or redundancy.

However, we are still some way from elucidating the biological function of Pavlovian conditioning. Learning about the information content of CSs in an efficient manner seems intuitively important to an organism, but how does this knowledge bestow a biological advantage on that organism? It is not *what* the organism learns that is of final importance, but how the organism *uses* that information to benefit itself and its inclusive fitness. Nevertheless, one important benefit of this information-gathering process is that it should allow the animal to allocate its time optimally between different biological functions. For instance, knowing that food is available only during certain signals (CSs) allows the animal to devote time exclusively to other biological functions (such as defending a territory, caring for offspring, being alert to predators, and so on) when that food signal is not present.

2 The prefiguring hypothesis: optimizing interaction with a forthcoming biologically important event

Hollis (1982, 1984a) has expounded a detailed thesis that the biological function of Pavlovian conditioning is to "enable the animal to *optimize interaction with the forthcoming biologically important event (UCS)* (known as the prefiguring hypothesis). The performance of a CR, although energetically costly, allows the animal to deal better with the UCS event, and, as such, the CR is essentially preparatory" (1982: 3). In effect, this states that the Pavlovian CR has a generalized function which allows the animal to deal better with food, predators, rivals, and mates: all activities essential to the survival and subsequent inclusive fitness of the animal. To support Hollis's assertion, it must be demonstrated that feeding, mating, avoiding predators, and defeating rivals or intruders is facilitated as a result of Pavlovian conditioning: animals that have learned Pavlovian associations should experience a selective advantage over conspecifics who have not had the benefit of this learning.

First, it has been known for some time that in the prototypical Pavlovian conditioning situation using hungry dogs, digestion is shortened when food is preceded by a CS, and that metabolic processes are activated by the CS which ensure that even large portions of food are absorbable (Bykov, 1959; Nicolaides, 1977). More formally, Zamble (1973) and Zamble, Baxter, and Baxter (1980) have shown that hungry rats can consume more dry food and thirsty rats can consume more water when the food and water are signaled than when they occur at unpredictable and irregular intervals. Zamble (1973) found that rats for whom 30-min access to food was signaled by a 15-min visual or auditory CS consumed up to 20 per cent more food than an unsignaled control group. The actual mechanism mediating this effect is unclear at present; it could be either behavioral or physiological. But what matters from the point of view of the present discussion is that animals for whom food delivery is reliably signaled do have an advantage in terms of the amount of food consumed in a fixed period of time.

However, we must add a note of caution to this. When assessing the contribution of a behavior or adaptive process to an organism's inclusive fitness (as we are when discussing the biological function of Pavlovian conditioning), we cannot assess that behavior or process directly in terms of fitness, but only in terms of some intermediate currency selected by past evolution as a good predictor of fitness (see Chapter 8). In the case of feeding, most theorists consider that the *net rate of energy intake* is a good starting point, and that animals will act to maximize it (see Chapter 8). Thus, actual amount of food consumed is not a particularly good indicator of efficiency unless we also know how much energy the animal is expending in obtaining, handling, and consuming that food. In this context, this play-off between calories consumed and energy expended is important, because we know that Pavlovian CSs which predict food also generate significant increases in energy-expending activity (as measured, for instance, by generalized stabilometer measures) (Bindra and Palfai, 1967; Sheffield, 1966; Zamble, 1967). Until we have good evidence that signaled food presentations result in a greater net rate of energy intake than unsignaled food presentations, we must assume that the greater levels of activity generated by an appetitive CS might cancel the benefits of more efficient consumption of the subsequent signaled UCS.

Pavlovian conditioning also appears to facilitate sexual interaction with a mate. Pavlovian CSs paired with conspecific mates result in conditioned secretion of sexual hormones during the CS (Graham and Desjardins, 1980). Signaled presentation of mates has also been shown to facilitate copulation in rats and Japanese quail. Zamble and Hadad (1980, quoted in Hollis, 1982) found that male rats that had signaled presentations of females with which they were subsequently allowed to copulate showed a significantly shorter latency to ejaculation than control subjects which had the Pavlovian signal explicitly unpaired with the female. Farris (1964) found that male quail which had a 10 sec buzzer paired with access to a female exhibited a significant decrease over trials in the latency to initiate courtship, and three out of four subjects mounted the female immediately on introduction. Unfortunately, courtship and mounting data were not presented for control subjects.

In a recent series of extensive experiments, Hollis (1984a, b) and Hollis, Martin, Cadieux, and Colbert (1984) have investigated the effect of signaled territorial intrusion on the ability of the blue gourami fish (*Trichogaster trichopterus*) to defend its territory. Male subjects that had the presentation of a conspecific male intruder signaled by a red light (CS) delivered significantly more bites and tail-beatings to their opponents than did subjects which had received explicitly unpaired presentations of the red light and intruder. Similarly, male subjects which had undergone Pavlovian conditioning showed conditional aggressive displays consisting of immediate approach to the CS and the site of intrusion with fins erect in an intraspecific threat display. Hollis (1984b) suggests that territorial defense is important to reproduction, and that any adaptive process which provides a defensive advantage should also yield a reproductive advantage. She writes that "the function of Pavlovian conditioning seems clear: By means of the conditional aggressive response — a display that is termed *charging* in the ethological literature (Forselius, 1957) — rivals are confronted at the territory boundary by an already aggressively displaying owner, strategically ready for battle" (Hollis, 1984b: 422). It also appears that stimuli which signal the explicit *absence* of an intruder are also valuable. The male blue gourami has to defend a territory, tend the nest, and forage for food, and a CS⁻ signaling no-intruder appears to reduce aggressiveness significantly. Thus, the CS⁻ would appear to inhibit aggression at a time when it would be counterproductive and hence avoid unnecessary or dangerous conflicts (Hollis, Martin, Cadieux, and Colbert, 1984).

In interspecific defense (antipredator defense) Pavlovian conditioning can provide an obvious advantage to an animal by activating anticipatory autonomic reactions necessary for rapid movement or mobilization. These physiological changes include decreased skin resistance responses (e.g. Holdstock and Schwartzbaum, 1965; cf. Mayes, 1979), and changes in heart and respiratory rate (e.g. Dykman, Mack, and Ackerman, 1965; Cohen and Durkovic, 1966). Nevertheless, it is not difficult to point out intuitively plausible advantages that Pavlovian conditioning might bestow on animals wishing to avoid predators but, in order to demonstrate the biological utility of this learning we must show that the chances of detection, capture, and injury by a predator are lessened if the predator is signaled.

This is a difficult proposition to assess, primarily because the majority of aversive Pavlovian conditioning studies have not used predators as UCSs but a ubiquitous, painful UCS such as electric shock. Laboratory studies designed to assess the degee of injury inflicted on a subject by a signaled or unsignaled predator are also open to obvious ethical considerations. The vast majority of aversive conditioning studies using electric shock as the UCS have little of empirical relevance to say about whether signaling the shock either reduces the painfulness of the shock or minimizes the physical injury it might cause. However, Macphail (1982: 62) has speculated that signaling electric shock in aversive conditioning studies with fish may allow these subjects to adopt an orientation to the electrodes in the tank which minimizes the amount of current transmitted through the fish's body.

Nevertheless, signaled shock may provide some "psychological" if not "physiological" benefit. Indeed, when given the inimical choice, animals prefer signaled to unsignaled shock presentations (Badia, Culbertson, and Harsh, 1973; Lockard, 1963). In these studies of preference for signaled shock, it has been recorded that rats make small postural adjustments during the CS which, although not changing the net amount of subsequent electric current flowing through the animal, do alter the current density that the animal experiences (Marlin, Berk, and Miller, 1978). Nevertheless, even when rats are prohibited from making these postural adjustments they still prefer signaled shock (Miller, Daniel, and Berk, 1974), and paradoxically — when a titration procedure is used — rats rate a signaled intermediate intensity tail-shock as being significantly *more* aversive than unsignaled intermediate intensity shock (cf. Miller and Balaz, 1981). So, even though they choose signaled over unsignaled shock, they find the former more aversive. A resolution of the "preference for signaled shock" phenomenon is difficult to find at present, although the laboratory situation in which it has been studied has obvious artificialities which might hide its adaptive significance. In a less contrained situation all other things being equal, escape or avoidance of an aversive event may be better effected if it is signaled than if it is not signaled. Thus, there may be a preprogramed evolutionarily determined tendency to prefer one's aversive events signaled. Unfortunately, in laboratory studies of the phenomenon — where the shock *cannot* be avoided — the experienced UCS is rated as *more* aversive if it is signaled. This, too, might have an adaptive significance: if signaled shock is perceived as more intense than unsignaled shock, it is likely to generate greater conditioning in fewer trials with any subsequent benefit that learning can bestow.

Nevertheless, all this begs the question being asked in this section: do we have evidence that signaled aversive events bestow a defensive advantage on the animal? As yet there is very little experimental evidence in which the value to inclusive fitness (or some relevant currency) of having aversive events signaled has been assessed. We can make some intuitive guesses about what the outcome of such studies might be, and why — but at the moment these are still only guesses.

What this section has attempted to do is assess whether Pavlovian conditioning possesses any generalized biological function. This can be done by assessing its value to inclusive fitness in terms of appropriate currencies such as maximizing net energy intake, optimizing mating opportunities, defeating intruders, and avoiding predators. There appears to be *no* firm evidence which suggests that Pavlovian conditioning does *not* benefit the animal in terms of one of these currencies, but equally the solid evidence in favor of the benefits of Pavlovian learning *estimated in terms of appropriate currencies* is sketchy. For instance, it is one thing to say that pairing a Pavlovian CS with food will insure a greater subsequent food consumption, it is quite another to say that that Pavlovian learning will result in a greater net rate of energy intake. The latter is the more legitimate currency in which to assess the value of a behavioral process to inclusive fitness.

3 *Summary*

This section has considered two ways in which Pavlovian conditioning might possess a generalized biological function. The prefiguring hypothesis of Hollis (1982, 1984a) suggests that Pavlovian conditioning might enable the animal to optimize interaction with a forthcoming biologically important event — regardless of which functional system that event is related to. The optimal time allocation hypothesis suggests that Pavlovian conditioning might serve a rather general information-gathering purpose. To this extent Pavlovian learning would be seen to enable the animal to allocate its time more efficiently both within and between different biological functions. For instance, if an animal has learned that food is available only during the presence of certain signals, then it can specifically allocate time when the signal is *not* present to other functions, such as defending a territory, being alert to predators, and so on. Being able to allocate its time optimally between different biological functions would be an important general contributor to an animal's inclusive fitness. Both the prefiguring hypothesis and the generalized information-gathering hypothesis suggest that Pavlovian learning contributes to an animal's inclusive fitness in rather different ways, but as yet we still lack studies which have investigated the different predictions that these hypotheses raise.

There is one final issue that needs to be raised in relation to Pavlovian conditioning as a generalized adaptive process whose biological function is measured in terms of a nonspecific contribution to inclusive fitness. This revolves around the question of how such a general adaptive process might have been selected for during an organism's evolutionary progress.

It seems clear that learning or flexibility of behavior cannot be isolated as some abstracted quality or attribute that can be selected for: it has to be associated with specific behavioral traits (cf. Plotkin, 1983). Selection takes place at the level of specific behavioral outcomes, not on the basis of some non-functional assessment of the utility of the process itself. This makes it much more likely that any Pavlovian process that proves to be adaptive would be selected for in relation to a specific biological function, such as adaptability in mating, adaptability in feeding, or adaptability in defense, and so on.

This raises the question of whether Pavlovian conditioning could ever have been selected for *as a generalized adaptive process*; it seems more likely that it would have been selected for as an adaptive aid to a particular behavioral repertoire serving a particular biological function, such as feeding. There is nothing, of course, to suggest that Pavlovian learning might not have been independently selected for several times during a species' evolution in order to serve several biological functions. If this were the case, then the underlying mechanisms which mediate Pavlovian conditioning in different biological systems need not be the same: it is the outcome that is selected for, not the means to that outcome. This would imply that details of the associative processes in one biological systems might be different from those in another (in some systems conditioned responding might be mediated by higher-level cognitive CS–UCS associations, while in other systems simple reflexive S–R learning may have been selected for). We shall discuss this possibility later in this chapter. Finally, one way in which a generalized functional view of Pavlovian conditioning might be salvaged from this discussion is by suggesting that Pavlovian conditioning was selected for in one biological system and was then transferred across functions as an adaptive process suitable to other systems (that is, it contained "ecologically surplus abilities," cf. Johnston, 1985, and p. 13 in this volume).

This would imply that details of the associative mechanisms which mediate Pavlovian conditioning should be the same across many biological functions. It might also imply that, because Pavlovian conditioning has become a learning process available to all biological functions, there might be occasions where Pavlovian conditioning proves to be detrimental to a particular biological function for which it was not originally selected, and the organism may subsequently have evolved safeguards against this counterproductivity.

Pavlovian conditioning as specific adaptations to individual biological functions

There are a number of instances where Pavlovian conditioning can be seen to benefit an animal, either (1) in a very specific kind of way (that is, in terms of helping the organism to deal with a problem which is either peculiar to that species, or peculiar to that species' ecological niche), or (2) in a fashion whereby the Pavlovian learning possesses characteristics which differentiate it from Pavlovian learning in other conditions or biological functions. Both of these types of examples lend some support to the contention that Pavlovian conditioning does not have a generalized biological function, but has evolved independently many times over in order to serve different functions in different circumstances. Before we discuss the logic of this proposal in more detail, let us examine some examples.

1 Taste aversion learning

In 1966 Garcia and Koelling discovered a phenomenon now known as taste aversion learning (TAL). They found that rats would readily associate the taste of a novel food with subsequent poisoning, but would rarely associate other audio-visual cues with toxicity. In their study they exposed rats to what they called a "bright-noisy" water solution — a saccharin-flavored solution associated with loud noises and flashing lights. Subsequently rats were given either sickness-inducing X rays or foot shock. They found that rats given X rays formed an aversion only to the taste cue, while those given the foot shock avoided only the loud noises and light. This has been replicated many times and has provided the basis for a substantial literature on TAL (cf. Domjan and Wilson, 1972; Miller and Domjan, 1981; Domjan, 1980; Rozin and Kalat, 1971; Kalat, 1985). What is also theoretically intriguing about TAL is that rats will associate taste with poisoning when the two events are separated by intervals of up to twenty-four hours (Garcia, Ervin, and Koelling, 1966; Smith and Roll, 1967; Etscorn and Stephens, 1973).

On the face of it TAL seemed to violate two laws of Pavlovian conditioning: (1) the *law of equipotentiality* of stimuli — all stimuli should be equally capable of being used as conditioned stimuli and subsequently able to enter into association with any UCS, and (2) the *law of contiguity* — animals should associate together only stimuli which are temporally contiguous.

TAL has been reported in many species other than rodents, such as quail (Wilcoxon, Dragoin, and Kral, 1971), blue jays (Brower, 1969), catfish (Little, 1977), bats (Terk and Green, 1980), cows (Zahorik and Houpt, 1977), coyotes

(Gustavson, 1977; Gustavson, Garcia, Hankins, and Rusiniak, 1974) and even in a terrestrial mollusk, the slug (Gelperin, 1975). Nevertheless, species that tend to select their food on the basis of visual rather than olfactory features are known to learn aversions to the color or other physical features of the food. Such examples include monkeys (Johnson, Beaton, and Hall, 1975; Gorry and Ober, 1970) and visually-feeding species of birds (Capretta, 1961; Wilcoxon, Dragoin, and Kral, 1969; Martin and Bellingham, 1979; Martin, Bellingham, and Storlien, 1977).

Clearly, what this plethora of evidence suggests is that animals have a predisposition to associate toxicity with those features of a food which they experience when foraging: rats use taste and olfactory cues to sample novel foods, while many species of birds grind their food after ingestion and select it on the basis of visual characteristics. These are the features of a food which will become associated with subsequent toxicity, and this can happen after long delays between sampling the food and subsequent poisoning.

The fact that TAL appeared to violate the laws of equipotentiality of stimuli and temporal contiguity originally led a number of theorists to suggest that TAL was a specific adaptation which had evolved to enable organisms —especially omnivorous foragers — to cope with the urgent problem of avoiding novel foods which might be toxic (e.g. Garcia and Ervin, 1968; Garcia, McGowan, and Green, 1972; Garcia, Hawkins, and Rusiniak, 1974; Seligman, 1970). Indeed, rats appear to have an innate tendency to sample just a small portion of a novel foodstuff and then wait for several hours before eating either more of the food or a different one (Rozin, 1969) — a strategy well-suited to long-delay learning. In the extreme version of this "special learning mechanism" account of TAL, Garcia, Hawkins, and Rusiniak (1974) have suggested that the rat has two basic but independent associative systems; one to learn about events in its external environment and one to learn about events in its internal environment: in effect, the former insures that taste becomes associated with poisoning only after long delays, and the latter insures that exteroceptive stimuli become associated with external aversive events when only short delays intervene.

In order to assess whether TAL is a specific adaptation which has evolved independently of the Pavlovian learning which serves other biological functions, there are two questions we might suitably ask at this stage. First, is TAL the optimally efficient method of avoiding toxins; and second, can the apparent violations of basic associative rules by TAL be interpreted in Pavlovian terms *without* having to postulate a separately-evolved learning mechanism?

First, why should omnivorous foragers such as the rat have developed a specialized food-aversion learning system when it can be argued that there are other, psychologically less complicated, methods of avoiding toxins? For instance, the vast majority of poisons actually taste bad (Richter, 1950; Kalat, 1985). Similarly, most human infants display an aversion to foods containing unpalatable toxic substances (such as alcohol and tobacco) when they are first exposed to these substances (Rozin, Gruss, and Berk, 1979). So why not just evolve the capacity to avoid bad-tasting foods?

The answer appears to be that TAL represents only one aspect of gustatory learning — the avoidance of toxins. The same learning mechanism also appears to take part in the learning of food preferences and the selection of balanced, nutritive diets. For instance, if thiamine-deficient rats are fed a flavored solution and are then injected with thiamine, the subjects will subsequently exhibit an increased preference for that flavor (Campbell, 1969; Zahorik and Maier, 1969). Thus, it could be argued that the mechanism which mediates TAL also "plays a major role in the animal's selection of foods as well as its avoidance of poisons" (Kalat, 1977: 83); it might be argued that the learning mechanism evolved to enable selection of suitable balanced diets but has since been adapted to help cope with the avoidance of toxins. The evidence on this point is difficult to assess. For instance, Rozin (1967) has demonstrated that what appear to be food preferences are in fact really the animal learning to avoid the alternatives. That is, they "learn" what foods are safe and nutritive by a process of elimination (cf. Kalat, 1985). As Kalat (1985) points out, we will only know whether animals learn food preferences directly by designing experiments that show they prefer a particular taste over other "safe" tastes. There does appear to be a smattering of support for this possibility (e.g. Zahorik, 1977; Revusky, 1974; Woods, Vasselli, and Milam, 1977). Meanwhile, it seems rather out of character with the optimizing penchant of evolutionary selection that an organism should develop a mechanism devoted solely to learning about the toxicity of foodstuffs, especially when it already possesses defenses such as neophobia and the tendency to avoid the bad or bitter tastes which normally accompany toxins.

This line of reasoning argues — either rightly or wrongly — that there is insufficient reason to evolve a learning mechanism devoted solely to learning about the toxicity of foods: the rat, as one example, already has pre-wired tendencies which help to minimize consumption of toxins. As an alternative, TAL may be only one feature of a more widely utilized mechanism for determining food preferences, or, more radically, it may simply be another learning phenomenon which — when examined closely — can be subsumed under the mantle of a generalized nonspecific Pavlovian learning mechanism. This latter possibility is worth exploring.

The two features of TAL which set it aside from other kinds of Pavlovian conditioning are (1) that rats have a strong tendency to associate taste rather than any other cue with toxicity, and (2) that they appear to be able to do this over longer CS–UCS intervals than is possible in conventional Pavlovian conditioning. An interesting experiment by Krane and Wagner (1975) addressed these two anomalies. They trained rats to drink from a tube with each lick producing a light–sound cue, contact with a saccharin-flavored solution, or no explicit cue. After drinking had ceased, the tube was made inaccessible and the subject was presented with a brief electric shock (UCS) either 5, 30 or 210 sec after withdrawal of the drinking tube (CS). When they subsequently allowed the rats further access to the drinking tube they found that subjects given the light-tone cue showed significant suppression of drinking when the CS–UCS interval was 5 sec but not when it was 210 sec. However, rats given the saccharin-flavored CS showed no avoidance of drinking at the 5 sec CS–UCS interval, but substantial suppression of drinking at the longer 210 sec CS–UCS interval.

What these results suggest is that taste *can* become associated with shock —but only when long delays intervene between drinking and the subsequent shock. This, Krane and Wagner claimed, was evidence that taste could become associated with any event as long as a reasonably lengthy delay intervened. Because of the intrinsic delay between taste and sickness in TAL, this meant that taste was the cue that unavoidably became associated with toxicosis. However, this still begs the question of why taste should enter into association with consequences only after a long delay. Krane and Wagner (1975: 887) claim that memories of audio-visual stimuli decay more rapidly than taste memories. Taste does not become associated with shock at brief CS–UCS intervals because the "trace" of the flavor is experienced both before and *after* shock presentation when the CS–UCS interval is only 5 sec, and it is well known that stimuli that are present *after* aversive stimuli offset act as "safety" signals and do not acquire aversive properties (e.g. Denny, 1971).

At first glance the Krane and Wagner experiment appears to provide important grist to the generalized learning theorists' mill, but it begs a number of important questions. Why, for instance, should one assume that "memories" of taste decay less quickly than memories of audio-visual stimuli? One might allude to the lingering "after-taste" left by flavored solutions, but there is plenty of evidence to suggest that peripheral after-tastes are not present at the time of sickness (cf. Revusky and Garcia, 1970; Rozin and Kalat, 1971). What is more, it has subsequently been demonstrated that long-delay learning *can* occur with audio-visual CSs when interference effects during the CS–UCS interval are minimized (e.g. Lett, 1973, 1979; Lieberman,

McIntosh, and Thomas, 1979; Sullivan, 1979). This suggests that audio-visual cues can be associated with long-delay UCSs, but this rarely happens when the UCS is toxicity. Another oddity which does not mesh well with the Krane and Wagner explanation is that animals only seem to develop food aversions when the food is actually ingested or swallowed (e.g. Domjan and Wilson, 1972; Palmerino, Rusiniak, and Garcia, 1980). This might not seem so surprising in a species such as the rat which subsequently learns to avoid the poisoned food by taste, but birds such as quail and pigeons will form strong aversions to *visual* food cues only when the food has been paired with a taste cue and ingested (Lett, 1980; Westbrook, Clarke, and Provost, 1980). This assumes that the birds first learn about the taste of a food in order to learn about the visual characteristics of the food in order to associate the latter with toxicity. Why not just associate the taste with toxicity? Well, perhaps there are good ecological reasons for quail and pigeons not associating taste alone with poisoning, since visual and taste characteristics are likely to be readily associated in a visual feeder. However, it does imply that the associative processes involved in poison avoidance are probably more involved than those sketched out by Krane and Wagner.

This all makes the problem look rather difficult to unravel. However, there are two other approaches that one can take in attempting to determine if TAL is simply a manifestation of a generalized learning process or a specialized adaptation. First, one could attempt to show that TAL is a selective association which results from perfectly normal processes which affect the interaction between CS and UCS. Or one could attempt to show that the apparent anomalies associated with TAL can be demonstrated quite readily in non-gustatory learning. Evidence on either score would support the notion that TAL was a specific manifestation of generalized learning processes.

Interactions between CS and UCS

There has been a certain amount of suggestion in the conditioning literature that the nature of the UCS will determine the nature of orienting reactions to the CS, and hence determine which aspects of the CS will be attended to and will subsequently enter into association with the UCS (e.g. Gillette, Martin, and Bellingham, 1980; Rescorla and Holland, 1976; Lolordo, 1979). In TAL, for instance, gastric poisoning as a UCS may in some way direct attention to oral elements of the CS, while an exteroceptive UCS such as foot shock may direct attention to audio-visual aspects of the CS. Nevertheless, the evidence for differential attention resulting from UCS-type in TAL is weak. For instance, Miller and Domjan (1981) equated subjects for differential orientations to shock and illness UCSs by giving equal exposure to shock and poisoning. They presented shock and poisoning to the same animals on successive days, but had only one of the UCSs paired with a CS. Nevertheless, aversions to a light CS occurred only in subjects which had this followed by foot shock, and taste aversion developed in subjects which only had the CS followed by poisoning. This result could not be accounted for in terms of differential CS-directed attention determined by UCS-type.

A second possibility in this context concerns the similarity between CS and UCS. It has been demonstrated on numerous occasions that conditioning to a CS will be much stronger if that CS shares characteristics in common with the UCS (Testa, 1974, 1975; Testa and Ternes, 1977; Rescorla and Gillan, 1980). Thus, taste and toxicosis could be considered similar in that they start slowly, persist for a long time, and end slowly. In contrast, exteroceptive audio-visual cues and aversive UCSs such as electric shock are usually brief, and begin and end abruptly. There is some indirect evidence to suggest that similarity in the temporal-intensity characteristics of taste and illness does facilitate conditioning. For instance, Goudie and Dickins (1978) found that TAL was facilitated if the duration and intensity of the CS was relatively similar to the duration and intensity of the subsequent illness UCS. There is little further evidence available to substantiate whether TAL does result from stimulus similarity effects at present. But since stimulus similarity effects are well substantiated in other conditioning paradigms, and it has been shown that such effects result from the facilitation of associative rather than generalization or sensitization processes (cf. Testa, 1975; Rescorla and Furrow, 1977; Rescorla and Gillan, 1980; Domjan, 1983), such an appraisal is worth considering further as a possible explanation of TAL.

TAL phenomena in non-gustatory learning

What is clear from the TAL literature is that taste is not the *only* stimulus feature that can become associated with toxicosis. There is substantial evidence that visual cues can become associated with toxicosis in visual feeders (see above) — and this may not be surprising. However, olfactory feeders such as rats can also learn to associate visual, spatial, or tactile cues with subsequent poisoning, given appropriate conditioning procedures (e.g. Morrison and Collyer, 1974; Galef and Dalrymple, 1981; Krane, 1980; Domjan and Hanlon, 1982), which strongly suggests that gastric illness as a UCS is not solely conditionable to a taste CS alone. What this might lead one to suspect is that there is something peculiar about the TAL conditioning procedure that selects taste to become associated with poisoning and only after long delays. If it is a peculiarity of the conditioning procedure, then under appropriate conditions we should be able to obtain stimulus selectivity and long-delay learning in other non-gustatory preparations.

What is interesting about TAL is that rats will sample a small portion of a novel food and then wait for any consequences before sampling either more of the same or a different foodstuff. This, of course, minimizes interference from competing taste/olfactory stimuli during the CS–UCS interval. Revusky (1971, 1977) has argued that a CS_A will become associated with a subsequent UCS to the extent that CS_A does not become associated with other events that follow it and the subsequent UCS does not become associated with other events that precede it. This explains long-delay TAL by stressing that in the delay between sampling a novel food and subsequent illness, the subject is likely to experience various other exteroceptive audio-visual stimuli but not other tastes. In support of this assertion, Revusky (1971) has shown that TAL can be substantially disrupted if a novel flavor is presented to the animal during the CS–UCS interval. Further support for this *concurrent interference* account of TAL comes from studies which have minimized interference during the CS–UCS interval in non-gustatory learning. Lett (1973, 1974), for instance, found that rats learned a spatial discrimination task in a T-maze with delays of up to 8 min between response and reinforcement when interference effects were minimized by removing the subject from the maze during the delay interval.

Lieberman, McIntosh, and Thomas (1979) provide a different account of long-delay learning in non-gustatory paradigms. They suggest that long-delay learning can occur quite readily if the event to be remembered is *marked* by a salient or unexpected stimulus. They discovered that long-delay learning could be found if the correct response in a T-maze was marked either by the subject being immediately picked out of the maze and handled or presented with a burst of noise or a flash of light. Domjan (1983) has suggested that the marking hypothesis of Lieberman, McIntosh, and Thomas (1979) could provide an explanation of TAL: the ingestive behavior and its accompanying sensations such as approach, mouthing, licking or masticating, and swallowing the food may serve to make that event salient and enhance its memorability. This possibility is further strengthened by two facts. First, robust TAL over long CS–UCS intervals only appears to occur when the food is swallowed (Domjan and Wilson, 1972; Palmerino, Rusiniak, and Garcia, 1980) — presumably such an activity enhances its saliency by facilitating after-tastes and oral digestive activities. Second, flavored substances used in TAL studies are usually novel to the animal — a factor sure to enhance their memorability.

Another unusual aspect of gustatory learning which originally appeared to be peculiar to TAL was *potentiation*. The presence of a novel-tasting foodstuff was found to facilitate conditioned aversion to associated odor cues in rats (Rusiniak, Hankins, Garcia, and Brett 1979; Spear and Kucharski, 1984), visual stimuli in pigeons and quail (Lett, 1980; Clarke, Westbrook and Irwin, 1979), and visual stimuli in rats (Galef and Osborne, 1978). This was odd, because in normal conditioning involving a compound CS, learning about one element (for example, taste) usually interferes with or overshadows learning about other elements (such as the visual aspects) (e.g. Kamin, 1969; cf. Mackintosh, 1974: 46). From an adaptive point of view, potentiation is a useful process in learning to avoid poisons because it enables the animal to avoid the poisoned food on the basis of olfactory or visual cues without having to consume or taste the food on subsequent encounters (cf. Domjan, 1983: 260). However, the potentiation-overshadowing dichotomy is not one which reflects a gustatory–non-gustatory learning dichotomy. Potentiation effects have subsequently been found outside of the feeding system in fear conditioning in rats (Pearce, Nicholas, and Dickinson, 1981), autoshaping in the pigeon (Rescorla, 1981), and rabbit nictitating membrane conditioning (Kehoe, Gibbs, Garcia, and Gormezano, 1979); and overshadowing has been demonstrated in TAL (Bouton, Jones, McPhillips, and Schwartzentruber, 1986). Neither phenomenon is unique to a particular preparation but appears to depend on procedural variables (cf. Domjan, 1983: 262–3).

Summary

The evidence presented above suggests a number of conclusions: (1) most of the phenomena once believed to be unique to TAL and distinguishing it as a separate learning process have since been demonstrated in non-gustatory learning (for example, long-delay learning, potentiation); (2) animals can generally associate gastric poisoning with features of food other than taste, given appropriate learning conditions; and (3) processes such as CS–UCS similarity effects, concurrent interference, and "marking" — which are all readily found in non-gustatory learning — can help to explain why in TAL it is taste that is associated with poisoning over relatively long intervals. Clearly, in TAL all of these factors may have combined to produce an optimally effective method of avoiding toxic foodstuffs, but such an explanation does not necessitate the postulation of a separately evolved learning mechanism.

2 Search image formation

There will obviously be occasions when rapid detection of a particular prey type is advantageous to a predator. First, there may be occasions when profitable prey (in terms of their contribution to net energy intake) are abundant enough to make capture of less profitable prey positively unprofitable (see Chapter 8); and second, if the predator can reduce the recognition time associated with profitable and unprofitable prey it will reduce the effort wasted in pursuing unprofitable prey before they are recognized as such. The phenomenon of *search image formation* appears to be one which benefits the predator in these kinds of situations (cf. Tinbergen, 1960; Dawkins, 1971), and reflects a change in the predator's ability to detect hidden prey resulting from previous experience with that prey type. Indeed, all of the evidence suggests that predators can forage more efficiently for one hidden prey type than for two (e.g. Pietrewicz and Kamil, 1979; Alcock, 1973), suggesting that, all other things being equal, attuning to one particular prey type is an optimal strategy.

The formation of a search image appears to take place by a process of learning about the characteristics and relative density and profitability of different prey types. However, there are at least two types of explanation based on associative processes. First, search image formation might be considered a perceptual change in that it represents a change in selective attention to profitable and unprofitable prey. If this were the case, predators would not only take less time to recognize and respond to the profitable prey to which they had formed a "search image," but they would also take *longer* to recognize unprofitable prey. Unfortunately, the evidence here is equivocal (Dawkins, 1971; cf. Kamil and Yoerg, 1982). However, while there is no evidence that the formation of a search image to profitable prey results in longer recognition times to unprofitable prey, there is ample evidence that a search image does reduce the latency to respond to a profitable prey and increases the probability of choosing that prey over other types of hidden prey (Alcock, 1973; Pietrewicz and Kamil, 1979).

Hollis (1982) considers that this resembles Pavlovian discrimination learning in which the characteristics of a profitable or abundant prey (CS^+) come to be distinguished from the characteristics of less profitable or less abundant prey (CS^-). When this learning has proceeded sufficiently, the CS^+ comes to elicit approach and consummatory behavior in the same way that many appetitive Pavlovian CSs do (such as in autoshaping). Although this notion is appealing, there are two facts which need to be emphasized: (1) not all Pavlovian CS^+s elicit approach and contact behavior — this depends on whether the CS itself possesses characteristics which inherently release approach responses (see Chapter 5); and (2) the characteristics of a less profitable or less abundant prey are, strictly speaking, not a CS^-, since those characteristics still signal an (albeit less profitable) edible prey. The characteristics of profitable and less profitable prey both signal reinforcers —but reinforcers of different magnitudes.

It is well known from the conditioning literature that if two stimuli signaling different magnitudes of reinforcement are presented independently and consecutively, both will still elicit CRs but CR strength will be proportional to reinforcer magnitude (e.g. Catania, 1963; cf. Mackintosh, 1974; see also Catania, 1966; Neuringer, 1967). However, it is also true that given a straight choice between stimuli which signal different reinforcer magnitudes, animals will opt for the one signaling the greater magnitude (Hill and Spear, 1963; Davenport, 1962; Clayton, 1964). When foraging for food in the wild, it is not clear that predators are faced with a straight concurrent choice, or whether they chance upon different prey sequentially. Where different prey types are abundant the animal may well be faced with what is the equivalent of a concurrent choice task, and select profitable prey while ignoring less profitable prey. Consistent with this implication of a Pavlovian interpretation is that the more abundant prey of all types are, the more similar the situation is to a concurrent choice, and the more likely animals should be to select the profitable prey at the expense of ignoring the less profitable. This implication has been supported in a study by Krebs, Erichsen, Webber, and Charnov (1977). They found that when large and small prey were presented to great tits (*Parus major*) on a moving belt, the birds were unselective when both prey were at a low density, but highly selective when the density of either large or small prey was increased. However, the implication that the more abundant different prey types are, the more the situation resembles a concurrent choice needs more direct empirical investigation.

Rather differently, Royama (1970) has suggested that predators do not necessarily learn to process the specific characteristics of the prey as a CS^+, but associate different environmental cues with different prey territories or prey profitability. Different types of prey are likely to be found in different types of areas and be signaled by different types of stimuli. So, differing kinds of insects may be signaled by the leaves or needles of trees, or different colored fungi on dead logs. It is quite clear that animals such as birds can discriminate different prey densities and profitability on the basis of the arbitrary stimuli which signal them (e.g. Smith and Sweatman, 1974; see Chapter 8), and it might be this kind of learning that accounted for Tinbergen's original observations on "search image formation" that individual birds often brought prey back to the nest in runs of the same prey type.

The obvious benefits of search image formation are (1) it reduces prey recognition time, and (2) it reduces the tendency to choose unprofitable prey in a multi-prey environment. Nevertheless, there are still a number of questions being begged here. First, does a prey have to be profitable before a search image of it is formed? If not, in situations where predators are forced to select less or nonprofitable prey for a period of time, forming a search image of that prey could result in the predator selecting the less profitable prey when subsequently given a choice of prey of differing profitability. However, whatever the possible biological anomalies that may arise with search image formation, it is quite likely that Pavlovian associative processes are involved somewhere. These may involve the specific features of the prey being associated with its relative profitability, or environmental features being associated with relative prey type or prey density.

3 *Food recognition and ingestion*

It is now fairly clear that many species have to learn to associate nutritional factors with appropriate species-specific feeding behaviors. For instance, experience appears to play an important role in the development of the relationship between nutritional factors and prey catching in cats (Baerends-van Roon and Baerends, 1979), hoarding in rodents and birds (Hinde, 1970; Sherry, 1985), biting and chewing in guinea pigs (Reisbick, 1973), and pecking in chickens (Hogan, 1973, 1984; Hogan-Warburg and Hogan, 1981). This association appears to proceed through a process of Pavlovian learning.

For instance, Hogan proposed that, on hatching

a chick has a functioning hunger or feeding system and a functioning pecking system, but that these two systems are functionally independent ... at hatching, there is no input from the hunger system to the pecking system. Only after appropriate experiences (of pecking followed by ingestion) do factors that control the hunger system become additional controlling factors for pecking.

(1984: 362)

This hypothesis yields four predictions: (1) pecking followed by ingestion of any object, nutritive or non-nutritive, should be sufficient for an association between hunger and pecking to be formed; (2) ingestion without pecking should not lead to such an association; (3) pecking without ingestion should not lead to such an association; and (4) when a chick has learned that pecking leads to ingestion, any factor which influences the hunger system should affect pecking. Hogan's (1984) experiments supported all of these implications with the additional proviso that appropriate pecking and ingestive experiences must occur about day 3 post hatching, or just after (cf. Hogan, 1973).

Hollis (1982) also reviews much of the evidence concerning the role of Pavlovian conditioning in food recognition processes and in the development of species-specific food-procuring behaviors. Much of the evidence in birds suggests that, while immediate post-hatching food-procuring behaviors rely very much on neurologically pre-organized reflexes (such as gaping or pecking the parent's bill), the parents eventually concentrate the hatchling's attention on the association between particular foodstuffs and nutrition. They do this either by regurgitating grain and seeds in response to the young pecking their bill (e.g. Lehrman, 1955), or by pecking at food on the ground (Sherry, 1977; Suboski, 1984; Suboski and Bartashunas, 1984).

What is perhaps most surprising about these data on feeding and nutrition is that behaviors that we might intuitively or traditionally have believed were intrinsically part of the feeding system are not so. Pecking in chicks appears to be associated with feeding only after appropriate experience, and this experience appears to involve Pavlovian associative learning. One might ask why many species do not appear to have evolved hunger systems in which the feeding behavior is not already pre-wired. There are probably many reasons for this. In particular, Hogan (1984) and Hall and Williams (1983) have pointed out that in all animals, through insects, fish, birds, and mammals, the method of providing nutrition changes between the embryo and the adult. Pavlovian conditioning appears to play two roles: (1) in aiding the transition from embryo to the adult feeding stages, and (2) in permitting a certain degree of flexibility in selection of food-procuring behaviors in the adult stage. If environmental factors change rather suddenly, requiring a species and its descendants to adopt a new feeding response to replace the traditional one, the Pavlovian process permits this flexibility. As Hogan (1984) points out, presumably we could attach hunger to ground scratching (or preening) instead of pecking in the chick if we prevented pecking from leading to ingestion and force-fed the chick every time it ground-scratched (or preened).

4 Aposematic coloration and avoidance learning

Prey species that are unpalatable tend to be brightly colored, and this phenomenon has come to be known as aposematic coloration (Cott, 1940, 1947; Edmunds, 1974). It is also known that predators (such as birds and some reptiles) actually associate the color of the prey with its taste (e.g. Brower, 1958; Coppinger, 1969; Morrell and Turner, 1970). In many senses it is a paradox that distasteful prey should evolve conspicuous coloration, since it obviously makes them less cryptic and more easily detectable. What is more, many prey that are not distasteful (such as the hover-fly) have also developed aposematic coloration so as to mimic the appearance of distasteful prey that share their environment. This deceit is known as *Batesian mimicry* (cf. Curio, 1976).

What we do know about aposematic coloration is that predators come to associate the conspicuous color of aposematic prey with their distastefulness through a process of classical conditioning (Gittleman, Harvey, and Greenwood, 1980; Roper and Wistow, 1986). Knowing this fact tells us something about why aposematic coloration and Batesian mimicry evolved in the first place. First, we know that the speed and strength of conditioning is a function of the saliency, discriminability, or intensity of the CS. Thus predators should learn more quickly to avoid aposematic colored prey than hidden or less discriminable prey. The evidence shows that, not only does avoidance learning proceed faster to conspicuous prey, but that the subsequent asymptotic levels of avoidance are higher when the prey is conspicuous than when it is hidden (Roper and Wistow, 1986). This is a situation in which knowledge of the processes of Pavlovian conditioning can help an understanding of the biological function of some seemingly paradoxical adaptations (cf. Hollis, 1984a). Many vertebrates utilize Pavlovian conditioning to distinguish palatable from distasteful prey, and thus some prey species have evolved characteristics (such as aposematic coloration) which insures that this learning occurs rapidly and efficiently.

This example does not illustrate a specific biological function of Pavlovian conditioning as such, since the survival of an aposematic prey depends on the predator, not the prey itself, evolving the characteristics of Pavlovian learning processes. However, it does indicate how the biological function of some adaptations cannot be understood unless we have a full understanding of all the processes which contribute to Pavlovian conditioning.

Specific adaptations or generalized biological function?

Since we can never have direct access to the evolution of psychological and behavioral processes, we must infer from the behavior of contemporary species how and why these processes might have evolved. There are a number of questions in this respect surrounding Pavlovian conditioning. What is its biological function? Did it evolve as a single multipurpose adaptive process, or did it evolve independently many times over to serve different biological functions? The answers to these questions are still sketchy, as will be clear from what has preceded. However, it might be possible to make some general statements about Pavlovian processes and their possible biological functions.

First, there are many ways in which Pavlovian conditioning can be conceived of as a useful adaptive aid to the survival of individual animals, and much of the evidence on this has been considered above. However, there is little or no evidence on how or whether Pavlovian conditioning increases inclusive fitness, and this is the only legitimate way in which the biological *function* of an adaptive process can be assessed. We still await the appropriate studies on this.

Second, it might be inferred that Pavlovian processes evolved independently to serve different biological functions if (1) Pavlovian conditioning possesses different dynamic or associative characteristics in different preparations or systems, and (2) if the associative or performance mechanisms underlying Pavlovian conditioning differ across preparations and response systems. There is no firm evidence to support the first of these two possibilities. It was traditionally felt that the associative and performance anomalies discovered in the "constraints on learning" literature of the 1970s (cf. Davey, 1981, ch. 5; Shettleworth, 1972a) might reflect different underlying mechanisms and hence the independent evolution of Pavlovian processes to serve different functions. However, in the last fifteen years, evidence has suggested that these anomalies can be accounted for within a generalized learning theory framework (cf. Domjan, 1983; Revusky, 1985). Associative oddities once thought to be specific to a particular response or learning system (such as TAL) have since been detected across other systems and may reflect procedural rather than adaptive constraints.

However, strong evidence for the evolution of separate Pavlovian mechanisms would be provided by information suggesting different associative mechanisms in different response systems. Since we now have suitable inferential techniques for detailing the characteristics of such mechanisms (see Chapter 4), and a burgeoning in the understanding of the neural bases of simple associations, collecting this evidence is a distinct reality. Consider the possibility that a particular CR is shown to be mediated by a mechanism which generates S–R rather than S–S learning — that is, the CR is generated by associations formed between the CS (or its internal representation) and the neural centers controlling the response system itself. Such a learning mechanism must have evolved to serve that particular response system and its particular biological function, and could not be easily generalized or adapted to serve other response systems and their biological functions, because the response system itself is an integral part of the associative mechanism. There is evidence that such S–R mechanisms exist in neurologically less complex species such as the sea slug, aplysia (Hawkins and Kandel, 1984; Quinn, 1984), and in some Pavlovian preparations such as the nictitating membrane response in rabbits (e.g. Moore, 1979). From the point of view of collecting strong evidence on differences in Pavlovian conditioning across species and biological functions, it would seem eminently more sensible to attempt to describe the associative mechanisms involved (either inferentially or neurologically) than to catalog similarities or anomalies in the dynamics of the various conditioning processes, as occurred during the 1970s.

From another point of view, we might ask a question which was posed at the outset of this chapter. Does Pavlovian conditioning serve *no* biological function, but exist as an accidental concatenation of other processes? First, it must be stated that the answer is most probably that it *does* serve either one or many biological functions — it would be absurd to believe that a phenomenon as ubiquitous as Pavlovian learning does not. However, if it did not serve a biological function, what kinds of evidence might lead us to suspect this? Studies might subsequently show that Pavlovian learning does not increase inclusive fitness, or we may demonstrate situations where the learning of a Pavlovian CR is positively counter-productive. For instance, the Pavlovian CR in some preparations may simply represent a behavioral "false start" (but see Chapter 5), and this false start may be detrimental in that it might fatigue or exhaust the animal before it encounters the UCS, or it may increase the threshold for response triggering on future occasions when the response would be more appropriate. These are the kinds of evidence we should look for if we wished to argue from the negative rather than positive side of the story.

Finally, general process theorists have argued that Pavlovian conditioning represents a generalized information-seeking process that has been utilized across most biological functions. Revusky (1985), for instance, has argued that learning can be considered as a general biological process in much the same way as mammalian respiration — the means may differ from species to species, but the ultimate goal is the same: the function of mammalian respiration is to take oxygen from the air, exchange it for waste products in the lungs, and distribute it through the circulatory system; the function of learning, such theorists argue, is to allow causal inferences and predictions to be made about the future which allow the animal to adapt in nearly all biological environments. Such a generalized approach, however, begs many questions about how such a process was selected for in the first place (see pp. 181–2).

Nevertheless, one implication of a generalized process approach to the function of Pavlovian conditioning is that it would surely generate occasions when such learning is inappropriate or maladaptive. Revusky (1977, 1985) has argued that there are many such situations that can be catalogued which are not simply anomalies generated by unnatural laboratory contingencies.

For instance, sensory preconditioning (see Chapter 4) has no obvious biological value when it occurs in TAL but it still, nevertheless, occurs (Reiss and Wagner, 1972; Taukulis and Revusky, 1975; Revusky, 1977). Similarly, the conditioned immune reactions that protect animals against sickness can produce harmful allergies and cancers, and aversive conditioning can also produce maladaptive and inappropriate fear reactions such as incapacitating phobias and specific fears (e.g. Eysenck and Kelley, 1986). Clearly, the fact that a conditioning process is either useless or maladaptive when it occurs in one particular biological function but remains biologically useful in another, does provide evidence for the existence of some generalization across functions.

Conclusion

At present, there are a plethora of mainly insubstantiated hypotheses on the role and biological function of Pavlovian conditioning. I will add some further speculations which I hope are not too outrageous, and are soundly based on the evidence presented in this chapter. First, the biological function of a behavioral process can best be ascertained when its effect on inclusive fitness, or some appropriate currency, has been assessed. In the case of Pavlovian conditioning this remains to be done.

Second, biological function, whether generalized or specific, needs to be considered in relation to how the process may have evolved. If one wishes to propose that Pavlovian conditioning is a generalized adaptive process, one would also have to explain how a generalized process which is not specific to any particular biological function could have been selected for.

Third, Pavlovian conditioning may be a generalized process which was selected for to serve one function but has been adapted to serve all other biological functions. If this were the case we would expect to find anomalies where Pavlovian conditioning is maladaptive or simply useless — there does appear to be a smattering of evidence that these anomalies exist.

Fourth, if evidence is found that associative mechanisms differ in different Pavlovian preparations, either within or between species, then this is good evidence that they evolved independently, possibly to serve different functions. We still await clearer inferential and neurobiological evidence on the nature of associative mechanisms in a range of differing species and Pavlovian preparations, but the initial evidence suggests that at least some response systems may utilize S–R associative processes while others utilize more centrally represented S–S relationships.

Chapter summary

1 If such a wide range of living species possess Pavlovian learning abilities, then it is reasonable to assume that it evolved to serve some biological function.

2 Pavlovian conditioning may have evolved a *generalized function* (e.g. to enable the animal to reduce the unpredictability of its environment) or a *specific function* which aids the animal only with certain biological functions.

3 The *optimal time allocation hypothesis* suggests that, since Pavlovian CSs act to signal biologically important events, Pavlovian conditioning enables the animal to allocate its time efficiently between various biological functions. The way in which animals process the relationship between CSs and UCSs suggests that they do this optimally and with minimum redundancy.

4 *The prefiguring hypothesis* suggests that the biological function of Pavlovian conditioning is to enable the animal to optimize interaction with the forthcoming biologically important event (the UCS). Much of the available evidence suggests that animals which do have biologically important events signaled (by Pavlovian CSs) are at a biological advantage to animals which do not have these events signaled.

5 There are some instances where Pavlovian learning in one biological function possesses characteristics which differentiate it from Pavlovian learning in other functions. *Prima facie*, this lends some support to the possibility that Pavlovian learning may have evolved separately to serve different biological functions.

6 One example of the above is *taste aversion learning*. Originally, the dynamics of this kind of Pavlovian learning were thought to be quite different from other kinds of Pavlovian learning. However, much of the contemporary evidence on taste aversion learning does not require the postulation of a separately evolved learning mechanism.

7 *Search image formation* allows the animal to recognize profitable prey rapidly, and many of the features of this learning appear to reflect a special kind of Pavlovian learning.

8 Many species have to learn to associate nutritional factors with appropriate species-specific feeding behaviors, and Pavlovian learning appears to serve this particular developmental function.

9 Many prey species that are unpalatable tend to be brightly colored (*aposematic coloration*), and many palatable prey species have mimicked this (known as *Batesian mimicry*). It is not obvious why palatable prey should make themselves so noticeable until one considers the dynamics of Pavlovian conditioning. That is, a predator will learn to avoid a brightly colored prey

more quickly than a hidden prey. This example shows how the biological function of some adaptations (such as Batesian mimicry) cannot be understood unless we have a full understanding of Pavlovian conditioning processes.

10 General process theorists have argued that Pavlovian conditioning represents a generalized information-seeking process that has been utilized by most biological functions. Evidence that Pavlovian conditioning has generalized to serve more biological functions than the one it was originally selected for is provided by the fact that on a number of occasions Pavlovian conditioning generates learning which is either inappropriate or useless. This suggests a generalized rather than specific function for such learning.

Chapter seven

Instrumental conditioning: learning mechanisms, performance, and function

Traditionally, instrumental or operant reinforcement has been considered to be the process by which the majority of an organism's "meaningful" behavior is generated (cf. Skinner, 1938; Blackman, 1974). The importance of instrumental learning to the animal psychologist arises from a couple of factors. First, instrumental learning as championed by B. F. Skinner provided a suitable atheoretical means of describing learning phenomena in terms of behavior–environment interactions. Second, from an adaptive point of view, if an animal failed to learn about the consequences of its actions then it would surely be at an extreme disadvantage — most organisms are in some way sensitive to the consequences of their actions, although this of course does not necessarily mean that they *learn* about the consequences of those actions. Learning to adapt to the consequences of its actions is therefore a useful psychological tool for an animal that lives in a changing and unpredictable environment.

Nevertheless, there are many plausible ways in which an animal may go about adapting to the consequences of its behavior without having to learn that a particular action is followed by a particular environmental consequence (R–S learning); and, indeed, some theroretical accounts of instrumental learning have attempted to subsume this kind of learning under the auspices of other associative learning mechanisms such as Pavlovian conditioning (cf. Bindra, 1974; Moore, 1973). This chapter will attempt to describe some contemporary theories of instrumental learning and discuss how instrumental learning mechanisms might be influenced by ecological determinants. Clear evidence accrued in the 1970s that certain types of responses in various species were not amenable to instrumental reinforcement (cf. Shettleworth, 1972a; Hinde and Stevenson-Hinde, 1973), and this suggested that even instrumental learning may be affected by biological and ecological constraints deriving from an organism's niche and lifestyle.

Whether these constraints directly influence associative mechanisms (e.g. Lolordo, 1979; Seligman, 1970) or whether they act at the level of instrumental performance (e.g. Breland and Breland, 1961, 1966; Boakes, Poli, Lockwood, and Goodall, 1978) is still an important issue in learning theory, but this will only be resolved when a better understanding of the mechanisms underlying instrumental learning is achieved.

A Cognitive approaches to instrumental learning: Pavlovian interpretations of instrumental learning

It is worth here just briefly considering some of the better-known failures of instrumental reinforcement that appeared in the constraints on learning literature of the 1960s and 1970s. Just as perceptual illusions tell us a good deal about the normal functions of the perceptual systems, then those instances where learning fails also give important insights into the workings of learning mechanisms.

For example, in a series of studies Breland and Breland (1961, 1966) found that there were certain conditions in which instrumental conditioning failed to work. In one study a hungry pig was reinforced with food for approaching a piggy-bank and dropping a coin from its mouth into the piggy-bank. However, after a period of training when the pig appeared to be learning the response quite adequately, the topography of the pig's behavior suddenly began to drift away from that which was suitable to depositing the coin in the the piggy-bank — the pig began to root the coin around and toss it in the air rather than place it directly into the slot of the piggy-bank. Even when the pig was made more hungry by increasing the deprivation level, the rooting and tossing of the coin persisted, with the result that receipt of the food reinforcer was delayed even longer. Such a reaction was clearly maladaptive if the animal wished to maximize reinforcement procurement.

In a second study, Breland and Breland attempted to teach raccoons to pick up coins and deposit them in a piggy-bank. Just as in the study with the pig, this behavior developed well, using instrumental reinforcement, until suddenly the behavior began to break up and the raccoons spent long periods rubbing the coins together and dipping them into the piggy-bank without letting go.

Breland and Breland (1966) labeled these phenomena "*misbehavior*" and attributed them to a process of *instinctive drift*. In both cases the "rooting and tossing" behavior of the pigs and the "dipping and rubbing" behavior of the raccoons are species-typical food-related behavior. In some way these "instinctive" behaviors had "drifted" into the learning process and disrupted

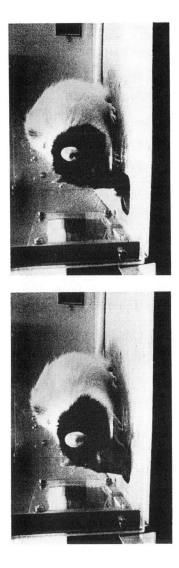
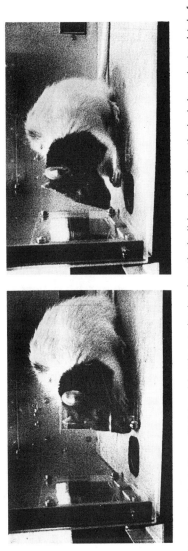

Figure 7.1 "Misbehavior in the rat": this subject is required to drop the ball-bearing down the hole in order to obtain food but usually fails to let the bearing drop and frequently retrieves it as it is about to fall down the hole. The rat spends much of its time pawing, mouthing and licking the bearing. (Photograph courtesy of R. A. Boakes)

execution of the required instrumental response.

Boakes, Poli, Lockwood, and Goodall (1978) have also recorded this kind of misbehavior in rats who were trained to press a lever to obtain a ball bearing and then deposit the ball bearing into a small hole to obtain food. Eventually, all subjects spent long periods chewing, pawing, and licking the ball bearing and preventing it from falling down the hole to deliver food (see Figure 7.1). This ritualistic misbehavior delayed food delivery for long periods, and was clearly contrary to that which was required by the instrumental contingency. Yet again, however, the so-called "misbehavior" *was* appropriate to the normal feeding habits of rats: hungry rats frequently spend their time handling and investigating any small object in their environment — whether those objects be food or not (cf. Barnett, 1956).

There are two ways in which these examples of misbehavior can be conceived. Either they represent the disruption of instrumental responses by competing species-typical behaviors which have been elicited by some aspect of the conditioning situation; or they suggest that our conception of the instrumental learning mechanism as one which simply permits any arbitrary response to become associated with a subsequent reinforcer is wrong. Some theorists have taken this latter view, and suggested that instrumental responding is in fact generated by the learning of stimulus-reinforcer rather than response–reinforcer associations. Such theorists claim that considering instrumental learning in these terms accounts for anomalies provided by misbehavior and some of the other well-documented constraints on learning (cf. Boakes, 1979; Mackintosh, 1983).

1 *Incentive motivation*

Incentive motivation theory was first proposed by Hull (1952) and Spence (1951, 1956) but has recently been elaborated in slightly adapted form by Bindra (1972, 1974). This account states that stimuli which are spatially or temporally associated with reward acquire *incentive motivation* — a property which energizes ongoing behavior. Bindra (1972, 1974) has argued that incentive stimuli (stimuli which have become paired with reinforcement delivery) serve two important functions in generating and directing behavior: (1) they motivate the animal by activating a generalized central motivational state, and (2) they elicit orienting responses in such a way that the animal's behavior is directed toward them. In this account, a hungry rat would learn to press a lever to obtain food in the following way: on the first few occasions the rat accidentally presses the lever, the rat experiences a close-up view of the lever immediately followed by food. Since all food deliveries are contingent upon the rat pressing the lever, food will always be preceded by a close-up view of the lever. Thus, the lever will become an incentive stimulus (in Bindra's account, an incentive stimulus is functionally equivalent to a Pavlovian CS), and subsequently the lever will induce an appropriate energizing motivational state and — because it is an incentive stimulus — the rat's behavior will be directed toward it. Thus "the principle of contingency learning between stimuli (which is conceptually derived from the classical conditioning paradigm) is sufficient for explaining learned behavioral modifications; the principle of response reinforcement is unnecessary" (Bindra, 1974: 207).

This account does have in its favor the fact that it addresses many of the anomalies in the constraints on learning literature. For instance, in the case of misbehavior, this account would stress that aspects of the conditioning situation *other than* where the instrumental response is to be made have acquired incentive value. In the case of the Brelands' pig and raccoons, the coins presumably became established as incentive stimuli and the subjects directed all behavior toward them. Incentive theory also accounts for all instances of CS-directed behavior such as autoshaping, and predicts that CS-directed behavior should be fairly resistant to modification by an omission contingency. If the CS is the only aspect of the conditioning environment reliably paired with food, then animals should still approach and contact the CS even when an instrumental omission contingency is applied. This certainly appears to be the case (e.g. Williams and Williams, 1969; Schwartz and Williams, 1972a), and where an omission contingency has been shown to reduce contact with a CS substantially, pigeon subjects still direct their behavior toward the CS either by pre-key-pecking (e.g. Lucas, 1975) or by marginally off-key-pecking (e.g. Barrera, 1974) (however, see Davey, Oakley, and Cleland, 1981).

Incentive motivation also takes good account of the effects stemming from the interaction between differing motivational states. For instance, when an aversive CS is superimposed on behavior maintained by appetitive reinforcement, this causes a suppression in the rate of appetitively motivated behavior (conditioned suppression, see p. 26; cf. Davey, 1981, ch. 4; Blackman, 1972), and conversely when an aversive CS is superimposed over behavior maintained by avoidance responding, that responding is frequently facilitated (e.g. Rescorla, 1967a; Sidman, Herrnstein, and Conrad, 1957). However, symmetrical effects are not necessarily found if an appetitive CS is superimposed on instrumentally-maintained responding. When an appetitive CS is presented during responding maintained by food reinforcement, that responding is frequently suppressed (positive conditioned suppression; Azrin and Hake, 1969; Miczek and Grossman, 1971; J. B. Smith, 1974).

A simple account of these phenomena which alludes to the additive effects of compatible motivational states and the competing effects of incompatible motivational states (e.g. Konorski, 1967; see also pp. 209–14) would predict enhancement of responding when an appetitive CS is superimposed over a baseline of appetitively-motivated instrumental responding. However, experiments by Lolordo (1971), Lolordo, McMillan, and Riley (1974), and Karpicke, Christoph, Peterson, and Hearst (1977) have demonstrated that positive conditioned suppression occurs only if the superimposed appetitive CS is localizable and positioned some distance from the instrumental manipulandum. The suppression of instrumental behavior during presentation of the superimposed CS results from the animal leaving the instrumental manipulandum to approach and contact the CS (Karpicke, Christoph, Peterson, and Hearst, 1977). Since Bindra states that all appetitive CSs elicit approach and contact behavior, then his incentive motivation theory can account for the apparent motivational anomaly of positive conditioned suppression.

Incentive motivation theory also attempts to account for aversively maintained instrumental responding (for example, avoidance or escape learning) by postulating that stimuli associated with aversive UCSs elicit withdrawal reactions. In a unidirectional alleyway which a rat must traverse to avoid shock, the avoidance response would be facilitated if the warning CS is placed in the start box (so that the avoidance response requires the animal to run away from it) and would be learned very slowly if the warning CS was placed in the goal-box (so that the rat had to run *toward* it). This prediction is supported by the experimental evidence available: rats do take significantly longer to learn the avoidance response if it involves approach to the warning signal (Bolles and Grossen, 1970; Katzev, 1967). The fact that it is very difficult in any situation to condition any avoidance response which does not involve withdrawal, running away, or removal of stimuli associated with the aversive UCS is also consistent with Bindra's theory (cf. Bolles, 1970).

2 *Pavlovian conditioning*

Attempts have also been made to interpret instrumental conditioning in more traditional Pavlovian terms. Moore (1973) has suggested that, in the pigeon as one example, instrumental responding can be considered as a Pavlovian process in which the animal learns that certain aspects of the environment (such as the pecking key) come to be associated with the reinforcer. This aspect of the environment becomes a Pavlovian CS eliciting UCS-like consummatory behavior directed toward that CS. Moore accounts for instrumental response shaping via successive approximations (cf. Davey, 1981: 40) by suggesting that it is a Pavlovian rather than a response-reinforcer association that is being strengthened during this procedure. Moore says that

> autoshaped birds, too, tend first to begin to face the key, then to begin to approach it, then to peck toward it and so forth. Apparently, successive approximations to key pecking can arise through the mere strengthening of a Pavlovian association between the key and grain.

> (Moore, 1973: 176)

So, this approach emphasizes two factors: (1) instrumental learning progresses as a function of stimulus-reinforcer associations, and (2) the nature of the reinforcer will to some extent determine the topography of the instrumental response (because the response is basically a Pavlovian CR).

There is some evidence consistent with these premises. First, the nature of the instrumental response does appear to be influenced in various ways by the nature of the reinforcer. For instance, instrumental key pecking in pigeons has been found to resemble the peck topography for feeding (R. F. Smith, 1967), and avoidance key pecking in pigeons is frequently accompanied by the full-blown aggressive responses normally elicited by shock (Rachlin, 1969); the duration of instrumental lever-presses in rats is determined by whether the reinforcer is a solid pellet or a liquid food (Hull, 1977); and, when the instrumental response closely resembles the reinforcer-consummatory behavior, the response will persist even when the reinforcement schedule is changed from a response-contingent to a response-independent one (Lowe and Harzem, 1977). Second, if the reinforcer-elicited behavior is incompatible with the required instrumental response, conditioning frequently fails. For instance, Shettleworth (1973, 1975) found that the frequency of face washing, scratching, and scent marking in hungry hamsters was affected little by an instrumental food contingency, whereas digging, rearing, and scrabbling rapidly increased in frequency if they produced food. Shettleworth suggests that digging, rearing, and scrabbling are all behaviors exhibited by hungry hamsters in anticipation of food, whereas face washing, scratching, and scent marking are not elicited by food. Similarly, Sevenster (1968) observed that when sticklebacks were reinforced for either rod biting or swimming through a ring in order to court a female, it was far easier to reinforce the latter response. This appears to be related to the fact that, in the stickleback, the behavior elicited by courting involves swimming in a zig-zag fashion. Thus, instead of biting the rod, many of the subjects would perform the courtship display elicited by the female and simply swim round the rod. Third, if approaching and contacting the CS is contrary to the required instrumental response, the instrumental contingency frequently fails to have effect. This is evident from studies where an omission contingency is imposed on auto-shaped responding — animals will still contact the CS even though doing so prevents food delivery (Williams and Williams, 1969; Schwartz and Williams, 1972a).

3 *Problems with Pavlovian accounts of instrumental learning*

On the face of it, these various Pavlovian accounts of instrumental conditioning look pretty enticing — if only because they appear to predict accurately those occasions when instrumental conditioning should fail. However, there are a number of grounds for doubting that a Pavlovian interpretation solely in terms of the learning of stimulus–reinforcer relationships is an adequate explanation of instrumental conditioning. First, this account implies that animals learn nothing about their particular actions and how they relate to reinforcers. We know that some animals can accurately discriminate their own behavior (e.g. Beninger, Kendall, and Vanderwolf, 1974), and since an instrumental response will always be temporally contiguous with reinforcer delivery, why shouldn't animals associate their behavior with the reinforcer in just the same way that they will associate a temporally contiguous environmental stimulus with reinforcement? To adapt to the consequences of one's actions by learning about external stimulus–reinforcer contingencies seems a fairly makeshift way of going about it — especially when this means that the process will fail if certain constraints are not met. However, what is perhaps more important in this context is that there are instances of instrumental learning which a straightforward Pavlovian interpretation has a great deal of trouble explaining.

First of all, the Pavlovian account requires that instrumental learning can occur only if there is some localizable aspect of the environment which becomes established as a Pavlovian CS, and that the animal can direct its behavior toward: that is, the only responses that can be learned are those which are directed toward some part of the environment, and which usually require manipulation of that part of the environment. This is clearly untrue. Instrumental responses which can be successfully reinforced and are nondirected are wheel running in rats (Bernheim and Williams, 1967; Bolles, Stokes, and Younger, 1966; Mackintosh and Dickinson, 1979), leg flexion in the restrained dog (Konorski, 1948; Wahlsten and Cole, 1972), and "head bobbing" in the pigeon (Jenkins, 1977). What is more, subtle aspects of a CS-directed response can be altered by instrumental contingencies without altering either the nature of the reinforcer or the general CS-directed orientation of the response. Davey, Oakley, and Cleland (1981) generated autoshaped lever-contact behavior in rats using a retractable-lever CS and a food UCS. When an omission contingency was imposed on CS-contact behaviors sufficiently forceful to record a lever press (but not on CS-contact behaviors which did *not* result in a lever press), the topography of CS-contact behaviors changed from pawing and biting to sniffing, mouthing, and nosing. It is difficult to see how these subtle changes in topography could result from a Pavlovian process which stresses that the topography of instrumental responses can only be changed by manipulating the nature of the reinforcer or the stimuli that the animal has associated with the reinforcer (see also Atnip, 1977).

One final prediction from this Pavlovian account of instrumental conditioning is that instrumental responses should be accompanied by other responses indicating reinforcer anticipation. There is substantial evidence, however, that emission of instrumental responses is quite independent of indicators of UCS anticipation. For instance, Williams (1965) trained dogs to press a panel for food on either a fixed-interval or a fixed-ratio schedule, and he recorded both rates of panel pressing and rates of salivation at different times during the inter-reinforcement interval. Although there was a good correlation between the probability of salivation and the probability of panel pressing on the fixed-interval schedule, on the fixed-ratio schedule panel pressing was initiated well before there were any signs of anticipatory salivation. Similarly, in avoidance learning there appears to be a very poor correlation between performance of the avoidance response and other indicators of UCS-anticipatory fear (Mineka, 1979; Starr and Mineka, 1977; Kamin, Brimer, and Black, 1963). Clearly, instrumental responses can occur at times when the organism is not exhibiting other signs of reinforcer anticipation and, presumably, in the presence of external or temporal cues which do not possess the predictive qualities necessary to become established as Pavlovian CSs.

Interactions between Pavlovian and instrumental learning

Some early theories of instrumental conditioning suggested that, although instrumental conditioning could not be accounted for solely by Pavlovian processes, Pavlovian stimuli could influence the rate and strength of instrumental responding (e.g. Rescorla and Solomon, 1967; Konorski, 1967). This implied that, regardless of how instrumental responses were mediated, this process could be infiltrated by Pavlovian contingencies; therefore, an understanding of how instrumental and Pavlovian processes interact should throw some light on the nature of the underlying instrumental mechanism.

Early interactionist accounts tended to stress that Pavlovian CSs had their effect on instrumental responding by influencing the strength of hedonistic or motivational variables. For instance, superimposing an aversive Pavlovian CS during ongoing instrumental avoidance responding can increase the rate of avoidance responding (Rescorla and Lolordo, 1965; Bull and Overmier, 1968; Grossen and Bolles, 1968; Martin and Reiss, 1969; Overmier, 1968), and an aversive CS will even elicit avoidance responses previously conditioned to other stimuli (Solomon and Turner, 1962). Conversely, applying an appetitive CS during appetitive instrumental performance has also been reported to increase response rate (Lolordo, McMillan, and Riley, 1974; Henton and Brady, 1970; Meltzer and Hamm, 1974, 1978; but see pp. 205–6). Furthermore, presenting a Pavlovian CS from an antagonistic motivational system to the one maintaining instrumental responding usually suppresses responding (e.g. Bull, 1970; Bull and Overmier, 1969; Davies and Kreuter, 1972; Blackman, 1972; Millenson and de Villiers, 1972). Despite a few contradictory results (e.g. Azrin and Hake, 1969; Baum and Gleitman, 1967; Hyde, 1969; Blackman, 1968; Pomerleau, 1970; Karpicke, Christoph, Peterson, and Hearst, 1977, the majority of this literature can be interpreted in such a way as to suggest that Pavlovian CSs or instrumental discriminative stimuli (S^Ds) elicit a motivational state appropriate to the reinforcer and that this motivational state in some way mediates the emission of the instrumental response. Thus, when stimuli which elicit identical motivational states are compounded, this will result in stronger mediation of any instrumental behaviors controlled by that motivational state.

Nevertheless, there are many specific ways in which this mediation could occur (cf. Boakes, 1979), and simply alluding to the mediation of instrumental responses by intervening motivational states does not provide any particularly new insights into instrumental learning mechanisms. For instance, can we be more specific about the nature of the mediating state and the associations which link it to antecedent stimuli and the subsequent instrumental response? During a transfer experiment, a Pavlovian CS is paired with a UCS before it is superimposed on the baseline of instrumental responding. Because of this sequence of events it may be that during the initial Pavlovian learning phase, the animal learns superstitious responses which subsequently are either compatible or incompatible with the instrumental response, thus producing either facilitation or suppression of responding. This is highly unlikely, since Pavlovian instrumental interactions are still observed when the Pavlovian pretraining is conducted with the animal physically restrained and in an apparatus distinctively different from that in which the instrumental training was carried out, thus minimizing the similarity between the S^Ds controlling superstitious operants and the S^Ds controlling the instrumental response (Bull, 1970; Bull and Overmier, 1969; Overmier and Payne, 1971; Overmier and Starkman, 1974).

However, we may wish to clarify the effects of motivational transfer by ascertaining the nature of the associative links connecting stimuli, responses, and mediational states. Historically, two views of these interactions have been propounded. Mowrer (1939, 1947), Trapold and Overmier (1972), and Overmier and Lawry (1979) have proposed a *serial* associative sequence, such that stimuli evoke the mediator, and the mediator evokes the response in a serial chain (that is, S–M–R), whereas others such as Hull (1931), Konorski (1967), and Spence (1956) have proposed *parallel* associative sequences in which direct stimulus-response (S–R) associations are established parallel to a mediating S–R–R sequence (*i.e.* $S \overset{M}{\underset{}{\diagup \diagdown}} R$). In both cases, the transfer of control experiments where Pavlovian CSs are superimposed on instrumental baselines have their effect via a mediator (M). The serial chain account suggests that a superimposed appetitive Pavlovian CS will facilitate appetitive instrumental responding by evoking the same mediator which also generates the instrumental response; according to the parallel view, the Pavlovian CS facilitates responding by a route independent to that which generates the instrumental response.

One method of assessing the validity of the serial vs. parallel approach is to attempt to demonstrate that in the stimulus–mediator–response (S–M–R) possibility, the S–M and M–R links are relatively independent. That is, it is possible to break one of the links and leave the other intact. In a fairly complex experimental study, Overmier and Brackbill (1977) attempted to show that the S–M link was unaffected by destruction of the M–R link. There were four phases in this study: (1) dogs were given free-operant avoidance training in a shuttlebox; (2) they were subsequently trained on a discrete-trial discriminative avoidance task in which they had to press a panel with their noses during a distinctive tone S^D in order to avoid shock; (3) for experimental subjects, the panel-pressing avoidance response was extinguished by presenting unsignaled, response-independent shocks; and (4) in this stage, the tone S^D conditioned in stage (2) was presented during shuttlebox avoidance performance established in stage (1). The results from stage (4) showed that shuttlebox avoidance performance was indeed facilitated during presentation of the tone S^D. These data strongly suggested that eliminating an avoidance response to a particular S^D did not impair the ability of that S^D to modulate performance of a different avoidance response.

Thus, the S–M link appears to remain, even following elimination of the M–R link. Furthermore, because the S–M link appeared to be intact following this procedure, and yet the S^D could not evoke the avoidance response in stage (3), the conclusion is that there is unlikely to be a direct S–R link which parallels the S–M–R link (cf. Overmier and Lawry, 1979).

In a parallel study to that outlined above, Overmier and Bull (1969) attempted to demonstrate that the S–M link could be broken without affecting the strength of the M–R link. In their experiment, (1) dogs were first trained on a discrete-trial shuttlebox avoidance task in the presence of a distinctive S^D; (2) following this, dogs were confined to a small chamber and the S^D was extinguished (that is, presented but never followed by shocks), and a new aversive CS conditioned by pairing this with shock; (3) finally, the dogs were replaced in the shuttlebox apparatus and presented with the new aversive CS and the previously extinguished S^D. The results indicated that in stage (3) the new aversive CS reliably evoked avoidance responses while the original S^D did not. Thus, the M–R link appears to remain even when the original S–M association is disrupted.

Having established that some kind of S–M–R process appears to be operating during instrumental learning and can be highlighted by Pavlovian-instrumental transfer experiments, let us now turn to a more detailed analysis of the nature of the mediator (M) itself.

1 *Mediation by motivational factors*

Traditionally the mediator has been considered to reflect some motivational or hedonistic state appropriate to the UCS or instrumental reinforcer. One example from aversive conditioning — whether Pavlovian or instrumental —is that this type of conditioning is considered to generate a hypothetical mediating state known simply as "fear" (e.g. Mowrer, 1939; Rescorla and Solomon, 1967). There are three implications of motivational accounts such as this: (1) qualitatively or quantitatively different UCSs or reinforcers relevant to the *same* motivational system (e.g. defense or "fear") will generate compatible mediating states; (2) UCSs or reinforcers relevant to *different* motivational systems (e.g. defense vs. feeding) will generate incompatible or different mediating states which will be mutually inhibitory; and (3) qualitatively or quantitatively different stimuli (CSs or S^Ds) which generate *similar* mediating states will interact to have an additive facilitatory effect on responding.

There is mounting evidence against all three of these implications. First, in homogeneous appetitive transfer studies, suppression is now reported as frequently as facilitation (see pp. 205–6) and in homogeneous aversive transfer studies it seems that facilitation or suppression can be obtained depending on the manipulation of various factors such as the duration of the CS, the intensity of the UCS, and whether the Pavlovian training is carried out either on or off the baseline of instrumental responding (e.g. Pomerleau, 1970; Bryant, 1972; Scobie, 1972, 1973). Second, response facilitation can be obtained when either an aversive or appetitive Pavlovian CS is superimposed on instrumental responding maintained by reinforcers relevant to a *different* motivational system (Overmier and Schwarzkopf, 1974; Overmier and Lawry, 1979). Third, appetitive CSs will enhance appetitive instrumental responding in transfer-of-control experiments only when the same type of reinforcer (for example, a food pellet) is used as the Pavlovian UCS and the instrumental reinforcer, but not when different reinforcers (such as food pellet vs. sucrose solution) are used (Kruse, Overmier, Konz, and Rokke, 1983; Baxter and Zamble, 1982).

2 *Mediation by specific reinforcer characteristics*

Both Trapold and Overmier (1972) and Overmier and Lawry (1979) have suggested that the factor mediating instrumental responding and thus implicated in Pavlovian-instrumental transfer-of-control studies is more directly related to the nature of the specific UCS or reinforcers used than more general motivational factors. Put more clearly, in instrumental studies the subject forms an internal representation of the outcome of responding (which, for instance, might encode features of the reinforcer), and it is this representation that mediates subsequent responding. Thus, when a Pavlovian CS is paired with a similar outcome or reinforcer, that CS will come to elicit the representation and facilitate instrumental responding.

There are three lines of evidence consistent with this kind of theory. First, in discriminative choice procedures where different instrumental responses are paired with different S^Ds, choice learning is substantially quicker and more efficient if the two responses produce discriminably different reinforcers. These may be food pellets vs. sucrose solution in appetitive choice, or different intensity shocks in aversive choice paradigms (Trapold, 1970; Brodigan and Peterson, 1976; Carlson, 1974; Overmier, Bull, and Trapold, 1971).

Second, when different mediators control *similar* responses, compounding the two stimuli actually facilitates responding. Overmier and Schwarzkopf (1974) conditioned dogs to jump a hurdle to avoid shock during a specific S^D. After avoidance discrimination was completed, the dogs were then shifted to jumping the hurdle to obtain food on a variable-interval schedule. Finally, on test trials, the aversive S^D was presented during appetitive hurdle jumping for food. They found that during these S^D presentations rate of hurdle jumping increased dramatically. While these results are clearly contrary to those predicted by a motivational mediation account, they are still consistent with an explanation which alludes to the mediation of instrumental responses by more specific representations of particular reinforcers. According to this latter account, hurdle jumping could be mediated by both a representation of the appetitive reinforcer *and* the representation of shock elicited by the aversive S^D. Thus, providing conditions under which both representations were jointly presented enhanced the response they both mediated (see also Overmier and Lawry, 1979).

Finally, presenting an appetitive Pavlovian CS during instrumental choice responding has been shown to facilitate only those choices which produce the same type of reinforcer as that conditioned to the CS (Kruse, Overmier, Konz, and Rokke, 1983; Baxter and Zamble, 1982).

3 *Summary*

Clearly, facilitation of instrumental performance in Pavlovian-instrumental transfer-of-control studies appears to occur only in situations where the Pavlovian UCS and the instrumental reinforcer are identical, or where the UCS and reinforcer are different but mediate identical responses. The implication of this for an understanding of the mechanisms underlying instrumental conditioning is that the instrumental response appears to be mediated by an internal representation of the outcome of that responding.

This conclusion leads to two further considerations. First, if the instrumental responding is mediated by representations of the characteristics of the reinforcer, then intervening directly to manipulate those characteristics should also influence instrumental responding. Second, what exactly does it mean in mechanistic terms to say that the response is mediated by an internal representation of the reinforcer? This implies that some sort of associative link has been established between centers controlling the reinforcer representation and the centers controlling emission of the instrumental response. But how is this association established when what occurs in reality is the exact opposite? The response is always followed by the reinforcer, not the reinforcer by the response! (See Dickinson, 1980, 1985, for discussion of "associationist" vs. "logical" theories of instrumental learning.)

Effects of reinforcer manipulation on instrumental responding

One obvious implication of the hypothesis that the instrumental response is mediated by reinforcer representations is that altering these representations, either by revaluing or restructuring them, should also affect instrumental responding, and what does appear to be clear from a reading of the relevant literature is that an animal undergoing instrumental conditioning certainly learns something about the nature of the reinforcer. Responding is not entirely independent of knowledge of the reinforcer as it would be if it were elicited solely by antecedent stimuli (or S–R associations) (cf. Davey, 1981: 226–7).

However, providing evidence that animals learn about the characteristics of an instrumental reinforcer is not the same as evidence that the instrumental response is actually mediated by this knowledge. Other studies have addressed this question more directly. In an extensive series of studies, Adams and Dickinson set out to discover under what conditions devaluation of a food reinforcer (by postconditioning pairing of the reinforcer with gastric poisoning, see pp. 116–17) would affect instrumental response rate (Adams, 1980, 1982; Adams and Dickinson, 1981a, b; Dickinson, Nicholas, and Adams, 1983). The procedure for this type of investigation involves first training the subject to make an instrumental response (for example, lever pressing) for food reinforcement (such as a sucrose pellet), and then subsequently devaluing the food by pairing it with gastric illness (taste aversion learning). Subjects are tested in three ways: (1) to see if lever pressing persists into an extinction period following devaluation; (2) by applying a consumption test to assess if the food really has become aversive; and (3) to see if the food has retained any residual response–reinforcing properties by determining if it can act to re-establish the original instrumental response. If representations of the food reinforcer were mediating the instrumental response then responding should be significantly suppressed following post-conditioning devaluation of the reinforcer.

Initially, these studies suggested that responding was suppressed by the devaluation of the reinforcer only after *moderate* amounts of training (that is, only after less than 100 massed reinforcements of the reinforced response). After extended instrumental training, the instrumental response appeared to be independent of the animals' current evaluation of the reinforcer: that is, the rats continued to respond even after the food reinforcer had been paired with illness and the animals refused to consume any more of the food (cf. Adams and Dickinson, 1981a).

These results suggest that during early training responding is mediated by the animals' evaluation of the goal or reinforcer, but with extended training, control of the response becomes independent of its original goal or outcome — the response appears to become a rather "reflexive habit" after extensive practice (e.g. Kimble and Perlmuter, 1970). However, subsequent experiments using the postconditioning revaluation technique in within-subjects designs and with added controls have indicated that, although there is some residual responding which does appear to be independent of the current status of the reinforcer, instrumental responding *does* remain sensitive to reinforcer devaluation even after extensive training. This suggests continued mediation by reinforcer representations (Colwill and Rescorla, 1985a, b).

Nevertheless it is interesting to note that although responding does appear to be modulated by the current status of the reinforcer, there is still some responding which is independent of it. If the conditioning literature is surveyed in detail there are a number of conditions under which instrumental responding tends to become detached from and autonomous of the goal. These are (1) after extensive training (Kimble and Perlmuter, 1970; Tolman, 1933); (2) following postconditioning satiation (cf. Morgan, 1974); (3) under conditions of severe deprivation (Bruce, 1935; Elliott, 1934; Tolman, 1948); and (4) after training on intermittent schedules (Capaldi and Myers, 1978; Chen and Amsel, 1980; Dickinson and Nicholas, 1983; Dickinson, Nicholas, and Adams, 1983).

Paradoxically, instrumental responding frequently persists even when "free-food" is made available in the conditioning chamber — a phenomenon known as "contrafreeloading" (Osborne, 1977); that is, rats ignore the adjacent free food and eat only the food they have worked for. These data suggest either that instrumental responding can be controlled concurrently by more than one factor (e.g. Colwill and Rescorla, 1985b), or that certain characteristics of the training procedures act to transfer control of the response from one set of factors (such as mediation by reinforcer representations) to another (such as control by antecedent stimuli, for example, S–R or associative links). Although we have solid evidence that instrumental responding can be mediated by reinforcer representations, we do not yet have a clear picture of how this control can be overridden in situations where this obviously occurs.

Associative aspects of reinforcer-mediated responding

There might be good evidence that instrumental responding is mediated by reinforcer representations, but this still begs the question of how such mediation is developed. The problem here is one that has been apparent since

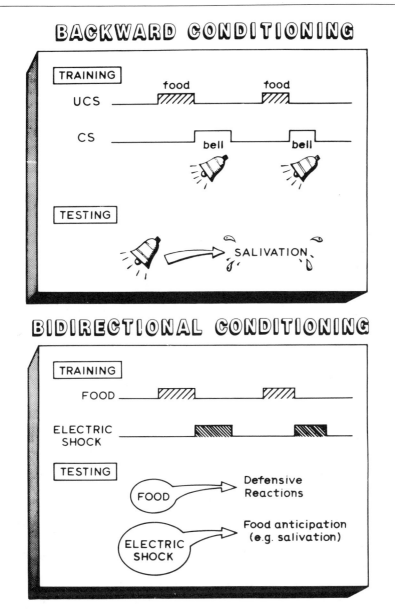

Figure 7.2 Schematic representation of backward conditioning and bidirectional conditioning procedures. See text for further explanation.

the time of Pavlov: how can an association develop between a reinforcer representation and an instrumental response when that relationship represents the reverse of what occurs in the environment? Traditionally there have been two approaches to this paradox. One is to appeal to processes of *backward conditioning*; the other is to appeal to the *bidirectionality of associations*.

1 *Backward conditioning*

Backward conditioning is the phenomenon whereby CRs develop when the CS actually *follows* the UCS (cf. Cautela, 1965; Razran, 1971; Spetch, Wilkie, and Pinel, 1981). The assumption is that a backward association between the CS and the preceding UCS mediates the appearance of a CR relevant to that UCS, and this notion can be used to explain reinforcer mediated instrumental responding in a similar way (see Figure 7.2). However, there has long been controversy over whether backward conditioning has been successfully demonstrated — many writers doubt its existence (e.g. Cautela, 1965; Mackintosh, 1974; Spooner and Kellogg, 1947).

To demonstrate backward conditioning it has to be shown that any detectable CRs are not the result of (1) either pseudoconditioning or sensitization, or (2) the forward pairings of the CS on one trial with the UCS presented on the following trial. Many early studies of backward conditioning did not employ controls sufficient to rule out these alternatives (cf. Mackintosh, 1974: 59). However, a number of more recent studies have been properly controlled and do indicate that backward conditioning can be unequivocally demonstrated. For instance, Keith-Lucas and Guttman (1975) presented rats with backward pairings of a toy hedgehog (CS) and electric shock (UCS), and after only a single backward UCS–CS pairing found significant CS-avoidance behavior in experimental subjects when compared with appropriate controls. Spetch, Wilkie, and Pinel (1981) reviewed these more recent controlled studies of backward conditioning, and concluded that a number of studies provided unequivocal evidence for the existence of backward conditioning (Wagner and Terry, 1975; Heth and Rescorla, 1973; Mahoney and Ayres, 1976; Burkhardt, 1980; Keith-Lucas and Guttman, 1975). These studies demonstrate that "a backward UCS–CS pairing produced a statistically significant change in behavior that resembled the effect of forward pairing of the same stimuli. Each study included control procedures that ruled out the possibility that the change in behavior was due to factors other than the backward pairings, such as pseudoconditioning or sensitization" (Spetch, Wilkie, and Pinel, 1981: 168).

However, there are a number of features which characterize these successful demonstrations of backward conditioning. First, conditioning can occur in a very small number of trials — even after just one backward UCS–CS pairing (e.g. Keith-Lucas and Guttman, 1975; Logue, 1979). Second, these successful demonstrations have all employed aversive UCSs such as electric shock or gastric illness. From an ecological point of view both of these characteristics make adaptive sense. An animal may be attacked by a hidden predator, thus experiencing the trauma of the attack before encountering features of the predator. If an animal should escape such an attack it would make adaptive sense to avoid future encounters with those predator features which were detected *following* the attack, and to learn to do so after as few pairings as possible. Thus, there is intuitively good reason to suppose that backward conditioning might exist, as well as empirical evidence in its favor.

Nevertheless, there appears to be little evidence that backward conditioning has been demonstrated in appetitive preparations. This may indicate one of two things: first, that backward conditioning is a learning specialization which has evolved to cope specifically with aversive encounters such as the one outlined above. Certainly, in appetitive conditioning it is difficult to conceive of many natural situations in which signals or correlates of such UCSs as food or mates would occur *after* rather than before the biological event associated with them. Second, it may be that we are not using the best methods available to detect backward associations. For instance, criteria for successful backward conditioning have varied between writers. Cautela (1965) suggests that the backward CS must elicit a CR appropriate to the UCS to demonstrate backward conditioning, and Spetch, Wilkie, and Pinel (1981) also imply that the CS should produce a change in behavior that resembles the effect of forward pairing of the same stimuli. These criteria might be far too strict, and rule out the possibility that backward conditioning might generate "behaviorally silent" associations (cf. Dickinson, 1980) which can only be detected indirectly. It would seem odd to suggest that animals do not detect the correlation between backward UCS–CS pairings, especially when they can learn forward pairings even when the two stimuli are not biologically important (sensory preconditioning).

Nevertheless, what we are interested in from the point of view of explaining the mechanism by which reinforcer representations generate instrumental responses is whether backward CSs do elicit internal representations of the preceding UCS. If they do, this would provide evidence that pairings of response and reinforcer in the instrumental situation could generate backward reinforcer–response associations. There are several ways in which behaviorally-silent backward associations might be detected. For instance, if the backward CS does elicit an internal representation of the UCS, then it should be able to act as a successful reinforcer for higher-order conditioning. Holland (1981) and Holland and Ross (1981) have already shown that CS-elicited reinforcer representations generated by forward conditioning can substitute for the events themselves during higher-order conditioning; it remains to be seen if the same results can be obtained with backward conditioning.

In summary, it may well be the case that backward conditioning does generate backward associations, but whether they are detected in behavioral changes would intuitively seem to depend on what use the animal can put this information to (that is, on performance factors). In backward aversive conditioning this information would need to be acted on rather quickly for the sake of survival, and thus the association would presumably be detected more readily than in appetitive backward conditioning studies.

Nevertheless, there is still one problem for a backward conditioning account of reinforcer-mediated responding. If a response-reinforcer relationship generates a backward association such that the reinforcer or reinforcer representation stimulates centers associated with the response — what is it that initially activates the reinforcer representation? There is an obvious possible answer to this — it could be that specific S^Ds or even contextual features of the conditioning environment become paired with reinforcement, and act as Pavlovian CSs which elicit the reinforcer representation (cf. Trapold and Overmier, 1972). This type of two-process interpretation, however, is not without its problems. How, for instance, could an animal learn to execute two entirely different responses in the presence of distinctively different S^Ds when the two responses produce the same type of reinforcer (cf. Friedman and Carlson, 1973; Peterson, Wheeler, and Armstrong, 1978; Trapold, 1970)? If both S^Ds evoke the same reinforcer representation, it is difficult to see how this single representation would differentially mediate different responses, even with the aid of backward conditioning. Clearly, as we have indicated in the previous section, there are still some good grounds for retaining the notion of simple S–R learning to account for certain phenomena which are not easily incorporated into reinforcer-mediated accounts of instrumental learning.

2 Bidirectional conditioning

Many of Pavlov's associates, and subsequently his students, have attempted to explain instrumental learning by appealing to the bidirectionality of associations (Pavlov, 1928, 1932; Beritov, 1924; Asratian, 1966, 1972).

Bidirectional conditioning hypothesis assumes that both forward and backward associations are formed in both Pavlovian and instrumental conditioning. In instrumental conditioning the pairing of response with reinforcer should generate associations from the cortical centers controlling the response to the reinforcer "centers" and *vice versa* (cf. Gormezano and Tait, 1976; Asratian, 1972). Thus, excitation of the reinforcer "center" will associatively stimulate the motor areas controlling the instrumental act. This approach is not greatly different from that which attempts to interpret reinforcer-mediated instrumental responding in terms of backward conditioning, and indeed, any evidence for backward conditioning can be taken as consistent with the existence of bidirectional associations (Mackintosh and Dickinson, 1979). Much of the research on bidirectional associations, however, has been carried out by pairing two UCSs (for example, UCS_1–UCS_2). If bidirectional associations exist, subsequently presenting UCS_1 should also elicit UCRs appropriate to UCS_2, and presenting UCS_2 should elicit UCRs typical of UCS_1. Support for bidirectional associations using this paradigm is sketchy, with much research being only anecdotally reported, poorly controlled, or providing, at best, only modest evidence for bidirectional associations (Asratian, 1952, 1965, 1972; Gormezano and Tait, 1976).

3 *Summary*

That backward associations represent the means by which reinforcer-mediated instrumental responding occurs cannot be ruled out. The actual available evidence on backward conditioning and bidirectionality of associations is at present scarce and in places flimsy — but it is clear that backward conditioning can be demonstrated, and it is also clear that investigators have not adopted the best methods available for detecting backward associations. They have attempted to rely on the traditional observation of CS-elicited CRs as indication of a backward association, a method which is constrained by performance factors and does not permit the possibility of behaviorally-silent associations.

One final piece of evidence regarding the possibility of response–reinforcer associations in instrumental learning concerns the rules by which an instrumental response will become associated with the reinforcer. Presumably, basic rules of association which apply to the formation of CS–UCS associations (such as blocking, overshadowing, predictive correlation and so on should also apply to response-reinforcer-associations. Studies which have directly approached this problem do report that the strength of an instrumental response varies in accordance with such predictions (Mackintosh and Dickinson, 1979; Pearce and Hall, 1979). It seems from results such as this that the direction is well signposted toward predictive models of both association and performance in instrumental learning — but there is still a long way to travel yet.

B The nature of the reinforcement process in instrumental learning

The preceding sections of this chapter have argued toward the conclusion that a majority of instrumental responding is mediated by conditioning-generated representations of the reinforcer or outcome of responding. However, there are still a number of other issues that need to be clarified. First, there are some instances where it is not entirely clear what the effective outcome of responding is (such as in avoidance responding, below). Second, where does the notion of reinforcer-mediated responding leave the traditional distinction between reinforcement and motivation? We will deal with these two issues separately.

Avoidance learning

In order to clarify the first of these two issues it is worth discussing the traditionally thorny problem of the reinforcers in avoidance of learning. How is it that the *absence* of an event (such as the avoiding of shock) comes to reinforce responding? "How can a shock which is *not* experienced, that is, which is avoided, be said to provide either a source of motivation or of satisfaction?" (Mowrer, 1947). The most durable explanation of this paradox has been two-factor theory (Miller, 1948; Mowrer, 1947),which accounts for the reinforcement of the avoidance response in terms of the reduction of a hypothetical state of "fear" which has been generated in Pavlovian fashion by environmental cues paired with shock. However, apart from the conceptual problems involved in dealing with a hypothetical motivation state (fear) which appears to have no obvious physiological correlates (McAllister and McAllister, 1971; Brady, Kelly, and Plumlee, 1969; Hineline, 1973), two-factor theory has difficulty coping with at least one important aspect of avoidance responding.

One problem with two-factor theory is that it does not specify why it is very difficult to generate certain kinds of avoidance behavior. For instance, there are numerous reports of failures to train rats to avoid shock efficiently by lever pressing in a Skinner-box (D'Amato and Schiff, 1964; Meyer, Cho, and Weseman, 1960; Smith, McFarland, and Taylor, 1961; Weissman, 1962) or of pigeons to avoid shock by pecking an illuminated key (Azrin, 1959; Hineline and Rachlin, 1969; Hoffman and Fleshler, 1959; Rachlin, 1969; Rachlin and Hineline, 1967). However, for other types of response, avoidance learning proceeds rapidly and efficiently. For instance, running an alleyway to avoid shock is learned very rapidly in as little as 6–7 trials (Theios, 1963); merely jumping out of a box may need as little as only one trial to establish robust avoidance behavior (Maatsch, 1959); shuttle-box avoidance learning may take around 100 trials for rats (Brush, 1966), while wheel running may be established as an efficient avoidance response in fewer than 40 trials (Bolles, Stokes, and Younger, 1966).

1 Species-specific defense reactions

Bolles (1970) has attempted to explain differences in the efficiency of avoidance responses by alluding to the organism's species-specific defense reactions (SSDRs). For instance,

> The mouse does not scamper away from the owl because it has learned to escape the painful claws of the enemy; it scampers away from anything happening in its environment, and it does so merely because it is a mouse. The gazelle does not flee from an approaching lion because it has been bitten by lions; it runs away from any large object that approaches it, and it does so because this is one of its species-specific defense reactions. Neither the mouse nor the gazelle can afford to *learn* to avoid: survival is too urgent, the opportunity to learn is limited, and the parameters of the situation make the necessary learning impossible. The animal which survives is one which comes into its environment with defensive reactions already a prominent part of its repertoire.
>
> (Bolles, 1970: 33)

Bolles suggested that to become an efficient avoidance response, (1) the avoidance response must be compatible with one of the organism's SSDRs, and (2) it must exert some change in the stimulus conditions in the environment and indicate "safety." Now, the rat is known to have a repertoire of defensive reactions called "fight, fright and flight." That is, when confronted with danger the rat will either run away, freeze, or adopt an aggressive strategy. It can be seen that avoidance responses which consist of one of these actions and which also produce environmental stimulus changes, are learned rapidly and effectively (for example, alleyway running and jumping out of a box). Responses which are compatible with an SSDR but do not produce immediate stimulus changes are learned less effectively (such as wheel running). Shuttle-box avoidance, where the rat is sometimes jumping back into a compartment where it has previously been shocked (that is, the response produces cues indicating danger rather than safety), is learned with some difficulty, while lever pressing, which is not obviously compatible with any of the rat's SSDRs, is the most difficult to learn. Indeed, when lever-press avoidance is learned, it often topographically resembles either freezing (Hoffman and Fleshler, 1962; Hoffman, Fleshler, and Chorny, 1961; Bolles, 1971) or aggressive biting (Pear, Moody, and Persinger, 1972).

The SSDR hypothesis would therefore suggest that instrumental avoidance learning is not simply the converse of appetitive instrumental learning, because the urgency of survival and the limited opportunities to learn avoidance responses successfully dictate that the animal should have evolved a slightly different strategy. This strategy involves employing innately-programed SSDRs when confronted by stimuli signaling danger, and unless the avoidance response utilized in the laboratory situation is compatible with these SSDRs it will not be learned.

However, ecologically appealing though the SSDR hypothesis seems, it still has a number of problems associated with it. First, it is clear that certain kinds of SSDRs cannot easily be learned as avoidance responses. Rats, for instance, do not easily learn to freeze to avoid shock (Bolles and Riley, 1973). Second, the SSDR hypothesis as outlined by Bolles is not particularly predictive. For example, what factors determine which of an organism's defense reactions will occur in which situation, and is there a hierarchy of defense reactions which dictates that certain SSDRs will be given precedence over others? Furthermore, as Riess (1971) has pointed out, if pseudo-aggressive responses involving rearing with forepaws extended are one of the rat's predominant SSDRs, then this behavior is tailor-made for lever pressing. Yet lever pressing is a poorly-learned avoidance response. Finally, despite its attempt to account for differences in the efficacy of avoidance learning between different responses, SSDR hypothesis still does not address the traditional problem of what reinforces the avoidance response when it is learned. For the answer to some of these questions it is worth turning to a behavior systems analysis of defensive behavior such as the one outlined in Chapter 5.

2 *Behavior systems and avoidance learning*

An alternative approach to explaining the anomalies in the efficacy of avoidance learning is to allude not to the incompatibility between SSDRs and the avoidance response but to differences in what might be the effective reinforcer for avoidance responding. Masterson and Crawford (1982) have modified the SSDR account of avoidance learning by adopting a behavior systems framework in which to structure avoidance behavior. This account has two important features: (1) the kind of SSDR elicited in an aversive conditioning procedure will depend on the availability of natural releasers or "supports" for modules of the species' defensive behavior system. For instance, an escape route will release modules of the "fleeing" sub-system (see Chapter 5, p. 167), and a confined, familiar space will release bradycardia and freezing; (2) the effective reinforcer for an avoidance behavior is not considered to be reduction of some hypothetical motivational state such as "fear," but the production by the response of the stimuli necessary to release or support innate defensive reactions. Thus, an effective reinforcer for avoidance responding is not UCS avoidance directly, but the ability to indulge in a defense reaction brought about by the production of the appropriate releasing stimulus. In support of this line of argument, Masterson (1970) and Crawford and Masterson (1978) were able to obtain rapid and efficient lever-pressing avoidance in rats when that response provided the opportunity to flee to a different compartment: when the direct or indirect outcome of the response is to produce a releaser for an SSDR such as fleeing, successful avoidance learning occurs.

However, even with this approach, the question remains as to what defensive releasers will act as effective reinforcers for avoidance responses, and whether it is these releasers or the opportunity to indulge in the defensive reaction itself which is reinforcing. Clearly, one would not intuitively expect pied flycatchers to increase the frequency of an arbitrary avoidance response in order to produce an owl which they could then mob (see Figure 5.5, p.167)! Similarly, the kinesthetic and vestibular cues produced by fleeing do not in and of themselves appear to be reinforcing, since fleeing is learned efficiently as an avoidance response only when it removes the animal from a dangerous place that has been paired with an aversive UCS or takes an animal to a consistently safe place (cf. Anisman and Wahlsten, 1974; Hamilton, 1972; Modaresi, 1975; Olton and Isaacson, 1968). It may well be the case that only a selected number of defensive releasers can act as effective avoidance reinforcers: namely, those stimuli which elicit or signal safety-oriented fleeing such as home-burrow fleeing or safe-object or safe-direction oriented fleeing.

Molar accounts of reinforcement

In recent years, some theorists have attempted to understand instrumental reinforcement by considering two basic factors: (1) that the animal must make decisions about how to allocate its time between different behaviors (such as feeding, parental care, finding a mate, and so on), and (2) that it may frequently have to make these decisions when the opportunity to indulge in one or more of these behaviors is restricted in some way. It is appropriate to discuss two of these approaches here.

1 *Response allocation and behavioral regulation*

Animals are always engaged in some kind of behavior, whether it be feeding, grooming, drinking, or even sleeping. What this means is that there can be no behavioral vacuum, and when changes occur in the rate of frequency of one behavior it will affect the distribution or rate of other behaviors. Similarly, not all behaviors are of equal *value* to the animal — it may "prefer" to indulge in certain kinds of activities (as measured, say, by the amount of time it allocates to that behavior relative to others), or certain behaviors may be of major biological importance (such as eating and drinking). Premack (1965, 1971c) was the first to assimilate these intrinsic differences in the value of behaviors into an account of instrumental reinforcement. He proposed that responses could be structured into a kind of "preference hierarchy" based on their probability of occurrence, and that more probable behaviors could be used to reinforce less probable behaviors. In this sense, reinforcement is not an absolute attribute of some "goal" activity, but is a relationship between a more probable behavior and a less probable behavior. Thus, in the standard instrumental conditioning situation where lever pressing produces food for a hungry rat, eating reinforces lever pressing because eating is usually a more probable behavior than lever pressing. Normally, differences in the behavior preference hierarchy can be produced by experimental manipulations which restrict the animal's opportunity to indulge in one or more particular behaviors. The standard manipulation here is to restrict the animal's opportunity to eat (food deprivation) such that given free choice between, say, lever pressing and eating, eating will be the much more probable behavior and hence act to reinforce lever pressing if a contingency is arranged between the two behaviors (e.g. Premack, 1962, 1965).

The next question to ask is by what processes more probable behaviors can act to reinforce less probable behaviors. In this respect, experiments have revealed two important factors. First, there is clearly competition between various activities for the available time, and restricting one behavior normally acts to increase others. For example, if a rat is allowed to live in an environment where it can allocate its time between exploration, eating, drinking from a water bottle, and running in a running-wheel, then restricting one of these activities will lead to an increase in one or more of the other activities (e.g. Dunham, 1971; Henton and Iverson, 1978; Hinson and Staddon, 1978; Staddon and Ayres, 1975; Staddon, 1977, 1983). Second, there appear to be regulatory mechanisms which tend to maintain the activities in a fixed proportion, and description of these mechanisms has been incorporated into what are known as *behavioral regulation* theories of reinforcement (e.g. Allison, 1983; Hanson and Timberlake, 1983; Timberlake, 1984; Staddon, 1983). These theories assume that animals allocate their time among activities in a manner which is in some way "optimal" for them (the way they do this in their natural environment will depend on their lifestyle and ecological factors which determine how they obtain essential biological resources), and that when opportunity to indulge in one particular activity is restricted (that is, the optimal distribution of activities is disrupted), the animal possesses a homeostatic regulatory mechanism which attempts to return the allocation of activities as near as possible to the optimal distribution.

There are two main kinds of manipulation that one can make in order to investigate how different activities interact. First, we can simply restrict the opportunity to indulge in an activity and see how this affects the overall distribution of activities (such as by removing a running-wheel from the rat's cage), or second, we can impose a contingency between two activities and see if this affects their relative distributions (for example, making the rat run in the wheel in order to obtain water). Both manipulations have basically the same effect: they disrupt the animal's optimal distribution of activities, and activate regulatory processes which attempt to return the animal as closely as possible back to that optimal distribution (cf. Staddon, 1979, 1983). In the case of many schedules of reinforcement, the imposed contingency does not allow the animal to return to the optimal allocation of activities. For example, a rat may have an optimal allocation of 30 sec drinking to each 30 sec of running in a wheel. We can now impose a contingency such that the animal has to run twice as much as it drinks (that is, it has to run for 60 sec in order to obtain 30 sec access to drinking). Under such contingencies, the animal simply cannot return to its optimal allocation, since twice as much running is required as drinking. Nevertheless, behavioral regulation theory assumes that returning as closely as possible to the optimal distribution is a goal of response allocation. In the case of the above example, the animal would probably compromise by increasing its preferred rate of running in order to produce something nearing its preferred rate of drinking. Thus, drinking will appear to "reinforce" running by this kind of regulatory process.

Behavioral regulation accounts of reinforcement differ in important ways from traditional accounts of reinforcement. First, they have ecological relevance in the sense that they assume that each animal has an optimal distribution of activities, and this distribution will depend on the animal's lifestyle and means of obtaining biologically important resources such as food, water, and sexual partners. Reinforcement effects occur when this optimal distribution (as measured by a free-response baseline) is disrupted or restricted in some way. Thus, reinforcement effects depend very much on the free-baseline activity distributions and not on any absolute or intrinsic attribute of a behavior (in strict contrast to traditional drive-reduction theories of reinforcement). Second, behavioral regulation accounts do not differentiate between instrumental responses and reinforcer consummatory responses — reinforcer consummatory responses (such as eating) are not considered to possess properties which distinguish them from instrumental responses (such as pressing a lever): what is important is the contingency relationship between them. Finally, behavioral regulation accounts assume that the factor which *motivates* instrumental responding is not some physiological need state, but the regulatory process which is continually attempting to return the animal to its optimal allocation of activities when this has been disrupted in some way.

2 *Economic theories of behavioral regulation*

Although behavioral regulation accounts of reinforcement stress that changes in the allocation of behaviors under reinforcement contingencies result from attempts to return to the optimal distribution of activities, we still need to clarify the rules which govern this process. For instance, when a reinforcement contingency makes it impossible for the animal to return to its *optimal* distribution, what rules govern the compromise it will eventually make? A number of theorists have noted the similarities between describing behavior changes in response to altered reinforcement contingencies and certain ideas concerning labor supply and consumer demand in microeconomics (e.g. Allison, 1983; Lea, 1978; Staddon, 1980, 1983).

Figure 7.3 illustrates a typical *labor supply curve* which relates wages earned to total work performed. Each line (A–E) represents an increasing amount of work required to obtain a fixed wage income, and as the curve moves from a high wage rate (A) to lower wage rates (B, C, and D), people attempt to maintain their wage income by working more. However, at particularly low wage rates (E), the total amount of work performed no longer increases in order to compensate for the low wages, and the labor

NUMBER OF REINFORCEMENTS OBTAINED
TOTAL WAGES EARNED

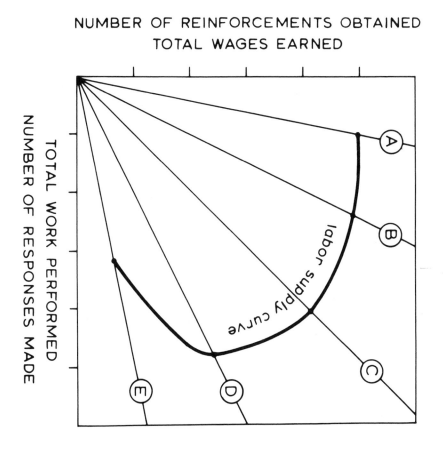

Figure 7.3 An idealized labor supply curve showing different wage rates (A–E) and the amount of work that individuals would be willing to do under each rate. See text for fuller explanation.

supply curve becomes "backward bending" as work level actually decreases. The backward bending labor supply curve results from the different preferences that people have for work as opposed to other activities. When wage rates are high people will have a lot of both money and opportunity to indulge in other activities (such as leisure). When the wage rate becomes particularly low (as in line E), people are less willing to forgo leisure in order to work for relatively poor incomes. This kind of labor supply curve can also be utilized to describe the behavior of animals working at making an instrumental response in order to obtain food. In this case, "wage rate" corresponds to the number of responses the animal has to make in order to obtain a food reinforcer. In a study using rats as subjects and varying the number of lever presses required to obtain 10 licks of sucrose, Kelsey and Allison (1976) found that as the number of lever presses required to obtain the reinforcer increased (by increasing the value of a fixed-ratio schedule), the rate of lever pressing at first increased but then decreased in a fashion similar to the backward-bending labor supply curve.

Another application of microeconomic theory to describing instrumental reinforcement effects concerns the notion of *consumer demand*. A consumer demand curve expresses the relationship between how much of a commodity is purchased and its price. Some commodities are very sensitive to their price, and consumption can fluctuate with changes in price. When the price of a commodity does affect its rate of consumption (for example, consumption may decrease as price increases), then demand for the commodity is called *elastic*. However, when consumption of a commodity is relatively unaffected by its price, then demand for that commodity is called *inelastic*. Whether demand for a commodity is elastic or inelastic depends on a number of factors, including the actual need for the product, the wealth of the consumer, and the availability of substitutes. These notions can be applied to animal learning in a number of ways, primarily by conceiving of the reinforcer as the commodity and the number of responses required to obtain the reinforcer as the price. Thus, price can be manipulated simply by increasing the value of a fixed-ratio reinforcement schedule. In studies using closed-economies (see pp. 231–3), where rats must obtain all their food requirements by pressing a lever in their home cages, demand for a commodity like food is relatively inelastic. That is, response rate will increase with corresponding increases in FR value (cf. Lea, 1978; Lea and Roper, 1977; Hogan and Roper, 1978). However, in circumstances where a substitute is available as an alternative to the reward, demand for that reward becomes elastic — that is, changes in FR value for the reward do not produce corresponding increases in response rate (cf. Kagel, Rachlin, Green, Battalio, Basmann, and Klemm, 1975).

Economic models of behavioral regulation have a number of implications for behavioral allocation and instrumental reinforcement. First, economic models assume that behavior changes occur in order to maintain some kind of optimal balance between activities and needs, and they provide mathematical formulations which allow us to make some predictions about behavior changes and describe the constraints that restrict instrumental learning. Second, economic models allow us a means to describe some of the interspecific differences in the factors which constrain adaptive behavior. For instance, although most animals generally exhibit inelastic demand for food by making more and more responses as the FR value increases (cf. Hogan and Roper, 1978), some species do not. In particular, hamsters show an elastic demand for food by failing to increase their response rate with increased FR values, and this appears to reflect the fact that they rely on previously hoarded food rather than increases in response rate to compensate for the increases in the "price" of food (Lea and Tarpy, 1986). Differences such as this between species of rodent are clearly dependent on ecological and life-history differences between the species, but they can also be summarized in terms of differences in the constraints described by economic models of behavior.

Motivation and closed economies: a behavior systems analysis

One important characteristic of molar accounts of reinforcement is that they do not differentiate between those processes which reinforce behavior and those which motivate behavior. However, this does not mean that a distinction cannot be made between reinforcement and motivation, only that within molar theories this distinction is unnecessary. In some other circumstances it may be theoretically interesting to make such a distinction because it helps to explain some anomalous findings. One such source of anomalous findings stems from the distinction between learning studies which are conducted in open or closed economies. An open-economy study is akin to the traditional experimental paradigm where the animal is in the learning situation for only a limted period each day, and is maintained in a relatively constant state of food or water deprivation. A closed-economy study, however, is one where an animal is in the learning situation for 24 hr a day and obtains its total daily food or water requirement solely as a result of performing instrumental responses in a home environment with no supplementary food or water required.

The vast majority of traditional learning studies have been conducted under open-economy conditions, with the consequence that conceptualizations of reinforcement and motivation have usually involved some notion similar to physiological "need reduction" (e.g. Hull, 1943). However, Collier (1983) and Collier and Rovee-Collier (1981) have pointed out that this has led to a tendency to construct theories of associative learning on the basis of the performance of animals which are actually operating under "emergency" conditions that they would not normally encounter in the wild. Studies conducted in a closed economy have shown that rats will never allow their body-weights to decline by more than 6–7 per cent (Collier, Hirsch, and Hamlin, 1972; Collier, Hirsch, and Kanarek, 1977), even when variations are made in the number of responses needed to procure food and the size of individual meals (Kanarek, 1975; Collier, Hirsch, and Hamlin, 1972; Hill and Collier, 1978).

The study of instrumental responding in closed economies has provided at least two interesting facts related to motivation. First, since rats in a closed economy will always attempt to maintain a stable daily energy intake, to make *smaller* meals contingent on responding (that is, reducing the magnitude of reward) actually *increases* response rate (Collier and Kaufman, 1977; Hill and Collier, 1978; Hursh, 1978). This is, of course, the opposite of what has traditionally been observed in deprived animals in open economies performing during restricted experimental sessions (cf. Hogan and Roper, 1978; Pubols, 1960; Davey, 1981: 91–3). Second, it appears from closed economy studies, and from the behavioral ecology literature (see Chapter 8) that food abundance and distribution, and the energy expended in searching for, capturing, handling, and consuming the food, will also determine the distribution of feeding activities. Animals are geared toward optimal feeding performance, and if it is expedient not to feed (in terms of the net energy intake being outweighed by the loss in energy incurred during feeding), then animals will not normally feed (cf. Collier, 1983).

If there is one important fact that can be derived from closed-economy studies it is that under normal feeding conditions animals rarely experience deprivation states of intensities similar to that induced in open-economy studies. Since in open-economy studies we assume it is the state of deprivation that "motivates" the animal to learn, what "motivates" animals to learn in closed-economy studies? An explanation for this can be derived from an analysis of the feeding strategies that animals have evolved in their natural environment. For instance, it is quite clear that in nature most animals feed *in anticipation of their needs* and not as a result of a state of deprivation (cf. Collier, 1983; Collier and Rovee-Collier, 1981; Fitzsimmons, 1972). Rats given *ad libitum* food are seldom physiologically hungry (Armstrong, Clarke, and Coleman, 1978; Lepkovsky, Lyman, Fleming, Nagumo, and Dimick, 1967) yet they still feed on a regular number of meals per day, usually during periods of darkness (Le Magnen, 1971; Nelson, Scheving, and Halberg, 1975). Other species show more extreme examples of this by starving when hungry and feeding when replete, simply because of the constraints and demands of their particular niche and lifestyle. For example, during spring and early summer, deer and moose need to consume enough vegetation suitable to providing adipose reserves to see them through the winter (Moen, 1973; Belovsky, 1978). Hibernators frequently have to gather their energy needs for a whole year in the course of two or three months of feeding (Barash, 1973).

From these kinds of facts it is clear that variables other than a physiological state we might loosely call "hunger" can motivate animals in appetitive learning situations, and in behavior systems terms these variables can be classified as factors which activate the feeding behavior system. In Chapter 5 we discussed some of the ways in which these system activators could be identified (see p. 160), and those principles also apply here to instrumental conditioning. Once a thorough ethological analysis of the species lifestyle has been carried out and system activators identified, a number of motivational phenomena that did not fit comfortably into traditional motivational frameworks become explicable. For example, Roper (1973, 1975) found that using nest material as a reinforcer had only a weak effect on the frequency of a key-pressing operant in mice. However, when mice were either pregnant or subjected to low temperatures, nest material became a very potent reinforcer for key pressing. In behavior system terms, both pregnancy and low temperatures are activators of the nesting behavior system, and act as motivational variables which render nest materials as an effective reinforcer. Similarly, hamsters are a species which do not require any food deprivation to learn in appetitive instrumental conditioning tasks (Charlton, 1984; Launay, 1981). The crucial factor here is that hamsters are prolific food hoarders with large cheek pouches that they use to transport food to their home food cache. Thus, the motivational factor or system activator in this instance is the evolved tendency to pouch and hoard food whenever it is encountered, and this "motivational factor" frequently results in more efficient learning than food deprivation itself.

Conclusion

In this chapter we have discussed a number of quite different factors related to an understanding of instrumental learning. These have included (1) a discussion of what is learned during instrumental conditioning, including the kinds of factors which might act to mediate and generate an instrumental response; (2) discussion of various ways of analyzing the reinforcement process; (3) discussion of the kinds of factors which contribute to the motivational component of learning.

Chapter summary

1 The constraints on learning literature of the 1960s and 1970s suggested that there were many situations in which instrumental conditioning did not work. These examples were called *misbehavior* and were thought to represent a process of *instinctive drift*.

2 These anomalies led a number of theorists to suggest that there was no such thing as an underlying instrumental reinforcement process, but that all instrumental conditioning could be explained in terms of other learning processes, such as Pavlovian conditioning.

3 One such theory was *incentive motivation*, which suggested that animals learned instrumental responses because (1) parts of the environment associated with the response acquired incentive motivation through Pavlovian conditioning, and (2) the animal's behavior became directed to all stimuli that had acquired incentive motivation.

4 Although Pavlovian-based accounts of instrumental conditioning were able to explain many of the anomalies in the constraints on learning literature, they were unable to account for a number of other aspects of instrumental conditioning and, thus, did not represent a full account of instrumental learning.

5 Studies which have investigated the interactions between Pavlovian and instrumental learning (*transfer-of-control experiments*) have suggested that the important factor which mediates facilitation of responding in these studies is not a compatible motivational state *per se*, but identical reinforcers. This evidence suggests that an internal representation of the reinforcer is important in mediating instrumental responding.

6 Postconditioning reinforcer devaluation studies in instrumental conditioning have also shown that the evaluation of the reinforcer is important in mediating instrumental responding.

7 While a representation of the reinforcer appears to be important in mediating the instrumental response, the mechanics of how this happens is still unclear. Neither *backward conditioning* nor *bidirectional associations* adequately address this problem.

8 Avoidance learning has traditionally been perplexing to learning theorists, because (1) there is no obviously experienced consequence of responding which could act as a reinforcer, and (2) many responses did not appear to be readily acquired as avoidance responses (e.g. bar pressing in rats; key pecking in pigeons).

9 The *species-specific defense reactions* (SSDR) hypothesis suggested that avoidance of aversive events was largely in-built and not learned. Thus, only

responses which were compatible with the animals' SSDRs could be learned as effective avoidance responses.

10 The effective reinforcer for avoidance responding appears to be safety. Thus, any response that has the consequence of producing safety cues will be reinforced. In particular, any response that permits the animal to flee from cues associated with the aversive event can be effectively learned.

11 Some theorists have attempted to understand instrumental reinforcement by considering (1) that an animal must make decisions about how to allocate its time between different behaviors, and (2) that it may have to make these decisions when the opportunity to indulge in one or more of these behaviors is restricted in some way. Two particular examples of these molar accounts of reinforcement are *response allocation and behavioral regulation* and *economic theories of behavioral regulation*.

12 Studies which have investigated the behavior of animals in *closed economies* (i.e. where an animal obtains its total daily food or water requirement solely as a result of performing instrumental responses in a home environment) have suggested that the kinds of deprivation conditions used to motivate animals in traditional, open-economy learning situations may not be universally applicable.

13 In their natural environment animals are rarely in an "emergency" deprivation state and their behavior is motivated by a range of factors related to their environmental niche and their lifestyle rather than any state of psychological deprivation. Understanding the factors which motivate an animal to feed in its natural environment helps us to understand some of the conditions under which stimuli become reinforcing.

Chapter eight

Behavioral ecology

Living organisms are usually faced with a number of competing demands during their lifetime. Generally, these demands extend to finding food, avoiding predators, securing a sexual partner, and so on. Coping efficiently with these demands has the consequence of increasing the likelihood that the genes of that organism will survive and propagate in future generations. This in turn insures that many of the attributes possessed by that organism for coping with these demands will also be passed on to future generations if they are genetically encoded. The implication of this process is that contemporary species of animals are likely to be those which have coped most effectively with this optimality problem, and are thus likely to possess relatively optimal behavioral and psychological processes for dealing with their life's problems. Argued in this way, optimality can be seen as a general constraint that impinges on most living organisms: dealing efficiently with the acquisition of food leaves more time to be alert to predators, and so on. There are at least two ways of going about tackling these ideas as far as we are concerned in this volume. First, we can work out mathematically what might be the optimal solution to a particular problem that the animal faces (such as choosing when to leave one food source in order to investigate others), and see if the animal's behavior does approximate this optimal solution. Second, we would be particularly interested in the role that learning plays in achieving optimal performance, and what kinds of mechanisms underlie this learning.

Optimality models

MacArthur and Pianka (1966) were probably the first to introduce the idea that in order to maximize its contribution to the gene pool an animal is faced with an optimization problem. For example, in relation, say, to feeding, animals should be attempting to obtain the maximum amount of food per unit time. This is not just sheer gluttony, nor just a safeguard against any uncertainty in the future food stock; an efficient feeder can allocate relatively more time to other biologically important functions than an inefficient feeder. The kinds of optimality problems an animal is likely to encounter are usually choice problems.

For instance, if the animal feeds in an environment where food is "patchily" distributed, then it has to make decisions about when to leave one patch and try out another (for instance, if a bird feeds on insects normally found in dead logs, it must decide when to give up foraging in one log and travel to find others). Similarly, if an animal feeds off a number of different prey types common in its habitat — each of which vary in their nutritive and calorific value — it must decide when to ignore a less profitable prey in order to pursue and capture a more lucrative one.

Decisions of this kind require a number of factors to be taken into account. Such factors include the amount of time and effort required to travel between patches, the overall prey density in the animal's environment, the amount of time and energy it takes the animal to capture and consume a particular prey type, and so on. Because so many factors are involved in arriving at a relatively optimal solution to these kinds of problems, we might reasonably suspect that animals which can solve such problems optimally are doing so by utilizing learning and memorial processes (McNamara and Houston, 1985).

The first question that is raised when attempting to discover whether animals do forage optimally is to define what an optimal solution might be. Clearly, we can only practically calculate a relatively crude approximation to the optimal solution. The reason for this is that animals optimize in order to maximize their inclusive fitness, and because we cannot measure fitness directly, it is necessary to make simplifying assumptions which might allow us to measure fitness according to some appropriate *currency*. For example, when investigating optimal feeding patterns we could make the assumption that animals are attempting to maximize their rate of food intake per unit time, and calculate the optimal solution in these terms. However, such a currency is unlikely to be particularly accurate because it does not take into account the amount of energy the animal is expending in acquiring and consuming the food. Because of this, a generally acceptable currency assumes that animals attempt to maximize their *net rate of energy intake*, measured in terms of calories per unit time. Under this kind of assumption it is clearly not optimal for an animal to consume a prey which requires more energy to capture and eat than it contains in nutriment. While net rate of energy intake is generally accepted as a useful currency for measuring optimality, it is not necessarily the only one.

For instance, Pulliam (1976) has used a time budget model to predict the optimal flock size for birds, given that each bird has to negotiate a trade-off in time between food intake, predation risk, and fighting, and the amount of time a bird needs to indulge in these behaviors will depend on the size of the flock. Using time allocation as a currency of fitness can be useful in that it allows the theorist to compare competition between different behaviors which serve different functions (for example, feeding vs. defense), but it does still beg the question of whether one time unit spent feeding is equivalent to the same time unit spent avoiding predators (cf. Krebs, Houston, and Charnov, 1981).

Thus, by using the appropriate currency and taking into account relevant factors we can calculate what would be the optimal solution for an animal in, say, a particular foraging situation. However, what conclusion do we reach if the animal's behavior does not fit this optimal solution? The main justification for using optimality models is the assumption that natural selection penalizes those organisms which do not behave optimally. Does the failure to observe optimal performance therefore invalidate this assumption? The answer is probably no, it does not. This is because there are a number of good reasons why we would not expect animals to behave in a *perfectly* optimal way.

First, evolutionary adaptation always lags behind environmental change, and so we could probably expect that the strategies that an animal currently possesses in order to achieve optimality may not yet have been modified by current environmental pressures. Second, in order to perform optimally in most situations an organism would have to be more or less omniscient. Even if an animal did possess all of the information-processing and memorial abilities necessary to achieve the "perfect" solution, it would still have to take time acquiring the relevant information. To this extent it would have to "sample" the different options in order to assess their value, and the mere fact of sampling could be sufficient to produce deviations from the perfect solution. This is something that we shall encounter in some of the following sections of this chapter. Finally, we must be clear that an optimality model based on particular assumptions and currencies is not designed to test the idea that animals are optimal (Maynard Smith, 1978), but only to test the assumptions inherent in that particular model. If the model is unsuccessful in its predictions, there is no reason why it cannot be replaced by another model using different assumptions and different currencies. Ideally, we are trying to find the best model for predicting the animal's behavior, and although there is some danger that this may extend the notion of optimality beyond its theoretical usefulness, it is not necessarily an invalid approach to the problem

(Lewontin, 1978). In fact, some approaches have circumvented this possible criticism by proposing that we should adopt what is known as an "inversive optimality" approach. That is, we should attempt to discover the rules which do govern an animal's behavior in, for instance, foraging situations, and then attempt to infer what function this maximizes (e.g. McFarland, 1978). This is the approach that has recently been adopted in some learning paradigms such as the study of matching in instrumental choice situations (see pp. 81–3).

Diet selection

Any prey item consumed as food by a predator has both a cost factor and a benefit factor. The cost is the amount of energy spent in searching for, capturing, and eating that prey. The benefit is in terms of the energy and nutritive value of that prey. Thus, the animal is constantly pressured to evaluate these two factors when foraging for food. In effective terms these two factors can be evaluated to calculate the net food value of a particular prey item, and this is usually denoted as net energy intake per unit handling time (E/h). MacArthur and Pianka (1966) assumed that this trade-off was important in determining which prey items a predator would either choose to ignore or capture while foraging in its habitat.

For instance, an environment will contain prey of different profitability (according to the E/h calculation), and a predator has the problem of deciding which prey to consume and which to ignore. Figure 8.1 ranks a hypothetical predator's food in order of profitability, and shows how average travel time between prey items decreases with increased breadth of diet; that is, the more a predator includes different prey items in its diet the less distance it has to travel to encounter one. However, while the time spent traveling to capture a prey item (t) decreases with increased breadth of diet, the profitability (E/h) of the prey eaten also decreases. By combining both the E/h and t functions it is possible to calculate the general curve of net food intake per unit time (E/T). The top half of Figure 8.1 shows that the E/T function increases, reaches a peak, and then declines. In this example, the E/T curve peaks at the fifth-ranked prey type, and this implies that including only the first five ranked prey items in the diet will provide the best net energy returns per unit foraging time. Including items ranked lower than five will reduce this net energy intake. Clearly, to perform optimally in this situation the predator should include prey items 1–5 in its diet, but reject prey items ranked 6 and worse.

One other prediction from this kind of model is that the richer the environment (in terms of the density of high-ranking prey items), the less will

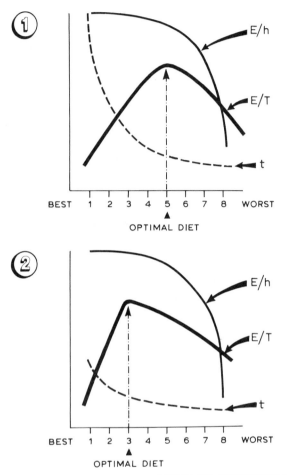

PREY TYPES RANKED IN ORDER OF PROFITABILITY

Figure 8.1 (1) An idealized model of optimal diet selection. As more prey are added to the diet the travel time (*t*) to encounter a prey decreases, but so does the average profitability of prey (E/h). When these two factors are taken into account, the net food intake per unit time (E/T) rises, then decreases, indicating that the optimal diet should include only the 5 most profitable prey. The lower figure (2) represents a good habitat with more abundant prey. In such circumstances, travel time (*t*) is reduced, and the peak of the curve describing net food intake per unit time (E/T) moves to the left, indicating that the animal should include only the 3 most profitable prey in its diet.

be the average travel time (t) to capture a prey. This will move the peak of the E/T curve toward the more profitable end of the ranking, and thus, in order to obtain optimal net energy intake, predators should include even fewer prey items in their diet (see bottom half of Figure 8.1).

There are two important implications of these optimality calculations: (1) predators should either include a prey type in their diet or reject it completely (there should be no partial preferences); and (2) the number of prey items a predator includes in its diet will be affected by the frequency of high-ranking prey but not by the frequency of lower-ranking types.

Both of these predictions have received support from experimental studies which have varied the density of differing prey types for predators (cf. Goss-Custard, 1981; Werner and Mittelbach, 1981; Kamil and Roitblat, 1985). For instance, Elner and Hughes (1978) studied diet selection in the shore crab (*Carcinus maenas*) which feeds on mussels (*Mytelus edulis*). They used three different-sized mussels varying in their profitability (E/h). When overall density of mussels was low, the crabs were unselective. At medium and high densities, the crabs ignored the least profitable of these mussels, and, in the high density condition, showed a strong preference for the most profitable mussel type.

Other studies have yielded similar findings in bluegill sunfish (*Lepomis macrochirus*) hunting for differing-sized daphnia (Werner and Hall, 1974, 1976, 1979; Werner, Mittelbach, Hall, and Gilliam, 1983); in redshanks (*Tringa totanus*) hunting for worms (Goss-Custard, 1977); and in barn owls (Herrera, 1974) and starfish (Menge, 1972).

Krebs, Erichsen, Webber, and Charnov (1977) tested the diet selection model in the laboratory using great tits (*Parus major*). The great tits were presented with either large or small pieces of mealworm passing in front of them on a conveyor belt. As predicted by the optimality account the birds were unselective when prey density was low, but selected only the larger items when prey density was high.

In a field study, Goss-Custard (1981) studied redshanks foraging for worms on mud flats. He found that the proportion of larger worms eaten was affected only by their own density and not by the density of smaller worms, and smaller worms were taken only when the density of large worms was low. Both results are consistent with predictions from MacArthur and Pianka's optimality model.

In an instrumental analog of the diet selection problem, Lea (1979) tested the optimality model using pigeons. The birds had to complete an initial fixed-interval (FI) requirement, after which they were given one of two stimuli. These stimuli were associated with either a short or long FI value and represented prey type. At this point the subject could either choose to complete that FI requirement (thus including that "prey item" in its diet) or reject it and start again. Manipulating either the long or short FI components was equivalent to manipulating prey density, and E/h could be manipulated by changing either the value of the initial FI component or the duration of access to food at the end of each trial. In general, the results were consistent with MacArthur and Pianka's model except that more partial preferences were observed than would have been predicted by the model.

Despite these encouraging findings, there is some evidence that the MacArthur and Pianka optimality model may be a little too simplistic. It seems to be clear that factors other than travel time (t) and prey profitability (E/h) need to be taken into the equation. For instance, Hughes (1979) has suggested that the time it takes an animal to *recognize* the prey as either profitable or unprofitable needs to be included in the E/h calculation, and this would presumably also be affected by learning factors. Elner and Hughes (1978) point out that it takes shore crabs 1–2 sec to reject an unprofitable prey, and this may frequently lead to the acceptance of unprofitable prey when the MacArthur and Pianka model predicts that it should be rejected. Similarly, Erichsen, Krebs, and Houston (1980) found that great tits would accept more unprofitable prey than was predicted when different-sized mealworms were disguised by being inserted into either opaque or clear pieces of straw. The birds could only "recognize" profitable from unprofitable prey by picking up the straws and investigating them.

Belovsky (1978, 1984a, b) has suggested that the optimal diet selection model also needs modifying to cope with the special foraging problems encountered by herbivores. Animals such as moose, beaver, kudu, and microtine rodents are subject to constraints on their digestive capacities and nutritional requirements. When these nutritional constraints are added to simple optimal diet models they appear to have some success in accounting for the available data (Belovsky, 1978, 1981, 1984a, b).

Finally, some deviations from an optimal diet selection model appear to reflect "sampling behavior" on the part of the animal. Such occasions occur when, for instance, subjects "partially select" low profitability prey when the model suggests they should completely reject them (e.g. Krebs, Erichsen, Webber, and Charnov, 1977; Goss-Custard, 1981; Werner and Mittelbach, 1981). This is perhaps not too surprising, since the animal's feeding habitat is rarely static in the way that it is when controlled in laboratory studies. It would seem sensible occasionally to sample a less profitable prey in order to update on changes in either prey frequency or profitability. Perhaps more importantly from our point of view, though, is the fact that such "sampling behavior" is probably indicative of the operation of learning mechanisms in optimal diet selection. We shall also encounter this possibility in discussing patch selection and persistence.

Patch selection

Very many animals find that their food is *patchily* distributed, and these patches can be found situated around their local habitat. The problem that such an animal faces when feeding is to ascertain the richness of the patch it is currently exploiting, and at what point it should move on to investigate other patches. There is considerable evidence that, given a choice, animals will tend to spend more time foraging in the richest patches (that is, patches with the highest prey density). This has been observed in great tits (*Parus major*) (Smith and Sweatman, 1974), ovenbirds (*Seirus aurocapillus*) (Zach and Falls, 1976), wagtails (*Motacilla flava*) (Davies, 1977), redshank (*Tringa totanus*) (Goss-Custard, 1981), kangaroos (*Macropus giganteus*) (Taylor, 1984), and bees (*Apis mellifer*) (Waddington and Holden, 1979).

This tendency to choose the richer source of food over less profitable sources is also well documented in instrumental analogs of foraging situations (e.g. Lea, 1981; Rachlin, Green, Kagel, and Battalio, 1976; see pp. 81–3). However, what is perhaps more important from the point of view of optimality is how an animal goes about discovering that one patch is richer than another, and whether it can make the appropriate decision to forage in the richer patch in the least necessary amount of time. This implies that patch selection can be modeled as if it were divided into two phases: a *sampling* phase, where the animal attempts to assess the richness of the alternative patches; and an *exploitation* phase, where the animal reaps the rewards of that choice. There is clearly evidence that animals do spend more time sampling prey from different patches before settling to exploit exclusively one particular patch. For instance, Smith and Sweatman (1974) found that on early training trials great tits showed only a small deviation from random search between patches of differing density. However, after about 10 trials the search pattern became distinctly nonrandom, and birds spent significantly more time searching high-density rather than low-density patches.

Nevertheless, the maximizing problem facing the animal in such patch selection tasks is to calculate the optimal amount of time to spend sampling before exploiting one particular patch. In a two-choice situation this can be calculated mathematically in terms of what is known as the *two-armed bandit* problem (Wahrenberger, Antle, and Klimko, 1977; Krebs, Kacelnik, and

Taylor, 1978). This conceives of the problem as the organism being faced with two one-armed bandits and a limited number of coins. The animal has to discover which of the one-armed bandits is more profitable as quickly as possible. The solution to this optimal sampling problem will depend on two factors: (1) the difference in food distribution (density or richness) between the two alternatives; and (2) the total time available for foraging. If the animal spends insufficient time sampling, it risks exploiting the poorer alternative; if it spends too long sampling, it risks not taking full advantage of the richer alternative.

Studies which have investigated the two-armed bandit problem have tended to suggest that animals' sampling performance does fit tolerably well with predictions from the two-armed bandit model. For instance, Kacelnik (1979) studied great tits which were permitted to hop on one of two perches in order to obtain food. Rewards for responding to the two perches were scheduled according to differing variable ratio (VR) schedules, and these values were changed on a day-to-day basis. Kacelnik attempted to discover how long the birds took to sample the two alternatives before exploiting one of the perches. He found that performance was described very well by an optimizing model based on a sampling period ("time horizon") of 150 responses. Also consistent with this optimizing model were the findings that increasing the difference in reward frequency between the two alternatives *reduced* the sampling period, and increasing the session time *increased* the length of the sampling period.

Kamil and Roitblat (1985) point out that there are a number of interesting aspects to this kind of research on patch selection. First, it is a problem that is generally ignored by laboratory studies of choice (cf. Kamil and Yoerg, 1982; see pp. 81–3). These laboratory studies are usually interested in the choice solution that the animal continually settles on (that is, they are interested in steady-state performance) rather than how that choice is actually arrived at. While an animal is under pressure to maximize reward in a concurrent choice task, it is also under pressure to arrive at its decisions in an optimal fashion. Second, two-armed bandit models of optimal sampling are probably a little simplistic as they stand at present. Kamil and Roitblat (1985) suggest that the time taken to travel between patches is also a factor that needs to be taken into consideration, because this requires time and energy. It is especially important in studies of *central place* foraging where animals travel between foraging sites and some central place such as a nest. If the time and energy required to travel between foraging sites and the central place is considerable (such as when parent birds are providing their nestlings with food), then one might expect the sampling "time window" to be substantially reduced (Kacelnik, 1984; Aronson and Givnish, 1983).

Patch persistence

An animal is not just faced with the problem of choosing which patch to exploit during its foraging activities; arguably a more difficult problem is deciding when to leave the current patch in order to explore others. Although a patch may have been relatively rich when the animal chose to exploit it, capturing prey will normally lead to the patch becoming *depleted*. At some point the patch will become so depleted of prey that it will now no longer be an attractive proposition and richer alternatives may be found elsewhere. The maximization problem facing the animal here is to leave the depleting patch at the point where the animal's average net energy intake per unit time would not be reduced by seeking food in other patches. As a general rule, an optimal predator should exploit a particular patch only as long as the expected rate of return in that patch is higher than the rate of return that can be expected by leaving and exploiting another patch.

1 *The marginal value theorem*

The first attempt to formalize the optimal solution to this problem was by Charnov (1976). Figure 8.2 shows the diminishing rate of net energy intake from a particular patch as a function of time in the patch (the curve $f(T)$) and the overall average net rate of food intake for that environment as a whole (the straight line E/T). Charnov argued that when the net rate of energy intake in the patch drops to a level equal to the overall average for the habitat, then the animal should leave that patch and search elsewhere. In Figure 8.2 this point is reached when the slope of the curve $f(T)$ equals the slope of E/T. This model is known as the *marginal value theorem* because the predator should stay in a patch until its rate of energy intake reaches a marginal value which is equal to the net rate of intake for the habitat as a whole. The time spent traveling between patches also needs to be included in this equation. If energy is expended traveling between patches, then the slope of E/T will be reduced and the amount of time an animal should spend in each patch before the marginal value is reached should be increased (see bottom panel of Figure 8.2).

The marginal value theorem makes a number of assumptions which may or may not apply in individual instances. For instance, first, it assumes that all patches will be depleted as the animal spends time foraging in that patch. This is generally true, and some animals will deplete patches faster than others, depending on the efficiency of their predatory strategies. However, there is a possibility that in some cases exploiting a patch will lead to its becoming repletive rather than depleted. This might well be the case where foraging in a

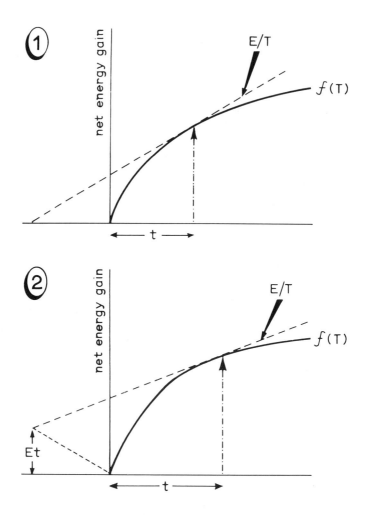

Figure 8.2 (1) The marginal value solution to the optimal time in a depleting patch. The average cumulative energy gain as a function of time in the patch is represented by f(T), while the line E/T represents the average energy gain per unit time for the habitat as a whole. The optimal predator should stay in the patch long enough to maximize the slope of E/T (in this case for the period *t*). Graph (2) represents the optimal solution given that the animal also has to take into account the energy expended on travelling between patches (Et). This reduces the slope of E/T and results in a longer optimal stay time (*t*).

particular patch actually helps to "scare up" further prey. However, as a general rule, repletive patches are likely to be much rarer than depleting patches. Second, the marginal value theorem assumes that the animal has knowledge about the overall rate of capture for the habitat as a whole and is keeping some record of the capture rate within the patch it is exploiting. Third, this theorem also assumes that the animal is spending all of its time foraging in patches or traveling between patches. It does not take into consideration other demands on the animal's time, such as avoiding predators or rearing young.

Given these assumptions and constraints, the marginal value theorem makes a number of predictions. First, a predator should leave any patch —regardless of its initial richness — when the marginal value for the habitat as a whole has been reached. This would obviously imply spending more time exploiting richer patches (because it would take longer to deplete a rich patch to the marginal value); and second, the greater the amount of time and energy required to travel between patches, the longer a predator should spend exploiting a particular patch (see bottom panel, Figure 8.2).

These predictions have, by and large, been upheld in experimental studies of optimal foraging: predators do tend to spend approximately the amount of time in each patch as predicted by the marginal value theorem. This has been demonstrated in titmice foraging for patchily distributed food (Smith and Sweatman, 1974), chickadees foraging for food in an indoor aviary (Krebs, Ryan, and Charnov, 1974), waterboatmen (*Notonecta glauca*) feeding on the larvae of *Culex molestus* (Cook and Cockrell, 1978), and wasps (*Nemeritis canescens*) searching for patchily distributed hosts in which to oviposit (Cook and Hubbard, 1977; Hubbard and Cook, 1978).

Similarly, Cowie (1977) has investigated the prediction that travel time between patches will influence the amount of time a predator should remain in a patch. While investigating the foraging behavior of great tits, Cowie manipulated travel time between patches (plastic cups filled with sawdust and containing pieces of worm) by placing lids on these cups which could be either hard or easy to remove. Thus, hard lids represented long travel times and easy lids short travel times. Cowie found that great tits spent longer exploiting a patch (cup) if the travel time was longer (that is, the lid was harder to remove), and the results compared favorably with predictions from marginal value theorem.

Nevertheless, even though these results do appear to be qualitatively consistent with marginal value theorem, there are often small but important deviations. For instance, predators often spend longer foraging in the poorest patches than would be predicted by the theorem (e.g. Smith and Sweatman,

1974; Hubbard and Cook, 1978). Presumably this may well reflect a sampling strategy which is necessary to acquire the information about prey density required by the optimal solution.

2 *Strategies for optimal foraging*

It is clear from this that the behavior of a wide range of organisms complies with optimal foraging theory, and these are organisms as neurologically and ecologically diverse as great tits and wasps. The next question that needs to be raised is how these animals are able to arrive at an optimal solution to their foraging problems. Evolutionary pressures require that they do evolve an optimal solution, but these pressures do not specify the means by which they achieve this solution. Therefore, the mechanisms for optimal foraging may be prewired or may require relatively sophisticated information processing, learning, and memorial skills.

Area-restricted search

Animals may possess mechanisms for remaining in a relatively rich patch which rely very little on learning abilities. For instance, thrushes, blackbirds, and sticklebacks exhibit what is known as *area-restricted search* (Smith, 1974a, b; Thomas, 1974). That is, whenever they encounter a prey item they will either decrease their speed of mobility or increase the tortuosity of their search path, thus insuring that they stay roughly in the same location. This implies that the more frequently the animals are encountering prey then the longer they will remain in that patch. Although there may be some learning involved in this strategy, it is clear that it could equally be a preprogramed response tendency elicited when a prey item is encountered.

In a slightly different approach to the problem, Waage (1979) investigated the behavioral mechanisms underlying patch use by the parasite wasp *Nemeritis canescens*. This organism searched for patchily distributed hosts in which to oviposit. An arena represented the habitat, and patches of prey (hosts) consisted of plastic dishes covered with sawdust. Waage discovered that *Nemeritis* exhibited two responses on encountering a patch of prey: (1) an orthokinetic response, which involved walking more slowly after entering the patch; and (2) a klinotactic response, involving sharp turns back into the patch whenever the patch edge was encountered. This latter response was an important determinant of time spent in the patch, because this edge response gradually waned with time so that *Nemeritis* eventually abandoned the patch. However, the waning of this edge response is due to gradual habituation of the reaction to the smell of the host patch, and this habituation process can be slowed by encountering a host and achieving successful oviposition. Thus, the richer a patch was in hosts, the slower the habituation of the edge response and the longer *Nemeritis* would remain in the patch. This example shows how learning mechanisms as basic as habituation and dishabituation can serve to enable the organism to approximate an optimal solution to its foraging problem.

Clearly, there may be other strategies which result in area-restricted searching and which provide an optimal solution, and these may depend on other more sophisticated learning abilities (cf. Lea, 1981: 380–2). One such learning phenomenon which may serve this purpose is the apparently para-doxical phenomenon of adjustive behavior, which is discussed elsewhere in this volume (cf. Falk, 1977; Chapter 3, pp. 83–91).

Giving-up time (GUT)

Krebs, Ryan, and Charnov (1974) have suggested that one useful strategy for an animal to adopt when attempting to forage optimally is to use the time intervals between successive captures as a measure of capture rate. Predators would then leave a patch when the time since the last capture equals or exceeds a criterion interval based on the overall capture rate in the habitat (cf. Hassell and May, 1974; Murdoch and Oaten, 1975). Thus the richer the habitat as a whole, the shorter would be the giving-up time in each patch. In their investigation of optimal foraging in chickadees, Krebs *et al.* (1974) presented birds with patches consisting of blocks of wood with holes containing pieces of concealed mealworm. The birds were trained on one prey item per patch and then tested in a mixed environment which consisted of two kinds of patches containing either one or three prey items. If birds were foraging simply on the basis of an "expectation" model (e.g. Gibb, 1958), then on the transition from training to testing the birds should leave each patch after capturing the one prey item they had come to expect during training. Krebs *et al.* found, however, that birds did not give up immediately after finding a single prey item, and they searched longer in the mixed condition than in the single prey training condition. In effect, their giving-up time depended on the average number of prey in the habitat rather than on the number of prey per patch, a result consistent with the GUT hypothesis.

However, there are a number of problems with the GUT hypothesis as formulated by Krebs *et al.* (1974). First, Cowie and Krebs (1979) have pointed out that the results of Krebs *et al.* (1974) could have been obtained even if the birds were behaving randomly. That is, as the environment as a whole becomes richer, it is obvious that the average interval between the last capture and leaving a patch will become shorter. While this is consistent with the GUT hypothesis, it is also consistent with much more trivial hypotheses. For instance, if an animal leaves a patch after being disturbed by the aviary door banging closed (the "random door-slam" hypothesis!) the interval between the last prey capture and leaving the patch is likely to be shorter the more dense prey are in the environment (Cowie and Krebs, 1979)! Second, there are a few studies which have failed to find a relationship beween giving-up time and overall prey density (e.g. Zach and Falls, 1976; Lima, 1984), which suggests that the strategies that animals adopt in such circumstances may be more varied or depend on more factors than those assumed by the GUT hypothesis.

The variable "memory window" hypothesis

Cowie (1977) hypothesized that in order to forage optimally, an animal might use a *memory window* of the last few patches visited in order to estimate its likely net gain in a new patch. If this were the strategy being used, then if the animal has just visited a number of relatively poor patches and then visits a relatively rich patch, it is likely to stay longer than optimal in the new rich patch, and as the memory of the bad patches fades, the average expectation increases and it will give up more readily in subsequent patches. An experiment by Cowie (1977) did not confirm this hypothesis. Instead of spending more time in a good patch following a bad-to-good transition and then decreasing, the time spent in patches gradually *increased* after such a transition. Although this does not support the memory-window hypothesis as outlined by Cowie, it does show that previous experience does influence the amount of time spent in a patch, but it is more in the form of a *time* expectation (that is, expecting to have to spend a certain amount of time in each patch) rather than a *rate* expectation (namely, expecting to capture so many prey in a given time period).

3 *Summary*

Clearly, many animals do exhibit performances which approximate the optimal strategy for foraging, and the marginal value theorem is just one attempt to estimate what might be the optimal solution to the animal's foraging problems. We have spent some time discussing the implications of the marginal value theorem, but let us not forget that it is just one model of optimal foraging. It may turn out that the assumptions of the marginal value theorem are too simplistic, and more refined models may be required (e.g. Iwasa, Higoshi, and Yamamura, 1981; Oaten, 1977; McNamara, 1982; Lima, 1984).

However, the behavior of foraging animals does tend to approximate what we might consider to be the optimal solution, and they appear to adopt many different strategies to achieve their solution. In some cases the mechanisms underlying optimal performance may be relatively unsophisticated (such as habituation processes in *Nemeritis*), but in others the animal may require very sophisticated learning and memorial abilities to achieve optimality, and more recent models of optimal foraging require that the animal processes and stores relatively large amounts of data (cf. Kamil and Roitblat, 1985). Nevertheless, as we have mentioned before, evolution demands that the animal perform optimally and does not specify what kind of mechanism should evolve to achieve this aim. However, we might reasonably assume that the various learning abilities possessed by animals are useful tools in achieving this optimality.

Risk-prone behavior

Another approach to the problem of how an animal should allocate its time among various potential food sources depends on current resource availability. Caraco (1980) hypothesized that if resource availability (in terms of food) is low, so that the animal cannot expect to meet its minimum requirements, then its behavior should become *risk-prone*. If, however, the animal can expect to meet its needs from the resources that it knows to be available, then its behavior will become *risk-averse*. Caraco characterizes this model in terms of the animal attempting to *minimize the risk of starvation*. For instance, if things are looking bad and it seems likely that the animal may not acquire sufficient sustenance, it is worth taking a gamble and exploiting a variable patch rather than a patch of fixed value which the animal knows will not meet its needs. Although there is a possibility that exploiting the variable patch may result in less food capture than the fixed patch, it may turn up trumps and provide the animal with its requirements. The main means of testing this hypothesis is by providing the animal with two food sources, one of which is fixed and the other variable. However, the *mean* value of the two sources is equal.

Caraco, Martindale, and Whittam (1980) tested the risk-prone hypothesis on yellow-eyed juncos (*Junco phaeonotus*). In the first experiment, birds were presented with a choice of either constant reward (2 seeds per trial) or variable reward (variable 0 or 4 seeds per trial). The subjects were food deprived for only 1 hour before an experiment and were thus maintained on a positive energy budget (that is, energy intake exceeded expenditure). In this case subjects opted significantly more often for the fixed alternative. In a second experiment, subjects were maintained on a negative energy budget (net energy intake was less than expenditure). In these circumstances, subjects opted significantly more often for the variable reward. These results support Caraco's risk-prone hypothesis, as have subsequent experiments on dark-eyed juncos (*Junco hyemalis*) (Caraco, 1981) and white-crowned sparrows (*Zonotrichia leucophrys*) (Caraco, 1982, 1983). Recently, other experiments have shown that birds are sensitive to the distribution of variable rewards around a mean, and to the skew of the distribution of rewards; white-crowned sparrows show a significant preference for reward that is positively skewed (that is, delivers 1 seed with $p = 0.75$ or 3 seeds with $p = 0.25$) rather than normally distributed (delivers 0 seeds with $p = 0.25$ or 2 seeds with $p = 0.75$) when maintained under a positive energy budget (Caraco and Chasin, 1984).

Thus, exhibiting risk-prone behavior is obviously an advisable strategy when threatened with starvation because of depleted resources. Although it is true to say that risk-prone behavior has really only been demonstrated in relatively small seed-eating birds (cf. Kamil and Roitblat, 1985), if it is a phenomenon common to a wide range of animals, it has important implications for behavior in learning situations. For instance, in appetitive learning tasks animals are normally made hungry by being given only limited daily access to food: circumstances which usually maintain the animal on a negative energy budget regardless of the amount of food the animal requires in the experimental situation. An implication of this — if risk-proneness applies to a wide range of animals — is that appetitive learning studies are likely to generate risk-prone tendencies, and may not reflect the behavioral inclinations of animals which, on a day-to-day basis, manage to maintain themselves on a positive energy budget (see also pp. 231–3 for further discussion of the implications of studying animals behaving under "emergency" conditions).

Conclusion

Evolutionary pressures are going to demand that an animal executes its biological functions in an optimal fashion, and so we might reasonably assume that animals have evolved the abilities to arrive at the optimal solutions to their life's problems. We can go about investigating this by deciding in advance what the optimal solution to a particular problem might be, and then seeing if the animal's behavior approximates this solution. There is clear evidence that animals do approximate the optimal solution to a number of problems, including selecting which prey to include in their diet, selecting which food patch to exploit, and deciding how long to remain in one patch before exploring another.

However, none of the fits is perfect. This may imply that the assumptions on which we have based our optimality models are inadequate and need to be revised. Or it may imply that animals do not possess the abilities necessary for arriving at the *perfectly* optimal solution. In most cases it would be fair to assume that a reasonable approximation to the perfect solution would suffice, or that the evolution of the abilities necessary to reach the optimal solution still lags behind the changes that are constantly occurring in the animal's habitat. Finally, while evolution might penalize those organisms that do not perform optimality, it does not specify how the animal should go about achieving the optimal outcome, or what mechanisms should underlie optimality.

Clearly, learning mechanisms are likely to be involved in optimal performance. The kinds of abilities required would include recognizing profitable from unprofitable prey, discriminating rich patches from poor patches, gathering and storing information on the density of prey types, and so on. Thus, if learning is a central contributor to optimal performance, it may be this function which has insured that learning has been selected for during the evolution of living organisms.

Chapter summary

1 Because organisms are faced with a number of competing demands during their lifetime, animals that have evolved efficient means of coping with these demands are likely to survive and pass on their genes to future generations.

2 If animals have evolved optimal strategies for coping with various life problems (such as procuring food), we can calculate what the optimal solution might be and see if the animal's behavior actually approximates this solution.

3 In the case of feeding, animals normally have to make a number of decisions related to their foraging behavior. They have to (1) decide which prey to accept and which to reject; (2) decide where to forage (patch selection), and (3) decide how long to stay feeding in a particular patch before moving on to another (patch persistence).

4 In diet selection, some prey are less valuable (nutritive) than others. When the net food value of individual prey items are calculated, the range of prey that an animal includes in its diet is predicted fairly well by an *optimal diet selection model*.

5 Since animals are not omniscient (they do not have immediate knowledge of the value of different prey items), deviations from optimal diet

selection models can be accounted for by the animal "sampling" different prey.

6 When an animal's food is "patchily" distributed, it tends to choose the richest of the proximally available patches in which to feed. This implies that patch selection has two phases: (1) a *sampling phase*, where the animal samples the richness of alternative patches, and (2) an *exploitation phase*, where the animal reaps the rewards of that choice.

7 The behavior of animals in sampling and exploiting patches appears to approximate the optimal solution which is predicted by a "*two-armed bandit*" model of patch selection.

8 Once an animal has begun to exploit a patch it will usually begin to deplete that patch of food. The animal, therefore, has to make a decision on when to leave the "depleting" patch and exploit another. One optimal solution to this problem is contained in the *marginal value theorem*. When studied, the behavior of animals whose food is patchily distributed appears to correspond reasonably well with predictions from this model.

9 Evolutionary pressures might require that an animal evolve optimal solutions to such life problems as feeding, but it does not specify the kind of mechanism that the animal should evolve to reach these optimal solutions. So, different species may have evolved quite different mechanisms for this purpose.

10 Another approach to the problem of how an animal should allocate its time among various potential food sources depends on current resources availability. If an animal's food resources are insufficient to meet its current minimum requirements its behavior should become *risk prone*; i.e. it should be more likely to reject current food resources in search of potentially richer resources which could minimize the risk of starvation. Experimental evidence is generally consistent with this thesis.

Chapter nine

Phase-specific learning: imprinting and avian song learning

Certain kinds of learning are characterized by the fact that they occur only during a specific — and often brief — period of the animal's lifetime. Furthermore, these kinds of learning have rather dramatic and long-lasting effects on the animal's subsequent behavior and lifestyle. This kind of learning is generally known as *phase-specific* learning, in that the behavior changes incurred by it are acquired during what appears to be a well-defined *sensitive period* of the animal's development. The effects are durable, often resistant to subsequent manipulation and appear to play an important role in determining many of the animal's long-term preferences.

Apart from describing phase-specific learning, there are two important theoretical issues raised by this phenomenon. First, does it represent a specialized learning process which is independent of, and has different features from, other more fundamental learning mechanisms? Clearly, phase-specific learning may be mediated by generalized associative mechanisms (such as, for example, Pavlovian or instrumental learning) but be special only in the sense that the period in which the responses can be learned is restricted in some way. Second, what is the biological function of phase-specific learning? If an animal has evolved the ability to learn certain responses only during restricted periods of its life, then one may reasonably assume that there exist pressures determined by the animal's environment and lifestyle which have selected for these tendencies. These questions can best be tackled by discussing two particularly prominent examples of phase-specific learning —imprinting and avian song learning.

Imprinting

Lorenz (1935) originally observed that the young of certain precocial birds (birds hatched with a complete covering of down and able to leave the nest immediately on hatching, such as duckling and chicks) would, on emerging from the egg, learn to approach and follow the nearest moving object. This attachment appeared to be subsequently difficult to break and also appeared to be formed only during a specific period of the birds' early development. Since the time of these original reports, two particular types of imprinting have been studied intensively. The original "following reaction" described by Lorenz is now known as *filial imprinting*, and this type of learning determines the preferred target for the following response mainly in young precocial birds. Also of interest, however, is *sexual imprinting* or the learning of social preferences. This type of learning will determine the subsequent mate preferences in both precocial and altricial birds.

Both types of learning share three important characteristics: (1) the existence of rather distinct sensitive phases when the learning will occur; (2) a comparatively high degree of durability and stability over time; and (3) a degree of selectivity about the kinds of stimuli which are most effective in determining durable preferences (that is, certain types of stimuli will be followed more readily than others).

1 *The nature of the imprinted object*

In laboratory studies of imprinting, hatchlings have been shown to imprint to a wide variety of stimuli and objects. These include people, boxes, cylinders, decoy ducks, model hens, rotating disks, and flickering lights (cf. Hess, 1973). However, there are certain target stimuli which are more effective in producing strong and durable following reactions. For instance, a vocal or noisy object is imprinted more readily than a silent one (Collias and Collias, 1956), and at longer post-hatch ages visual stimuli are more effective than auditory stimuli (Gottlieb and Klopfer, 1962). There is also a critical aspect to the size of the target stimulus: if it is too small it will tend to be treated simply as a possible food (Fabricius and Boyd, 1954).

However, one particularly salient feature of a stimulus which elicits strong imprinting reactions is movement. Ducklings, for instance, will imprint more readily to moving rather than stationary objects (Klopfer, 1971), and objects which emit "jerky" or lifelike movements are preferred to objects which emit smooth "gliding" movements (Fabricius, 1951). Furthermore, in both filial and sexual imprinting, preferences are developed more readily for stimuli which resemble the hatchling's own species (Immelmann, 1972); and Hess and Hess (1969) found that mallard ducklings when imprinted on the first day of life will show a faster following reaction to a mallard decoy than to a human being.

Figure 9.1 A typical set-up for the experimental study of the imprinted following response in chicks. The imprinting stimulus is a stuffed jungle fowl and the chick is housed in a running wheel which measures activity toward the imprinting stimulus. (Photograph courtesy of B. McCabe)

Clearly, there are characteristics of the target stimulus which can have differential effects on the probability of imprinting and on the speed of the following response. The fact that hatchlings appear to prefer target stimuli which resemble or possess features of their own species — even if they have been incubator hatched and have never had access to a conspecific — does suggest that imprinting may possess some genetically-determined biases which facilitate the establishment of preferences for the hatchling's own species (Immelmann, 1972, 1985; Hess, 1973) (see Figure 9.1).

2 *The sensitive period*

Jaynes (1956) exposed New Hampshire chick hatchlings to cardboard cubes at different intervals after hatching. The majority of those exposed at 1–6 hours after hatching met the criterion for imprinting. However, only 71 per cent of those exposed at 6–12 hours imprinted, 40 per cent of those exposed at 24–30 hours, 60 per cent of those exposed at 30–36 hours, and only 20 per cent of those exposed at 48–54 hours. Thus, there was an inverse relationship between post-hatch age and tendency to imprint.

Different species, of course, will tend to have different sensitive periods, and the time course of these periods seems to be highly adaptive. Immelmann (1985) suggests that the time course of the sensitive period will be related very much to (1) the fact that young precocial birds need to identify their parents almost immediately after hatching, and (2) in altricial species of birds the preferences learned through imprinting need to be acquired before the bird reaches nutritional independence. Support for this suggestion comes from the fact that in many species of birds the length of the sensitive period is related to the age at which the young bird leaves its parents and their breeding grounds. For instance, the period for sexual imprinting in zebra finches is around 40 days, which corresponds very closely to the time which the young stay close to the parents before leaving. However, in greylag geese, which remain in close proximity to their parents for about 10 months, the sensitive period for sexual imprinting lasts for over 150 days (Immelmann, 1972).

The duration of the sensitive period for imprinting does appear to be related to both hormonal and neuronal changes. For instance, the sensitive period for filial imprinting in ducklings appears to be related to changes in the corticosterone levels in the blood (Landsberg, 1980); while androgens have a positive effect and estrogens a negative effect on sexual imprinting in male zebra finches. Treatment with testosterone in these birds actually resulted in stronger social preferences during the sensitive period than in subjects which were untreated (Pröve, 1984). Similarly, sensitive periods appear to be related to periods of neuronal plasticity in the central nervous system. This neuronal plasticity permits rapid learning and the establishment of relatively permanent behavioral changes, while the end of the sensitive period is characterized by a rapid decrease in neuronal plasticity (Bateson, Horn, and Rose, 1975; Bateson, 1984). Correlations between the sensitive period for filial and sexual imprinting and developmental degeneration in various forebrain and visual centers of the brain have been found in mallards, silky chicks, and zebra finches (Bischof and Herrmann, 1984; Wolff, 1981).

Nevertheless, although the sensitive period does reflect a kind of "window on the world" which permits learning only during the time that the animal is allowed to look through the window, the actual duration of the sensitive period is not rigorously fixed within species. For instance, the duration of the sensitive period can be influenced markedly by the conditions during rearing and the nature of the rearing, training, and testing conditions (e.g. Moltz and Stettner, 1961; Sluckin and Salzen, 1961; Brown, 1975; Brown and Hamilton, 1977). This again suggests some environmentally-determined plasticity in the learning process.

3 Imprinting as the formation of preferences

As well as filial and sexual imprinting, there appear to be other kinds of preference formation which share learning characteristics similar to imprinting. Such processes include the establishment of preferences for habitat, locality, food types, host preferences in parasitic species, and song-learning in passerine birds (Immelmann, 1975; Hess, 1973; see below). The learning of such preferences all appear to occur during a sensitive period and have durable and long-lasting effects.

Locality imprinting

There is evidence that a young animal may learn to prefer the immediate environment that it first perceives, and this may subsequently determine the locality in which it will eventually breed (Thorpe, 1945). For instance, Hess (1972) allowed one group of ducklings to hatch in a simulated open ground nest and a second group to hatch in an elevated nest box. Some were kept in this environment for 1 day, some for 2 days. When these ducks eventually came to nest and breed in the wild, those that had remained in the nest for 2 days eventually nested either in the elevated nest boxes or on the ground, depending on the conditions in which they had originally been reared.

Processes similar to imprinting also appear to operate during the learning of routes for migratory birds. Such species must be able to find their way between their breeding and wintering grounds which can often be many thousands of miles apart. An important factor for successful migration appears to be the learning of sun and star compasses, and experimental planetarium studies have shown that there is a sensitive period for learning to read these compasses, usually between fledging and the start of the first autumnal migration. If a bird is exposed to the natural sky during this period it will migrate successfully; if no exposure takes place during this sensitive period it will never subsequently learn to read the star compass correctly even given repeated exposures (cf. Keeton, 1980).

Food preferences

Most birds and mammals develop preferences in their feeding habits, and preference for certain kinds of foods appears to develop during a specific period of the animal's development. For instance, the food preferences of chicks appear to be determined by experience with food objects during a sensitive period in the first 3–4 days post-hatching. Hess (1962, 1964) found that, on hatching, chicks would prefer to peck at a white circle on a blue background rather than a white triangle on a green background. He then reinforced chicks of differing age groups with food for pecking at the less-preferred stimulus. Figure 9.2 shows that pecking at the non-preferred stimulus could be influenced by food reinforcement only during the period of 3–5 days post-hatching, and the modification in pecking preferences during this sensitive period appears to be relatively permanent (Hess, 1973). Both of these characteristics suggest that this kind of food preference learning resembles other kinds of imprinting processes.

Imprinting in mammals

So far, we have discussed imprinting primarily in relation to precocial and altricial birds. What evidence is there that learning processes like imprinting exist in other groups of animals? A process which closely resembles imprinting can be identified in the formation of the mother–young bond in sheep and goats. Collias (1953) found that if the lamb is removed from the ewe at birth and returned 2–3 hours later, the ewe will refuse to accept the lamb. However, if the lamb is removed 1 hour after birth and returned 2–3 hours later, it will subsequently be accepted by the ewe. Thus, the sensitive period for the formation of this mother–young bond appears to be 1–2 hours after birth — a finding which has been replicated in goats (Klopfer, Adams, and Klopfer, 1964). This kind of filial imprinting differs from that in precocial birds in that the learning appears to be done by the parent and not the offspring. However, since sheep and goats give birth on a number of

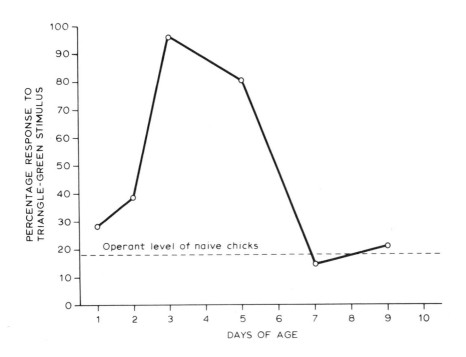

Figure 9.2 Preference for pecking at a triangle-green stimulus only had a lasting effect when the chick subjects were reinforced for this behavior between the ages of 3–5 days. (After Hess, 1973)

occasions during their lifetime, this learning can recur more than once. It thus differs from the relatively stable and durable filial and sexual imprinting that occurs in birds.

4 Learning mechanisms in imprinting

It is important to be clear about what is special about imprinting as a learning process. It is that preference learning occurs only during a sensitive period, and that the preference that is formed is fairly durable and resistant to change. It is also important to be clear about what is learned. A "preference" is not a behavior as such, and we infer preference either from the fact that an animal is willing to approach and follow a stimulus or from the fact that it chooses that stimulus in preference to others in a choice test. These are all points we must be clear about before we can begin to discuss what learning processes might be involved in imprinting.

Traditionally, theorists have been concerned about discovering the role that both Pavlovian and instrumental conditioning might play in imprinting, or, if they are not involved, what specialized learning processes can be devised to account for imprinting. The characteristics that make imprinting special as a learning phenomenon by no means exclude the involvement of Pavlovian or instrumental learning, as we shall see below. It is the relative resistance of the imprinting behavior to subsequent change that makes it unlikely, however, that an explanation of imprinting could be couched *solely* in terms of conditioning principles. While simple associative factors might contribute to the acquisition of the preference, some other factors need to be invoked to explain its subsequent durability.

Imprinting as associative learning

Moltz (1960, 1963) originally claimed that filial imprinting could be thought of simply as a sequence of Pavlovian followed by instrumental conditioning. He suggests that on emerging from the egg, hatchlings have little fear of the world around them and orient toward any relatively large, attention-provoking object. By a process of Pavlovian association the object which is oriented toward (the target or imprinted stimulus) becomes associated with these low anxiety levels such that, when the hatchling does eventually begin to acquire fear to unfamiliar objects, the imprinted stimulus becomes a source of anxiety reduction which instrumentally reinforces the following response. Certainly, there is some evidence that imprinted stimuli do have fear or arousal reducing effects (Bateson, 1969; Hoffman, 1968), and indeed, animals do appear to approach stimuli which have been paired with fear reduction (Leclerc, 1985; see p. 27).

Imprinted objects also acquire reinforcing properties and act in much the same way as do conditioned reinforcers (see pp. 69–70). For instance, young ducklings or chicks can easily be trained to press a pedal to switch on a motor bringing the imprinted object into motion, and will also perform an instrumental response in order to present themselves with different angled views of the imprinted object (Bateson and Reese, 1969). However, there are a number of problems with a simple associative model of this kind. First, while imprinting can in some instances be reversed by certain kinds of procedures (e.g. Salzen and Meyer, 1967, 1968), the following response appears, by and large, to be insensitive to punishment during the sensitive period —something not predicted if conditioning processes are acting alone. Subjecting young chicks to electric shocks contingent upon approaching the imprinted object during the sensitive period actually fails to prevent approach behavior (Kovach and Hess, 1963). Second, imprinted responses do not appear to show a readiness to extinguish when reinforcements are subsequently withheld. For instance, altering the pecking preference of a 3–4-day-old chick with food reinforcement appears to have a permanent effect, even when food reinforcement is subsequently discontinued (Hess, 1962, 1964). Third, if the following response were a simple conditioned behavior then we might expect that *any* target stimulus would be equally effective in establishing approach and follow responses. However, it is quite clear that some stimuli — especially stimuli possessing characteristics that resemble the hatchling's own species —are more effective as filial and sexual imprinting stimuli. While we now know that Pavlov's principle of equipotentiality of stimuli is probably incorrect (see pp. 125–7), it is still difficult to understand why conspecific features are so salient unless there is some genetically predetermined tendency to prefer those features (cf. Hess, 1973; Immelmann, 1985: 283–5).

Nevertheless, none of the foregoing precludes the possibility that associative mechanisms are at work somewhere in imprinting; but if they are, they still need to be clearly identified, and traditional conditioning principles would not appear to provide a complete picture of the imprinting process.

Imprinting as a special learning mechanism

Lorenz (1935) first pioneered the view that imprinting was a special learning mechanism dedicated to a particular function such as kin recognition. Many theorists were subsequently skeptical of this claim — if only because it appeared to violate scientific principles of parsimony and run contrary to generalized laws of learning that were popular during the 1960s and 1970s (e.g. Bateson, 1966; Hoffman and Ratner, 1973). Nevertheless, even some years ago theorists did admit to the possibility of genetically-determined biases in imprinting. The tendency of precocial hatchlings to imprint more readily to stimuli which possess conspecific features is important in this respect, and led Hess (1973) to suggest that

> we must consider that young chicks innately possess a schema of the natural imprinting object, so that the more a social object fits this schema, the stronger the imprinting that occurs to the object. This innate disposition with regard to the type of object learned indicates that social imprinting is not just simply an extremely powerful effect of the environment upon the behavior of an animal. Rather, there has been an evolutionary pressure for the young bird to learn the right thing — the

natural parent — at the right time — the first day of life — the time of the sensitive period that has been genetically provided for.

(Hess, 1973: 380)

There are two issues here that should be clarified: one suggests that there is a good deal of *genetic predisposition* in imprinting, the second suggests that imprinting is a *specialized learning process* which differs from other more conventional learning processes. The two are quite independent issues. For instance, we have already seen in earlier chapters that some animals might bring a genetically-determined predisposition to a learning situation, but the actual learning appears to be mediated by conventional learning mechanisms (see, for instance, taste aversion learning, Chapter 6, pp. 183–90). In such cases the genetic or species predisposition determines what kinds of stimuli will be attended to, and as a consequence, what other stimuli they will become associated with. The fact that ducklings imprint more readily to conspecifics than other more neutral stimuli may be another example of this genetically-determined stimulus selectivity (see also pp. 125–7).

However, there is some evidence on the neurophysiology of imprinting which throws some light on these issues. One concerns the brain centers involved in imprinting, the other concerns the states of neuronal plasticity that exist during sensitive periods. Bateson and his colleagues have demonstrated that filial imprinting in domestic chicks enhances biochemical activity in the roof of the forebrain. For instance, when chicks were allowed to imprint using only one eye (the other being covered by a patch), the biochemical activity was 15 per cent higher on the trained side of the forebrain roof than on the untrained side (Horn, Rose, and Bateson, 1973). Similarly, there is a correlation between the strength of the imprinting response and biochemical activity in the roof of the anterior forebrain (Bateson, Horn, and Rose, 1975). The critical brain center which appeared to be the focus of these effects was the intermediate region of the medial hyperstriatum ventrale (IMHV) (cf. Horn, McCabe, and Bateson, 1979), and this center had connections to visual projection areas (Bradley and Horn, 1978). In subsequent studies involving ablation of IMHV, this area was found to be crucial to the recognition of the imprinted object. Subjects which had IMHV lesions showed no subsequent preference for the object with which they had earlier received imprinting training (McCabe, Horn, and Bateson, 1981). Furthermore, while IMHV lesioned chicks failed to learn the characteristics of a moving imprinted object, they could still successfully learn instrumental responses involving a visual discrimination for heat reinforcement (cf. Bateson, 1984). This suggests that IMHV is not a generalized center mediating visual recognition, but is specialized in mediating certain kinds of recognition — especially those concerned in imprinting, and possibly with the storage of information acquired during imprinting.

In other neurophysiological studies the readiness to learn early in life can often be found to be correlated with the formation of new synapses and dendritic branching and to terminate with the disconnection of neurons and their physiological death (e.g. Wolff, 1981; Bischof and Herrmann, 1984). Such periods of neural plasticity often coincide with sensitive periods for imprinting. The evidence is beginning to suggest that this may not only account for phase-specific learning but that it might also account for the relative durability of the learning that occurs during a sensitive period. For instance, Immelmann suggests that

> In view of the possible correlations between sensitive phases and neuronanatomical development, it seems likely that the critical mechanism underlying the temporal limits of plasticity might consist of genetically determined programs for the time course of neuronal plasticity. These programs could determine at what age and for how long morphological changes are possible and thus put constraints on the age period during which information can be stored with a high degree of permanance.
>
> (Immelmann, 1985: 283)

The fact that at the end of a sensitive period particular brain centers may become effectively neuronally inert may indeed account for the permanence of information learned during the sensitive period. If information acquired during imprinting is stored in a specific center which is characterized by this brief period of neuronal plasticity followed by neuronal inactivity thereafter, then this could go some way to explaining the relative permanence of preferences acquired during sensitive periods of imprinting.

5 Summary

What the above evidence is beginning to suggest is that (1) animals may indeed have genetically predetermined tendencies to imprint to some objects rather than others, but this does not necessarily imply that imprinting is a specialized learning system but may simply reflect stimulus selectivity predispositions found in learning generally; and (2) special areas of the brain appear to be important in the storage of information learned during imprinting and these areas may be characterized by the phasic nature of their neuronal plasticity. This results in information acquired during imprinting being relatively resistant to change later in life.

This still leaves open the question of what mechanisms are implicated in the actual *learning* about imprinted objects. These may indeed be basic associative mechanisms, but we must await further evidence on this point.

Song learning in birds

There are just under 9 000 extant species of bird in the world, of which around 4 000 are perching songbirds (the passerines), that are differentiated from other species by their striking and often complex vocalizations. While most passerine species possess their own distinctive song, individual members of a species may elaborate on and augment the basic species theme. Similarly, while some aspects of a species song appear to be innately determined, individual birds clearly have to learn important features of their species song. This learning is interesting in that, while it employs many distinct characteristics, it is in particular phase-specific and durable — characteristics which set it aside from simple forms of adaptive learning and which make comparisons with imprinting possible.

An example of the characteristics of this song learning is provided in a study on white-crowned sparrows (*Zonotrichia leucophrys*) by Marler (1970). The song of the white-crowned sparrow consists of an initial whistle followed by a more individual complex trill. The whistle is highly stereotyped, but the trill represents a locality dialect which is learned by the bird. Within the first 150 days post-hatching, premature singing begins with both the whistle and the trill developing through a series of stages which gradually begin to approximate the adult song. At about 8 months of age, when the bird reaches sexual maturity, the song crystallizes and no further learning takes place, either in that year or in subsequent years. Thus, as the bird reaches sexual maturity it is as though the learning mechanism is switched off, and what has been learned up to that point remains durable and resistant to change. First, let us look at the characteristics of the learning processes that contribute to song learning.

1 *Characteristics of the learning process*

We know that learning is an essential aspect of the development of a mature bird's song because birds that are reared in isolation will develop abnormal songs (Kroodsma, 1982). Nevertheless, as we shall see below, although learning is essential, there are also some predispositional features of this learning.

266

Acoustical feedback

While some aspects of song structure develop even in birds that have been deafened, severing the auditory feedback loop will result in birds learning abnormal songs (Konishi, 1965). This feedback appears to be important only in songbirds, however, since the calls of many nonsinging birds such as doves and chickens are unaffected by early deafening (Konishi and Nottebohm, 1969). Thus, songbirds must hear themselves sing in order to learn the species song correctly. However, even in deafened birds, there are clear species differences in the songs that emerge, suggesting at least some genetic predetermination (e.g. Marler and Sherman, 1982).

Imitation and improvisation

Imitation appears to have an important, but complex, effect on song learning. For instance, birds that are raised with exposure to their conspecific song usually develop songs which are more clearly normal than birds reared in isolation. Some species, such as the northern mockingbird, may mimic many species, whereas others, such as North American sparrows, will never mimic heterospecific songs (Baylis, 1982; Dowsett-Lemaire, 1979; Marler and Peters, 1980). However, many species of bird are as likely to improvise as to imitate directly, although the imitation process appears to facilitate this improvisation. They tend to utilize the conspecific song as a kind of template around which they can improvise.

Juncos, for instance, appear to utilize a model as a template for developing their own individualized and highly stereotyped song. As a consequence, juncos share very few song syllables in common (Marler, 1967; Marler, Kreith, and Tamura, 1962). Hearing a conspecific model performing the species-specific song can also act as a *trigger* for the song-learning process. For instance, some birds can readily learn heterospecific sounds, but only if they are intermingled with conspecific sounds (cf. Marler and Peters, 1980). The presence of the conspecific sounds appears to act as a trigger which permits the subject to imitate what follows. Nevertheless, some other species of bird rely almost entirely on improvisation rather than imitation. Blackbirds, for instance, can recombine syllables to form completely new songs even when reared in acoustical and social isolation (Hall-Craggs, 1962; Thielcke-Poltz and Thielcke, 1960).

Sensitive periods

In passerine birds, song learning appears only during what seems to be a sensitive period during early development. There appear to be two stages to this developmental process: first, the sensitive period itself when learning occurs, and second, the process of *crystallization* when no further learning takes place (Kroodsma, 1981; Marler, 1970). The sensitive period itself varies from species to species. In species such as the white-crowned sparrow, the song sparrow, and the zebra finch, the sensitive period occurs very early in the first year (Immelmann, 1969; Kroodsma, 1977, 1978). In other species, the sensitive period may last for the whole of the first year and crystallization will be less well defined. Such species include the European and cardinal chaffinch (Lemon, 1975; Nottebohm, 1970). However, a few other species, although learning the rudiments of their song early in the first year, do not have a well-defined crystallization stage and may continue learning in subsequent years. This produces a large song repertoire which may have important biological functions for those species concerned (for example, female canaries exposed to the songs of males with large repertoires lay more eggs than those exposed to males with small song repertoires: Kroodsma, 1976). Nevertheless, well-defined sensitive periods and crystallization stages are more commonly the rule than the exception.

Memorial abilities

During song learning there is a sensory phase, when the bird is exposed to the model song, followed by a sensorimotor phase, where the bird begins to produce an amorphous imitation of the model, through to the development of the full song and eventual crystallization. What is interesting is that the sensory and sensorimotor stages may be separated by several months during which the bird neither hears the model nor rehearses the song (Marler and Peters, 1982). Similarly, when the song has crystallized it remains relatively unchanged, even though the bird does not rehearse the song during the non-breeding season (Konishi and Nottebohm, 1969).

Genetic predispositions

Even when birds have been experimentally deafened early in life, Marler and Sherman (1982) found significant species differences in the frequency characteristics and the duration, structure, and repertoire size of the songs that these birds eventually learned, suggesting that at least some aspects of the song are preprogramed. Similarly, in species such as song sparrows and canaries, certain aspects of the song temporal pattern develop quite normally in deafened individuals even though the refinements of the song may be abnormal (Guettinger, 1981; Marler and Sherman, 1982). Also, the fact that around 85 per cent of song birds learn to mimic only their own species songs and reject heterospecific songs does possibly suggest a genetic predisposition (although in some cases it may be the social conditions during rearing which determine this preference; cf. Immelmann, 1969).

2 Is song learning a specialized learning process?

Any theoretical account of the learning process that underlies song acquisition must take into account a number of salient facts. First, the learning tends to occur during a brief sensitive period early in life and subsequently is relatively resistant either to change or forgetting. Second, there are certain genetic predispositions and species-specific factors which need attention: certain components of the song appear to be learned regardless of acoustical and social isolation, and a large number of species prefer their own species song and reject others. Third, song learning appears to possess remarkable memorial capacities: birds retain sensory information for months on end before performing the song, and also retain the song even after non-use during the months of the nonbreeding season.

Associative learning

There appears to be little evidence that song learning in birds is shaped either by instrumental or Pavlovian contingencies (cf. Marler, 1984), but that the presence of certain triggering conditions is sufficient for the learning to take place. However, two points should be raised here. First, there is some evidence that contingent social interaction may be necessary and sufficient for song learning to proceed in some species (Payne, 1981); and if there is any shaping from instrumental contingencies social interaction may be the most viable reinforcer. Second, hearing the conspecific song can act as a very powerful reinforcer itself to some species of bird. For instance, Stevenson (1969) found that presentations of the conspecific song to chaffinches contingent upon a perching response acted to increase the frequency of that response.

Specialized brain centers

A number of studies have shown that certain forebrain nuclei (for example, nucleus hyperstriatum ventrale, pars caudale (HVc) and the nucleus robustus archistriatalis (RA) occur only in birds capable of song learning and are absent in suboscine or nonpasserine birds which lack this capacity (Nottebohm, 1980; Paton, Manogue, and Nottebohm, 1981; Konishi, 1985). Similarly, variations in the size of the HVc and RA nuclei can be found within species: for instance, canaries with larger numbers of syllables to their song tend to have larger HVcs and RAs than those with a smaller number of syllables (Nottebohm, Kasparian, and Pandazis, 1981), and the size of HVc and RA nuclei fluctuate seasonally, becoming larger in the spring season when the canary is most vocal (Nottebohm, 1981). These nuclei appear to be involved in both the sensory and sensorimotor aspects of song production since they contain both motor and auditory neurones (e.g. McCasland and Konishi, 1981; Konishi, 1985).

Single-unit recordings from the HVc suggest that both motor and auditory nuclei are involved in song learning, because certain neurones of the HVc have been shown to fire only just prior to and during the delivery of a specific learned piece of the bird's song (McCasland, 1983; Margoliash, 1983). Lesion studies of the HVc nucleus also support its involvement in song learning. HVc-lesioned canaries, for instance, show fewer changes in their songs than birds lesioned in the hypoglossus region (Nottebohm, 1980; Nottebohm, Manning, and Nottebohm, 1976; Nottebohm, Stokes, and Leonard, 1976). Furthermore, there even appears to be a lateralization of function in the HVc nuclei; lesions of the left HVc cause greater loss or song deterioration than a lesion of the right HVc (Nottebohm, Manning, and Nottebohm, 1976).

It is not entirely clear yet what the existence of these specialized brain nuclei means for theories of song learning. The discovery of a specific brain center related to song learning does appear to correspond with the finding of similar specialized centers for imprinting, and may obviously reflect the evolution of special learning requirements. It is possible that these song control nuclei may contain the auditory templates that appear to exist within different species (e.g. Marler, 1984), or they may possess the neural characteristics necessary to delineate sensitive periods for song learning (see pp. 264–5). We must await further neurophysiological studies for clarification of these issues.

3 Summary

We can say tentatively that song learning does appear to be a specialized learning process. Songs are not obviously learned by processes of instrumental or Pavlovian conditioning, and song learning appears to possess certain predispositions which indicate the possible existence of auditory templates within species. In many species the conspecific song is learned rapidly during a short period of early development, and is durable over many seasons without being lost during periods of disuse. The existence of brain nuclei specializing in song learning and production suggests that song learning may be a highly specialized process, but how these nuclei mediate any specialization that may exist has yet to be determined.

The biological function of phase-specific learning

The general features which characterize phase-specific learning are (1) the existence of sensitive periods when the learning occurs, and (2) the high degree of stability and durability that this learning bestows on the animal. Both imprinting and avian song learning possess these characteristics in varying degrees. The next question to ask is why phase-specific learning should have evolved as a specialized learning adaptation possessing these characteristics.

It can be seen from the contents of this chapter that phase-specific learning has been discovered and studied almost exclusively in birds (cf. Immelmann and Suomi, 1981), and the existence of such learning may well be related to the rapid ontogenetic development in these animals. Birds reach their adult size and weight within 1 per cent of their normal life expectancy compared with a figure of over 30 per cent for most mammals. This rapid ontogenetic development appears to have the benefit of enabling birds to reach the ideal ratio between body-weight and a constant wing surface as quickly as possible (cf. Immelmann, 1985; Mason, 1979). Phase-specific learning may represent the learning and memorial equivalent of the bird's rapid bodily development, with conventional learning processes perhaps being inadequate to cope with the kinds of information that need to be acquired in the brief period between hatching and adulthood.

Furthermore, while phase-specific learning does have distinct characteristics it is adaptable in that sensitive periods do appear to adapt to specific ecological conditions. In precocial birds, for instance, the sensitive period begins as early as a few hours after hatching when the hatchling needs to recognize and follow the parents. With altricial species these periods are prolonged by the fact that the young bird has more time available in which to learn the characteristics of the parents. In many species the termination of the sensitive period is geared to the age at which the young bird leaves the parents, and this process appears to protect what is already learned and prevent "misimprinting" on either wrong species or wrong habitats. Very brief sensitive periods have, for instance, been found in species which disperse and form flocks very early and where the dangers of "misimprinting" are high (cf. Immelmann, 1985). All of these ecological conditions favor the evolution of a durable early-learning mechanism which is particularly sensitive to certain environmental stimuli.

271

Chapter summary

1 Certain types of learning are characterized by the fact that they occur only during a specific, brief period of the animal's lifetime. This kind of learning is called *phase specific* and occurs during a *sensitive period* of the animal's development.

2 There are two main types of phase-specific learning that have been studied. These are *imprinting* and avian *song learning*.

3 The young of certain precocial birds (such as chicks and ducklings) would, on emerging from the egg, learn to approach and follow the nearest moving object. This attachment is known as imprinting, is subsequently difficult to break, and occurs during a specific period of the bird's early development.

4 Hatchlings will imprint to many different stimuli but appear to have a preference for their own species.

5 The actual duration of the sensitive period for imprinting does not appear to be rigorously fixed but is determined by hormonal and neuronal changes.

6 As well as filial imprinting (attachment to conspecifics) there appear to be other kinds of preference formation which share similar characteristics to imprinting. These include locality imprinting, food preferences, and mother–young attachments in some mammals.

7 We are still unclear as to the actual mechanisms which underlie imprinting. However, (1) animals do appear to have genetically predetermined tendencies to imprint to some objects rather than others, and (2) special areas of the brain appear to be important in the storage of information learned during imprinting. These latter areas are characterized by the phasic nature of their neuronal plasticity which gives imprinting its characteristic of being resilient to change in later life.

8 Many species of bird have their own distinctive song. The acquisition of such songs appears to reflect a combination of genetically-predetermined factors and individual learning. The learning component is normally characterized by its phase-specific nature and its durability.

9 Birds reared in complete isolation often develop abnormal songs, suggesting that learning is a vital component of song acquisition. Important factors include acoustical feedback, imitation and exposure to relevant information during a *sensitive period* of song development.

10 Song learning appears to be a specialized learning process because (1) songs are not obviously learned by processes of conditioning, and (2) song learning possesses certain predispositions which indicate the existence of auditory templates within species.

11 There appears to be a specific brain center related to song learning, which corresponds to the fact that similar specialized centers exist for imprinting. These brain centers appear to contain the auditory templates for song learning and possess the phasic neuronal plasticity necessary for delineating a sensitive period for song learning.

12 Phase-specific learning has been identified primarily in birds, and it may be a specialized form of learning which has evolved in this group to provide rapid cognitive development which matches their very rapid ontogenetic development.

Chapter ten

Learning and intelligence

As recently as 1980 a stalwart of the study of intelligence, A. R. Jensen, was led to write that

> in terms of measured learning and problem-solving capacities, the single-celled protozoans (for example, the amoeba) rank at the bottom of the scale, followed in order by the invertebrates, the lower vertebrates, the lower mammals, the primates, and man. The vertebrates have been studied most intensively and show fishes at the bottom of the capacity scale, followed by amphibians, reptiles and birds. Then comes the mammals, with rodents at the bottom followed by the ungulates (cow, horse, pig and elephant, in ascending order), then the carnivores (cats and dogs), and finally the primates, in order: new world monkeys, old world monkeys, the apes (gibbon, orangutan, gorilla, chimpanzee), and, at the pinnacle, humans.
>
> (Jensen, 1980: 175)

This ranking is not intuitively contentious; we might at first glance quibble only with one or two discrete particulars of this scaling, but the sensible layman would not deny that a human or an ape would be more intelligent and adaptable than a protozoan, a rat or a cat or a dog. However, intuitively reasonable as this scaling seems, it is by no means easy to link this kind of intelligence ranking to objective criteria. For instance, although we might be able to show that humans were better at learning conceptually-based tasks than pigeons, the homing abilities of pigeons would undoubtedly allow them to win out over most humans if the task were simply to return home successfully from an unknown location; similarly, although humans would be ranked higher than, say, sharks on the ability to see fine detail and solve abstract problems, they would be ranked lower than sharks on the ability to detect low-frequency pressure waves or electric fields in the immediate vicinity. What these examples illustrate is the non-linear nature of adaptive abilities. Living creatures have, in general, evolved a variety of specialized capacities which allow them to cope reasonably efficiently with the problems they are likely to encounter in their own ecological niche.

There are two issues that arise out of this. First, is there any separable feature of animal behavior which we can call intelligence and which we can identify as an evolved characteristic? Second, since adaptive capacities evolve to cope with the demands of an animal's natural environment, to what extent is intelligence a suitable capacity to evolve in order to cope with these demands?

The nature of animal intelligence

1 Anthropomorphic definitions

First, we must deal with the fundamental problem of what is to be considered as animal intelligence. All too often this is considered in relation to human intelligence and revolves around attributes such as abstraction, conceptualization, and — very often — the mere fact that an animal exhibits what appears to be complex behavior. There are many pitfalls in describing apparently complex behavior as intelligent, the most famous of which is the example of Clever Hans (Pfungst, 1911). Clever Hans was a horse that had seemingly learned to solve complex mathematical problems and communicate the answer by tapping its foot. Although many scientists were convinced that Clever Hans was reasoning out the answers, subsequent closer scrutiny revealed that the horse was reacting to subtle cues provided by the person who had set the task. This person might nod their head as Clever Hans tapped out the answer and then stop when Clever Hans had reached the correct number. The horse was simply reacting to discrete cues unwittingly provided by the observer.

In other cases, behavior might be seen as "purposeful" in the sense of being a reasoned solution to a particular task. There are, again, many instances where such first impressions are misleading. For instance, Wolfgang Köhler (1925) conducted many experiments on the problem-solving abilities of apes and described his findings in terms of *insight learning*. Insight learning is characterized by Köhler as the ability to reorganize cognitively the elements of a problem until a possible functional solution is arrived at (the moment of insight). In one of these studies, a chimpanzee had to rake in a banana which is out of its reach and has to join two fitting sticks end to end in order to be able to do so. Normally, the subjects can solve this problem after a period

275

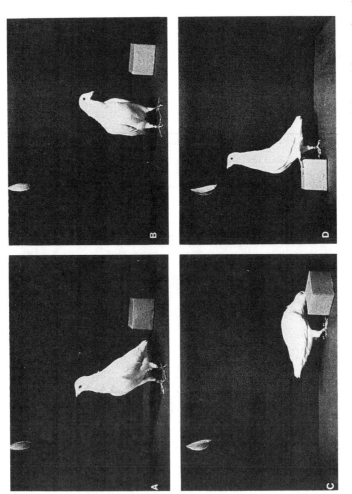

Figure 10.1 "Insight" in the pigeon. This subject had been separately reinforced for moving the box to a green spot in the center of the chamber and on other occasions for standing on a box already placed in the center of the chamber and pecking at the plastic banana hanging from the ceiling. The four photographs (A-D) represent a test session when the pigeon was faced with the problem of pecking the banana with the box at the side of the chamber and no green spot to move the box to. In only a short time pigeons had solved the problem by moving the box to the center of the chamber and mounting it to peck the banana. (Photographs courtesy of R. Epstein)

time apparently by "reasoning out" a solution. However, subsequent studies have demonstrated that what on the face of it appears to be a purposefully reasoned solution to the task does contain many experiential and nonpurposeful elements. Both Birch (1945) and Schiller (1952) found that apparently insightful solutions are not obtained unless the chimpanzees had previous manipulatory experience with the elements of the problem (for example, the fitting sticks). Very often chimpanzees fit together sticks in an apparently insightful way even when there is no problem to solve. In another of Köhler's tasks, chimpanzees were required to stack boxes in the center of the room in order to stand on them and obtain a banana that was otherwise out of reach. Köhler believed that the solution to this problem was the result of insightful reasoning directed at a particular goal, and Schiller (1952) found that if chimpanzees were given boxes simply to play with (and no problem to solve) they "actually stacked them and climbed on the tower jumping upward from the top repeatedly with arms lifted above the head and stretching towards the ceiling. For the human observer it was hard to believe that there was no food above them to be reached" (Schiller, 1952).

There is also the tendency to attribute human-like intellectual characteristics, such as reasoning, to animals which more closely approximate humans in their evolutionary lineage and appearance. In an interesting variation on Köhler's box-stacking problem, Epstein, Kirshnit, Lanza, and Rubin (1984) attempted to demonstrate behavior formalistically similar to that seen in Köhler's apes, but in pigeons. In some sessions the pigeons were rewarded with food for pushing a small cardboard box onto a green spot on the center of the floor of the chamber; in other sessions they were rewarded with food for standing on the box (which had already been placed in the center of the chamber by the experimenter) and pecking at a small toy banana suspended above the box. When these two behaviors (directional pushing and standing on the box) were established, a test session was carried out whereby the toy banana was suspended from the ceiling and the box was located some distance from the banana, and no green spot was present. The pigeons initially showed unsuccessful attempts to reach the banana by flying up and pacing around it, but then "each subject began rather suddenly to push the box in what was clearly the direction of the banana.... Each subject stopped pushing in the appropriate place, climbed, and pecked the banana" (Epstein *et al.*, 1984: 61) (see Figure 10.1). The behavioral characteristics of Köhler's apes and Epstein's pigeons at the point at which the solution to the problem is achieved are almost identical, yet whereas we might be too willing to explain the ape's behavior as intelligent or as the result of reasoning, we might be much more inclined to look for some basic processes in the case of the pigeons.

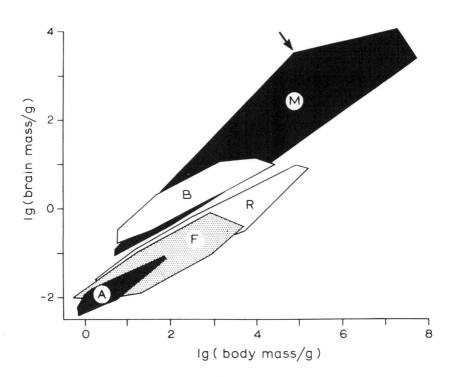

Figure 10.2 Brain–body relations in living species from 5 vertebrate classes: A = amphibia, F = fishes, R = reptiles, B = birds, and M = mammals. The arrow indicates the point where humans lie on this figure. See text for further explanation. (After Jerison, 1973)

One other instance when we are willing to attribute the characteristic of intelligence to behavior is when it is not necessarily formally complex but appears to require a substantial amount of information processing in order to execute it successfully. For instance, many predators capture their prey not simply by chasing and catching them but by intercepting them at some future point where their paths intersect. This presumably requires a decision on (1) whether the prey is worth pursuing in the first place (that is, whether it is possible to catch it), and (2) the best route to adopt to intercept the prey. Diving gannets (*Sula bassani*) dive into the water when catching prey with sufficient velocity to dive under a particular shoal of fish and spear their prey on the way back to the surface. This in itself requires information about the distance of the dive, the distance below the surface of the shoal of fish and the projected velocity on hitting the water (Lee and Reddish, 1981). Such abilities are also possessed by invertebrates. Flies can use a time-to-contact strategy to control landing on static horizontal surfaces (Wagner, 1982), and Collett and Land (1978) have shown that hoverflies are able to intercept the complex path of another fly. These abilities *look* sophisticated and intelligent because we are aware of the amount of information that would be required *for us* to describe and predict these activities. For example, we have discussed in Chapter 8 how animals appear to forage for food optimally in a patchy environment. We know they are foraging optimally because we have the mathematical abilities to calculate what the optimal solution might be. But this of course does not mean that the animal is using those same calculations to arrive at the optimal solution. The wasp *Nemeritis*, for instance, can arrive at the optimal solution to its ovipositing problem by utilizing processes as basic as orthokinesis, klinotaxis, and habituation (see pp. 248–9).

What the above examples illustrate are some of the more obvious ways in which animal behavior might be mistakenly labeled as "intelligent" based on approximations to what we describe in humans as intelligent behavior. However, there are other more fundamental reasons for rejecting the notion that animal intelligence is just a scaled-down version of human intelligence. As Hodos (1982) points out, this comparison ignores the special nature of human intelligence, which is greatly dependent on our language abilities and the cognitive skills that derive from this. Most other animal species do not possess language abilities yet may have developed special capabilities suitable for their own environments which would only be of limited value to humans. It is therefore unhelpful to assess the intelligence of animals on the basis of cognitive tasks which depend in humans on linguistic abilities.

2 *The evolutionary approach*

Jerison (1973, 1982, 1983) has taken a rather unorthodox approach to the definition of animal intelligence by suggesting that animal intelligence is the behavioral correlate of encephalization (brain size). He has developed an objective measure of the brain size that a species actually has when compared to the brain size that would be expected on the basis of body size alone (known as the encephalization quotient, EQ). Thus, the greater the brain size relative to body size the greater is the EQ. Figure 10.2 illustrates body–brain relationships in living species from five vertebrate classes. The closer a species falls to the top left-hand corner of the figure the greater is its EQ. This shows that not only do some classes have greater EQs than others (for example, mammals have greater EQs than birds, and birds than fish, and so on), but there are also significant differences within classes; the EQ of humans and dolphins is greater than the EQ of other mammals; within the bird class, chickens and pigeons are among the least encephalized, song birds are "average," and crows and parrots are the most encephalized.

Nevertheless, how does this relate to intelligence? Jerison (1985a, b) argues that after accounting for the number of neurones required to cope with routine body functions (this number will be larger the greater the actual body size of the animal), all "excess" neurones contribute to extra information-processing capacity, and that the evolution of encephalization reflects the need for greater information processing. Thus, since information-processing capacity is determined by cortical surface area (brain size), then "animal intelligence and the problems of its analysis may be much better understood if we reverse the implicit causal arrow and think of it as the behavioral correlate of encephalization" (Jerison, 1985a: 28). The implication here is that when distantly related species share comparable EQs, we should consider them as comparable in intelligence. This does not mean that they have evolved equivalent encephalization for similar reasons, and the adaptations may be quite different. For instance, some species of deer and wolves share similar EQs, yet they live in ecological balance as prey and predator in a set of related niches (Mech, 1970). Van Valen (1973) suggests that in such circumstances, species evolve in order to keep their place in the niche relative to other species. Thus, the deer will have evolved adaptive strategies to counter-balance any adaptive gain evolved by its predator, the wolf. This is one example of how phylogenetically unrelated species may have evolved to similar grades of encephalization.

Nevertheless, the EQ approach of Jerison does beg a number of questions in relation to the issue of intelligence and learning. Although it does emphasize the role of evolutionary pressures in determining intelligence, it does not readily specify how those pressures will be translated into behavioral adaptations. Indeed, in some cases these pressures may call for increased simplicity rather than increased complexity. Furthermore, although it is reasonable to conceive of intelligence as the behavioral correlate of encephalization, it is not at all clear how we should begin to search for these behavioral correlations, and, in effect, we are still left with the problem of specifying what adaptive characteristics on what tasks define intelligence.

3 *The ecological approach*

One of the original approaches to the modern study of animal intelligence was pioneered by Bitterman (1965, 1975), whose efforts were directed toward the

Table 10.1 The behavior of five different species in four different test situations as classified by Bitterman (1965, 1975). The behavior is characterized as either rat-like or fish-like depending on their performance on these tasks (see text for further elaboration).

	Spatial problems		Visual problems	
	Reversal	Probability	Reversal	Probability
Monkey	Rat	Rat	Rat	Rat
Rat	Rat	Rat	Rat	Rat
Pigeons	Rat	Rat	Rat	Fish
Turtle	Rat	Rat	Fish	Fish
Fish	Fish	Fish	Fish	Fish

search for divergence and nonlinearity in learning mechanisms as reflected in the performance of different species on a variety of different learning tasks. This comparative approach led Bitterman to believe that there were clear qualitative differences in intellectual functioning between a number of species (rat, pigeon, turtle, and fish) on two particular experimental procedures — serial reversal learning and probability learning. In serial reversal learning the subject has to learn an S^+/S^- discrimination to a set criterion before the reinforcement contingencies between S^+ and S^- are reversed (that is, S^+ becomes S^- and S^- becomes S^+). The object of successive reversals is to see if the subject can reach the learning criterion after each reversal with fewer and fewer errors. Probability learning is a discrimination task in which reinforcement is available for responding to one of two stimuli on every trial, but where the probability of reinforcement is higher for responding to one of the two stimuli (S^+) than to the other (S^-). For example, S^+ may be reinforced on 70 per cent of the trials, leaving S^- to be reinforced on the remaining 30 per cent. In this example, adopting a *maximizing* strategy (that is, always responding to the higher probability stimulus on every trial) would yield reinforcement on 70 per cent of the trials, whereas *matching* (responding to the higher probability stimulus on roughly the same percentage basis as it is reinforced namely 70 per cent) would yield reinforcement on only 58 per cent of the trials (70×0.7 plus 30×0.3). Thus, arguably, maximizing is the more adaptive strategy. On the basis of the results of his experiments Bitterman was led to classify animals from different vertebrate categories as either "fish-like" or "rat-like" in the qualities of their performance (see Table 10.1). The conclusion drawn by Bitterman is that rats are not just qualitatively different from fish in the nature of their learning performance but are superior in terms of developed intelligence (Bitterman, 1965) (see pp. 284–90).

Nevertheless, there have been serious criticisms of this kind of comparative approach to animal intelligence, both on theoretical grounds (Hodos and Campbell, 1969) and empirical grounds (Johnston, 1981a; Macphail, 1982). We will discuss some of the emphirical evidence in the next section of this chapter, but first let us confine ourselves to the theoretical issues.

One of the main problems of the comparative approach employed by Bitterman is that, while it attempts to compare the abilities of quite different species, it ignores the possible role of evolutionary mechanisms in selecting for these abilities (cf. Hodos and Campbell, 1969; Johnston, 1985; Gottlieb, 1985). There are three important factors that need to be stressed in this respect. First, the evolution of learning abilities will depend upon what problems the animal needs to solve in its own environmental niche. Thus, learning abilities and intelligence will evolve largely because the animal requires them in its own niche. Second, evolution selects only for outcomes, not for mechanisms; thus, while different species may face similar problems posed by their ecological niches, they need not evolve similar mechanisms to cope with these problems. While one species may evolve a learning mechanism to cope with the problem, other species may evolve maturational, morphological, or preprogramed behavioral adaptations. In such circumstances the species that has evolved a learning mechanism to deal with the problem is not necessarily better adapted than those species which have evolved other means — all of these species are equally adapted. Third, when species are faced with new problems in their environmental niche the adaptive solution does not automatically call for increased complexity (such as the evolution of learning abilities), but may frequently call for increased simplicity (Hodos, 1982).

These factors have a number of implications for the notion of animal intelligence. First, evolutionary trends do not follow a unilinear progression from simpler to more complex (cf. Hodos, 1982) as is often assumed in the use of the notion of general intelligence to describe differences in learning abilities between species. Furthermore, comparing phylogenetically unrelated species on arbitrary tasks pays no attention to how such an ability as general intelligence *might* have evolved (cf. Hodos and Campbell, 1969; Gottlieb, 1984). Since turtles are not descended from fish, pigeons from turtles, or rats from pigeons, any differences in abilities on arbitrary learning tasks has little or nothing to say about the evolution of any characteristic we wish to call "intelligence." Second, the comparative approach compares species on arbitrary learning tasks with no regard to the natural problems those species have to deal with. This has two implications. First, the laboratory task facing the animal may not be one which that animal is faced with in its own environmental niche. If this is the case, capacities appropriate to dealing with the problem could never have been specifically selected for. And second, since problems in nature are usually dealt with by different, problem-specific devices evolved for those purposes, the problems encountered in arbitrary laboratory tasks may have to be solved by abilities not designed for that purpose but pressed into service to make the best of the job in hand. Thus, the comparative psychologist is not necessarily tapping some capacity we can call general intelligence, but at best is observing how good a fit there is between a purpose-specific ability and its performance on some task which it was not necessarily selected to deal with.

All this has led some ecological learning theorists to propose that the notion of animal intelligence is theoretically meaningless (e.g. Johnston, 1981a), and that we should talk instead of the adaptedness of an animal to its environmental niche regardless of what capacities or abilities have evolved to deal with living in that niche. In this sense an ant is as adapted as a dolphin, but each has evolved quite different behavioral abilities to deal with the problems encountered in their differing niches. One possible approach to salvaging the notion of animal intelligence within this ecological context is to study species not on the basis that they are distantly related but on the basis that they occupy contrasting ecological niches. It may be possible to identify the variety of problems facing an animal in its ecological niche and use this as some kind of index to the capacities it has evolved to deal with them. We may then be able to determine if different learning, perceptual, or behavioral abilities correlate with various ecological conditions (e.g. Gottlieb, 1984), and eventually be able to define the probable behavioral attributes that species must exhibit for success in a particular ecological niche (such correlations are known as *adaptive profiles*, e.g. Dewsbury, Baumgardner, Sawrey, and Webster, 1982; Fragaszy and Mason, 1983).

Finally, although the ecological approach does emphasize the adaptedness of a species to its niche, there is another way of defining animal intelligence within this framework. A number of writers have argued that simply being adapted to a particular niche is no guarantee of survival — particularly if a catastrophic and irreversible change in the conditions within that niche occurs (cf. Huxley, 1957; Rensch, 1959; Gottlieb, 1984). In this respect, those species which evolve abilities to deal with sudden changes in their niche, or which are able to exploit new niches, are likely to hold a selective advantage over those species which have not evolved such abilities. To all intents and purposes we are saying that those species which evolve abilities to cope with problems that they have not yet encountered will gain a selective advantage. However, since they have not yet encountered those future problems, those problems cannot represent the pressures which might select for such abilities — so how might such abilities evolve, if at all? Nevertheless, capacities which have evolved for a specific purpose may contain *ecologically surplus abilities* (Johnston, 1981b, 1985; Gans, 1979; Bock, 1959), and be suited to coping with other concurrent problems or possible future problems, and speciation itself provides some random variation to the evolution of cognitive abilities (e.g. Gould, 1980; Gould and Eldridge, 1977). Such surplus capacities may represent the ability to cope with unforeseen problems in an animal's niche and provide a useful means of defining animal intelligence. This does appear to salvage some usefulness for the arbitrary learning tasks approach of the comparative psychologists. The ability to solve a problem that a species does not have to face in its niche is at least some indication of surplus abilities and — within limits — some indication of how that species might fare in changed ecological conditions. Nevertheless, to have any heuristic value this approach needs to insure that the arbitrary tasks presented to an animal mimic the likely problems a species will face given the possible ecological changes that might occur in its niche.

Intelligence and arbitrary learning tasks

Despite the reservations just mooted about the arbitrary learning task approach to animal intelligence, this approach has evoked considerable interest in recent years. This interest has largely centered on the debate as to whether or not different species exhibit *qualitatively* different performances on these tasks. The controversy surrounds the assertion of Macphail (1982) that there is no evidence for qualitative differences in intelligence between vertebrate species — in strict contrast to Bitterman's (1975) original conclusions (see Table 10.1). We have already discussed some of the evidence relating to this controversy elsewhere (the comparative analyses of Pavlovian and instrumental conditioning in chapters 2 and 3), but it is worth looking at some of the evidence here that relates to performance on more complex learning tasks.

1 *Serial reversal learning*

Bitterman's classification of animals on the basis of their performance on serial reversal learning tasks suggests that fish differ from turtles, pigeons, and rats in their performance on spatial problems, and that fish and turtles differ from pigeons and rats on visual problems (see Table 10.1). Thus, fish failed to exhibit any improvement with successive reversals (Behrend,

Domesick, and Bitterman, 1965; Warren, 1960), turtles apparently showed improvement over reversals on spatial but not visual problems (Bitterman, 1965), and both pigeons (Bullock and Bitterman, 1962; Gossette, Gossette, and Riddell, 1966) and rats (Bitterman, 1965) show improvement in both spatial and visual reversals. Subsequent studies suggested that many species of birds show improvement over reversals, but some species more than others. For instance, magpies and mynah birds (both passerine species) are more efficient than chicks and quail (both galliformes) (Gossette, Gossette, and Riddell, 1966), and corvids such as American blue jays are more efficient than pigeons (Kamil, Jones, Pietrewicz, and Maudlin, 1977; Mackintosh, Wilson, and Boakes, 1985). Within the class of mammals, species such as capuchin monkeys, squirrel monkeys, macaques, raccoons, skunks, weasels, mink, and ferrets have all been shown to demonstrate improved performance over successive reversals (Gossette, Kraus, and Speiss, 1968; Gossette and Kraus, 1968; Doty and Combs, 1969; Schrier, 1966), as do a variety of marsupials (e.g. Buchmann and Grecian, 1974; Friedman and Marshall, 1965).

Before investigating this evidence further it is worth considering what learning ability is required to perform efficiently on a serial reversal task. The animal cannot simply use the physical characteristics of the stimuli to predict the correct response because the predictive value of the stimuli with regard to reward change with successive reversals. Clearly, what is required is that the animal must use the outcome of one trial to determine its response on the next trial. Of the two alternative stimuli (A and B), A will always be rewarded if A was chosen and rewarded on the previous trial or if B was chosen and not rewarded on the previous trial. This all amounts to a "win–stay, lose–shift" strategy being the most efficient to deal with the problem, and perfect reversal performance using such a strategy would be reflected by only a single error on each reversal. Successful one-trial reversal performance has been obtained in rats, rhesus monkeys, pigeons, and marsupials (Dufort, Guttman, and Kimble, 1954; Schrier, 1966; Buchmann and Grecian, 1974; Gossette and Hood, 1967), although this is strongly dependent on procedural and contextual factors (cf. Macphail, 1982). Nevertheless, the fact that these species do display one-trial reversal performance and, in some cases, can transfer this ability to completely new sets of stimuli (e.g. Kamil, Jones, Pietrewicz, and Maudlin, 1977) does suggest the use of an abstracted strategy such as "win–stay, lose–shift."

The one anomalous class of species in Bitterman's original classification that apparently fails to show any serial reversal learning is fish. However, more recent studies have shown that Bitterman's original failure can be attributed to contextual factors rather than the lack of any learning abilities

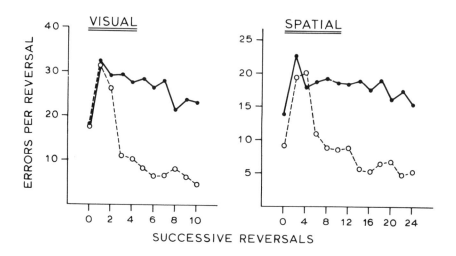

Figure 10.3 Serial reversal learning on visual and spatial tasks in rats (open circles) and goldfish (filled circles). (After Mackintosh, Wilson, and Boakes, 1985)

suitable to serial reversal learning. Mackintosh and Cauty (1971) found that fish would show a significant improvement over reversals if the food magazine was located close to the response keys — in Bitterman's studies food was delivered some distance from the response keys and usually at the back of the tank. Nevertheless, even though the goldfish in the Mackintosh and Cauty study did show improvement, it was considerably less improvement than that shown by rats (see Figure 10.3).

Thus, it can be concluded that all vertebrate species so far studied do demonstrate serial reversal learning given appropriate procedural and contextual conditions. Some species even exhibit the most efficient form of serial reversal learning, which is one-trial reversal. However, there are clear quantitative differences between species on this kind of task. What does this imply about the relative learning abilities of these species? First of all, it could be that different species are adopting different strategies to cope with the problem. We have already mentioned that a number of bird and mammalian species show one-trial reversal performance typical of a "win–stay, lose–shift" strategy; so far, such one-trial reversal performance has not been obtained in fish (cf. Macphail, 1982). But fish do show an improvement over reversals, so

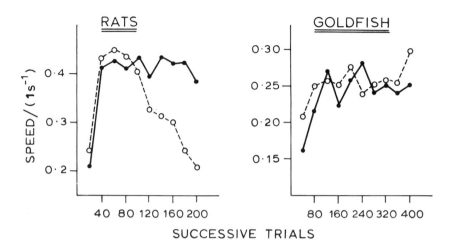

Figure 10.4 Speed of responding on rewarded (filled circles) and non-rewarded (open circles) trials on a serial alternation task in rats and goldfish. (After Mackintosh, Wilson, and Boakes, 1985)

what strategy might they be adopting? It has been argued that rather than using a different and less efficient strategy to cope with the reversal learning problem, fish may simply have a quantitatively poorer capacity for dealing with the information required to use this strategy. The "win–stay, lose–shift" strategy requires the ability to attend to the relevant aspects of the stimuli and the ability to remember what the outcome was of the previous trial. Fish may be weaker on one or both of these factors. There is no clear evidence relating to the attentional factors (cf. Mackintosh, 1969; Macphail, 1982: 72–9), but there is some evidence that fish are poorer than, say, rats, at remembering the outcome of the previous trial.

One task which requires the animal to use the outcome of one trial to predict the outcome of the next is alternation learning. In this case, a response is reinforced only on alternate trials. Rats learn in this situation to respond more slowly on nonreinforced trials (as predicted by the fact that the previous response was reinforced), but goldfish frequently show no differential responding (see Figure 10.4). So it is at least possible that fish may be using the same strategy as, say, rats in the reversal learning task, but that the component cognitive abilities required for this strategy are less well developed in fish than in rats.

One final, but important, consideration in relation to this comparative evidence concerns the kinds of strategies that different species might bring to this task in terms of, for example, their natural foraging strategies. Clearly, a "win–stay, lose–shift" strategy might be utilized more readily by a species whose natural foraging repertoire contains such a strategy. Contrary to this hypothesis, it has been suggested that rats naturally adopt a "win–shift" strategy when foraging because, being omnivorous foragers, their food sources are relatively dispersed and require time to be replenished when depleted (Olton and Schlosberg, 1978). This "win–shift" strategy may be innate in the sense that it is found in very young rat pups (cf. Olton and Schlosberg, 1978). Alternatively, pigeons usually have food sources that tend to be "concentrated and dependable" (Bond, Cook, and Lamb, 1981) and are thus more likely to adopt a "win–stay" strategy. However, when rats and pigeons are compared on spatial serial reversal performance, the results are contrary to what might be expected on the basis of a foraging hypothesis: rats, which are supposedly more likely to adopt a "win–shift" strategy in natural situations, show more efficient reversal learning (which requires a "win–stay" strategy) than do pigeons (Mackintosh, 1969).

2 *Probability learning*

Bitterman's original findings on probability learning performance (Table 10.1) suggested that fish and turtles tend to *match* (that is, match the percentage of responses to S^+ to the percentage reinforcement of that choice), whereas rats tended to *maximize* (choose exclusively the S^+ stimulus). Pigeons tended to match on visual probability learning tasks but maximize on spatial problems. Clearly, the most efficient strategy is to maximize, as this will yield reward on a 70:30 probability task on 70 per cent of the trials. Matching will yield reward on only 58 per cent of trials (70×0.7 plus 30×0.3). Bitterman's assertion that fish were qualitatively inferior to rats on this task was subsequently disputed by Mackintosh (1969), who claimed that (1) rats do not maximize in the sense of responding exclusively to S^+ on *every* trial; (2) fish sometimes exceed matching performance and on occasions can be shown to maximise (Woodard and Bitterman, 1973); (3) birds, such as pigeons, do not appear exclusively to maximise or match but frequently show performance that is in between the two (Graf, Bullock, and Bitterman, 1964); and (4) whether rats maximize or match appears to depend on the type of apparatus used. When trained in a conventional jumping stand rats tend to maximize, but when trained in an apparatus built to resemble the kind of apparatus normally used with fish (in terms of relative size, type of stimuli, and so on), rats actually match (Weitzman, 1967).

However, although this evidence implies that there are no qualitative differences between species, in that fish (e.g. Woodard and Bitterman, 1973), reptiles (Kirk and Bitterman, 1965), birds (Macphail and Reilly, 1983; Graf, Bullock, and Bitterman, 1964; Shimp, 1966; Mackintosh, Lord, and Little, 1971), and rats (Mackintosh, 1969) have all been shown to maximize under certain conditions, Mackintosh (1969) has proposed that there are clear quantitative differences between species from different classes, and that these differences can be ascribed to differences in the stability of attention to the relevant stimulus dimensions. Thus, goldfish (whose attentional capacities are supposed to be relatively poor) will perform at a significantly lower level than efficient maximizing, birds somewhat less so, and rats least of all. However, as Macphail (1982) points out, there is no reason to believe that a weakness in attention to the relevant stimulus dimensions is an attribute of the organism: it may equally well be an attribute of the different procedures and apparatuses used to study different species. This possibility is lent some support by the fact that pigeons can perform at near to perfect maximizing levels given appropriate procedures (Macphail and Reilly, 1983; Mackintosh, Lord, and Little, 1971), and efficient performance does in some cases appear to depend on characteristics of the training apparatus (e.g. Weitzman, 1967).

All of this assumes that different species are adopting a maximizing strategy and that failure to achieve maximum efficiency with this strategy (resulting in some cases as matching) is a result of either poor attentional capacities or interfering contextual factors. However, there is some evidence to suggest that fish in some circumstances do not adopt an inefficient maximizing strategy which eventually results in what looks like matching. Nonrandom matching (matching that does not appear to be the result of systematic strategies) has frequently been reported in fish (Behrend and Bitterman, 1966; Woodard and Bitterman, 1973) but never in mammals (e.g. Mackintosh, 1970; Weitzman, 1967; Wilson, Oscar, and Bitterman, 1964a, b; Bitterman, 1971). At the very least this suggests that mammals have a greater capacity than fish for adopting strategies in probability learning tasks.

3 Summary

What Macphail (1982) has concluded from his exhaustive review of these learning tasks is that there is no evidence for a *qualitative* difference in abilities between vertebrate species. Fish, reptiles, birds, and mammals have all been shown to perform at greater than chance level on these tasks given appropriate contextual conditions. While this conservative conclusion may be true, there are two other aspects of it to take into account. First, there are *quantitative* differences between performances in different classes of species. At present it is not clear whether these represent differences in attentional or memorial abilities between species or whether they reflect contextual factors (cf. Macphail, 1985). Second, there is little clear indication of what learning mechanisms or strategies different species are utilizing to solve these problems when they are able to do so. It is certainly not clear that they are bringing natural problem-specific capacities to bear on the task or whether they are utilizing makeshift processes which had been selected for other purposes.

Finally, it is important to put all of these findings back into an ecological context by attempting to understand the kinds of natural situations in which an animal might need serial reversal or probability learning skills. Whether a species did need these skills or not in its environmental niche would certainly help to throw light on the reasons for the efficiency or inefficiency with which that species could solve the task. Efficient serial reversal learning requires the adopting of a "win–stay, lose–shift" strategy. This is certainly useful for an animal that has to forage in its habitat for food that is patchily distributed in clumps. For instance, a bird may feed on insects found hidden in crevices in trees or logs; once having located a tree or log containing insects the best strategy would seem to be to stay with that tree or log until searching in crevices fails to produce food and then move on. Efficient probability learning, on the other hand, requires the skill of identifying which option has been rewarded most frequently in the past and then choosing that option when faced with a choice. The natural analogy of this strategy would seem suitable mainly for predators whose prey is mobile and can move from location to location. All other things being equal, when searching for prey the predator is best served by choosing to forage at the location where the prey has most frequently been found in the past (maximizing) rather than at the location where it was last found (matching). However, whether the species that perform well on serial reversal and probability learning tasks are ones whose lifestyles reflect these natural problems still remains to be investigated.

Concept learning

Concept learning normally involves two particular attributes. First, the learning cannot be acquired by discrimination of a single physical attribute of the stimuli involved; and second, that learning cannot be achieved by use of a simple template of the stimuli concerned since the learning should be able to transfer successfully to stimuli whose physical characteristics the animal has never previously encountered.

We will deal here with three particular instances of concept learning in animals: sameness–difference discriminations, number concepts, and visual concepts.

1 *Sameness–difference discriminations*

There are two particular experimental procedures that are used to investigate the acquisition of sameness–difference concepts. First, the *matching* task presents the animal simultaneously with three stimuli, two of which are identical. The animal is required to respond to either of the two identical stimuli. Second, in an *oddity* task the procedure is similar, except that the animal is required to respond to the stimulus that is different from the other two. It is quite clear that animals can master these kinds of tasks without forming a concept of "sameness" or of "oddity" but by basing their responding on configurational cues (see Macphail, 1982: 211–12). However, if the subjects are responding on the basis of a concept of "sameness" or "oddity," then they should exhibit positive transfer to a completely novel set of stimuli which they had not experienced during training. Although animals such as pigeons have been shown to perform relatively efficiently on matching and oddity tasks, many studies suggest they may not be using the notions of "sameness" and "oddity" to do so (e.g. Carter and Werner, 1978; Berryman, Cumming, Cohen, and Johnson, 1965), and transfer from one problem to another when demonstrated is usually very weak (e.g. Zentall and Hogan, 1975, 1978). However, transfer of performance to novel stimuli on trial 1 of the transfer has been successfully achieved in chimpanzees, rhesus monkeys, cebus monkeys, and squirrel monkeys (Moon and Harlow, 1955; Strong and Hedges, 1966; Thomas and Boyd, 1973), while non-primate mammals such as rats, cats and raccoons perform less well on such tasks (Strong and Hedges, 1966; Boyd and Warren, 1957; Warren, 1960; Wodinsky and Bitterman, 1953).

It does appear from this very brief review that primates may be the only animals able to form "sameness" or "oddity" concepts — they are the only types of species to have shown persistently successful performance on trial 1 of transfer to novel stimuli. However, Macphail (1982) has pointed out several procedural differences in these inter-specific studies which might account for the difference in performance. For instance, the primate studies have generally used objects as stimuli, while the pigeon studies have used two-dimensional visual stimuli, and it is known that sameness–oddity learning, even in monkeys, is better with three-dimensional objects (Meyer, Treichler, and Meyer, 1965).

2 *Number concepts*

There are two principal ways in which we can investigate whether animals possess a number concept. First, we can attempt to discover whether they are able to discriminate between groups of units compared simultaneously side by side (a *simultaneous apprehension* procedure), and second, we can attempt to discover if animals can discriminate the number of events in a series of sequentially presented events and use that number as a cue for responding (a *counting* procedure). This second procedure is more analogous to what we might understand as counting, and studies have investigated the abilities of animals to discriminate the number of times they emit a unit of their behavior as well as whether they can discriminate the number of external stimuli they have been presented with.

Simultaneous apprehension of number

In a series of famous experiments, Koehler (1950) attempted to show that birds did possess some kind of number concept in a simultaneous discrimination task. Ravens and parrots, for instance, when presented with a number of boxes having lids with differing numbers of spots on them, could pick out the box showing the same number of spots as that on a simultaneously presented "sample" card (the spots on the boxes and cards were arranged in various arrays so as to rule out discrimination on the basis of patterning or size of the array). More recently, Thomas, Fowlkes, and Vickery (1980) were able to demonstrate number concepts in squirrel monkeys using the simultaneous discrimination technique. Thomas's subjects were able to discriminate between two cards on the basis of the number of circles on the cards (while varying the size of the circles and their patterning on the card). In such studies as these, Koehler (1950) found that the limit for number discrimination varied from five to six in piegons, to six in jackdaws, and seven in ravens and parrots. In the Thomas study one monkey was able to discriminate between seven and eight, and the other monkey between eight and nine. These studies do not, however, suggest that these animals have counting abilities but that they do have the ability at some perceptual level to discriminate arrays varying in the number of their individual components (up to a particular limit depending on the species concerned).

Counting procedures

Much of the early work investigating counting abilities in animals was unsystematic and methodologically inadequate in that it failed to control for — among other things — "Clever Hans" effects, odor cues, and successful discrimination based on timing rather than number (cf. Wesley, 1961). For instance, in counting experiments we have to be sure that the animal is responding to the number of stimuli it has experienced or the number of responses it has made rather than the time taken to present those stimuli or make those responses.

In one study, Koehler (1950) trained pigeons to eat peas that were delivered down a chute. They were then trained to eat only a specific number and were given an electric shock if they exceeded that number. Even when the intervals between pea deliveries were varied to make temporal cues irrelevant, pigeons could perform this task successfully up to a limit of six. In a study by Chen (1967), rats were trained to run up an alleyway into a circular compartment and run round this compartment for a fixed number of times before returning down the alleyway to obtain food. Three-quarters of the rats in this study mastered this task when up to three laps were required, and could still perform efficiently when the size of the circular compartment was altered so as to disrupt any kinesthetic or temporal cues that might have been controlling the behavior. Davis, Memmott, and Hurwitz (1975) trained rats to press a lever to obtain food on a VI 30 sec schedule, and during each session presented a maximum of three fixed-duration shocks at irregular intervals during the session. They found that after the third shock had been delivered the response rate of the rats increased dramatically, suggesting that they had been able to count the number of shocks delivered in the session.

Hobson and Newman (1981) have reviewed some of the evidence on counting procedures with animals, and conclude that counting in some cases is very accurate, even when inter-event intervals are varied to confound control by temporal factors (e.g. Rilling, 1967). However, as Church and Meck (1984) have pointed out, in order to rule out control by temporal factors completely one has to vary not just the inter-unit interval but also the duration of each unit. For instance, we know that rats can sum the duration of a series of discrete units by turning off some hypothetical clock in the gaps between each unit (e.g. Roberts and Church, 1978; Meck, Church, and Olton, 1985). Thus, instead of counting they may be summing the time of each unit and responding when a critical cumulative time is reached. However, even when the duration of each unit to be counted is varied as well as the inter-unit interval, rats can discriminate the number of sequential stimuli presented (either two or four) (Fernandes and Church, 1982; see also Meck and Church, 1983). Furthermore, the formation of number concepts in rats appears to be cross-modal. They can successfully transfer a learned number discrimination from auditory to visual stimuli (Meck and Church, 1983; Church and Meck, 1984).

All this evidence suggests quite strongly that many species of mammals and birds do possess the ability to form a number concept and to count the presentation of successive stimuli up to a particular limit. Possessing the ability to form number concepts and to count discrete numbers of successive units in a given period of time is particularly important in being able to calculate the *rate* at which events are occurring. As we have seen in previous chapters (for instance, chapters 3 and 8), this is a particularly useful ability when it comes to carrying out certain biological functions, such as feeding, efficiently. Since animals are under the selective pressure to forage optimally, it is perhaps not surprising that many species of animals will have evolved numerical abilities which assist them in this task.

3 *Visual concepts*

The majority of studies carried out on visual concepts has used pigeons — largely because of their visual acuity and easy adaptation to the learning environment. Possibly the best-known example of visual concept learning is the work on the learning of *natural concepts* by Herrnstein and his colleagues (e.g. Herrnstein and Loveland, 1964; Herrnstein, Loveland, and Cable, 1976; Herrnstein and de Villiers, 1980). In one study it was found that pigeons could discriminate between photographs containing trees (of different varieties, at different distances, and with or without leaves) and photographs showing a stick of celery or a vine, and in other experiments in this study, pigeons were able to discriminate accurately photographs of an individual woman from photographs of other people, and to discriminate photographs that contained bodies of water from those that did not (Herrnstein, Loveland, and Cable, 1976). Indeed, pigeons need as few as six and no more than thirty-six positive and negative instances to discriminate and generalize photographs of human faces (Malott and Siddall, 1972), and can learn to discriminate an oak leaf from non-oak leaves even more quickly (Cerella, 1979). Furthermore, many species of animals appear to be able to transfer successful discrimination from two-dimensional photographs to their real three-dimensional counterparts. For instance, Trillmich (1976) found that budgerigars that had learned to discriminate between photographs of two other budgerigars transferred this discrimination to the live birds, but the reverse transfer failed. Both Davenport and Rogers (1970, 1971) and Cabe (1976, 1980) have shown that apes and pigeons respectively can transfer a discrimination learned with objects to their photographic equivalents, but Cabe and Healey (1979) found that pigeons could not transfer an object discrimination to their line-drawing equivalent.

At this point it is worth discussing two alternative interpretations of these data. First, these animals either learn the concepts from scratch by experiencing individual instances or, second, they may have some built-in means of identifying certain categories which are biologically or ecologically important to them (such means might include phylogenetically prewired templates, and so on). Certainly, pigeons are particularly successful at discriminating natural conceptual classes such as trees, water, or people, but have some difficulty learning more artificial categories such as cubes or cartoon characters (Cerella, 1977, 1980, 1982). Herrnstein (1984) speculated that the relative speed with which pigeons learn natural categories over artificial categories could not be accounted for in terms of individual experience, but may be the result of collective experience encoded in the animal's genes — in effect, evolutionary pressures may have selected for individuals which can learn biologically important concepts quickly. It is indeed the case that it might be important for a pigeon to learn to discriminate trees quickly, as they represent roosting and nesting locations, means of escaping ground-based predators, and so on. The need to identify water is fairly obvious, and even learning to discriminate people rapidly might represent the need to distinguish predators from other benign species in the habitat.

However, the results of one particular experiment argue against this evolutionary perspective. Herrnstein and de Villiers (1980) taught pigeons to discriminate underwater photographs containing fish from those that did not contain fish. The pigeons in this study learned the discrimination in as few trials as it took to learn the tree, water, and people discriminations. As Herrnstein (1984) points out, fish have no biological or ecological relevance to pigeons and the two species have never shared an environment in the last 50 million years.

Perhaps some light can be cast on the difference between learning natural and most artificial concepts by looking more closely at the way in which pigeons learn artificial concepts. Cerella (1980) trained pigeons to discriminate cartoon pictures of Charlie Brown from other "Peanuts" characters, and although they learned this discrimination (with some difficulty), they generalized the learning in ways which suggested that their discriminations were based on local features of the two-dimensional patterns rather than by more global two-dimensional or three-dimensional invariances. For instance, pigeons would still respond to incomplete, scrambled, and inverted positive stimuli (see Figure 10.5).

Morgan, Fitch, Holman, and Lea (1976) trained pigeons to discriminate the letter "A" from the numeral "2" using a variety of different typefaces and handwritten examples. In nearly all cases, responding to the "A" was greater

Figure 10.5 Test "Charlie Brown" stimuli used by Cerella (1980). From left to right, incomplete, scrambled, and inverted positive stimuli. (From Cerella, 1982)

than to the "2," and generalization to twenty-two additional typefaces was more or less complete. In fact, although "A" is a man-made artificial category, the pigeons seemed to learn this faster than they do most other artificial concepts, and as quickly as natural concepts. What is instructive about this example is that when Morgan *et al.* attempted to distinguish which features of the "A" were important for making the discrimination, they concluded that "no single feature could be called necessary and sufficient" (1976: 65) to account for the discrimination.

In a related study, Blough (1982) found similar results suggesting that for the pigeon, discriminating an "A" is not an all-or-none decision but a quantitative one. Morgan *et al.* called this concept a *polymorphous* one (after Ryle, 1951), in that it is defined by degrees of overlap between features rather than by necessary and sufficient conditions. To illustrate this point, Lubow (1974) taught pigeons to discriminate between man-made objects and natural features in black and white aerial photographs. In analyzing the controlling features, Lubow found that the important aspect was some combination of right-angles, straight lines, and high contrast regions, but none on its own was a necessary or sufficient feature.

In a more detailed study of polymorphous concepts, Lea and Harrison (1978) taught artificial concepts to pigeons in which they had to respond to

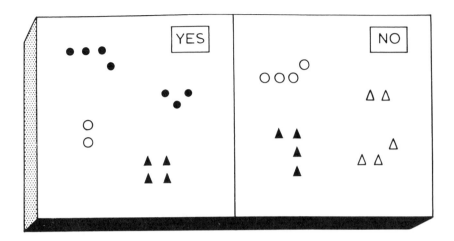

Figure 10.6 Positive (Yes) and negative (No) instances of a polymorphous concept. The rule is that positive instances contain at least 2 of symmetry, blackness, or circularity. (After Dennis, Hampton, and Lea, 1973)

three distinct features if they were to perform correctly. These kinds of discrimination were readily learned by the pigeons — even though Cambridge undergraduate students found it extremely difficult or impossible to extract explicitly the rules governing these polymorphous concepts (Dennis, Hampton, and Lea, 1973, see Figure 10.6).

What appears to be happening here is that the majority of the artificial concepts we attempt to teach animals in these experiments are ones in which the relevant features are fairly readily verbally definable, and the discrimination has to be based on an all-or-none decision about the feature. What seems to be the case is that animals such as pigeons do not base their discriminations on all-or-none factors (such as necessary and sufficient conditions), but respond in a more graded way based on the interaction of a number of features such as are required for the solution of polymorphous concepts. This makes the learning of so-called natural categories easier for the animal than most artificial categories because this quantitive strategy is more applicable in the former case. As Herrnstein (1984) points out, "categories that are fairly easy to describe physically do not seem to be significantly easier for animals, and may even be harder, than categories that are hard to describe in those terms. For example, pigeons appear to find patches of colored light a harder category to form than photographs of trees" (1984: 257–8), and as Lea (1984) concludes, although we have good grounds for believing that animals such as pigeons do form concepts, "current data give no grounds for postulating that the pigeons actually possess or form concepts similar to those used by the experimenters in selecting the stimuli" (1984: 377).

Spatial memory

Most animals need to have a good working knowledge of the locations of biologically important resources in their environment. For instance, they need to know the quickest route back to their nest site or home burrow, how to get to sheltered or safe places in the event of danger, and where suitable food resources are located. We know that many animals have some mechanism which allows them to locate sites within their habitat relatively accurately. This is especially true when related to feeding activities. For example, members of the Paridae and Corvidae bird families (for example, marsh tits and nutcrackers, respectively) frequently cache food which they later relocate, recover, and eat (e.g. Cowie, Krebs, and Sherry, 1981; Turcek and Kelso, 1968). On the other hand, some birds appear to use spatial cues to avoid locations where they have just eaten. Hawaiian honeycreepers (*Loxops virens*), for example, feed on the nectar of the mamane flower, and avoid returning to those flowers they have recently visited and removed nectar from (Kamil, 1978). Quite clearly, the ability to identify locations could be the result of fairly basic processes such as taxes or simple cue discrimination, but we should examine the possibility that animals are able to construct a relatively sophisticated spatial map of their environment which would involve the use of a combination of psychological processes including discrimination, memory, and cognitive representations.

Memory for spatial location has recently been studied in the *eight-arm radial maze*, a maze which has eight arms radiating from a central start point. In the simple studies, a pellet of food is placed at the end of each arm and the subject rat placed in the central start area. The rat is allowed to enter any arm of the maze and consume the food in that arm. The rat is then replaced in the central start area but the food eaten by the rat is not replaced. This continues until the food at the end of all eight arms has been consumed. Clearly, the most efficient strategy for the rat is to remember which arms it has already entered and to avoid those arms on future trials. This is what occurs: with continued practice rats rarely re-enter an arm that they have already visited (Olton, 1978; Olton and Samuelson, 1976). Control experiments have ruled out a number of simplistic interpretations of these results. For instance, rats do not locate baited arms on the basis of the odor of food from those arms, because even when depleted arms are immediately rebaited with food, rats still avoid them and enter arms they have not previously visited (Olton and Samuelson, 1976). Similarly, rats do not use odor cues to mark the entrances to arms they have just visited (and so avoid them on future choices). Even when the entire maze is doused in after-shave lotion to mask such cues, rats still perform efficiently and enter only those arms they have not previously visited (Olton and Samuelson, 1976). Even when the arms of the maze are interchanged between choices, rats still only enter arms on the basis of their *location* (Olton, Collinson, and Werz, 1977).

How do rats achieve this efficient foraging performance? Certainly, rats do have some natural features to their foraging behavior which are suitable to efficient performance in the eight-arm radial maze. For example, rats appear to adopt a general "win–shift" strategy when feeding, largely because their food sources are dispersed, rapidly depleted, and require time to be replenished (cf. Olton and Samuelson, 1976; Haig, Rawlins, Olton, Mead, and Taylor, 1983). They also tend to avoid places recently visited and explore novel aspects of their environment (cf. Gaffan and Davies, 1981). Species whose food sources are naturally more "concentrated and dependable" — and are thus less likely to adopt a "win–shift" strategy — appear to perform less well in the radial maze; one such example is the pigeon (Bond, Cook, and Lamb, 1981; but see also Roitblat, Tham, and Gollub, 1982; Wilkie, Spetch, and Chew, 1981). Nevertheless, although these species-specific feeding attributes might explain why one species might be more efficient in the radial maze than another species, it does not explain *how* rats are able to be so efficient.

There is considerable evidence that rats do learn a spatial map of the maze using distal cues in the room (such as the location of chairs, tables, posters, and so on) to locate different arms (cf. Roberts, 1984). In an insightful study, Morris (1981) trained rats to swim to a slightly submerged platform in a water tank. The platform was hidden from sight by making the water opaque by adding milk. What Morris found was that, regardless of the starting point where the rats were placed in the tank (even if it was a completely novel starting point), they were able to swim almost directly to where the submerged platform was located. This implies that they were not using specific responses to find the platform but appeared to have the platform located on a cognitively represented spatial map.

A spatial map is extremely useful for those species which cache food for consumption at some later time. Not only does this require the ability to construct spatial maps but also substantial memorial abilities in remembering the location of caches within that map. Cowie, Krebs, and Sherry (1981) dispensed radioactively labeled sunflower seeds to marsh tits (*Parus palustris*), many of which were cached by the birds. After locating the cached seeds with an oscillation counter, the experimenters then placed control seeds either close (within 10 m) or far (100 m) from the cached seed. They found that the marsh tits found the cached seeds more rapidly than the control seeds, suggesting that they were using memory rather than direct cues to locate the seeds. The fact that direct cues are not used in cache location has also been shown by Sherry, Krebs, and Cowie (1981). They removed all cached seeds after the caching session and either 3 or 24 hrs later allowed the subject birds (marsh tits) to search the experimental habitat. They found that the birds made significantly more visits to the locations where they had previously cached seeds, even though there were no seeds to act as cues. Further studies have shown that marsh tits avoid locations where they had already cached seeds when caching more seeds, and that there is a recency effect when recovering seeds cached at two separate times (Shettleworth and Krebs, 1982).

Work on cache memory in nutcrackers (*Nucifraga caryocatactes*) is also instructive because, whereas marsh tits may have a cache memory limit of a few days, nutcrackers appear to leave food caches for months before retrieving them. For instance, Balda (1980) found that cache recovery in nutcrackers was highly accurate, using retention intervals of 7–31 days —even when seeds had been removed to avoid the use of direct cues. Vander Wall (1982) used two nutcrackers in a single environment. Each bird was allowed to cache its own seeds, and in subsequent recovery tests each bird recovered its own seeds and never the seeds of the other bird. This strongly supports the memory and spatial map explanation rather than the direct cues hypothesis, as does the fact that when Vander Wall moved landmarks such as logs and rocks the cache recovery of both nutcrackers was substantially reduced.

All of these studies suggest that many animals are able to form cognitively represented spatial maps based largely on visual cues, and that locations on this map can be remembered for relatively long periods of time. This is an ability that is clearly superior to a simple route-learning strategy for species which forage over a relatively large and physically varied habitat.

Language learning

A wide variety of animals can communicate to one another using visual, auditory, tactile, or olfactory cues. Normally, the information that is communicated is simple but highly relevant to that particular species' biological functioning. For instance, the information communicated may convey that the transmitter is of a particular sex, is either an aggressive or a benign intruder, or in a particular biological state such as sexually receptive. In some species, such as honeybees, the information conveyed by these communicative systems can be quite complex. Honeybees perform several communicative dances, of which the "waggle dance" is the most important. The "waggle dance" is a figure of eight movement performed by bees that have just returned from a foraging trip, and it can convey information related to the distance, direction and richness of the nectar source that has just been visited (Von Frisch, 1967, 1972, 1974).

Nevertheless, whereas communication systems serve fairly obvious and important biological functions, there is no clear evidence from studies of free-living animals that any species other than humans possesses a flexible, syntax-based language system. In most cases animal communication is distinguished from human communication by the fact that the former involves a fairly rigid response to specific internal or external stimuli, and to this extrent nonhuman animals "cannot tell lies" (Black, 1968). However, although individual experience may result in the communicative systems of some animals becoming more flexible, "there is no evidence that [animals] continue to recombine qualitatively different vocal units, separately meaningful, into new messages with new meanings. In other words, they have no syntax" (Marler, 1975: 33).

Nevertheless, that animals do not appear to utilize language systems in their natural environments does not mean that they do not have the cognitive capacities necessary for learning a language. Many species, such as chimpanzees, appear to be able to convey quite complex information to one another using a combination of visual gesturing and vocalizations without the need to develop an integrated language system (e.g. Van Lawick-Goodall, 1968; Menzel, 1974; Menzel and Halperin, 1975; Smith, 1973); but this still begs the question of whether they could utilize a language system if required to do so.

There have been a series of attempts to teach language to apes in recent years, and these have since been extended to studies using nonprimate species such as sea lions, woodpeckers, and African gray parrots (e.g. Chauvin and Muckensturm-Chauvin, 1980; Pepperberg, 1981, 1983). The original reasons for carrying out these studies were varied. In some cases, it was to attempt to demonstrate that language learning is not a uniquely human ability; in other cases it was to investigate some of the learning processes that could give rise to language abilities. In still other studies, the intention was simply to investigate the intellectual abilities of the species concerned and to formulate a theory of mind (namely, how the capacity to attribute mind or intention to other individuals is developed — e.g. Premack and Woodruff, 1978). So, how have animals fared in these studies?

1 *What is language?*

The first problem encountered when studying the ability of animals to learn language is what exactly constitutes a language. While there is much speculation over what should constitute linguistic competence, Thorpe (1974) has catalogued a fairly comprehensive list of features which characterize human language. Of the sixteen features listed, eight are clearly identifiable in a variety of nonhuman animal communication systems, while the remaining eight are not. These latter eight are: (1) *discreteness*: the language consists of discrete elements which are functionally independent; (2) *tradition*: the meaning of words or symbols are transmitted by learning; (3) *learnability*: learners of the language system learn it from one another; (4) *duality*: symbols and words are often meaningless on their own, but have meaning when combined in specific ways; (5) *displacement*: the language system is able to refer to things or events which are remote in space and time; (6) *productivity*: novel communications can be transmitted by previously unused combinations of words or symbols; (7) *reflectiveness*: the language system contains the means to communicate about the communication system itself; (8) *prevarication*: the ability to communicate information which is not immediately apparent or relevant (for example, the ability to tell a lie).

So, in order to demonstrate that a nonhuman animal has acquired a human-like language, we must not only demonstrate that the animal has the capacity to acquire the syntactical skills necessary to use language, but also exhibits most of the eight characteristics outlined above. There have been a number of seminal language-learning studies involving apes; it is worth discussing these individually.

2 *Language-learning studies in apes*

Vicki

A number of attempts to teach language to chimpanzees using speech have failed to produce results of any significance (e.g. Jacobsen, Jacobsen, and Yoshioka, 1932; Kellogg and Kellogg, 1933; Hayes and Hayes, 1955; Hayes and Nissen, 1971). Hayes and Hayes (1955) attempted to train a young female chimpanzee called Vicki to use a vocal language by first reinforcing any vocal emissions and then shaping these vocalizations into meaningful words. Vicki learned only a limited number of vocalizations, including "mama," "papa," "cup," and "up," and using a clicking of the teeth for a ride in the car, "tsk" for a cigarette, and "ch" for a drink. However, rather than utilize the vocal language she was being trained to learn, Vicki would often use gestures and "pantomiming" to obtain her ends. Nevertheless, although the language learning aspects to this study were something of a failure, the study did emphasize the advanced cognitive skills possessed by Vicki in a number of ways.

Washoe

Since the primary communicative mechanism of chimpanzees is visual and they show good manual dexterity, Gardner and Gardner (1969) attempted to teach an eight-month-old female chimpanzee, Washoe, American Sign Language (ASL) — a form of communication which primarily uses hand gestures as symbols. The training consisted first of teaching her the signs by moulding her hands into the appropriate positions, and then reinforcing her for using the sign in requests. After 21 months of training Washoe had acquired about 40 signs, including nouns, verbs, adjectives, adverbs, and prepositions, and could transfer these signs to new contexts and combine them in apparently meaningful ways. Gardner and Gardner (1969) utilized a self-paced, double-blind testing situation to give some objective measure of the validity of Washoe's signing. In one such test, deaf individuals who were familiar with ASL agreed with the assessment of experienced observers on what Washoe was "saying" in 98 per cent of the instances recorded. Washoe also used signs spontaneously and in different meaningful combinations. For example, when requesting soda, Washoe would sign "please sweet drink," "gimme sweet," "please hurry sweet drink," "please gimme sweet drink" (Gardner and Gardner, 1971). Washoe was also productive in combining known signs to label new objects, such as combining the signs for "water" and "bird" to denote a duck. Although Washoe apparently showed vocabulary, use of basic syntactic ordering, and reference to objects not directly observable (displacement), it is arguable whether her achievements merit the label "language learning." First, the structure of ASL is quite different from the structure and characteristics of spoken English, and second, even the Gardners admit that many of Washoe's responses may have been inadvertently cued by the experimenters (the "Clever Hans" phenomenon).

Sarah

Premack (1970, 1971a, b) began studying language learning in chimpanzees by proposing a functional description of language in which he hoped a more universal semantic and logical structure could be found than existed in human language. One of the initial problems in the Washoe study was that Washoe first of all had to learn to make the signs before language learning could progress; Premack side-stepped this problem by attempting to teach language to Sarah, a nine-month-old chimpanzee, using arbitrarily shaped pieces of colored plastic as symbols. These symbols could then be arranged in sequence on a magnetized board to make up sentences. Premack assumed that every rule of language could be reduced to simpler units, and that by defining procedures for teaching these units it would be possible to provide language to animals which did not already possess such an ability. A vocabulary was built up by simultaneously pairing the appropriate symbol with the object it represented (for example, a banana). "No" was introduced as a negation against certain actions. Through extensions of these procedures Sarah was eventually taught the usage of symbols for "same–different," the interrogative "?", "name of" to request new symbols for objects which did not already have one, and the contingency phrase "if-then." Finally, she was able to learn the basics of syntax and logic by understanding the importance of the temporal sequencing of symbols in phrases such as "the spoon is in the cup" and "the apple is in the bucket." Sarah could also describe the features of an object represented by its symbol even when the object itself was absent. For instance, in response to the symbol for "apple" (a blue square plastic chip), she described it as red (not blue) and round (not square), and as having a stem. Thus, while Sarah shows some use of syntax and the ability to master logical relations, the procedures used by Premack demonstrate that a syntactically-based language system can be acquired through the use of a functional and analytical approach.

Lana

Lana was a female chimpanzee who was taught an artificial language system called "Yerkish" (Rumbaugh, Gill, and Von Glaserfeld, 1973; Rumbaugh and Gill, 1976). Lana was provided with a computer console consisting of a number of keys containing symbols which had a specific object or action referent. When the keys were pressed, each symbol was illuminated in sequence on a display board. The computer controlled Lana's access to food, water, an open window, and also to interactions with her handler. Lana was also taught colors, the names of a variety of items, and several prepositions which allowed her to make reference to objects by name, attribute or location

(Gill and Rumbaugh, 1974). Although Lana initiated conversations quite frequently and spontaneously, these conversations were primarily initiated either in order to receive something or to correct something which was not in accordance with routine — she rarely initiated conversation simply to comment on things as human children often do (Rumbaugh, Gill, Von Glaserfeld, Warner, and Pisani, 1975).

Other ape studies

Since these early studies of language learning in apes, a variety of subsequent projects have emerged which have attempted to investigate the extent of the language-learning abilities of apes (e.g. Terrace, 1979; Fouts, 1974; Patterson, 1978), the ability of apes to communicate with one another using a learned language system (Fouts and Rigby, 1976), and their spontaneity in conversing about matters which are remote from their immediate needs (e.g. Savage-Rumbaugh, Sevcik, Rumbaugh, and Rubert, 1985; Savage-Rumbaugh, Pate, Lawson, Smith, and Rosenbaum, 1983). In terms of our original criteria for language, Washoe, Sarah, and Lana collectively appear in their communications to demonstrate discreteness, duality, displacement, product-ivity, and reflectiveness, while other studies indicate tradition and learnability. What is not so clear is whether apes are learning syntax in the way that humans do, or that the syntax that they apparently learn is anything more than rudimentary (cf. Terrace, Pettito, Sanders, and Bever, 1979; Thompson and Church, 1980). Nevertheless, using such taught languages, studies are beginning to reveal that apes are capable of making non-goal-oriented comments on the world, and are capable of communicating their own intentions before their actions occur (Savage-Rumbaugh et al., 1985; Savage-Rumbaugh et al., 1983). The appearance of such an intentional communicative capacity does indicate that apes may possess a "concept of mind" and be able to attribute intention and purpose to the actions of other individuals (Premack and Woodruff, 1978). This would appear to have the evolutionary advantage of being able to monitor the results of one's own actions and to predict the actions of others. Springing from this capacity is the logical consequence of then being able to control the actions of others by conveying through a language or communication system not only what you yourself intend to do but what you would have others do.

Conclusion

From an ecological point of view there are two primary questions that need to be asked about learning and intelligence. First, does the animal's ·natural environment contain selection pressures which might lead to the evolution of sophisticated cognitive and learning skills? And second, what selective benefit might those sophisticated skills bestow on an animal? Clearly, very many species of animals are particularly well-adapted to their niche without needing to evolve even basic learning skills, let alone more sophisticated ones.

Nevertheless, sophisticated learning skills such as those discussed in this chapter do appear to have biological benefit to some species, either in specific instances or in general. We can, for example, identify foraging problems in particular species which correspond reasonably well to serial reversal and probability learning tasks. However, although it is clear that a variety of classes of animals can cope relatively efficiently with such learning tasks, as yet we have no indication that those species which are most efficient in these tasks are the ones which have to face an identical foraging problem in their natural environments. Other sophisticated learning abilities such as concept formation, counting, and the development of basic communicative and linguistic systems have more generalized adaptive benefits in the context of a variety of biological functions such as feeding, defense, mate selection, and so on, and many of these skills possess their adaptive function by facilitating biologically important reactions or by contributing to optimal performance.

For instance, no two predators may possess physically similar features yet may be identified on the basis of a number of converging features which can be responded to differentially (a polymorphous concept); learning the concept of a predator in this way should result in quicker recognition of predators and also in the immediate recognition of species of predators which the animal has not previously encountered. Similarly, possessing some basic number or counting ability would seem important for estimating the rate of important events (such as prey captures) in the animal's environment. The ability to estimate the characteristics of events such as their rate is likely to be a useful contributor to the optimal allocation of behavior within and between biological functions.

Comparative studies of sophisticated learning abilities across vertebrate classes do not obviously appear to reveal any qualitative differences in intelligence (cf. Macphail, 1982), although the study of certain capacities, such as language learning, does require more investigation in nonprimate species. Nevertheless, there are clear quantitative differences in abilities between classes of animals, and these may reflect qualitative differences in the component processes (such as attention and memory) which all contribute to relatively sophisticated learning abilities such as serial reversal, probability learning, and concept learning.

Finally, while a strict ecological approach to learning and intelligence would suppose that species would not develop sophisticated learning skills unless they had encountered selection pressures necessary to evolve these capacities, the possession of *surplus* intellectual abilities can easily prove an advantage in circumstances where the species environment undergoes a radical or catastrophic change. In such circumstances, species possessing surplus learning or intellectual abilities may be able to utilize them in coping with new problems set by the changed ecological conditions in their niche or, alternatively, to exploit new and perhaps radically different niches. One species which has demonstrated the value of this capacity to utilize sophisticated learning abilities to adapt and exploit new environments in this way is, of course, *Homo sapiens*.

Chapter summary

1 There is often a tendency to classify an animal's behavior as intelligent if it looks intelligent according to an anthropomorphic definition of that term. However, behavior that "looks" intelligent is often the result of relatively simplistic learning processes.

2 Jerison (1973) has suggested that animal intelligence can be conceived of as the behavioral correlate of encephalization (brain size) and has developed a measure of animal intelligence known as the *encephalization quotient* (EQ).

3 Comparative approaches to animal intelligence have traditionally investigated the performance of different species on a variety of different learning tasks. However, while such an approach attempts to compare the abilities of different species, it ignores the possible role of evolutionary mechanisms in selecting for these abilities.

4 Ecological approaches to animal intelligence have concentrated primarily on the adaptedness of an animal to its environmental niche rather than on the evolution of a generalized capacity called "intelligence."

5 However, adaptedness to a particular niche is no guarantee of survival —especially if a catastrophic and irreversible change occurs in the conditions within that niche. Therefore, animals which have developed *surplus capacities* that may permit them to cope with unforeseen problems may provide a useful ecological means of defining animal intelligence.

6 Arbitrary learning tasks such as *serial reversal learning* and *probability learning* tasks have recently been used to assess whether different species cope with these tasks in qualitatively different ways. The evidence suggests that, although there is no clear evidence for qualitative differences between different vertebrate species, there are clear quantitative differences.

7 Many mammalian and avian species appear to be able to form concepts,

including sameness–difference concepts, number concepts, and visual concepts.

8 Birds appear to be able to learn *natural concepts* (e.g. trees, water, people) much faster than artificial concepts (e.g. cubes, triangles, cartoon characters). This appears to be because birds do not base their discriminations on all-or-none factors (such as necessary and sufficient conditions), but respond in a more graded way based on the interaction of a number of features such as are required for the solution of *polymorphous concepts*.

9 Most animals need to have a good working knowledge of their environment, and many species of birds can quickly relocate hidden food caches after lengthy retentional intervals, and studies using an *eight-arm radial maze* have suggested that rats can develop a good *spatial map* of their environment which contains information about the locations of food.

10 Many animals possess communication systems necessary for conveying important biological information to one another. These systems vary in complexity, but none appears to possess all the characteristics which distinguish a human-like language.

11 Attempts to teach animals a human-like language have met with varying degrees of success. Some studies using apes have demonstrated the acquisition of discreteness, duality, displacement, productivity, reflectiveness, tradition, and learnability in the learned language system. However, it is not so clear that apes learn syntax in the same way as humans, but recent studies suggest they are capable of making non-goal-oriented comments on the world and may possess a "concept of mind."

Journal and periodical abbreviations

Acta Biol. Exp. = Acta Biologica Experimentalis
Acta Neurobiol. Exp. = Acta Neurobiologica Experimentalis
Adv. Ecol. Res. = Advances in Ecological Research
Adv. Sci = Advances in Science
Adv. Study Behav. = Advances in the Study of Behavior
Am. J. Ment. Defic. = American Journal of Mental Deficiency
Am. Nat. = American Naturalist
Am. Psychol. = American Psychologist
Am. Sci = American Scientist
Am. Zool. = American Zoologist
Anim. Behav. = Animal Behaviour
Anim. Behav. Monogr. = Animal Behaviour Monographs
Anim. Learn. Behav. = Animal Learning and Behavior
Ann. Rev. Ecol. Syst. = Annual Review of Ecology and Systematics
Ann. Rev. Psychol. = Annual Review of Psychology
APA = American Psychological Association
Auk = Auk

Behav. = Behaviour
Behav. Anal. Let. = Behaviour Analysis Letters
Behav. Biol. = Behavioral Biology
Behav. Brain Res. = Behavioral and Brain Research
Behav. Brain Sci. = Behavioral and Brain Sciences
Behav. Ecol. Sociobiol. = Behavioral Ecology and Sociobiology
Behav. Genet. = Behavior Genetics
Behav. Neural Biol. = Behavioral and Neural Biology
Behav. Neurosci. = Behavioral Neurosciences
Behav. Processes = Behavioral Processes
Behav. Res. Meth. Instrum. = Behavior Research Methods and
  Instrumentation

Behav. Res. Therap. = Behaviour Research and Therapy
Behav. Suppl. = Behaviour Supplements
Behav. Therap. = Behavior Therapy
Biol. Psychiat. = Biological Psychiatry
Biol. Psychol. = Biological Psychology
Biol. Rev. = Biological Review
Brain Lang. = Brain and Language
Brain Res. = Brain Research
Br. Birds = British Birds
Bull. Anim. Behav. = Bulletin of Animal Behavior
Bull. Inst. Oceanograph. Monaco = Bulletin of the Institute of Oceanography, Monaco
Bull. Psychon. Soc. = Bulletin of the Psychonomic Society

Canad. J. Zool. = Canadian Journal of Zoology
Comm. Behav. Biol. = Communications in Behavioral Biology
Comp. Psychol. Monogr. = Comparative Psychology Monographs
Condor = Condor
Cond. Reflex = Conditioned Reflex
Copeia = Copeia

Dev. Psychobiol. = Developmental Psychobiology
Diseases Nerv. Syst. = Diseases of the Nervous System

Ecol. = Ecology
Ecol. Mon. = Ecology Monographs
Exp. Neurol. = Experimental Neurology

Genet. Psychol. Monogr. = Genetic Psychology Monographs

Harvard Educ. Rev. = Harvard Educational Review

IRCS Med. Sci. = IRCS Medical Science

J. Anim. Ecol. = Journal of Animal Ecology
J. Comp. Neurol. = Journal of Comparative Neurology
J. Comp. Physiol. Psychol. = Journal of Comparative and Physiological Psychology
J. Comp. Psychol. = Journal of Comparative Psychology
J. Exp. Anal. Behav. = Journal of the Experimental Analysis of Behavior
J. Exp. Psychol. = Journal of Experimental Psychology
J. Exp. Psychol.: Anim. Behav. Processes = Journal of Experimental Pyschology: Animal Behavior Processes
J. Exp. Psychol.: General = Journal of Experimental Psychology: General

J. Exp. Psychol.: Hum. Percep. Perf. = Journal of Experimental Psychology: Human Perception and Performance

J. Exp. Res. Person. = Journal of Experimental Research in Personality

J. Gen. Psychol. = Journal of General Psychology

J. Genet. Psychol. = Journal of Genetic Psychology

J. Hist. Behav. Sci. = Journal of the History of the Behavioral Sciences

J. Human Evol. = Journal of Human Evolution

J. Neurosci. = Journal of Neuroscience

J. Nutrition = Journal of Nutrition

Learn. Motiv. = Learning and Motivation

Merrill Palmer Q. = Merrill Palmer Quarterly

Naturwiss. = Naturwissenschaften

Patt. Recog. = Pattern Recognition

Pav. J. Biol. Sci. = Pavlovian Journal of Biological Science

Percept. = Perception

Percept. Mot. Skills = Perception and Motor Skills

Pharmacol. Biochem. Behav. = Pharmacology, Biochemistry, and Behavior

Phil. Trans. R. Soc. Lond. = Philosophical Transactions of the Royal Society, London

Physiol. & Behav. = Physiology and Behavior

Physiol. Psychol. = Physiological Psychology

Physiol. Rev. = Physiology Review

Proc. Aristotel. Soc. Suppl. = Proceedings of the Aristotelian Society Supplement

Proc. Internat. Ornith. Cong. = Proceedings of the International Ornithology Congress

Proc. R. Soc. Lond. = Proceedings of the Royal Society, London

Proc. XV Conf. High Nerv. Act. = Proceedings of the 15th Conference on Higher Nervous Activity

Proc. 73rd Am. Psychol. Assoc. = Proceedings of the 73rd American Psychological Association

Prog. Psychobiol. Physiol. Psychol. = Progress in Psychobiology and Physiological Psychology

Psychol. Bull. = Psychological Bulletin

Psychol. Monogr. = Psychological Monographs

Psychol. Rec. = Psychological Record

Psychol. Rep. = Psychological Reports

Psychol. Rev. = Psychological Review

Psychon. Monogr. Suppl. = Psychonomic Monograph Supplements
Psychon. Sci. = Psychonomic Science
Psychopharmacol. = Psychopharmacology
Psychophysiol. = Psychophysiology

Q. J. Exp. Psychol. = Quarterly Journal of Experimental Psychology
Q. Rev. Biol. = Quarterly Review of Biology

Sym. Soc. Exp. Biol. = Symposium of the Society for Experimental Biology

Theor. Pop. Biol. = Theoretical Population Biology
Trends Neurosci. = Trends in Neuroscience

Z. Tierpsychol. = Zeitschrift für Tierpsychologie
Z. Vgl. Physiol. = Zeitschrift für Vergleichende Physiologie

Bibliography

Adams, C. D. (1980) "Post-conditioning devaluation of an instrumental reinforcer has no effect on extinction performance," *Q. J. Exp. Psychol.* 32: 447–58.
(1982) "Variations in the sensitivity of instrumental responding to reinforcer devaluation," *Q. J. Exp. Psychol.* 34B: 77–98.
Adams, C. D. and Dickinson, A. (1981a) "Actions and habits: variations in associative representations during instrumental learning," in N. E. Spear and R. R. Miller (eds) *Information Processing in Animals: Memory Mechanisms.* Hillsdale, NJ: Erlbaum, 143–65.
(1981b) "Instrumental responding following reinforcer devaluation," *Q. J. Exp. Psychol.* 33B: 109–21.
Alberts, J. R. (1978a) "Huddling by rat pups: multisensory control of contact," *J. Comp. Physiol. Psychol.* 92: 220–30.
(1978b) "Huddling by rat pups: group behavioral mechanisms of temperature regulation and energy conservation," *J. Comp. Physiol. Psychol.* 92: 231–45.
Alberts, J. R. and Brunjes, P. C. (1978) "Ontogeny of thermal and olfactory determinants of huddling in the rat," *J. Comp. Physiol. Psychol.* 92: 897–906.
Alcock, J. (1972) "The evolution of the use of tools by feeding animals," *Evolution* 26: 464–73.
Alcock, N. (1973) "Cues used in searching for food by red-winged blackbirds (*Agelaius phoeniceus*)," *Behav.* 46: 174–88.
Alkon, D. L. (1974) "Associative training of Hermissenda," *Journal of General Physiology* 64: 70–84.
Allison, J. (1983) *Behavioral Economics*, New York: Praeger.
Alloy, L. B. and Tabachnik, N. (1984) "Assessment of covariation by humans and animals: the joint influence of prior expectations and current situational information," *Psychol. Rev.* 91: 112–49.
Amiro, T. W. and Bitterman, M. E. (1980) "Second-order appetitive conditioning in goldfish," *J. Exp. Psychol.: Anim. Behav. Processes* 6: 41–8.
Angermeier, W. F. (1960) "Some basic aspects of social reinforcements in albino rats," *J. Comp. Physiol. Psychol.* 53: 364–7.
(1962) "The effect of a novel noxious stimulus upon the social operant behavior of the rat," *J. Genet. Psychol.* 100: 151–4.
Anisman, H. and Wahlsten, D. (1974) "Response initiation and directionality as

factors influencing avoidance performance," *J. Comp. Physiol. Psychol.* 87: 1119–28.

Annable, A. and Wearden, J. H. (1979) "Grooming movements as operants in the rat," *J. Exp. Anal. Behav.* 32: 297–304.

Annau, Z. and Kamin, L. J. (1961) "The conditioned emotional response as a function of the intensity of the US," *J. Comp. Physiol. Psychol.* 54: 428–32.

Applewhite, P. and Morowitz, H. J. (1966) "The micrometazoa as model systems for studying the physiology of memory," *Yale Journal of Biological Medicine* 39: 60–105.

Armstrong, E. A. (1950) "The nature and function of displacement activities," *Sym. Soc. Exp. Biol.* 4: 361–84.

Armstrong, S., Clarke, J., and Coleman, G. (1978) "Light–dark variation in laboratory rat stomach and small intestine content," *Physiol. & Behav.* 21: 785–8.

Aronson, R. B. and Givnish, T. J. (1983) "Optimal central place foragers: a comparison with null hypotheses," *Ecology* 64: 395–9.

Ashmole, N. P. (1963) "The regulation of numbers of tropical oceanic birds," *Ibis* 103b: 458–73.

Asratian, E. A. (1952) "On the physiology of temporary connections," *Proc. XV Conf. High. Nerv. Act.*, Moscow.

(1965) *Compensatory Adaptations, Reflex Activity, and the Brain*, Oxford: Pergamon Press.

(1966) "Instrumental conditioned reflexes," *Cond. Reflex* 2: 258–72.

(1972) "Genesis and Localization of conditioned inhibition," in R. A. Boakes and M. S. Halliday (eds) *Inhibition and Learning*, London: Academic Press.

Atnip, G. W. (1977) "Stimulus- and response-reinforcer contingencies in autoshaping, operant, classical and omission training procedures in rats," *J. Exp. Anal. Behav.* 28: 59–69.

Azrin, N. H. (1959) "Some notes on punishment and avoidance," *J. Exp. Anal. Behav.* 2: 260.

Azrin, N. H. and Hake, D. F. (1969) "Positive conditioned suppression: conditioned suppression using positive reinforcers as the unconditioned stimuli," *J. Exp. Anal. Behav.* 12: 117–73.

Azrin, N. H. and Hutchinson, R. R. (1967) "Conditioning of the aggressive behavior of pigeons by a fixed-interval schedule of reinforcement," *J. Exp. Anal. Behav.* 10: 395–402.

Azrin, N. H., Hutchinson, R. R., and Hake, D. F. (1963) "Pain-induced fighting in the squirrel monkey," *J. Exp. Anal. Behav.* 6: 620.

(1966) "Extinction-induced aggression," *J. Exp. Anal. Behav.* 9: 191–204.

Badia, P., Culbertson, S., and Harsh, J. (1973) "Choice of longer or stronger signalled shock over shorter or weaker unsignalled shock," *J. Exp. Anal. Behav.* 19: 25–32.

Baer, P. E. and Fuhrer, M. J. (1968) "Cognitive processes during differential trace and delayed conditioning of the GSR," *J. Exp. Psychol.* 78: 81–8.

(1970) "Cognitive processes in the differential trace conditioning of electrodermal and vasomotor activity," *J. Exp. Psychol.* 84: 176–8.

(1973) "Unexpected effects of masking: differential EDR conditioning without relational learning," *Psychophysiol.* 10: 95–9.

Baerends, G. P. (1971) "The ethological analysis of fish behavior," in W. S. Hoar and D. J. Randall (eds) *Fish Physiology*, New York: Academic Press.
(1975) "An evaluation of the conflict hypothesis as an explanatory principle for the evolution of displays," in G. P. Baerends, C. Beer, and A. Manning (eds) *Essays on Function and Evolution in Behavior*, Oxford: Clarendon Press.
(1976) "On drive, conflict and instinct, and the functional organization of behavior," in M. A. Corner and D. F. Swaab (eds) *Perspectives in Brain Research* 45: 427–47.

Baerends-van Roon, J. and Baerends, G. P. (1979) "The morphogenesis of the behavior of the domestic cat, with a special emphasis on the development of prey-catching," *Proceedings of the Royal Netherlands Academy of Sciences* 72.

Baker, A. G. and Baker, P. A. (1985) "Does inhibition differ from excitation? Proactive interference, contextual conditioning, and extinction," in R. R. Miller and N. E. Spear (eds) *Information Processing in Animals: Conditioned Inhibition*, Hillsdale, NJ: Erlbaum.

Baker, A. G. and Mackintosh, M. J. (1977) "Excitatory and inhibitory conditioning following uncorrelated presentations of CS and UCS," *Animal Learning and Behavior* 5: 315–19.

Baker, A. G. and Mercier, P. (1982) "Extinction of the context and latent inhibition," *Learn. Motiv.* 13: 391–416.

Balaz, M. A., Capra, S., Hartl, P., and Miller, R. R. (1981) "Contextual potentiation of acquired behavior after devaluing direct context-US associations," *Learn. Motiv.* 12: 383–97.

Balda, R. P. (1980) "Recovery of cached seeds by a captive *Nucifraga caryotactes*," *Z. Tierpsychol.* 52: 331–46.

Ball, W. and Tronick, E. (1971) "Infant responses to impending collision: optical and real," *Science* 171: 818–20.

Barash, D. P. (1973) "The social biology of the Olympic marmot," *Animal Behavior Monographs* 6: 173–244.

Barnett, S. A. (1956) "Behavior components in the feeding of wild and laboratory rats," *Behaviour* 9: 24–43.
(1975) *The Rat: A Study in Behavior*, Chicago: University of Chicago Press.

Baron, A., Kaufman, A., and Stauber, K. A. (1969) "Effects of instructions and reinforcement feedback on human operant behavior maintained by fixed-interval reinforcement," *J. Exp. Anal. Behav.* 12: 701–12.

Barrera, F. J. (1974) "Centrifugal selection of signal directed pecking," *J. Exp. Anal. Behav.* 22: 341–55.

Barrett, B. H. and Lindsley, O. R. (1962) "Deficits in acquisition of operant discrimination and differentiation shown by institutionalized retarded children," *Am. J. Ment. Defic.* 67: 424–36.

Bateson, P. P. G. (1966) "The characteristics and context of imprinting," *Biol. Rev.* 41: 177–220.
(1969) "The development of social attachments in birds and man," *Adv. Sci.* 25: 279–88.
(1985) "The neural basis of imprinting," in P. Marler and H. S. Terrace (eds) *The Biology of Learning*, New York: Springer-Verlag, 325–39.

Bateson, P. P. G., Horn, G., and Rose, S. P. R. (1975) "Imprinting: correlations between behavior and incorporation of (14C) Uracil into chick brain," *Brain Res.* 84: 207–20.

Bateson, P. P. G. and Reese, E. P. (1969) "Reinforcing properties of conspicuous stimuli in the imprinting situation," *Anim. Behav.* 17: 692–9.

Baum, M. and Gleitman, H. (1967) "'Conditioned anticipation' with an extinction baseline: the need for a disinhibition control group," *Psychon. Sci.* 8: 95–6.

Baum, W. M. (1981) "Optimization and the matching law as accounts of instrumental behavior," *J. Exp. Anal. Behav.* 36: 387–403.

Baxter, D. J. and Zamble, E. (1982) "Reinforcer and response specificity in appetitive transfer of control," *Anim. Learn. Behav.* 10: 201–10.

Baylis, J. R. (1982) "Avian vocal mimicry: its function and evolution," in D. E. Kroodsma and E. H. Miller (eds) *Acoustic Communication in Birds*, New York: Academic Press.

Bayroff, A. G. and Lard, K. E. (1944) "Experimental social behavior of animals: III. Imitational learning of white rats," *J. Comp. Physiol. Psychol.* 37: 165–71.

Bedford, J. and Anger, D. (1968) "Flight as an avoidance response in pigeons," Paper presented at the Psychonomic Society, St Louis, Mo.

Behrend, E. R. and Bitterman, M. E. (1962) "Avoidance conditioning in the goldfish; exploratory studies of the CS-US interval," *American Journal of Psychology* 75: 18–34.

—— (1963) "Sidman avoidance in the fish," *J. Exp. Anal. Behav.* 6: 47–52.

—— (1966) "Probability-matching in the goldfish," *Psychon. Sci.* 6: 327–8.

Behrend, E. R., Domesick, V. B., and Bitterman, M. E. (1965) "Habit reversal in fish," *J. Comp. Physiol. Psychol.* 60: 407–11.

Belovsky, G. E. (1978) "Diet optimization in a generalist herbivore: the moose," *Theor. Pop. Biol.* 14: 105–34.

—— (1981) "Optimal activity times and habitat choice of moose," *Oecologia* 48: 22–30.

—— (1984a) "Herbivore optimal foraging: a comparative test of three models," *Am. Nat.* (in press).

—— (1984b) "Summer diet optimization by beaver," *Am. Midl. Nat.* (in press).

Beninger, R. J., Kendall, S. B., and Vanderwolf, C. H. (1974) "The ability of rats to discriminate their own behaviors," *Canadian Journal of Psychology* 28: 79–91.

Bentall, R. P. and Lowe, C. F. (1982) "Developmental aspects of human operant behavior: the role of instructions and self-instructions," *Behav. Anal. Let.* 2: 186.

Berger, B. D., Yarczower, M., and Bitterman, M. E. (1965) "Effect of partial reinforcement on the extinction of a classically conditioned response in the goldfish," *J. Comp. Physiol. Psychol.* 59: 399–405.

Beritov, I. S. (1924) "On the fundamental nervous processes in the cortex of the cerebral hemispheres," *Brain* 47: 109–48, 358–76.

Bernheim, J. W. and Williams, D. R. (1967) "Time-dependent contrast effects in a multiple schedule of food reinforcement," *J. Exp. Anal. Behav.* 10: 243–9.

Berryman, R., Cumming, W. W., Cohen, L. R., and Johnson, D. F. (1965) "Acquisition and transfer of simultaneous oddity," *Psychol. Rep.* 17: 767–75.

Bicker, G. and Spatz, H. C. (1976) "Maze-learning ability of *Drosophila melanogaster*," *Nature* 260: 371.

Bicknell, A. T. and Richardson, A. M. (1973) "Comparison of avoidance learning in two species of lizards, *Crotaphytus collaris* and *Dipsosaurus dorsalis*," *Psychol. Rep.* 32: 1055–65.

Biferno, M. A. and Dawson, M. E. (1977) "The onset of contingency awareness and electrodermal classical contitioning: an analysis of temporal relationships during acquisition and extinction," *Psychophysiol.* 14: 164–71.

Bijou, S. W. and Baer, D. M. (1966) "Operant methods in child behavior and development," in W. K. Honig (ed.) *Operant Behavior: Areas of Research and Application,* New York: Appleton-Century-Crofts.

Bilbrey, J. and Winokur, S. (1973) "Controls for and constraints on autoshaping," *J. Exp. Anal. Behav.* 20: 323–32.

Bindra, D. (1972) "A unified account of classical conditioning and operant training," in A. H. Black and W. F. Prokasy (eds) *Classical Conditioning II: Current Research and Theory,* New York: Appleton-Century-Crofts, 453–81.
(1974) "Motivational view of learning, performance and behavior modification," *Psychol. Rev.* 81: 199–213.

Bindra, D. and Palfai, T. (1967) "Nature of positive and negative incentive motivational effects on general activity," *J. Comp. Physiol. Psychol.* 63: 288–97.

Bintz, J. (1971) "Between- and within-subject effect of shock intensity on avoidance in goldfish (*Carassius auratus*)," *J. Comp. Physiol. Psychol.* 75: 92–7.

Birch, H. G. (1945) "The relation of previous experience to insightful problem solving," *J. Comp. Psychol.* 38: 367–83.

Bischof, H-J. and Herrmann, K. (1984) "Ontogenetic development of sensory and song control areas in the zebra finch brain," *Behav. Brain Res.* (in press).

Bitterman, M. E. (1964) "Classical conditioning in the goldfish as a function of the CS–US interval," *J. Comp. Physiol. Psychol.* 58: 359–66.
(1965) "Phyletic differences in learning," *Am. Psychol.* 20: 396–410.
(1971) "Visual probability learning in the rat," *Psychon. Sci.* 22: 191–2.
(1975) "The comparative analysis of learning," *Science* 188: 699–709.

Bitterman, M. E., Menzel, R., Feitz, A., and Schafer, S. (1983) "Classical conditioning of proboscis extension in honeybees (*Apis mellifera*)," *J. Comp. Psychol.* 97: 107–19.

Black, A. H. (1971) "Autonomic aversive conditioning in infrahuman subjects," in F. R. Brush (ed.) *Aversive Conditioning and Learning,* New York: Academic Press, 3–104.

Black, M. (1968) *The Labyrinth of Language,* New York: Praeger.

Blackman, D. E. (1968) "Conditioned suppression or facilitation as a function of the behavioral baseline," *J. Exp. Anal. Behav.* 11: 53–61.
(1972) "Conditioned anxiety and operant behavior," in R. M. Gilbert, and J. D. Keehn (eds) *Schedule Effects: Drugs, Drinking and Aggression,* Toronto: University of Toronto Press, 26–49.
(1974) *Operant Conditioning: An Experimental Analysis of Behavior,* London: Methuen.

Blanchard, R. J. and Blanchard, D. C. (1969a) "Crouching as an index of fear," *J. Comp. Physiol. Psychol.* 67: 370–5.
(1969b) "Passive and active reactions to fear-eliciting stimuli," *J. Comp. Physiol. Psychol.* 68: 129–35.

Blanchard, R. J., Fukunaga, K. K., and Blanchard, D. C. (1976) "Environmental control of defensive reactions to a cat," *Bull. Psychon. Soc.* 8: 179–81.

Blanchard, R. J. and Honig, W. K. (1976) "Surprise value of food determines its effectiveness as a reinforcer," *J. Exp. Psychol.: Anim. Behav. Processes* 2: 67–74.

Blanchard, R. J., Mast, M., and Blanchard, D. C. (1975) "Stimulus control of defensive reactions in the albino rat," *J. Comp. Physiol. Psychol.* 88: 81–8.

Blest, A. D. (1957) "The function of eyespot patterns in the Lepidoptera," *Behav.* 11: 209–56.

Blough, D. S. (1958) "A method for obtaining psychophysical thresholds from the pigeon," *Science* 126: 304–5.

(1982) "Pigeon perception of letters of the alphabet," *Science* 218: 397–8.

Boakes, R. A. (1977) "Performance on learning to associate a stimulus with positive reinforcement," in H. Davis and H. M. B. Hurwitz (eds) *Operant-Pavlovian Interactions*, Hillsdale, N.J.: Erlbaum.

(1979) "Interactions between Type I and Type II processes involving positive reinforcement," in A. Dickinson and R. A. Boakes (eds) *Mechanisms of Learning and Motivation*, Chichester: John Wiley, 233–68.

Boakes, R. A., Poli, M., Lockwood, M. J., and Goodall, G. (1978) "A study of mis-behavior: token reinforcement in the rat," *J. Exp. Anal. Behav.* 29: 115–34.

Bock, W. J. (1959) "Preadaptation and multiple evolutionary pathways," *Evolution* 13: 194–211.

Boice, R. (1970) "Avoidance learning in active and passive frogs and toads," *J. Comp. Physiol. Psychol.* 70: 154–6.

Bolles, R. C. (1970) "Species-specific defense reactions and avoidance learning," *Psychol. Rev.* 77: 32–48.

(1971) "Species-specific defense reactions," in F. R. Brush (ed.) *Aversive Conditioning and Learning*, New York: Academic Press, 183–233.

Bolles, R. C. and Grossen, N. E. (1970) "Function of the CS in shuttle-box avoidance learning by rats," *J. Comp. Physiol. Psychol.* 70: 165–9.

Bolles, R. C. and Riley, A. L. (1973) "Freezing as an avoidance response: another look at the operant respondent distinction," *Learn. Motiv.* 4: 268–75.

Bolles, R. C., Stokes, L. W., and Younger, M. S. (1966) "Does CS termination reinforce avoidance behavior?" *J. Comp. Physiol. Psychol.* 62: 201–7.

Bols, R. J. (1977) "Display reinforcement in the Siamese fighting fish, *Betta splendens*: aggressive motivation or curiosity?" *J. Comp. Physiol. Psychol.* 91: 233–44.

Bond, A. B., Cook, R. G., and Lamb, M. R. (1981) "Spatial memory and the performance of rats and pigeons in the radial-arm maze," *Anim. Learn. Behav.* 9: 575–80.

Booker, R. and Quinn, W. G. (1981) "Conditioning of leg position in normal and mutant Drosophila," *Proceedings of the National Academy of Science USA*, 78: 3940–4.

Bottjer, S. W., Scobie, S. R., and Wallace, J. (1977) "Positive behavioral contrast, autoshaping, and omission responding in the goldfish (*Carassius auratus*)," *Anim. Learn. Behav.* 5: 336–42.

Bouton, M. E. and Bolles, R. C. (1979) "Contextual control of the extinction of conditioned fear," *Learn. Motiv.* 10: 445–66.

Bouton, M. E., Jones, D. L., McPhillips, S. A., and Schwartzentruber, D. (1986) "Potentiation and overshadowing in odor-aversion learning: role of method of odor presentation, the distal-proximal cue distinction, and the conditionability of odor," *Learn. Motiv.* 17: 115–38.

Boyd, B. O. and Warren, J. M. (1957) "Solution of oddity problems by cats," *J. Comp. Physiol. Psychol.* 50: 258–60.

Bradley, P. and Horn, G. (1978) "Afferent connections of *hyperstriatum ventrale* in the chick brain," *Journal of Physiology* 278: 46P.

Brady, J. V., Kelly, D., and Plumlee, L. (1969) "Autonomic and behavioral responses of the rhesus monkey to emotional conditioning," *Annals of the New York Academy of Science* 159: 959–75.

Brandon, S. E. and Bitterman, M. E. (1978) "Analysis of autoshaping in goldfish," *Anim. Learn. Behav.* 7: 57–62.

Breland, K. and Breland, M. (1961) "The misbehavior of organisms," *Am. Psychol.* 16: 661–4.

(1966) *Animal Behavior*, New York: Macmillan.

Brett, J. R. and MacKinnon, D. (1954) "Some aspects of olfactory perception in migrating adult Coho and Spring salmon," *Journal of the Fishery Research Board of Canada* 11: 310–18.

Brewer, W. F. (1974) "There is no convincing evidence for operant and classical conditioning in humans," in W. B. Weimer and D. J. Palermo (eds) *Cognition and the Symbolic Processes*, Hillsdale, NJ: Erlbaum.

Brimer, C. J. and Dockrill, F. J. (1966) "Partial reinforcement and the CER," *Psychon. Sci.* 5: 185–6.

Brodigan, D. L. and Peterson, G. B. (1976) "Two-choice discrimination performance of pigeons as a function of reward expectancy, pre-choice delay, and domesticity," *Anim. Learn. Behav.* 2: 121–4.

Brogden, W. J. (1939a) "The effect of frequency of reinforcement upon the level of conditioning," *J. Exp. Psychol.* 24: 419–31.

(1939b) "Sensory pre-conditioning," *J. Exp. Psychol.* 25: 323–32.

(1939c) "Unconditioned stimulus-substitution in the conditioning process," *American Journal of Psychology* 52: 46–55.

Brogden, W. J., Lipman, E. A., and Culler, E. (1938) "The role of incentive in conditioning and extinction," *American Journal of Psychology* 51: 109–17.

Bronson, G. W. (1968) "The development of fear in man and other animals," *Child Development* 39: 409–31.

Bronstein, P. M. and Hirsch, S. M. (1976) "Ontogeny of defensive reactions in Norway rats," *J. Comp. Physiol. Psychol.* 90: 620–9.

Brower, J. van Z. (1958) "Experimental studies of mimicry in some North American butterflies. I. The monarch, *Danaeus plexippus*, and viceroy, *Limenitis archippus archippus*," *Evolution*, 12: 32–47.

Brower, T. P. (1969) "Ecological chemistry," *Sci. Am.* 220: 22–9.

Brown, P. L. and Jenkins, H. M. (1968) "Auto-shaping of the pigeon's key peck," *J. Exp. Anal. Behav.* 11: 1–8.

Brown, R. T. (1975) "Following and visual imprinting in ducklings across a wide age range," *Dev. Psychobiol.* 8: 27–33.

Brown, R. T. and Hamilton, A. S. (1977) "Imprinting: effects of discrepancy from rearing conditions on approach to a familiar imprinting object in a novel situation," *J. Comp. Physiol. Psychol.* 91: 784–93.

Browne, M. (1974) "Autoshaping and the role of primary reinforcement and overt movements in the acquisition of stimulus-stimulus relations," Unpublished doctoral dissertation, Indiana University.

Bruce, R. H. (1935) "A further study of the effect of variation of reward and drive upon the maze performance of rats," *J. Comp. Psychol.* 20: 157–82.

Bruner, A. and Revusky, S. H. (1961) "Collateral behavior in humans," *J. Exp. Anal. Behav.* 4: 349–50.

Brush, F. R. (1966) "On the differences between animals that learn and do not learn to avoid electric shock," *Psychon. Sci.* 5: 123–4.

Bryant, R. C. (1972) "Conditioned suppression of free-operant avoidance," *J. Exp. Anal. Behav.* 17: 257–60.

Buchmann, O. L. K. and Grecian, E. A. (1974) "Discrimination-reversal learning in the marsupial *Isoodon obesulus* (Marsupialia, Peramelidae)," *Animal Behav.* 22: 975–81.

Buchwald, A. M. (1959) "Extinction after acquisition under different verbal reinforcement combinations," *J. Exp. Psychol.* 57: 43–8.

Bull, J. A. (1970) "An interaction between appetitive Pavlovian CSs and instrumental avoidance responding," *Learn. Motiv.* 1: 18–26.

Bull, J. A. and Overmier, J. B. (1968) "The additive and subtractive properties of extinction of inhibition," *J. Comp. Physiol. Psychol.* 66: 511–14.
(1969) "The incompatibility of appetitive and aversive conditioned motivation," *Proceedings of the 77th Convention of the APA* 4: 97–8.

Bullock, D. H. and Bitterman, M. E. (1962) "Habit reversal in the pigeon," *J. Comp. Physiol. Psychol.* 55: 958–62.

Burkhardt, P. E. (1980) "One trial backward fear conditioning in rats as a function of UCS intensity," *Bull. Psychon. Soc.* 15: 9–11.

Buzsaki, G. (1982) "The 'where is it?' reflex: autoshaping the orienting response," *J. Exp. Anal. Behav.* 37: 461–84.

Bykov, K. M. (1959) *The Cerebral Cortex and the Internal Organs*, Moscow: Foreign Languages Publishing House.

Cabe, P. A. (1976) "Discrimination of stereometric and planometric displays by pigeons," *Percept. Mot. Skills* 42: 1243–50.
(1980) "Picture perception in nonhuman subjects," in M. A. Hagen (ed.) *The Perception of Pictures*, New York: Academic Press.

Cabe, P. A. and Healey, M. L. (1979) "Figure-background color differences and transfer of a discrimination from objects to line drawings with pigeons," *Bull. Psychon. Soc.* 13: 124–6.

Campbell, C. S. (1969) "The development of specific preferences in thiamine-deficient Master's thesis, University of Illinois.

Capaldi, E. D. and Myers, D. E. (1978) "Resistance to satiation of consummatory and instrumental performance," *Learn. Motiv.* 9: 179–201.

Capretta, P. J. (1961) "An experimental modification of food preferences in chickens," *J. Comp. Physiol. Psychol.* 54: 238–42.

Caraco, T. (1980) "On foraging time allocation in a stochastic environment," *Ecol.* 61: 119–28.
(1981) "Energy budgets, risk, and foraging preferences in dark-eyed juncos (*Junco hyemalis*)," *Behav. Ecol. Sociobiol.* 8: 213–17.
(1982) "Aspects of risk-aversion in foraging white-crowned sparrows," *Anim. Behav.* 30: 719–27.
(1983) "White-crowned sparrows (*Zonatrichia leucophrys*): foraging preferences in a risky environment," *Behav. Ecol. Sociobiol.* 12: 63–9.

Caraco, T. and Chasin, M. (1984) "Foraging preferences: response to reward skew," *Anim. Behav.* 32: 76–85.

Caraco, T., Martindale, S., and Whittam, T. S. (1980) "An empirical demonstration of risk-sensitive foraging preferences," *Anim. Behav.* 28: 820–30.

Carew, T. J., Hawkins, R. D., and Kandel, E. R. (1983) "Differential classical conditioning of a defensive withdrawal reflex in *Aplysia californica*," *Science* 219: 397.

Carew, T. J., Walters, E. T., and Kandel, E. R. (1981) "Classical conditioning in a simple withdrawal reflex in *Aplysia californica*," *J. Neurosci.* 1: 1426.

Carlson, J. G. (1974) "Preconditioning the effects of shock-correlated reinforcement," *J. Exp. Psychol.* 103: 409–13.

Carlton, P. L. and Vogel, J. R. (1967) "Habituation and conditioning," *J. Comp. Physiol. Psychol.* 63: 348–51.

Carter, D. E. and Werner, T. J. (1978) "Complex learning and information processing by pigeons: a critical analysis," *J. Exp. Anal. Behav.* 29: 565–601.

Catania, A. C. (1963) "Concurrent performances: a baseline for the study of reinforcement magnitude," *J. Exp. Anal. Behav.* 6: 299–300.
(1966) "Concurrent operants," in W. K. Honig (ed.) *Operant Behavior: Areas of Research and Application*, New York: Appleton-Century-Crofts, 213–70.

Catania, A. C. and Reynolds, G. S. (1968) "A quantitative analysis of the responding maintained by interval schedules of reinforcement," *J. Exp. Anal. Behav.* 11: 327–83.

Cautela, J. R. (1965) "The problem of backward conditioning," *Journal of Psychology* 60: 135–44.

Cerella, J. (1977) "Absence of perspective processing in the pigeon," *Patt. Recog.* 9: 65–8.
(1979) "Visual classes and natural categories in the pigeon," *J. Exp. Psychol.: Hum. Percep. Perf.* 5: 68–77.
(1980) "The pigeon's analysis of pictures," *Patt. Recog.* 12: 1–6.
(1982) "Mechanisms of concept formation in the pigeon," in M. A. Goodale and R. J. W. Mansfield (eds) *Analysis of Visual Behavior*, Cambridge, Mass.: MIT Press.

Chacto, C. and Lubow, R. E. (1967) "Classical conditioning and latent inhibition in the white rat," *Psychon. Sci.* 9: 135–6.

Channell, S. and Hall, G. (1981) "Facilitation and retardation of discrimination learning after exposure to the stimuli," *J. Exp. Psychol.: Anim. Behav. Processes* 7: 437–46.

Charlton, S. G. (1983) "Differential conditionability: reinforcing grooming in golden hamsters," *Anim. Learn. Behav.* 11: 27–34.
(1984) "Hoarding-induced lever pressing in Golden Hamsters (*Mesocricetus auratus*): illumination, time of day, and shock as motivating operations," *J. Comp. Psychol.* 98: 327–32.

Charnov, E. L. (1976) "Optimal foraging: the marginal value theorem," *Theor. Pop. Biol.* 9: 129–36.

Chauvin, R. and Muckensturm-Chauvin, B. (1980) *Behavioral Complexities*, New York: International Universities Press.

Chen, C-S. (1967) "Can rats count?" *Nature* 214: 15–17.

Chen, J. S. and Amsel, A. (1980) "Recall (versus recognition) of taste and immunization against aversive taste anticipations based on illness," *Science* 209: 851–3.

Cherek, D. R., Thompson, T., and Heistad, G. T. (1973) "Responding maintained by the opportunity to attack during an interval food reinforcement schedule," *J. Exp. Anal. Behav.* 19: 113–23.

Chilliag, D. and Mendelson, J. (1971) "Schedule-induced airlicking as a function of bodyweight deficit in rats," *Physiol. & Behav.* 6: 603–5.

Church, R. M. and Meck, W. H. (1984) "The numerical attribute of stimuli," in H. L. Roitblat, T. G. Beaver, and H. S. Terrace (eds) *Animal Cognition*, Hillsdale, NJ: Erlbaum, 445–64.

Clark, E. (1959) "Instrumental conditioning in lemon sharks," *Science* 130: 217–18.

Clarke, J., Westbrook, R. F., and Irwin, J . (1979) "Potentiation instead of overshadowing in the pigeon," *Behav. Neural Biol.* 25: 18–29.

Clayton, K. N. (1964) "T-maze learning as a joint function of the reward magnitudes for the alternatives," *J. Comp. Physiol. Psychol.* 58: 333–8.

Cleland, G. G. and Davey, G. C. L. (1982) "The effects of satiation and reinforcer devaluation on signal-centered behavior in the rat," *Learn. Motiv.* 13: 343–60. (1983) "Autoshaping in the rat: the effects of localizable visual and auditory signals for food," *J. Exp. Anal. Behav.* 40: 47–56.

Cohen, D. H. and Durkovic, R. G. (1966) "Cardiac and respiratory conditioning, differentiation, and extinction in the pigeon," *J. Exp. Anal. Behav.* 9: 681–8.

Cohen, J. A. and Price, E. O. (1979) "Grooming in the Norway rat: displacement activity or 'boundary shift'?" *Behav. Neural Biol.* 26: 177–89.

Cohen, P. S. and Looney, T. A. (1973) "Schedule-induced mirror responding in the pigeon," *J. Exp. Anal. Behav.* 19: 395–408.

Colby, J. J. and Smith, N. F. (1977) "The effect of three procedures for eliminating a conditioned taste aversion in the rat," *Learn. Motiv.* 8: 404–13.

Colgan, D. M. (1970) "Effect of instructions on the skin resistance response," *J. Exp. Psychol.* 86: 108–12.

Collett, T. S. and Land, M. F. (1978) "How hoverflies compute interception courses," *Journal of Comparative Physiology* 125: 191–204.

Collias, N. E. (1953) "Some factors in maternal rejection by sheep and goats," *Bulletin of the Ecological Society of America* 34: 78.

Collias, N. E. and Collias, E. C. (1956) "Some mechanisms of family integration in ducks," *Auk*, 73: 378–400.

Collier, G. H. (1983) "Life in a closed economy: the ecology of learning and motivation," in M. D. Zeiler and P. Harzem (eds) *Advances in Analysis of Behavior* 3: 223–74.

Collier, G. H., Hirsch, E., and Hamlin, P. (1972) "The ecological determinants of reinforcement in the rat," *Physiol. & Behav.* 9: 705–16.

Collier, G. H., Hirsch, E., and Kanarek, R. (1977) "The operant revisited," in W. K. Honig and J. E. R. Staddon (eds) *Handbook of Operant Behavior*, Englewood Cliffs, NJ: Prentice-Hall.

Collier, G. H. and Kaufman, L. W. (1977) "The economics of magnitude of reinforcement," Paper presented at the Psychonometric Society meeting. Washington, DC.

Collier, G. H. and Rovee-Collier, C. K. (1981) "A coforaging behavior: laboratory simulations," in A. C. Kamil and T. Sargent (eds) *Foraging Behavior: Ecological, Ethological and Psychological Approaches*, New York: Garland STPM Press. (1983) "An ecological perspective of reinforcement and motivation," in E. Satinoff and P. Teitelbaum (eds) *Handbook of Behavioral Neurobiology*, New York: Plenum, 427–41.

Collins, L., Young, D. B., Davies, K., and Pearce, J. M. (1983) "The influence of partial reinforcement on serial autoshaping with pigeons," *Q. J. Exp. Psychol.* 35B: 275–90.

Colwill, R. M. and Rescorla, R. A. (1985a) "Postconditioning evaluation of a reinforcer affects instrumental responding," *J. Exp. Psychol.: Anim. Behav. Processes* 11: 120–32.
(1985b) "Instrumental responding remains sensitive to reinforcer devaluation after extensive training," *J. Exp. Psychol.: Anim. Behav. Processes* 11: 520–36.

Cook, R. M. and Cockrell, B. J. (1978) "Predator ingestion rate and its bearing on feeding time and the theory of optimal diets," *J. Anim. Ecol.* 47: 529–47.

Cook, R. M. and Hubbard, S. F. (1977) "Adaptive search strategies in insect parasites," *J. Anim. Ecol.* 46: 115–25.

Coppinger, R. P. (1969) "The effect of experience and novelty on avian feeding behaviour with reference to the evolution of warning colouration in butterflies," *Behav.* 35: 45–60.

Corfield-Sumner, P. K., Blackman, D. E., and Stainer, G. (1977) "Polydipsia induced in rats by second-order schedules of reinforcement," *J. Exp. Anal. Behav.* 27: 265–73.

Cott, H. B. (1940) *Adaptive Colouration in Animals*, London: Methuen.
(1947) "The edibility of birds: illustrated by five years' experiments (1941–1946) on the food preferences of the hornet, cat and man," *Proceedings of the Zoological Society*, London 116: 371–524.

Couvillon, P. A. and Bitterman, M. E. (1980) "Some phenomena of associative learning in honey bees," *J. Comp. Physiol. Psychol.* 94: 878–85.

Couvillon, P. A., Klosterhalfen, S., and Bitterman, M. E. (1983) "Analysis of overshadowing in honeybees," *J. Comp. Psychol.* 97: 154–66.

Cowie, R. J. (1977) "Optimal foraging in Great Tits (*Parus major*)," *Nature* 268: 137–9.

Cowie, R. J. and Krebs, J. R. (1979) "Optimum foraging in patchy environments," in R. M. Anderson, B. D. Turner, and L. R. Taylor (eds) *Population Dynamics*, Oxford: Blackwell Scientific Publications.

Cowie, R. J., Krebs, J. R., and Sherry, D. F. (1981) "Food storing by marsh tits," *Anim. Behav.* 29: 1252–9.

Cowles, R. P. (1908) "Habits, reactions, and associations in *Ocypoda arenaria*," *Papers of the Tortugas Laboratory, Carnegie Institute, Washington* 2: 1–41.

Craig, W. (1918) "Appetites and aversions as constituents of instincts," *Biological Bulletin Woods Hole* 34: 91–107.

Crawford, F. T. and Holmes, C. E. (1966) "Escape conditioning in snakes employing vibratory stimuli," *Psychon. Sci.* 4: 125–6.

Crawford, M. and Masterson, F. (1978) "Components of the flight response can reinforce bar-press avoidance learning," *J. Exp. Psychol.: Anim. Learn. Processes* 4: 144–51.

Crisler, G. (1930) "Salivation is unnecessary for the establishment of the salivary conditioned reflex induced by morphine," *American Journal of Psychology* 94: 553–6.

Croll, R. and Chase, R. (1980) "Plasticity of olfactory orientation to foods in the snail *Achtina fulica*," *Journal of Comparative Physiology* 136: 266–77.

Crow, T. J. and Alkon, D. L. (1978) "Retention of an associative behavioral change in Hermissenda," *Science* 201: 1239–41.

Crowell, C. R. and Anderson, D. C. (1972) "Variations in intensity, interstimulus interval, and interval between preconditioning CS exposures and conditioning with rats," *J. Comp. Physiol. Psychol.* 79: 291–8.

Cullen, E. (1957) "Adaptations in the kittiwake to cliff-nesting," *Ibis* 99: 275–302.

Curio, E. (1975) "The functional organization of anti-predator behaviour in the pied-flycatcher: a study of avian visual perception," *Anim. Behav.* 23: 1–115.
(1976) *The Ethology of Predation*, New York: Springer-Verlag.

Czaplicki, J. A., Porter, R. H., and Wilcoxon, H. C. (1975) "Olfactory mimicry involving garter snakes and artificial models and mimics," *Behav.*, 54: 60–7.

D'Amato, M. R. (1973) "Delayed matching and short-term memory in monkeys," in G. H. Bower (ed.) *The Psychology of Learning and Motivation*, 7, New York: Academic Press.

D'Amato, M. R. and O'Neill, W. (1971) "Effect of delay-interval illuminations on matching behavior in the capuchin monkey," *J. Exp. Anal. Behav.* 15: 327–33.

D'Amato, M. R. and Salmon, D. P. (1982) "Tune discrimination in monkeys (*Cebus apella*) and in rats," *Anim. Learn. Behav.* 10: 126–34.

D'Amato, M. R. and Schiff, D. (1964) "Long-term discriminated avoidance performance in the rat," *J. Comp. Physiol. Psychol.* 57: 123–6.

Davenport, J. W. (1962) "The interaction of magnitude and delay of reinforcement in spatial discrimination," *J. Comp. Physiol. Psychol.* 55: 267–73.

Davenport, R. K. and Rogers, C. M. (1970) "Intermodal equivalence of stimuli in apes," *Science* 168: 279–80.
(1971) "Perception of photographs by apes," *Behav.* 39: 318–20.

Davey, G. C. L. (1981) *Animal Learning and Conditioning*, London: Macmillan.
(1983) "An associative view of human classical conditioning," in G. C. L. Davey (ed.) *Animal Models of Human Behavior*, Chichester: John Wiley.
(ed.) (1987a) *Cognitive Processes and Pavlovian Conditioning in Humans*, Chichester: John Wiley.
(1987b) "The integration of human and animal models of Pavlovian conditioning: associations, cognitions and attributions," in G. C. L. Davey (ed.) *Cognitive Processes and Pavlovian Conditioning in Humans*, Chichester: John Wiley.

Davey, G. C. L. and Arulampalam, T. (1981) "Second-order electrodermal conditioning in humans," *IRCS Med. Sci.* 9: 567–8.
(1982) "Second-order 'fear' conditioning in humans: persistence of CR2 following extinction of CR1," *Behav. Res. Therap.* 20: 391–6.

Davey, G. C. L. and Cleland, G. G. (1982a) "The effect of partial reinforcement on the acquisition and extinction of sign-tracking and goal-tracking in the rat," *Bulletin of the Psychonomic. Society* 19: 115–18.
(1982b) "Topography of signal-centered behavior in the rat: effects of deprivation state and reinforcer type," *J. Exp. Anal. Behav.* 38: 291–304.
(1984) "Food anticipation and lever-directed activities in rats," *Learn. Motiv.* 15: 12–36.

Davey, G. C. L., Cleland, G. G., and Oakley, D. A. (1982) "Applying Konorski's model of classical conditioning to signal-centered behavior in the rat: some functional similarities between hunger CRs and sign-tracking," *Anim. Learn. Behav.* 10: 257–62.

Davey, G. C. L., Oakley, D., and Cleland, G. G. (1981) "Autoshaping in the rat:

effects of omission on the form of the response," *J. Exp. Anal. Behav.* 36: 75–91.

Davey, G. C. L., and McKenna, I. (1983) "The effects of postconditioning revaluation of CS1 and UCS following Pavlovian second-order electrodermal conditioning in humans," *Q. J. Exp. Psychol.* 35B: 125–33.

Davey, G. C. L., Phillips, J. H., and Witty, S. (1989) "Signal-directed behavior in the rat: interactions between the nature of the CS and the nature of the UCS," *Anim. Learn. Behav.*, in press.

Davey, G. C. L., Phillips, S., and Cleland, G. G. (1981) "The topography of signal-centered behavior in the rat: the effects of solid and liquid food reinforcers," *Behav. Anal. Let.* 1: 331–7.

Davidson, R. E. and Richardson, A. M. (1970) "Classical conditioning of skeletal and autonomic responses in the lizard (*Crotaphytus collaris*)," *Physiol. & Behav.* 5: 589–94.

Davidson, R. S. (1966) "Operant stimulus control applied to maze behavior: heat escape conditioning and discrimination reversal in *Alligator mississippiensis*," *J. Exp. Anal. Behav.* 9: 671–6.

Davies, N. B. (1977) "Prey selection and social behaviour in wagtails (Aves: Motacillidae)," *J. Anim. Ecol.* 46: 37–57.

Davis, H. and Kreuter, C. (1972) "Conditioned suppression of avoidance response by a stimulus paired with food," *J. Exp. Anal. Behav.* 17: 277–85.

Davis, H., Memmott, J., and Hurwitz, H. M. B. (1975) "Autocontingencies: a model for subtle behavioral control," *J. Exp. Psychol.: Gen.* 104: 169–88.

Davis, J. L. and Coates, S. R. (1978) "Classical conditioning of the nictitating membrane response in the domestic chick," *Physiol. Psychol.* 6: 7–10.

Davis, W. J. and Gillette, R. (1978) "Neural correlates of behavioral plasticity in command neurons of Pleurobranchaea," *Science* 199: 801–4.

Dawkins, M. (1971) "Perceptual changes in chicks: another look at the 'search image' concept," *Anim. Behav.* 19: 566–74.

Dawson, M. E. (1973) "Can classical conditioning occur without contingency learning? a review and evaluation of the evidence," *Psychophysiology* 10: 82–6.

Dawson, M. E. and Biferno, M. A. (1973) "Concurrent measurement of awareness and electrodermal classical conditioning," *J. Exp. Psychol.* 101: 55–62.

W. W. (1979) "Automatic classical conditioning as a function of awareness of stimulus contingencies," *Biol. Psychol.* 9: 23–40.

Dawson, M. E. and Furedy, J. J. (1976) "The role of awareness in human differential autonomic classical conditioning: the necessary-gate hypothesis," *Psychophysiol.* 13: 50–3.

Dawson, M. E. and Grings, W. W. (1968) "Comparison of classical conditioning and relational learning," *J. Exp. Psychol.* 76: 227–31.

Dawson, M. E. and Schell, A. M. (1985) "Information processing and human autonomic classical conditioning" in P. K. Ackles, J. R. Jennings and M. G. H. Coles. (eds) *Advances in Psychophysiology*, Vol. 1, Greenwich, CT.: JAI Press. (1987) "The role of 'controlled' and 'automatic' cognitive processes in human autonomic classical conditioning," in G. C. L. Davey (ed.) *Cognitive Processes and Pavlovian Conditioning in Humans*, Chichester: John Wiley.

Deane, G. E. (1969) "Cardiac activity during experimentally induced anxiety," *Psychophysiol.* 6: 17–30.

Debold, R. C., Miller, N. E., and Jensen, D. O. (1965) "Effect of strength of drive determined by a new technique for appetitive classical conditioning of rats," *J. Comp. Physiol. Psychol.* 59: 102–8.

Delprato, D. J. (1980) "Hereditary determinants of fear and phobias: a critical review," *Behav. Therap.* 11: 79–103.

Demarest, J. (1983) "The ideas of change, progress, and continuity in the comparative psychology of learning," in D. W. Rajecki (ed.) *Comparing Behavior: Studying Man Studying Animals*, Hillsdale, NJ: Erlbaum.

Dennis, I., Hampton, J. A., and Lea, S. E. G. (1973) "New problems in concept formation," *Nature* 243: 101–2.

Denny, M. R. (1971) "Relaxation theory and experiments," in F. R. Brush (ed.) *Aversive Conditioning and Learning*, New York: Academic Press, 235–95.

de Toledo, L. (1968) "Changes in heart rate and skeletal activity during conditioned suppression in rats," Unpublished Ph.D. dissertation, McMaster University.

de Toledo, L. and Black, A. H. (1966) "Heart rate: changes during conditioned suppression in rats," *Science* 152: 1404–6.

Dews, P. B. (1962) "The effect of multiple S-delta periods on responding on a fixed-interval schedule," *J. Exp. Anal. Behav.* 5: 319–74.
(1965) "The effects of multiple S-delta periods on responding on a fixed-interval schedule. III. Effects of changes in pattern of interruptions," *J. Exp. Anal. Behav.* 8: 427–33.
(1966) "The effect of multiple S-delta periods on responding on a fixed-interval schedule. V. Effect of periods of complete darkness and omission of food," *J. Exp. Anal. Behav.* 9: 573–8.

Dews, P. B. and Morse, W. H. (1958) "Some observations on an operant in human subjects and its modification by dextro-amphetamine," *J. Exp. Anal. Behav.* 1: 359–64.

Dewsbury, D. A., Baumgardner, D. J., Sawrey, D. K., and Webster, D. G. (1982) "The adaptive profile: Comparative psychology of red-backed voles (*Clethrionomys grapperi*)," *J. Comp. Physiol. Psychol.* 96: 649–60.

DiCara, L. V., Braun, J. J., and Pappas, B. A. (1970) "Classical conditioning and instrumental learning of cardiac and gastrointestinal responses following removal of neocortex in the rat," *J. Comp. Physiol. Psychol.* 73: 208–16.

Dickinson, A. (1980) *Contemporary Animal Learning Theory*, Cambridge: Cambridge University Press.
(1985) "Actions and habits: the development of behavioral autonomy," *Phil. Trans. R. Soc. Lond.* 308: 67–78.
(1986) "Re-examination of the role of the instrumental contingency in the sodium-appetite irrelevant incentive effect," *Q. J. Exp. Psychol.* 38B.

Dickinson, A., Hall, G., and Mackintosh, N. J. (1976) "Surprise and the attenuation of blocking," *J. Exp. Psychol.: Anim. Behav. Processes* 2: 213–22.

Dickinson, A. and Mackintosh, N. J. (1978) "Classical conditioning in animals," *Ann. Rev. Psychol.* 29: 587–612.
(1979) "Reinforcer specificity in the enhancement of conditioning by posttrial surprise," *J. Exp. Psychol.: Anim. Behav. Processes* 5: 162–77.

Dickinson, A. and Nicholas, D. J. (1983) "Irrelevant incentive learning during training on ratio and interval schedules," *Q. J. Exp. Psychol.* 35B: 235–47.

Dickinson, A., Nicholas, D. J., and Adams, C. D. (1983) "The effect of the instrumental training contingency on susceptibility to reinforcer devaluation," *Q. J. Exp. Psychol.* 35B: 35–51.

Dickinson, A., Shanks, D., and Evenden, J. (1984) "Judgement of act-outcome contingency: the role of selective attribution," *Q. J. Exp. Psychol.* 36A: 29–50.

Dieterlen, F. (1959) "Das Verhalten des syrischen Gildhamsters (*Mesocricetus auratus*, Waterhouse)," *Z. Tierpsychol.* 16: 47–103.

Domjan, M. (1980) "Ingestional aversion learning: unique and general processes," in J. S. Rosenblatt, R. A. Hinde, C. Beer, and M. Busnel (eds) *Advances in the Study of Behavior* 11, New York: Academic Press.
(1983) "Biological constraints on instrumental and classical conditioning: implications for general process theory," in G. H. Bower (ed.) *The Psychology of Learning and Motivation*, New York: Academic Press, 17.

Domjan, M. and Hanlon, M. J. (1982) "Post-avoidance learning to food-related tactile stimuli: avoidance of texture cues," *Anim. Learn. Behav.* 10: 293–300.

Domjan, M. and Wilson, N. E. (1972) "Contribution of ingestive behaviors to taste-aversion learning in the rat," *J. Comp. Physiol. Psychol.* 80: 403–12.

Doré, F. (1980) "Latent inhibition: learning about events that predict nothing," Paper presented to the 48th conference of the French-Canadian Association for the Advancement of Science.

Doty, B. A. and Combs, W. C. (1969) "Reversal learning of object and positional discriminations by mink, ferrets and skunks," *Q. J. Exp. Psychol.* 21: 58–62.

Dowsett-Lemaire, F. (1979) "The imitation range of the song of the marsh warbler, *Acrocephalus palustris*, with special reference to imitations of African birds," *Ibis* 121: 453–68.

Dufort, R. H., Guttman, N., and Kimble, G. A. (1954) "One-trial discrimination reversal in the white rat," *J. Comp. Physiol. Psychol.* 47: 248–9.

Dunham, P. J. (1971) "Punishment: method and theory," *Psychol. Rev.* 78: 58–70.

Durlach, P. J. (1983) "The effect of signaling intertrial USs in autoshaping," *J. Exp. Psychol.: Anim. Behav. Processes* 9: 374–89.

Durlach, P. J. and Grau, J. W. (1984) "General activity as a measure of context conditioning in autoshaping," Unpublished ms.

Dykman, R. A., Mack, R. L., and Ackerman, P. T. (1965) "The evaluation of autonomic and motor components of the nonavoidance conditioned response in the dog," *Psychophysiology* 1: 209–30.

Eckerman, D. A. (1967) "Stimulus control by part of a complex S-delta," *Psychon. Sci.* 7: 299–300.

Edmunds, M. (1974) *Defence in Animals*, Harlow, Essex: Longman.

Eisenberg, J. F. (1981) *The Mammalian Radiations*, Chicago: Chicago University Press.

Eisenstein, E. M. (1967) "The use of invertebrate systems for studies of the basis of learning and memory," in G. C. Quarton, T. Melneshuk, and F. O. Schmitt (eds) *The Neurosciences, a Study Program*, New York: Rockefeller University Press, 653–65.

Eisenstein, E. M. and Cohen, M. J. (1965) "Learning in an isolated prothoracic ganglion," *Anim. Behav.* 13: 304.

Elliott, M. H. (1934) "The effect of hunger on variability of performance," *American Journal of Psychology* 46: 107–12.

Elner, R. W. and Hughes, R. N. (1978) "Energy maximization on the diet of the shore crab *Carcinus maenas*," *J. Anim. Ecol.* 47: 103–16.

Epstein, R., Kirshnit, C. E., Lanza, R. P., and Rubin, L. C. (1984) "'Insight' in the pigeon: antecedents and determinants of an intelligent performance," *Nature* 308: 61–2.

Epstein, S. and Clarke, S. (1970) "Heart rate and skin conductance during experimentally induced anxiety: effects of anticipated intensity of noxious stimulation and experience," *J. Exp. Psychol.* 84: 105–12.

Erichsen, J. T., Krebs, J. R., and Houston, A. I. (1980) "Optimal foraging and cryptic prey," *J. Anim. Ecol.* 49: 271–6.

Estes, W. K. (1969) "New perspectives on some old issues in association theory," in N. J. Mackintosh and W. K. Honig (eds) *Fundamental Issues in Associative Learning*, Halifax, NS: Dalhousie University Press.

Estes, W. K. and Skinner, B. F. (1941) "Some quantitative properties of anxiety," *J. Exp. Psychol.* 29: 390–400.

Etscorn, F. and Stephens, R. (1973) "Establishment of conditioned taste aversions with a 24-hour CS–US interval," *Physiol. Psychol.* 1: 251–53.

Ewer, R. F. (1971) "The biology and behavior of a free-living population of black rats (*Rattus rattus*)," *Anim. Behav. Monogr.* 4: 127–74.

Eysenck, H. J. and Kelley, M. J. (1987) "The interaction of neurohormones with Pavlovian A and Pavlovian B conditioning in the causation of neurosis, extinction and incubation of anxiety," in G. C. L. Davey (ed.) *Cognitive Processes and Pavlovian Conditioning in Humans*, Chichester: John Wiley.

Fabricius, E. (1951) "Zur ethologie junger Anatiden," *Acta Zool. Fenn.* 68: 1–175.

Fabricius, E. and Boyd, H. (1954) "Experiments on the following reactions of ducklings," *Wildfowl Trust Annual Report*: 84–9.

Falk, J. L. (1961) "Production of polydipsia in normal rats by an intermittent food schedule," *Science*, 133: 195–6.

—— (1964) "Studies on schedule-induced polydipsia," in W. J. Wagner (ed.) *Thirst: First International Symposium on Thirst in the Regulation of Body Water*, 95–116.

—— (1966) "Schedule-induced polydipsia as a function of fixed-interval length," *J. Exp. Anal. Behav.* 9: 37–9.

—— (1969) "Conditions producing psychogenic polydipsia in animals," *Annals of the New York Academy of Science* 157: 569–93.

—— (1971) "The nature and determinants of adjunctive behavior," *Physiol. Behav.* 6: 577–88.

—— (1977) "The origin and functions of adjunctive behavior," *Anim. Learn. Behav.* 5: 325–35.

Fantino, E. and Duncan, B. (1972) "Some effects of interreinforcement time upon choice," *J. Exp. Anal. Behav.* 17: 3–14.

Farley, J. and Alkon, D. L. (1983) *Primary Neural Substrates of Learning and Behavioral Change*, New York: Cambridge University Press.

Farris, H. E. (1964) "Behavioral development, social organization, and conditioning of courting behavior in the Japanese quail (*Coturnix coturnix japonica*)," Unpublished Ph.D. thesis, University of Michigan.

—— (1967) "Classical conditioning of courting behavior in the Japanese quail, *Coturnix coturnix japonica*," *J. Exp. Anal. Behav.* 10: 213–17.

Farris, H. E. and Breuning, S. E. (1977) "Post-conditioning habituation and classically conditioned head withdrawal in the red-eared turtle (*Chrysemys scripta elegans*)," *Psychol. Rec.* 27: 303–13.

Felton, M. and Lyon, D. O. (1966) "The post-reinforcement pause," *J. Exp. Anal. Behav.* 9: 131–4.

Fernandes, D. M. and Church, R. M. (1982) "Discrimination of the number of sequential events by rats," *Anim. Learn. Behav.* 10: 171–6.

Ferraro, D. P., Schoenfeld, W. N., and Snapper, A. G. (1965) "Sequential response effects in the white rat during conditioning and extinction on a DRL schedule," *J. Exp. Anal. Behav.* 8: 255–60.

Ferster, C. B. and Skinner, B. F. (1957) *Schedules of Reinforcement*, New York: Appleton-Century-Crofts.

Finch, G. (1938) "Salivary conditioning in atropinized dogs," *American Journal of Psychology* 124: 136–41.

Fitzgerald, R. D. (1963) "Effects of partial reinforcement with acid on the classically conditioned salivary response in dogs," *J. Comp. Physiol. Psychol.* 56: 1056–60. (1966) "Some effects of partial reinforcement with shock on classically conditioned heart-rate in dogs," *American Journal of Psychology* 79: 242–9.

Fitzgerald, R. D., Vardaris, R. M., and Brown, J. S. (1966) "Classical conditioning of heart-rate deceleration in the rat with continuous and partial reinforcement," *Psychon. Sci.* 6: 437–8.

Fitzgerald, R. D., Vardaris, R. M., and Teyler, J. J. (1966) "Effects of partial reinforcement followed by continuous reinforcement on classically conditioned heart-rate in the dog," *J. Comp. Physiol. Psychol.* 62: 483–6.

Fitzsimmons, J. T. (1972) "Thirst," *Physiol. Rev.* 52: 465–561.

Flory, R. K. (1969) "Attack behavior as a function of minimum inter-food interval," *J. Exp. Anal. Behav.* 12: 825–8.

Flory, R. K. and Ellis, B. B. (1973) "Schedule-induced aggression against a slide-image target," *Bull. Psychon. Soc.* 2: 287–90.

Flory, R. K. and O'Boyle, M. K. (1972) "The effect of limited water availability on schedule-induced polydipsia," *Physiol. Behav.* 8: 147–9.

Foree, D. D. and Lolordo, V. M. (1973) "Attention in the pigeon: the differential effects of food-getting vs. shock-avoidance procedures," *J. Comp. Physiol. Psychol.* 85: 551–8. (1975) "Stimulus-reinforcer interactions in the pigeon: the role of electric shock and the avoidance contingency," *J. Exp. Psychol.: Anim. Behav. Processes* 104: 39–46.

Forselius, S. (1957) "Studies of anabantid fishes," *Zool. Bidr. Uppsala* 32: 93–597.

Fouts, R. S. (1974) "Language, origins, definitions and chimpanzees," *J. Human Evol.* 3: 475–82.

Fouts, R. S. and Rigby, R. L. (1976) "Man–chimpanzee communication," in T. A. Seberk (ed.) *How Animals Communicate*, Bloomington, Ind.: Indiana University Press.

Fowler, H. (1971) "Suppression and facilitation by response contingent shock," in F. R. Brush (ed.) *Aversive Conditioning and Learning*, New York: Academic Press, 537–604.

Fragaszy, D. M. and Mason, W. A. (1983) "Comparisons of feeding behavior in captive squirrel and titi monkeys (*Saimiri sciureus* and *Callicebus moloch*)," *J. Comp. Psychol.* 97: 310–26.

Frank, J. and Staddon, J. E. R. (1974) "Effects of restraint on temporal discrimination behavior," *Psychol. Rec.* 24: 123–30.

Frankhauser, G., Vernon, J. A., Frank, W. H., and Slack, W. V. (1955) "Effects of size and number of brain cells on learning in larvae of the salamander (*Triturus viridescens*)," *Science* 122: 692–3.

Friedman, G. J. and Carlson, J. G. (1973) "Effects of a stimulus correlated with positive reinforcement upon discrimination learning," *J. Exp. Psychol.* 97: 281–6.

Friedman, H. and Marshall, D. A. (1965) "Position reversal training in the Virginia opossum: evidence for the acquisition of a learning set," *Q. J. Exp. Psychol.* 17: 250–4.

Froseth, J. Z. and Grant, D. A. (1961) "Influence of intermittent reinforcement upon acquisition, extinction and spontaneous recovery in eyelid conditioning with fixed acquisition series," *J. Gen. Psychol.* 64: 225–32.

Fuhrer, M. J. and Baer, P. E. (1980) "Cognitive factors and CS–UCS interval effects in the differential conditioning and extinction of skin conductance responses," *Biol. Psychol.* 10: 283–98.

Gaffan, E. A. and Davies, J. (1981) "The role of exploration in win-shift and win-stay performance on a radial maze," *Learn. Motiv.* 12: 282–99.

Gagliardi, G. J., Gallup, G. G., and Boren, J. L. (1976) "Effect of different pupil to eye size ratios on tonic immobility in chickens," *Bull. Psychon. Soc.* 8: 58–60.

Galef, B. G. (1978) "Differences in affiliation behavior of weanling rats selecting eating and drinking sites," *J. Comp. Physiol. Psychol.* 92: 431–7.

Galef, B. G. and Clark, M. M. (1972) "Mothers' milk and adult presence: two factors determining initial dietary selection by weaning rats," *J. Comp. Physiol. Psychol.* 78: 220–5.

Galef, B. G. and Dalrymple, A. J. (1981) "Toxiciosis-based aversions to visual cues in rats: a test of the Testa and Ternes hypothesis," *Anim. Learn, Behav.* 9: 332–4.

Galef, B. G. and Osborne, B. (1978) "Novel taste facilitation of the association of visual cues with toxicosis in rats," *J. Comp. Physiol. Psychol.* 92: 907–16.

Gamzu, E. and Schwam, E. (1974) "Autoshaping and automaintenance of a key-press response in squirrel monkeys," *J. Exp. Anal. Behav.* 21: 361–71.

Gamzu, E. R. and Williams, D. R. (1971) "Classical conditioning of a complex skeletal response," *Science* 171: 923–5.
(1973) "Associative factors underlying the pigeon's key pecking in autoshaping procedures," *J. Exp. Anal. Behav.* 19: 225–32.

Gans, C. (1979) "Momentarily excessive construction as the basis for protoadaptation," *Evolution* 33: 227–33.

Garcia, J. (1981) "Tilting at the windmills of academe," *Am. Psychol.* 36: 149–58.

Garcia, J. and Ervin, F. R. (1968) "Gustatory-visceral and telereceptor-cutaneous conditioning — adaptations in internal and external milieus," *Comm. Behav. Biol.* 1 (Pt. A): 389–415.

Garcia, J., Ervin, F. R., and Koelling, R. A. (1966) "Learning with prolonged delay of reinforcement," *Psychon. Sci.* 5: 121–2.

Garcia, J., Hawkins, W. G., and Rusiniak, K. W. (1974) "Behavioral regulation of the milieu interne in man and rats," *Science* 185: 824–31.

Garcia, J. and Koelling, R. A. (1966) "Relation of cue to consequence in avoidance learning," *Psychon. Sci.* 4: 123–4.

Garcia, J., McGowan, B. K., and Green, K. F. (1972) "Biological constraints on conditioning," in M. E. P. Seligman and J. L. Hager (eds) *Biological Boundaries of Learning*, New York: Appleton-Century-Crofts, 21–43.

Gardner, B. T. and Gardner, R. A. (1971) "Two-way communication with an infant chimpanzee," in A. Schrier and F. Stollnitz (eds) *Behavior of Non-human Primates*, New York: Academic Press, 117–84.

Gardner, R. A. and Gardner, B. T. (1969) "Teaching sign language to a chimpanzee," *Science* 165: 664–72.

Gardner, W. M. (1969) "Autoshaping in the bobwhite quail," *J. Exp. Anal. Behav.* 12: 279–81.

Gelperin, A. (1975) "Rapid food aversion learning by a terrestrial mollusc," *Science* 189: 567–70.

Gentry, W. D. (1968) "Fixed-ratio schedule-induced aggression," *J. Exp. Anal. Behav.* 11: 813–17.

Gentry, W. D. and Schaeffer, R. W. (1969) "The effect of FR response requirement on aggressive behavior in rats," *Psychon. Sci.* 14: 236–8.

Gibb, J. A. (1958) "Predation by tits and squirrels on the eucosmimid *Ernarmonia conicolana*," *J. Anim. Ecol.* 27: 275–96.

Gibbon, J. (1981) "The contingency problem in autoshaping," in C. M. Locurto, H. S. Terrace, and J. Gibbon (eds) *Autoshaping and Conditioning Theory*, New York: Academic Press.

Gibbon, J. and Balsam, P. (1981) "Spreading associations in time," in C. M. Locurto, H. S. Terrace, and J. Gibbon (eds) *Autoshaping and Conditioning Theory*, New York: Academic Press.

Gill, T. V. and Rumbaugh, D. M. (1974) "Mastery of naming skills by a chimpanzee," *J. Human Evol.* 3: 483–92.

Gillette, K., Martin, G. M., and Bellingham, W. P. (1980) "Differential use of food and water cues in the formation of conditioned aversions by domestic chicks (*Gallus gallus*)," *J. Exp. Psychol.: Anim. Behav. Processes* 6: 99–111.

Gittleman, J. L., Harvey, P. H., and Greenwood, P. J. (1980) "The evolution of conspicuous colouration: some experiments in bad taste," *Anim. Behav.* 28: 897–9.

Golani, I., Wolgin, D., and Teitelbaum, P. (1979) "A proposed natural geometry of recovery from akinesia in the lateral hypothalamic rat," *Brain Res.* 164: 237–67.

Goldstein, A. C., Spies, G., and Sepinwall, J. (1964) "Conditioning of the nictitating membrane in the frog, *Rana p. pipiens*," *J. Comp. Physiol. Psychol.* 57: 456–8.

Gonzalez, F. A. (1974) "Effects of varying the percentage of key illuminations paired with food in a positive automaintenance procedure," *J. Exp. Anal. Behav.* 22: 483–9.

Gonzalez, R. C., Eskin, R. M., and Bitterman, M. E. (1962) "Alternating and random partial reinforcement in the fish with some observations on asymptotic resistance to extinction," *American Journal of Psychology* 74: 561–8.

Gonzalez, R. C., Longo, N., and Bitterman, M. E. (1961) "Classical conditioning in the fish: exploratory studies of partial reinforcement," *J. Comp. Physiol. Psychol.* 54: 452–6.

Gonzalez, R. C., Milstein, S., and Bitterman, M. E. (1962) "Classical conditioning in the fish: further studies of partial reinforcement," *American Journal of Psychology* 75: 421–8.

Gormezano, I. (1966) "Classical conditioning," in J. B. Sidowski (ed.) *Experimental Methods and Instrumentation in Psychology*, New York: McGraw-Hill, 385–420. (1972) "Investigations of defense and reward conditioning in the rabbit," in A. H. Black and W. F. Prokasy (eds) *Classical Conditioning*, vol. 2, New York: Appleton-Century-Crofts, 151–81.

Gormezano, I. and Coleman, S. R. (1973) "The law of effect and CR contingent modification of the UCS," *Cond. Reflex* 8: 41–56. (1975) "Effect of partial reinforcement on conditioning, conditional probabilities, asymptotic performance, and extinction of the rabbit's NMR," *Pav. J. Biol. Sci.* 10: 13–22.

Gormezano, I. and Hiller, G. W. (1972) "Omission training of the jaw-movement response of the rabbit to a water US," *Psychon. Sci.* 29: 276–8.

Gormezano, I. and Kehoe, E. J. (1976) "Classical conditioning: some methodological-conceptual issues," in W. K. Estes (ed.) *Handbook of Learning and Cognitive Processes*, vol. 2, Hillsdale, NJ: Erlbaum.

Gormezano, I. and Tait, R. W. (1976) "The Pavlovian analysis of instrumental conditioning," *Pav. J. Biol. Sci.* 11: 37–55.

Gorry, T. H. and Ober, S. E. (1970) "Stimulus characteristics of learning over long delays in monkeys," Paper presented to the Psychonomic Society, San Antonio, Texas.

Goss-Custard, J. D. (1977) "Optimal foraging and the size selection of worms by redshank, (1981) "Feeding behavior of redshank (*Tringa totanus*), and optimal foraging d," *Anim. Behav.* 25: 10–29. theory," in A. C. Kamil and T. D. Sargent (eds) *Foraging Behavior: Ethological and Psychological Approaches*, New York: Garland STPM Press.

Gossette, R. R., Gossette, M. F., and Riddell, W. (1966). "Comparison of successive discrimination reversal performances among closely and remotely related avian species," *Anim. Behav.* 14: 560–64.

Gossette, R. L. and Hombach, A. (1969) "Successive discrimination reversal (SDR) performance of American alligators and American crocodiles on a spatial task," *Percept. Mot. Skills* 28: 63–7.

Gossette, R. L. and Hood, P. (1967) "The reversal index (RI) as a joint function of drive and incentive levels," *Psychon. Sci.* 8: 217–18.

Gossette, R. L. and Kraus, G. (1968) "Successive discrimination reversal performance of mammalian species on a brightness task," *Percept. Mot. Skills* 27: 675–8.

Gossette, R. L., Kraus, G., and Speiss, J. (1968) "Comparison of successive discrimination reversal (SDR) performances of seven mammalian species on a spatial task," *Psychon. Sci.* 12: 193–4.

Gottlieb, G. (1984) "Evolutionary trends and evolutionary origins: relevance to theory in comparative psychology," *Psychol. Rev.* 91: 448–56. (1985) "Anagenesis: theoretical basis for the ecological void in comparative psychology," in T. D. Johnston and A. T. Pietrewicz (eds) *Issues in the Ecological Study of Learning*, Hillsdale, NJ: Erlbaum, 59–72.

Gottlieb, G. and Klopfer, P. H. (1962) "The relation of developmental age to auditory and visual imprinting," *J. Comp. Physiol. Psychol.* 55: 821–6.

Goudie, A. J. and Dickins, D. W. (1978) Nitrous oxide-induced conditioned taste aversions in rats: the role of duration of drug exposure and its relation to the taste aversion self-administration 'paradox,'" *Pharmacol. Biochem. Behav.* 9: 587–92.

Gould, S. J. (1980) *The Panda's Thumb*, New York: Norton.

Gould, S. J. and Eldridge, N. (1977) "Punctuated equilibria: the tempo and mode of evolution reconsidered," *Paleobiol.* 63: 115–51.

Graf, V., Bullock, D. H., and Bitterman, M. E. (1964) "Further experiments on probability-matching in the pigeon," *J. Exp. Anal. Behav.* 7: 151–7.

Graham, J. M. and Desjardins, C. (1980) "Classical conditioning: induction of luteinizing hormone and testosterone secretion in anticipation of sexual activity," *Science* 210: 1039–41.

Granda, A. M., Matsumiya, Y., and Stirling, C. E. (1965) "A method for producing avoidance behavior in the turtle," *Psychon. Sci.* 2: 187–8.

Grant, D. S. (1976) "Effect of sample presentation time on long-delay matching in the pigeon," *Learn. Motiv.* 7: 580–90.

(1981a) "Short-term memory in the pigeon," in N. E. Spear and R. R. Miller (eds) *Information Processing in Animals: Memory Mechanisms*, Hillsdale, NJ: Erlbaum.

(1981b) "Stimulus control of information processing in pigeon short-term memory," *Learn. Motiv.* 12: 19–39.

(1984) "Rehearsal in pigeon short-term memory," in H. L. Roitblat, T. G. Bever, and H. S. Terrace (eds) *Animal Cognition*, Hillsdale, NJ: Erlbaum, 99–116.

Grant, D. S., Brewster, R. G., and Stierhoff, K. A. (1983) "'Surprisingness' and short-term retention in pigeons," *J. Exp. Psychol.: Anim. Behav. Processes* 9: 63–79.

Grant, D. S. and Roberts, W. A. (1973) "Trace interaction in pigeon short-term memory," *J. Exp. Psychol.* 101: 21–9.

Grastyan, E. and Vereczkei, L. (1974) "Effects of spatial separation of the conditioned signal from the reinforcement: a demonstration of the conditioned character of the orienting response," *Behav. Biol.* 10: 121–46.

Grau, J. W. and Rescorla, R. A. (1984) "Role of context in autoshaping," *J. Exp. Psychol.: Anim. Behav. Processes* 10: 324–89.

Gray, J. A. (1965) "Stimulus intensity dynamism," *Psychol. Bull.* 63: 180–96.

Gray, T. and Appignanesi, A. A. (1973) "Compound conditioning: elimination of blocking effect," *Learn. Motiv.* 4: 374–80.

Grether, W. F. (1938) "Pseudo-conditioning without paired stimulation encountered in attempted backward conditioning," *J. Comp. Psychol.* 25: 91–6.

Grings, W. W. (1965) "Verbal-perceptual factors in the conditioning of autonomic responses," in W. F. Prokasy (ed.) *Classical Conditioning: a Symposium*, New York: Appleton-Century-Crofts.

Grings, W. W. and Dawson, M. E. (1973) "Complex conditioning," in W. F. Prokasy and D. C. Raskion (eds) *Electrodermal Activity in Psychological Research*, New York: Academic Press.

Grossen, N. E. and Bolles, R. C. (1968) "Effects of classical conditioned 'fear signal' and 'safety signal' on nondiscriminated avoidance behavior," *Psychon. Sci.* 11: 321–2.

Groves, P. M. and Thompson, R. F. (1970) "Habituation: a dual-process theory," *Psychol. Rev.* 77: 419–50.

Gruber, S. H. and Schneiderman, N. (1975) "Classical conditioning of the nictitating membrane response of the lemon shark (*Negaprion brevirostris*)," *Behav. Res. Meth. Instrum.* 7: 430–4.

Guettinger, H. R. (1981) "Self differentiation of song organization rules by deaf canaries," *Z. Tierpsychol.* 56: 323–40.

Gustavson, C. R. (1977) "Comparative and field aspects of learned food aversions," in L. M. Barker, M. R. Best, and M. Domjan (eds) *Learning Mechanisms in Food Selection*, Waco, Tex.: Baylor University Press.

Gustavson, C. R., Garcia, J., Hankins, W. G., and Rusiniak, K. W. (1974) "Coyote predation control by aversive conditioning," *Science* 184: 581–3.

Guthrie, E. R. (1935) *The Psychology of Learning*, New York: Harper.

Guttman, N. and Kalish, H. I. (1956) "Discriminability and stimulus generalization," *J. Exp. Psychol.* 51: 79–88.

Haig, K. A., Rawlins, N. P., Olton, D. S., Mead, A., and Taylor, B. (1983) "Food searching strategies of rats: variables affecting the relative strength of stay and shift strategies," *J. Exp. Psychol.: Anim. Behav. Processes* 9: 337–48.

Hailman, J. P. (1965) "Cliff-nesting adaptations in the Galapagos swallow-tailed 62. gull," *Wilson Bulletin* 77: 346–62
(1976) "Uses of the comparative study of behavior," in R. B. Masterson, W. Hodos, and H. Jerison (eds) *Evolution, Brain and Behavior: Persistent Problems*, Hillsdale, NJ: Erlbaum, 13–22.

Hall, G. and Minor, H. (1984) "A seach for context–stimulus associations in latent inhibition," *Q. J. Exp. Psychol.* 36B: 145–69.

Hall, G. and Pearce, J. M. (1979) "Latent inhibition of a CS during CS–US pairings," *J. Exp. Psychol.: Anim. Behav. Processes* 5: 31–42.

Hall, W. G. and Williams, C. L. (1983) "Suckling isn't feeding, or is it? A search for developmental continuities," *Adv. Study Behav.* 13: 219–54.

Hall-Craggs, J. (1962) "The development of song in the blackbird (*Turdus merula*)," *Ibis* 104: 277–300.

Halliday, M. S. and Boakes, R. A. (1971) "Behavioral contrast and response independent reinforcement," *J. Exp. Anal. Behav.*, 16: 429–434.
(1972) "Discrimination involving response-independent reinforcement: implications for behavioral contrast," in R. A. Boakes and M. S. Halliday (eds) *Inhibition and Learning*, London: Academic Press, 73–97.
(1974) "Behavioral contrast without response rate reduction," *J. Exp. Anal. Behav.* 22: 453–62.

Hamilton, L. W. (1972) "Intrabox and extrabox cues in avoidance responding: effect of septal lesions," *J. Comp. Physiol. Psychol.* 78: 268–73.

Hammond, L. J. (1968) "Retardation of fear acquisition by a previously inhibitory CS," *J. Comp. Physiol. Psychol.* 66: 756–9.

Hanson, S. J. and Timberlake, W. (1983) "Regulation during challenge: a general model of learned performance under schedule constraint," *Psychol. Rev.* 90: 261–82.

Haralson, J. V. and Groff, C. I. (1975) "Classical conditioning in the sea anemone, *Cribrina xanthogrammica*," *Physiol. Behav.* 15: 455–60.

Harrison, J. M. (1979) "The control of responding by sounds: unusual effect of reinforcement," *J. Exp. Anal. Behav.* 32: 167–81.

Hassell, M. P. and May, R. M. (1974) "Aggregation of predators and insect parasites and its effect on stability," *J. Anim. Ecol.* 43: 567–94.

Hawkins, R. D. and Kandel, E. R. (1984) "Is there a cell-biological alphabet for simple forms of learning?" *Psychol. Rev.* 91: 375–91.

Hay, D. A. (1975) "Strain differences in maze-learning ability of *Drosophila melanogaster*," *Nature* 257: 44–6.

Hayes, K. J. and Hayes, C. (1955) "The cultural capacity of chimpanzees," in J. A. Garan (ed.) *The Non-human Primates and Human Evolution*, Detroit, Mich.: Wayne University Press.

Hayes, K. J. and Nissen, C. H. (1971) "Higher mental functions of a home-raised chimpanzee," in A. M. Schrier and F. Stollnitz (eds) *Behavior of Nonhuman Primates*, New York: Academic Press, 59–115.

Hayes, W. N. and Saiff, E. I. (1967) "Visual alarm reactions in turtles," *Anim. Behav.* 15: 102–6.

Hearst, E. (1975) "Pavlovian conditioning and directed movements," in G. Bower (ed.) *The Psychology of Learning and Motivation*, vol. 9, New York: Academic Press.

(1979) "Classical conditioning as the formation of interstimulus associations: stimulus substitution, parasitic reinforcement, and autoshaping," in A. Dickinson and R. A. Boakes (eds) *Mechanisms of Learning and Motivation*, Hillsdale, NJ: Erlbaum.

Hearst, E. and Franklin, S. R. (1977) "Positive and negative relations between a signal and food: approach–withdrawal behavior to the signal," *J. Exp. Psychol.: Anim. Behav. Processes* 3: 37–52.

Hearst, E. and Gormley, D. (1976) "Some tests of the additivity (autoshaping) theory 50.

Hearst, E. and Jenkins, H. M. (1974) "Sign tracking: the stimulus-reinforcer relation and directed action," Austin, Tex.: Psychonomic Society.

Heinrich, B. (1976) "The foraging specializations of individual bumblebees," *Ecol. Mon.* 46: 105–28.

(1985) "Learning in invertebrates," in P. Marler and H. S. Terrace (eds) *The Biology of Learning*, New York: Springer-Verlag, 135–47.

Heinrich, B., Mudge, P. R., and Deringis, P. A. (1977) "Laboratory analysis of flower constancy in foraging bumblebees: *Bombus ternarius* and *B. terricola*," *Behav. Ecol. Sociobiol.* 2: 247–65.

Hemmes, N. S. (1973) "Behavioral contrast in the pigeon depends on the operant," *J. Comp. Physiol. Psychol.* 85: 171–8.

(1975) "Pigeon's performance under differential reinforcement of low rate schedules depends upon the operant," *Learn. Motiv.* 6: 344–57.

Henderson, T. and Strong, T. (1972) "Classical conditioning in the leech. *Macrobdella dititra*, as a function of CS and US intensity," *Cond. Reflex* 7: 210–15.

Hennessey, T. M., Rucker, W. B., and McDiarmid, C. G. (1979) "Classical conditioning in paramecia," *Anim. Learn. Behav.* 7: 417–23.

Henton, W. W. and Brady, J. V. (1970) "Operant acceleration during a pre-reward stimulus," *J. Exp. Anal. Behav.* 13: 205–9.

Henton, W. W. and Iverson, I. H. (1978) *Classical Conditioning and Operant Conditioning*, New York: Springer-Verlag.

Herman, L. M. (1975) "Interference and auditory short-term memory in the bottlenosed dolphin," *Anim. Learn. Behav.* 3: 43–8.

Herman, L. M. and Thompson, R. K. R. (1982) "Symbolic identity, and probe delayed matching to sounds by the bottlenosed dolphin," *Anim. Learn. Behav.* 10: 22–34.

Herrera, C. M. (1974) "Trophic diversity of the Barn owl, *Tyto alba*, in continental western Europe," *Ornis. Scand.* 5: 181–91.

Herrnstein, R. J. (1958) "Some factors influencing behavior in a two-response situation," *Transactions of the New York Academy of Science* 21: 35–45.

(1961) "Relative and absolute strength of response as a function of frequency of reinforcement," *J. Exp. Anal. Behav.* 4: 267–72.

(1970) "On the law of effect," *J. Exp. Anal. Behav.* 13: 243–66.

(1984) "Objects, categories, and discriminative stimuli," in H. L. Roitblat, T. G. Bever, and H. S. Terrace (eds) *Animal Cognition*, Hillsdale, NJ: Erlbaum, 233–61.

Herrnstein, R. J. and de Villiers, P. A. (1980) "Fish as a natural category for people and pigeons," in G. H. Bower (ed.) *The Psychology of Learning and Motivation*, vol. 14, New York: Academic Press.

Herrnstein, R. J. and Loveland, D. H. (1964) "Complex visual concept in the pigeon," *Science* 146: 549–51.

Herrnstein, R. J., Loveland, D. H., and Cable, C. (1976) "Natural concepts in pigeons," *J. Exp. Psychol.: Anim. Behav. Processes* 2: 285–302.

Herrnstein, R. J. and Vaughan, W. (1980) "Melioration and behavioral allocation," in J. E. R. Staddon (ed.) *Limits to Action*, New York: Academic Press.

Hershkowitz, M. and Samuel, D. (1973) "The retention of learning during metamorphosis of the crested newt (*Triturus cristatus*)," *Anim. Behav.* 21: 83–5.

Hess, E. H. (1962) "Imprinting and the critical period concept," in E. L. Bliss (ed.) *Roots of Behavior*, New York: Hoeber, 254–63.

(1964) "Imprinting in birds," *Science* 146: 1128–39.

(1972) "The natural history of imprinting," *Annals of the New York Academy of Science* 193: 124–36.

(1973) *Imprinting*, New York: Van Nostrand Reinhold.

Hess, E. H. and Hess, D. B. (1969) "Innate factors in imprinting," *Psychon. Sci.* 14: 129–30.

Heth, C. D. and Rescorla, R. A. (1973) "Simultaneous and backward fear conditioning in the rat," *J. Comp. Physiol. Psychol.* 82: 434–43.

Heyman, G. M. (1983) "Optimization theory: close but no cigar," *Behav. Anal. Let.* 3: 17–26.

Hill, W. F. and Spear, N. E. (1963) "Choice between magnitudes of reward in a T-maze," *J. Comp. Physiol. Psychol.* 56: 723–6.

Hill, W. L. and Collier, G. H. (1978) "The economics of response rate as a feeding strategy," Paper presented at the Eastern Psychological Association, Washington, DC.

Hilton, A. (1969) "Partial reinforcement of a conditioned emotional response in rats," *J. Comp. Physiol. Psychol.* 69: 178–93.

Hinde, R. A. (1970) *Animal Behaviour*, New York: McGraw-Hill.

Hinde, R. A. and Stevenson-Hinde, J. (1973) *Constraints on Learning*, London: Academic Press.

Hineline, P. N. (1973) "Varied approaches to aversion: a review of *Aversive Conditioning and Learning*, edited by F. Robert Brush," *J. Exp. Anal. Behav.* 19: 531–40.

Hineline, P. N. and Rachlin, H. (1969) "Escape and avoidance of shock by pigeons pecking a key," *J. Exp. Anal. Behav.* 12: 533–8.

Hinson, J. M. and Staddon, J. E. R. (1978) "Behavioral competition: a mechanism for schedule interactions," *Science* 202: 432–4.

——— (1983) "Matching, maximising, and hill-climbing," *J. Exp. Anal. Behav.* 40: 321–31.

Hobson, S. L. and Newman, F. (1981) "Fixed-ratio counting schedules," in M. L. Commons and J. A. Nevin (eds) *Quantitative Analyses of Behavior: I. Discriminative Properties of Schedules*, Cambridge, Mass.: Ballinger.

Hodos, W. (1982) "Some perspectives on the evolution of intelligence and the brain," in D. R. Griffin (ed.) *Animal Mind – Human Mind*, New York: Springer-Verlag, 33–56.

Hodos, W. and Campbell, C. B. G. (1969) "*Scala naturae*: Why there is no theory in comparative psychology," *Psychol. Rev.* 76: 337–50.

Hoffman, H. S. (1968) "The control of distress vocalization by an imprinted stimulus," *Behav.* 30: 175–91.

Hoffman, H. S. and Fleshler, M. (1959) "Aversive control with the pigeon," *J. Exp. Anal. Behav.* 2: 213–18.

——— (1962) "The course of emotionality in the development of avoidance," *J. Exp. Psychol.* 64: 288–94.

Hoffman, H. S., Fleshler, M., and Chorny, H. (1961) "Discriminated bar-press avoidance," *J. Exp. Anal. Behav.* 4: 309–16.

Hoffman, H. S. and Ratner, A. M. (1973) "A reinforcement model of imprinting: implications for socialization in monkeys and men," *Psychol. Rev.* 80: 527–44.

Hogan, J. A. (1964) "Operant control of preening in pigeons," *J. Exp. Anal. Behav.* 7: 351–4.

——— (1967) "Fighting and reinforcement in the Siamese fighting fish (*Betta splendens*)," *J. Comp. Physiol. Psychol.* 64: 356–9.

——— (1973) "How young chicks learn to recognize food," in R. A. Hinde and J. G. Stevenson-Hinde (eds) *Constraints on Learning*, New York: Academic Press.

——— (1974) "Responses in Pavlovian conditioning studies," *Science* 186: 156–7.

——— (1984) "Pecking and feeding in chicks," *Learn. Motiv.* 15: 360–76.

Hogan, J. A., Kleist, S., and Hutchings, C. S. L. (1970) "Display and food as reinforcers in the Siamese fighting fish (*Betta splendens*)," *J. Comp. Physiol. Psychol.* 70: 351–7.

Hogan, J. A. and Roper, T. J. (1978) "A comparison of the properties of different reinforcers," *Adv. Stud. Behav.* 8: 156–255.

Hogan-Warburg, A. J. and Hogan, J. A. (1981) "Feeding strategies in the development of food recognition in young chicks," *Anim. Behav.* 29: 143–54.

Holdstock, T. L. and Schwartzbaum, J. S. (1965) "Classical conditioning of heart rate and galvanic skin response in the rat," *Psychophysiol.* 2: 25–38.

Holland, P. C. (1977) "Conditioned stimulus as a determinant of the form of the Pavlovian conditioned response," *J. Exp. Psychol.: Anim. Behav. Processes* 3: 77–104.

——— (1979a) "The effects of qualitative and quantitative variations in the US on individual components of the Pavlovian appetitive conditioned behavior in rats," *Anim. Learn. Behav.* 7: 424–32.

——— (1979b) "Differential effects of omission contingencies on various components of Pavlovian appetitive conditioned behavior in rats," *J. Exp. Psychol.: Anim. Behav. Processes* 5: 178–93.

(1980a) "CS–US interval as a determinant of the form of Pavlovian appetitive conditioned responses," *J. Exp. Psychol.: Anim. Behav. Processes* 6: 155–74.
(1980b) "Influence of visual conditioned stimulus characteristics on the form of Pavlovian appetitive conditioned responding in rats," *J. Exp. Psychol.: Anim. Behav. Processes* 6: 81–97.
(1981) "Acquisition of representation-mediated conditioned food aversions," *Learn. Motiv.* 12: 1–18.
(1983) "Representation-mediated overshadowing and potentiation of conditioned aversions," *J. Exp. Psychol.: Anim. Behav. Processes* 9: 1–13.
(1984a) "Origins of behavior in Pavlovian conditioning," *The Psychology of Learning and Motivation*, 129–74, New York: Academic Press.
(1984b) "Unblocking in Pavlovian appetitive conditioning," *J. Exp. Psychol.: Anim. Behav. Processes* 10: 476–97.
Holland, P. C. and Forbes, D. T. (1983) "Mediated extinction of a flavor aversion," *Learn. Motiv.*, in press.
Holland, P. C. and Rescorla, R. A. (1975) "The effect of two ways of devaluing the unconditioned stimulus after first- and second-order appetitive conditioning," *J. Exp. Psychol.: Anim. Behav. Processes* 1: 355–63.
Holland, P. C. and Ross, R. T. (1981) "Within-compound associations in serial compound conditioning," *J. Exp. Psychol.: Anim. Behav. Processes* 7: 228–41.
Holland, P. C. and Straub, J. J. (1979) "Differential effects of two ways of devaluing the unconditioned stimulus after Pavlovian appetitive conditioning," *J. Exp. Psychol.: Anim. Behav. Processes* 5: 65–8.
Holldobler, B. and Wilson, E. O. (1983) "The evolution of communal nest-weaving in ants,' *Am. Sci.* 71: 490–9.
Hollis, K. L. (1982) "Pavlovian conditioning of signal-centered action patterns and autonomic behavior: a biological analysis of function," in J. S. Rosenblatt, R. A. Hinde, C. Beer, and M. C. Busnel (eds) *Advances in the Study of Behavior*, New York: Academic Press, 1–64.
(1984a) "Causes and function of animal learning," in P. Marler and H. S. Terrace (eds) *The Biology of Learning*, New York: Springer-Verlag, 357–71.
(1984b) "The biological function of Pavlovian conditioning: the best defense is a good offense," *J. Exp. Psychol.: Anim. Behav. Processes* 10: 413–25.
Hollis, K. L., Martin, K. A., Cadieux, E. L., and Colbert, M. M. (1984) "The biological function of Pavlovian conditioning: learned inhibition of aggressive behavior in territorial fish," *Learn. Motiv.* 15: 459–78.
Honig, W. K. (1978) "Studies of working memory in the pigeon," in S. H. Hulse, H. Fowler, and W. K. Honig (eds) *Cognitive Processes in Animal Behavior*, Hillsdale, NJ: Erlbaum.
Horn, G., McCabe, B. J., and Bateson, P. P. G. (1979) "An autoradiographic study of the chick brain after imprinting," *Brain Res.* 168: 361–73.
Horn, G., Rose, S. P. R., and Bateson, P. P. G. (1973) "Monocular imprinting and regional incorporation of tritated uracil into the brains of intact and 'split-brain' chicks," *Brain Res.* 56: 227–37.
Horridge, G. A. (1962) "Learning leg position by the ventral nerve cord in headless insects," *Proc. R. Soc. Lond. B*, 157: 33.
Hubbard, S. F. and Cook, R. M. (1978) "Optimal foraging by parasitoid wasps," *J. Anim. Ecol.* 47: 593–604.

Huber, J. C., Rucker, W. B., and McDiarmid, C. G. (1974) "Retention of escape training and activity changes in single paramecia," *J. Comp. Physiol. Psychol.* 86: 258–66.

Hughes, R. N. (1979) "Optimal diets under the energy maximization premise: the effects of recognition time and learning," *Am. Nat.* 113: 209–21.

Hull, C. L. (1931) "Goal attraction and directing ideas conceived as habit phenomena," *Psychol. Rev.* 38: 487–506.

(1943) *Principles of Behavior*, New York: Appleton-Century-Crofts.

(1952) *A Behavior System*, New Haven, Conn.: Yale University Press.

Hull, J. H. (1977) "Instrumental response topographies of rats," *Anim. Learn. Behav.* 5: 207–12.

Hursh, S. R. (1978) "The economics of daily consumption controlling food and water reinforced responding," *J. Exp. Anal. Behav.* 29: 475–91.

Hutchinson, R. R., Azrin, N. H., and Hunt, G. M. (1968) "Attack produced by intermittent reinforcement of a concurrent operant response," *J. Exp. Anal. Behav.* 11: 485–95.

Huxley, J. (1966) "Introduction: a discussion on ritualization of behavior in animals and man," *Phil. Trans. R. Soc. Lond.* 251: 249–71.

Huxley, J. S. (1957) "The three types of evolutionary progress," *Nature* 180: 454–5.

Hyde, T. S. (1969) "Effects of Pavlovian conditioned stimuli on discriminative instrumental baseline responding," Unpublished Ph.D. dissertation, University of Minnesota.

Immelmann, K. (1969) "Song development in the zebra finch and other estrildid finches," in R. A. Hinde (ed.) *Bird Vocalizations*, London: Cambridge University Press, 61–74.

(1972) "Sexual and other long-term aspects of imprinting in birds and other species," *Adv. Study Behav.* 4: 147–74.

(1975) "Ecological significance of imprinting and early learning," *Ann. Rev. Ecol. Syst.* 6: 15–37.

(1985) "The natural history of bird learning," in P. Marler and H. S. Terrace (eds) *The Biology of Learning*, New York: Springer-Verlag, 271–88.

Immelmann, K. and Suomi, S. J. (1981) "Sensitive phases in development," in K. Immelmann, G. W. Barlow, L. Petrinovich, and M. Main (eds) *Behavioral Development*, Cambridge: Cambridge University Press, 395–431.

Innis, N. K., Reberg, D., Mann, B., Jacobson, J., and Turton, D. (1983) "Schedule-induced behaviour for food and water: effects of interval duration," *Behav. Anal. Let* 3: 191–200.

Innis, N. K., Simmelhag-Grant, V. L., and Staddon, J. E. R. (1983) "Behavior induced by periodic food delivery: the effects of interfood interval," *J. Exp. Anal. Behav.* 39: 309–22.

Iwasa, Y., Higoshi, M., and Yamamura, N. (1981) "Prey distribution as a factor determining the choice of optimal foraging strategy," *Am. Nat.* 117: 710–23.

Jacobsen, C. F., Jacobsen, M. M., and Yoshioka, J. G. (1932) "Developments of an infant chimpanzee during her first year," *Comp. Psychol. Monogr.* 9: 1–94.

Jacobson, A. L., Fried, C., and Horowitz, S. D. (1967) "Classical conditioning, pseudoconditioning and sensitization in the planarian," *J. Comp. Physiol. Psychol.* 64: 73–9.

Jarrard, L. E. and Moise, S. L. (1970) "Short-term memory of the stumptail macaque: effect of physical restraint of behavior on performance," *Learn. Motiv.* 1: 267–75.

Jarvik, M. E., Goldfarb, T. L., and Carley, J. L. (1969) "Influence of interference on delayed matching in monkeys," *J. Exp. Psychol.* 81: 1–6.

Jaynes, J. (1956) "Imprinting: the interaction of learned and innate behavior: I. development and generalization," *J. Comp. Physiol. Psychol.* 49: 201–6.

Jenkins, H. M. (1977) "Sensitivity of different response systems to stimulus-reinforcer and response-reinforcer relations," in H. Davis and H. M. B. Hurwitz (eds) *Operant-Pavlovian Interactions*, Hillsdale, NJ: Erlbaum, 47–62.

Jenkins, H. M., Barnes, R. A., and Barrera, F. J. (1981) "Why autoshaping depends on trial spacing," in C. M. Lucurto, H. S. Terrace, and J. Gibbon (eds) *Autoshaping and Conditioning Theory*, New York: Academic Press.

Jenkins, H. M., Barrera, F. J., Ireland, C. and Woodside, B. (1978) "Signal-centered action patterns of dogs in appetitive classical conditioning," *Learn. Motiv.* 9: 272–96.

Jenkins, H. M. and Harrison, R. H. (1960) "Effects of discrimination training on auditory generalization," *J. Exp. Psychol.*, 59: 246–53.
(1962) "Generalization gradients of inhibition following auditory discrimination learning," *J. Exp. Anal. of Behav.*, 5: 435–41.

Jenkins, H. M. and Moore, B. R. (1973) "The form of the autoshaped response with food or water reinforcers," *J. Exp. Anal. Behav.* 20: 163–81.

Jensen, A. R. (1980) *Bias in Mental Testing*, London: Methuen.

Jerison, H. J. (1973) *Evolution of the Brain and Intelligence*, New York: Academic Press.
(1982) "The evolution of biological intelligence," in R. J. Sternberg (ed.) *Handbook of Human Intelligence*, London: Cambridge University Press, 723–91.
(1983) "The evolution of the mammalian brain as an information processing system," in J. F. Eisenberg and D. G. Kleiman (eds) *Advances in the Study of Mammalian Behavior*, American Society of Mammalogists, 113–46.
(1985a) "Animal intelligence as encephalization," *Phil. Trans. R. Soc. Lond.* 308: 21–35.
(1985b) *Issues in Brain Evolution*, Oxford Surveys of Evolutionary Biology, 2, in press.

Johnson, C., Beaton, R., and Hall, K. (1975) "Poison-based avoidance learning in nonhuman primates: use of visual cues," *Physiol. & Behav.* 14: 403–7.

Johnston, T. D. (1981a) "Contrasting approaches to a theory of learning," *Behav. Brain Sci.* 4: 125–73.
(1981b) "Selective costs and benefits in the evolution of learning," in J. S. Rosenblatt, R. A. Hinde, C. Beer, and M. C. Busnel (eds) *Advances in the Study of Behavior*, New York: Academic Press, 65–106.
(1985) "Introduction: Conceptual issues in the ecological study of learning," in T. D. Johnston and A. T. Pietrewicz (eds) *Issues in the Ecological Study of Learning*, Hillsdale, NJ: Erlbaum, 1–24.

Johnston, T. D. and Turvey, M. T. (1980) "An ecological metatheory for theories of learning," in G. H. Bower (ed.) *The Psychology of Learning and Motivation*, vol. 14, New York: Academic Press, 147–205.

Kacelnik, A. (1979) "Studies of foraging behavior and time budgeting in great tits (*Parus major*)," Unpublished D.Phil. thesis, Oxford University.
(1984) "Central place foraging in starlings (*Sturnus vulgaris*). I. Patch residence time," *J. Anim. Ecol.* 53: 283–99.
Kagel, J. H., Rachlin, H., Green, L., Battalio, R. C., Basmann, R., and Klemm, W. R. (1975) "Experimental studies of consumer demand behavior using laboratory animals," *Econ. Inqu.* 13: 22–38.
Kalat, J. W. (1975) "Taste-aversion learning in infant guinea pigs," *Dev. Psychobiol.* 8: 383–7.
(1977) "Biological significance of food-aversion learning," in N. W. Milgram, L. Krames, and T. M. Alloway (eds) *Food-Aversion Learning*, New York: Plenum Press.
(1985) "Taste-aversion learning in ecological perspective," in T. D. Johnston and A. T. Pietrewicz (eds) *Issues on the Ecological Study of Learning*, Hillsdale, NJ: Erlbaum, 119–41.
Kamil, A. C. (1978) "Systematic foraging by a nectar-feeding bird, the amakihi (*Loxops virens*)," *J. Comp. Physiol. Psychol.* 92: 388–96.
Kamil, A. C., Jones, T. B., Pietrewicz, A., and Maudlin, J. E. (1977) "Positive transfer from successive reversal training to learning set in blue jays (*Cyanocitta cristata*)," *J. Comp. Physiol. Psychol.* 91: 79–86.
Kamil, A. C. and Roitblat, H. L. (1985) "The ecology of foraging behavior: implications for animal learning and memory," *Ann. Rev. Psychol.* 36: 141–69.
Kamil, A. C. and Yoerg, S. J. (1982) "Learning and foraging behavior," in P. P. G. Bateson and P. H. Klopfer (eds) *Perspectives in Ethology*, London: Plenum, 325–64.
Kamin, L. J. (1968) "'Attention-like' processes in classical conditioning," in M. R. Jones (ed.) *Miami Symposium on the Prediction of Behavior: Aversive Stimulation*, Miami: University of Miami Press.
(1969) "Predictability, surprise, attention, and conditioning," in B. A. Campbell and R. M. Church (eds) *Punishment and Aversive Behavior*, New York: Appleton-Century-Crofts.
Kamin, L. J., Brimer, C. J., and Black, A. H. (1963) "Conditioned suppression as a monitor of fear of the CS in the course of avoidance training," *J. Comp. Physiol. Psychol.* 56: 497–501.
Kanarek, R. B. (1975) "Availability and caloric density of the diet as determinants of meal patterns in cats," *Physiol. & Behav.* 15: 611–18.
Karpicke, J., Christoph, G., Peterson, G., and Hearst, E. (1977) "Signal location and positive versus negative conditioned suppression in the rat," *J. Exp. Psychol.: Anim. Behav. Processes* 3: 105–18.
Katz, A., Webb, L., and Stotland, E. (1971) "Cognitive influences on the rate of GSR extinction," *J. Exp. Res. Person.* 5: 208–15.
Katzev, R. (1967) "Extinguishing avoidance responses as a function of delayed warning signal termination," *J. Exp. Psychol.* 75: 339–44.
Kaufman, A., Baron, A., and Kopp, R. M. (1966) "Some effects of instructions on human operant behavior," *Psychon. Monogr. Suppl.* 1: 243–50.
Keehn, J. D. (1969) "Consciousness, discrimination and the stimulus control of behavior," in R. M. Gilbert and N. S. Sutherland (eds) *Animal Discrimination Learning*, London: Academic Press, 273–98.

Keeton, W. T. (1980) "Avian orientation and navigation: new developments in an old mystery," in R. Nohring (ed.) *Acta XVII Congressus Internationalis Ornithologicus*, Berlin: Deutsche Ornithologen-Gesellschaft, 137–57.

Kehoe, E. J., Gibbs, C. M., Garcia, A., and Gormezano, I. (1979) "Associative transfer and stimulus selection in classical conditioning of the rabbit's nictitating membrane response to serial compound CS," *J. Exp. Psychol.: Anim. Behav. Processes* 5: 1–19.

Keith-Lucas, T. and Guttman, N. (1975) "Robust single-trial delayed backward conditioning," *J. Comp. Physiol. Psychol.* 88: 468–76.

Kelleher, R. T., Fry, W., and Cook, L. (1959) "Interresponse time distribution as a function of differential reinforcement of temporally spaced responses," *J. Exp. Anal. Behav.* 2: 91–106.

Keller, K. (1974) "The role of elicited responding in behavioral contrast," *J. Exp. Anal. Behav.* 21: 249–57.

Kellogg, W. N. and Kellogg, L. A. (1933) *The Ape and the Child: a Study of Environmental Influence upon Early Behavior*, New York: McGraw-Hill.

Kelsey, J. E. and Allison, J. (1976) "Fixed-ratio lever pressing by VMH rats: work vs. accessibility of sucrose reward," *Physiol. & Behav.* 17: 749–54.

Kemp, F. D. (1969) "Thermal reinforcement and thermoregulatory behaviour in the lizard (*Dipsosaurus dorsalis*): an operant technique," *Anim. Behav.* 17: 446–51.

Kendrick, D. F., Rilling, M., and Stonebraker, T. B. (1981) "Stimulus control of delayed matching in pigeons: directed forgetting," *J. Exp. Anal. Behav.* 36: 241–51.

Khavari, K. A. and Eisman, E. H. (1971) "Some parameters of latent learning and generalized drives," *J. Comp. Physiol. Psychol.* 77: 463–9.

Kierylowicz, H., Soltysik, S., and Divac, I. (1968) "Conditioned reflexes reinforced by direct and indirect food presentation," *Acta Biol. Exp.* 28: 1–10.

Killeen, P. (1969) "Reinforcement frequency and contingency as factors in fixed-ratio behavior," *J. Exp. Anal. Behav.* 12: 391–5.

Kimble, G. A. (1961) *Hilgard and Marquis' Conditioning and Learning*, New York: Appleton-Century-Crofts.

Kimble, G. A. and Perlmuter, L. C. (1970) "The problem of volition," *Psychol. Rev.* 77: 361–84.

King, G. D. (1974) "Wheel-running in the rat induced by a fixed time presentation of water," *Anim. Learn. Behav.* 2: 325–8.

Kirby, A. J. (1968) "Explorations of the Brown-Jenkins auto-shaping phenomenon," Unpublished Ph.D. thesis, Dalhousie University.

Kirk, K. L. and Bitterman, M. E. (1965) "Probability-learning by the turtle," *Science* 148: 1484–5.

Kissileff, H. R. (1969) "Food-associated drinking in the rat," *J. Comp. Physiol. Psychol.* 67: 284–300.

Kleinginna, P. R. (1970) "Operant conditioning in the indigo snake," *Psychon. Sci.* 18: 53–5.

Klopfer, P. H. (1971) "Imprinting: determining its perceptual basis in ducklings," *J. Comp. Physiol. Psychol.* 75: 378–85.

Klopfer, P. H., Adams, D. K., and Klopfer, M. S. (1964) "Maternal 'imprinting in goats,'" *Proceedings of the National Academy of Science* 52: 911–14.

Knutson, J. F. and Kleinknecht, R. A. (1970) "Attack during differential reinforcement of low rate of responding," *Psychon. Sci.* 19: 289–90.

Koehler, O. (1950) "The ability of birds to 'count,'" *Bull. Anim. Behav.* 9: 41–5.

Koenig, K. P. and Castillo, D. D. (1969) "False feedback and longevity of the conditioned GSR during extinction: some implications for aversion therapy," *J. Exp. Psychol.* 74: 505–10.

Köhler, W. (1925) *The Mentality of Apes*, London: Routledge & Kegan Paul; 3rd edn, 1973.

Konishi, M. (1965) "The role of auditory feedback in the control of vocalization in the white-crowned sparrow," *Z. Tierpsychol.* 22: 770–83.

(1985) "A logical basis for single-neuron study of learning in complex neural systems," in P. Marler and H. S. Terrace (eds) *The Biology of Learning*, New York: Springer-Verlag, 311–24.

Konishi, M. and Nottebohm, F. (1969) "Experimental studies in the ontogeny of avian vocalizations," in R. Hinde (ed.) *Bird Vocalizations*, London: Cambridge University Press.

Konorski, J. (1948) *Conditioned Reflexes and Neuron Organization*, Cambridge: Cambridge University Press.

(1967) *Integrative Activity of the Brain*, Chicago: University of Chicago Press.

Konorski, J. and Miller, S. (1937) "On two types of conditioned reflex," *J. Gen. Psychol.* 16: 264–72.

Konorski, J. and Szwejkowska, G. (1956) "Reciprocal transformations of heterogeneous conditioned reflexes," *Acta Biol. Exp.* 17: 141–65.

Kovach, J. K. and Hess, E. H. (1963) "Imprinting: effect of painful stimulation on the following behavior," *J. Comp. Physiol. Psychol.* 56: 461–4.

Krane, R. V. (1980) "Toxiphobia conditioning with exteroceptive cues," *Anim. Learn. Behav.* 8: 513–23.

Krane, R. V. and Wagner, A. R. (1975) "Taste-aversion learning with a delayed shock US: implications for the 'generality of the laws of learning,'" *J. Comp. Physiol. Psychol.* 88: 882–9.

Krebs, J. R., Erichsen, J. T., Webber, J. I., and Charnov, E. L. (1977) "Optimal prey selection in the great tit (*Parus major*)," *Anim. Behav.* 25: 30–8.

Krebs, J. R., Houston, A. I., and Charnov, E. L. (1981) "Some recent developments in optimal foraging," in A. C. Kamil and T. D. Sargent (eds) *Foraging Behavior: Ecological, Ethological and Psychological Approaches*, London: Garland Press, 3–18.

Krebs, J. R., Kacelnik, A., and Taylor, P. (1978) "Test of optimal sampling by foraging great tits," *Nature* 275: 27–31.

Krebs, J. R., Ryan, J. C., and Charnov, E. L. (1974) "Hunting by expectation or optimal foraging? A study of patch use by chickadees," *Anim. Behav.* 22: 953–64.

Krekorian, C. O., Vance, V. J., and Richardson, A. M. (1968) "Temperature-dependent maze learning in the desert iguana, *Dipsosaurus dorsalis*," *Anim. Behav.* 16: 429–36.

Krieckhaus, E. F. and Wolf, G. (1968) "Acquisition of sodium by rats: interaction of innate mechanisms and latent learning," *J. Comp. Physiol. Psychol.* 65: 197–201.

Kroodsma, D. E. (1976) "Reproductive development in a female songbird: differential stimulation by quality of male song," *Science* 192: 574–5.

(1977) "A reevaluation of song development in song sparrows," *Anim. Behav.* 25: 390–9.

(1978) "Aspects of learning in the ontogeny of bird song: where, from whom, when, how many, which, how accurately?" in G. Burghardt and M. Berkoff (eds) *The Development of Behavior*, New York: Garland Press.

(1981) "Ontogeny of bird song," in K. Immelmann, G. W. Barlow, L. Petrinovich, and M. Main (eds) *Behavioral Development: the Bielefeld Interdisciplinary Project*, New York: Cambridge University Press, 518–32.

(1982) "Learning and the ontogeny of sound signals in birds," in D. E. Kroodsma and E. H. Miller (eds) *Acoustic Communication in Birds*, New York: Academic Press, 1–23.

Kruse, J. M., Overmier, J. B., Konz, W. A., and Rokke, E. (1983) "Pavlovian conditioned stimulus effects upon instrumental choice behavior are reinforcer specific," *Learn. Motiv.* 14: 165–81.

Kruuk, H. (1976) "The biological function of gulls' attraction towards predators," *Anim. Behav.* 24: 146–53.

Lack, D. (1966) *Population Studies of Birds*, London: Oxford University Press.

Landenberger, D. E. (1966) "Learning in the Pacific starfish, *Piaster giganteus*," *Anim. Behav.* 14: 414–18.

Landis, C. and Hunt, W. A. (1939) *The Startle Pattern*, New York: Farrar & Rinehart.

Landsberg, J. W. (1980) "Hormones and filial imprinting," in R. Nohring (ed.) *Acta XVII Congressus Internationalis Ornithologicus*, Berlin: Deutsche Ornithologen-Gesellschaft, 837–41.

Laties, V. G. and Weiss, B. (1963) "Effects of a concurrent task on Fixed-Interval responding in humans," *J. Exp. Anal. Behav.* 3: 431–6.

Laties, V. G., Weiss, B., Clark, R. L., and Reynolds, M. D. (1965) "Overt 'mediating' behavior during temporally spaced responding," *J. Exp. Anal. Behav.* 8: 107–16.

Laties, V. G., Weiss, B., and Weiss, A. B. (1969) "Further observations on overt 'mediating' behavior and the discrimination of time," *J. Exp. Anal. Behav.* 12: 43–57.

Launay, M. (1981) "Running response reinforcement by food-hoarding in the Golden Hampster," *Behav. Processes* 6: 261–8.

Laverty, L. M. (1980) "The flower-visiting behavior of bumblebees: floral complexity and learning," *Canadian Journal of Zoology* 58: 1324–35.

Lea, S. E. G. (1978) "The psychology and economics of demand," *Psychol. Bull.* 85: 441–66.

(1979) "Foraging and reinforcement schedules in the pigeon: optimal and non-optimal aspects of choice," *Anim. Behav.* 27: 875–86.

(1981) "Correlation and contiguity in foraging behaviour," in P. Harzem and M. D. Zeiler (eds) *Predictability, Correlation and Contiguity*, Chichester: John Wiley, 355–405.

(1984) "In what sense do pigeons learn concepts?" in H. L. Roitblat, T. G. Bever, and H. S. Terrace (eds) *Animal Cognition*, Hillsdale, NJ: Erlbaum, 263–76.

Lea, S. E. G. and Harrison, S. N. (1978) "Discrimination of polymorphous stimulus sets by pigeons," *Q. J. Exp. Psychol.* 30: 521–37.

Lea, S. E. G. and Roper, T. J. (1977) "Demand for food on fixed-ratio schedules as a function of the quality of concurrently available reinforcement," *J. Exp. Anal. Behav.* 27: 371–80.

Lea, S. E. G. and Tarpy, R. M (1986) "Hamsters' demand for food to eat and hoard as a function of deprivation and cost," *Anim. Behav.* 12: 454–69.

Leander, J. D., Lippman, L. G., and Meyer, M. E. (1968) "Fixed-interval performance as related to subjects' vocalizations of the reinforcement contingency," *Psychol. Rec.* 18: 469–74.

Leclerc, R. (1985) "Sign-tracking behavior in aversive conditioning: its acquisition via a Pavlovian mechanism and its suppression by operant contingencies," *Learn. Motiv.* 16: 63–82.

Leclerc, R. and Reberg, D. (1980) "Sign-tracking in aversive conditioning," *Learn. Motiv.* 11: 302–17.

Lee, D. N. and Reddish, P. E. (1981) "Plummeting gannets: a paradigm of ecological optics," *Nature* 293: 293–4.

Legg, C. R. (1983) "Interspecific comparisons and the hypothetico-deductive approach," in G. C. L. Davey (ed.) *Animal Models of Human Behavior*, Chichester: John Wiley, 225–46.

Lehrman, D. S. (1955) "The physiological basis of parental feeding behav. in the ring dove (*Steptopelia risoria*)," *Behavior* 7: 241–86.

Le Magnen, J. (1971) "Advances in studies on the physiological control and regulation of food intake," in E. Stellar and J. M. Sprague (eds) *Progress in Physiological Psychology*, vol. 4, New York: Academic Press.

Lemon, R. E. (1975) "How birds develop song dialects," *Condor* 77: 385–406.

Leonard, D. W. and Theios, J. (1967) "Classical eyelid conditioning in rabbits under prolonged single alternation conditions of reinforcement," *J. Comp. Physiol. Psychol.* 64: 237–46.

Lepkovsky, S., Lyman, R., Fleming, D., Nagumo, M., and Dimick, M. K. (1967) "Gastrointestinal regulation of water and its effect on food intake and rate of digestion," *American Journal of Physiology* 188: 327–31.

Lett, B. T. (1973) "Delayed reward learning: disproof of the traditional theory," *Learn. Motiv.* 4: 237–46.

—— (1974) "Visual discrimination learning with a 1-min delay of reward," *Learn. Motiv.* 5: 174–81.

—— (1979) "Long-delay learning: implications for learning and memory theory," in N. S. Sutherland (ed.) *Tutorial Essays in Psychology*, Hillsdale, NJ: Erlbaum.

—— (1980) "Taste potentiates color-sickness associations in pigeons and quail," *Anim. Learn. Behav.* 8: 193–8.

Levitsky, D. and Collier, G. (1968) "Schedule-induced wheel running," *Physiol. Behav.* 3: 571–3.

Lewontin, R. C. (1978) "Adaptation," *Am. Sci.* 239: 212–30.

Leyland, C. M. (1977) "Higher order autoshaping,' *Q. J. Exp. Psychol.* 29: 607–19.

Lieberman, D. A., McIntosh, D. C., and Thomas, G. V. (1979) "Learning when reward is delayed: a marking hypothesis," *J. Exp. Psychol.: Anim. Behav. Processes* 5: 224–42.

Likely, D. G. (1974) "Autoshaping in the rhesus monkey," *Anim. Learn. Behav.* 2: 203–6.

Lima, S. L. (1984) "Downy woodpecker foraging behavior: efficient sampling in simple stochastic environments," *Ecol.* 65: 166–74.

Lindsley, O. R. (1960) "Characteristics of the behavior of chronic psychotics as revealed by free-operant conditioning methods," *Diseases Nerv. Syst.* (Monograph supplements) 21: 66–78.

Lippman, L. G. and Meyer, M. E. (1967) "Fixed-interval performance as related to instructions and to subjects' verbalizations of the contingency," *Psychon. Sci.* 8: 135–6.

Little, E. E. (1977) "Conditioned aversion to amino acid flavours in the catfish (*Ictalurus Punctatus*)," *Physiol. Behav.* 19: 743–7.

Lockard, J. S. (1963) "Choice of a warning signal or no warning signal in an unavoidable shock situation," *J. Comp. Physiol. Psychol.* 56: 416–21.

Locurto, C. (1981) "Contributions of autoshaping to the partitioning of conditioned behavior," in C. M. Locurto, H. S. Terrace, and J. Gibbon (eds) *Autoshaping and Conditioning Theory*, New York: Academic Press, 101–35.

Locurto, C., Terrace, H. S., and Gibbon, J. (1976) "Autoshaping, random control and omission training in the rat," *J. Exp. Anal. Behav.* 26: 451–62.

(1981) *Autoshaping and Conditioning Theory*, New York: Academic Press.

Logan, F. A. (1951) "A comparison of avoidance and non-avoidance eyelid conditioning," *J. Exp. Psychol.* 42: 390–3.

Logue, A. W. (1979) "Taste aversion and the generality of the laws of learning," *Psychol. Bull.* 86: 276–96.

Lolordo, V. M. (1971) "Facilitation of food-reinforced responding by a signal for response-independent food," *J. Exp. Anal. Behav.* 15: 49–55.

(1979) "Selective associations," in A. Dickinson and R. A. Boakes (eds) *Mechanisms of Learning and Motivation*, Chichester: John Wiley, 367–398.

Lolordo, V. M., McMillan, J. C., and Riley, A. L. (1974) "The effects upon food-reinforced pecking and treadle-pressing of auditory and visual signals for response-independent food," *Learn. Motiv.* 5: 24–41.

Looney, T. A. and Cohen, P. S. (1982) "Aggression induced by intermittent positive reinforcement," *Neurosci. Biobehav. Rev.* 6: 15–37.

Loop, M. S. (1976) "Auto-shaping — a simple technique for teaching a lizard to perform a visual discrimination task," *Copeia* 574–6.

Lorenz, K. Z. (1935) "Der Kumpan in der Umwelt des Vogels," in K. Lorenz (ed.) *Studies in Animal and Human Behaviour*, 1970, vol. 1: 101–258, translated by R. Martin, Cambridge, Mass.: Harvard University Press.

(1939) "Vergleichende Verhaltensforschung," *Zool. Anz. Supplement* 12: 69–102.

Losey, G. S. and Margules, L. (1974) "Cleaning symbiosis provides a positive reinforcer for fish," *Science* 184: 179–80.

Lovibond, P. F., Preston, G. C., and Mackintosh, N. J. (1984) "Context specificity of conditioning, extinction, and latent inhibition," *J. Exp. Psychol.: Anim. Behav. Processes* 10: 360–75.

Lowe, C. F. (1979) "Determinants of human operant behavior," in M. D. Zeiler and P. Harzem (eds) *Advances in Analysis of Behavior*, vol. 1, Chichester: John Wiley, 159–92.

(1983) "Radial behaviorism and human psychology," in G. C. L. Davey (ed.) *Animal Models of Human Behavior*, Chichester: John Wiley, 71–93.

Lowe, C. F., Beasty, A., and Bentall, R. P. (1983) "The role of verbal behavior in human learning: infant performance on fixed-interval schedules," *J. Exp. Anal. Behav.* 39: 157–64.

Lowe, C. F., Davey, G. C. L., and Harzem, P. (1974) "Effects of reinforcement magnitude on interval and ratio schedules," *J. Exp. Anal. Behav.* 22: 553–60.

Lowe, C. F. and Harzem, P. (1977) "Species differences in temporal control of behavior," *J. Exp. Anal. Behav.* 28: 189–201.

Lowe, C. F., Harzem, P., and Bagshaw, M. (1978) "Species differences in temporal control of behavior II: Human performance," *J. Exp. Anal. Behav.* 29: 351–61.

Lowe, C. F., Harzem, P., and Hughes, S. (1978) " Determinants of operant behavior in humans: some differences from animals," *Q. J. Exp. Psychol.* 30: 373–86.

Lubow, R. E. (1974) "High-order concept formation in the pigeon," *J. Exp. Anal. Behav.* 21: 475–83.

Lubow, R. E., Markman, R. E., and Allen, J. (1968) "Latent inhibition and classical conditioning of the rabbit pinna response," *J. Comp. Physiol. Psychol.* 66: 688–94.

Lubow, R. E., Rifkin, B., and Alek, M. (1976) "The context effect: the relationship between stimulus pre-exposure and environmental pre-exposure determines subsequent learning," *J. Exp. Psychol.: Anim. Behav. Processes* 2: 38–omission training," *Anim. Learn. Behav.* 3: 33–6.

Lucas, G. A. (1975) "The control of key pecks during automaintenance by prekeypeck omission training," *Anim. Learn. Behav.* 3: 33–6.

Maatsch, J. L. (1959) "Learning and fixation after a single shock trial," *J. Comp. Physiol. Psychol.* 52: 408–10.

McAllister, W. R. and McAllister, D. E. (1971) "Behavioral measurement of conditioned fear," in F. R. Brush (ed.) *Aversive Conditioning and Learning*, New York: Academic Press.

MacArthur, R. H. and Pianka, E. R.ment," *Am. Nat.* 100: 603–9.

MacArthur, R. H. and Wilson, E. O. (1967) *The Theory of Island Biogeography*, Princeton, NJ: Princeton University Press.

McCabe, B. J., Horn, G., and Bateson, P. P. G. (1981) "Effects of restricted lesions of the chick forebrain on the acquisition of filial preferences during imprinting," *Brain Res.* 205: 29–37.

McCasland, J. S. (1983) "Neuronal control of bird song production," Ph.D. thesis, California Institute of Technology.

McCasland, J. S. and Konishi, M. (1981) "Interaction between auditory and motor activities in an avian song control nucleus," *Proceedings of the National Academy of Science, USA*, 78: 7815–19.

McComb, D. (1969) "Cognitive and learning effects in the production of GSR conditioning data," *Psychon. Sci.* 16: 96–7.

McFarland, D. J. (1978) "The assessment of priorities by animals," in M. Dempster and D. J. McFarland. (eds) *Animal Economics*, London: Academic Press.

McGill, T. E. (1960) "Response of the leopard frog to electric shock in an escape-learning situation," *J. Comp. Physiol. Psychol.* 53: 443–5.

McGuire, T. R. and Hirsch, J. (1977) "Behavior-genetic analysis of *Phormia regina*: conditioning, reliable individual differences, and selection," *Proceedings of the National Academy of Science, USA*, 74: 5193–7.

McKearney, J. W. (1969) "Fixed-interval schedules of electric shock presentation: extinction and recovery of performance under different shock intensities and FI durations," *J. Exp. Anal. Behav.* 12: 301–13.

(1972) "Schedule-dependent effects: effects of drugs and maintenance of responding with response-produced electric shocks," in R. M. Gilbert and J. D. Keehn (eds) *Schedule Effects: Drugs, Drinking and Aggression*, Toronto: University of Toronto Press, 3–25.

Mackintosh, N. J. (1969) "Comparative studies of reversal and probability learning:

rats, birds and fish," in R. M. Gilbert and N. S. Sutherland (eds) *Animal Discrimination Learning*, London: Academic Press, 137–62.

(1970) "Attention and probability learning," in D. Mostofsky (ed.) *Attention: Contemporary Theory and Analysis*, New York: Appleton-Century-Crofts, 173–91.

(1971) "An analysis of overshadowing and blocking," *Q. J. Exp. Psychol.* 23: 118–25.

(1974) *The Psychology of Animal Learning*, London: Academic Press.

(1975a) "A theory of attention: variations in the associability of stimuli with reinforcement," *Psychol. Rev.* 82: 276–98.

(1975b) "Blocking of conditioned suppression: role of the first compound trial," *J. Exp. Psychol.: Anim. Behav. Processes* 2: 335–45.

(1983) *Conditioning and Associative Learning*, Oxford: Oxford University Press.

Mackintosh, N. J., Bygrave, D. J., and Picton, B. M. B. (1977) "Locus of the effect of a surprising reinforcer in the attenuation of blocking," *Q. J. Exp. Psychol.* 29: 327–36.

Mackintosh, N. J. and Cauty, A. (1971) "Spatial reversal learning in rats, pigeons, and goldfish," *Psychon. Sci.* 22: 281–2.

Mackintosh, N. J. and Dickinson, A. (1979) "Instrumental (Type II) conditioning," in A. Dickinson and R. A. Boakes (eds) *Mechanisms of Learning and Motivation*, Chichester: John Wiley, 143–70.

Mackintosh, N. J., Lord, J., and Little, L. (1971) "Visual and spatial probability learning in pigeons and goldfish," *Psychon. Sci.* 24: 221–3.

Mackintosh, N. J., Wilson, B., and Boakes, R. A. (1985) "Differences in mechanisms of intelligence among vertebrates," *Phil. Trans. R. Soc. Lond.* 308: 53–65.

McNamara, J. (1982) "Optimal patch use in a stochastic environment," *Theor. Pop. Biol.* 21: 269–88.

McNamara, J. and Houston, A. (1985) "A simple model of information use in the exploitation of patchily distributed food," *Anim. Behav.* 33: 553–60.

Macphail, E. M. (1968) "Avoidance responding in pigeons," *J. Exp. Anal. Behav.* 11: 625–32.

(1982) *Brain and Intelligence in Vertebrates*, Oxford: Clarendon Press.

(1985) "Vertebrate intelligence: the null hypothesis," *Phil. Trans. R. Soc. Lond.* 308: 37–51.

Macphail, E. M. and Reilly, S. (1983) "Probability learning in pigeons (*Columba livia*) is not impaired by hyperstriatal lesions," *Physiol. Behav.* 31: 279–84.

Mahoney, W. J. and Ayres, J. J. B. (1976) "One-trial simultaneous and backward fear conditioning as reflected in conditioned suppression of licking in rats," *Anim. Learn. Behav.* 4: 357–62.

Maki, W. S. (1979a) "Discrimination learning without short-term memory: dissocation of memory processes in pigeons," *Science* 204: 83–5.

(1979b) "Pigeon's short-term memories for surprising vs. expected reinforcement and nonreinforcement," *Anim. Learn. Behav.* 7: 31–7.

(1981) "Directed forgetting in pigeons," in N. E. Spear and R. R. Miller (eds) *Information Processing in Animals: Memory Mechanisms*, Hillsdale, NJ: Erlbaum.

(1984) "Some problems for a theory of working memory," in H. L. Roitblat, T. G. Bever, and H. S. Terrace (eds) *Animal Cognition*, Hillsdale, NJ: Erlbaum, 117–34.

Maki, W. S. and Hegvik, D. K. (1980) "Directed forgetting in pigeons," *Anim. Learn. Behav.* 8: 567–74.

Maki, W. S., Moe, J. C., and Bierley, C. M. (1977) "Short-term memory for stimuli, responses and reinforcers," *J. Exp. Psychol.: Anim. Behav. Processes* 3: 156–77.

Maki, W. S., Olsen, D., and Rego, S. (1981) "Directed forgetting in pigeons: analysis of cue functions," *Anim. Learn. Behav.* 9: 189–95.

Malott, R. W. and Siddall, J. W. (1972) "Acquisition of the people concept in pigeons," *Psychol. Rep.* 31: 3–13.

Mandel, I. J. and Bridger, W. H. (1967) "Interaction between instructions and ISI in conditioning and extinction of the GSR," *J. Exp. Psychol.* 74: 36–43.

Mandriota, F. J., Thompson, R. L., and Bennett, M. V. L. (1968) "Avoidance conditioning of the rate of electric organ discharge in mormyrid fish," *Anim. Behav.* 16: 448–55.

Marchant, R. G., III, Mis, F. W., and Moore, J. W. (1972) "Conditioned inhibition of the rabbit's nictitating membrane response," *J. Exp. Psychol.* 95: 408–11.

Margoliash, D. (1983) "Acoustic parameters underlying the responses of song-specific neurones in the white-crowned sparrow," *J. Neurosci.* 3: 1039–57.

Marler, P. (1956) "Behavior of the chaffinch, *Fringilla coelebs*," *Behav.* 5: 1–184.
—— (1967) "Comparative study of song development in sparrows," *Proc. Internat. Ornith. Cong.* 14: 231–44.
—— (1970) "A comparative approach to vocal learning: song development in white-crowned sparrows," *J. Comp. Physiol. Psychol.* 71: 1–25.
—— (1975) "On the origin of speech from animal sounds," in J. F. Kavanagh and J. E. Cutting (eds) *The Role of Speech in Language*, Cambridge, Mass.: MIT Press, 11–37.
—— (1977) "Perception and innate knowledge," in W. H. Heidcamp (ed.) *The Nature of Life*, Baltimore, Md.: University Park Press, 111–39.
—— (1984) "Songlearning: innate species differences in the learning process," in P. Marler and H. S. Terrace (eds) *The Biology of Learning*, New York: Springer-Verlag, 289–309.

Marler, P., Kreith, M., and Tamura, M. (1962) "Song development in hand-raised Oregon juncos," *Auk* 79: 12–30.

Marler, P. and Peters, S. (1980) "Birdsong and speech: evidence for special processing," in P. Eimas and J. Miller (eds) *Perspectives in the Study of Speech*, Hillsdale, NJ: Erlbaum, 75–112.
—— (1982) "Subsong and plastic song: their role in the vocal learning process," in D. E. Kroodsma and E. H. Miller (eds) *Acoustic Communication in Birds*, New York: Academic Press, 25–50.

Marler, P. and Sherman, V. (1982) "Song structure without auditory feedback: emendations of the auditory template hypothesis," *J. Neurosci.* 3: 517–31.

Marler, P. and Terrace, H. S. (1984) *The Biology of Learning*, New York: Springer-Verlag.

Marlin, N. A., Berk, A. M., and Miller, R. R. (1978) "Modification and avoidance of unmodifiable and unavoidable footshock," *Bull. Psychon. Soc.* 11: 203–5.

Martin, G. M. and Bellingham, W. P. (1979) "Learning of visual food aversions by chickens (*Gallus gallus*) over long delays," *Behav. Neural. Biol.* 24: 58–68.

Martin, G. M., Bellingham, W. P., and Storlien, L. H. (1977) "Effects of varied color experience on chickens' formation of color and texture aversions," *Physiol. Behav.* 18: 415–20.

Martin, I. and Levey, A. B. (1969) *Genesis of the Classical Conditioned Response*, Oxford: Pergamon Press.

Martin, L. K. and Reiss, D. (1969) "Effects of US intensity during previous discrete delay conditioning on conditioned acceleration during avoidance extinction," *J. Comp. Physiol. Psychol.* 69: 196–200.

Mason, W. (1979) "Ontogeny of social behavior," in G. J. Vandenberg and P. Marler (eds) *Social Behavior and Communication*, New York: Plenum, 1–28.

Masterson, F. A. (1970) "Is termination of a warning signal an effective reward for the rat?" *J. Comp. Physiol. Psychol.* 72: 471–5.

Masterson, F. A. and Crawford, M. (1982) "The defense motivation system: a theory of avoidance behavior," *Behav. Brain Sci.* 5: 661–96.

Matthews, C. B. A., Shimoff, E., Catania, C., and Sagvolden, T. (1977) "Uninstructed responding to ratio and interval contingencies," *J. Exp. Anal. Behav.* 27: 453–67.

Mayes, A. (1979) "The physiology of fear and anxiety," in W. Sluckin (ed.) *Fear in Animals and Man*, New York: Van Nostrand Reinhold, 24–55.

Maynard Smith, J. (1978) *The Evolution of Sex*, Cambridge: Cambridge University Press.

Mayr, E. (1974) "Behavior programs and evolutionary strategies," *Am. Sci.* 62: 650–9.

Mech, L. D. (1970) *The Wolf: the Ecology of an Endangered Species*, New York: Natural History Press.

Meck, W. H. and Church, R. M. (1983) "A mode control model of counting and timing processes," *J. Exp. Psychol.: Anim. Behav. Processes* 9: 320–34.

Meck, W. H., Church, R. M., and Olton, D. S. (1985) "Hippocampus, time, and memory," *Behav. Neurosci.*, in press.

Meltzer, D. and Hamm, R. J. (1974) "Conditioned enhancement as a function of the percentage of CS–US pairings and CS duration," *Bull. Psychon. Soc.* 4: 467–70. (1978) "Differential conditioning of conditioned enhancement and positive conditioned suppression," *Bull. Psychon. Soc.* 11: 29–32.

Mendelson, J. and Chilliag, D. (1970) "Schedule-induced air licking in rats," *Physiol. Behav.* 5: 535–7.

Menge, B. A. (1972) "Foraging strategy of a starfish in relation to actual prey availability and environmental predictability," *Ecol. Mon.* 42: 25–50.

Menzel, E. W. (1974) "A group of young chimpanzees in a one-acre field," in A. M. Schrier and F. Stollnitz (eds) *Behavior of Nonhuman Primates*, vol. 5, New York: Academic Press.

Menzel, E. W. and Halperin, S. (1975) "Purposive behavior as a basis for objective communication between chimpanzees," *Science* 189: 652–4.

Menzel, R. (1983) "Neurobiology of learning and memory: the honeybee as a model system," *Naturwiss.* 70: 504–11.

Menzel, R., Erber, J., and Masuhr, T. (1974) "Learning and memory in the honeybee," in L. Barton Browne (ed.) *Experimental Analysis of Insect Behavior*, New York: Springer-Verlag, 195–217.

Meyer, D. R., Cho, C., and Weseman, A. F. (1960) "On problems of conditioned discriminated lever-press avoidance responses," *Psychol. Rev.* 67: 224–8.

Meyer, D. R., Treichler, F. R., and Meyer, P. M. (1965) "Discrete-trial training techniques and stimulus variables," in A. M. Schrier, H. F. Harlow, and F. Stollnitz (eds) *Behavior of Nonhuman Primates: Modern Research Trends*, New York: Academic Press, 1–49.

Miczek, K. A. and Grossman, S. P. (1971) "Positive conditioned suppression: effects of CS duration," *J. Exp. Anal. Behav.* 15: 243–7.

Mikhailoff, S. (1923) "Experience reflexologique: expériences nouvelles sur *Pagurus striatus, Leander xiphiaas* et *treillanus*," *Bull. Inst. Oceanograph. Monaco* 375.

Millenson, J. R. and de Villiers, P. A. (1972) "Motivational properties of conditioned anxiety," in R. M. Gilbert and J. R. Millenson (eds) *Reinforcement: Behavioral Analyses*, New York: Academic Press, 98–128.

Miller, L. (1952) "Auditory recognition of predators," *Condor* 54: 89–92.

Miller, N. E. (1948) "Studies of fear as an acquirable drive: I. Fear as motivation and fear reduction as reinforcement in the learning of new responses," *J. Exp. Psychol.* 38: 89–101.

— (1969) "Learning of visceral and glandular responses," *Science* 163: 434–45.

Miller, R. R. and Balaz, M. A. (1981) "Differences in adaptiveness between classically conditioned responses and instrumentally acquired responses," in N. E. Spear and R. R. Miller (eds) *Information Processing in Animals: Memory Mechanisms*, Hillsdale, NJ: Erlbaum, 49–80.

Miller, R. R., Daniel, D., and Berk, A. M. (1974) "Successive reversal of a discriminated preference for tailshock," *Anim. Learn. Behav.* 2: 271–4.

Miller, R. R. and Spear, N. E. (1985) *Information Processing in Animals: Conditioned Inhibition*, Hillsdale, NJ: Erlbaum.

Miller, V. and Domjan, M. (1981) "Specificity of cue to consequence in aversion learning in the rat: control for US-induced differential orientations," *Anim. Learn. Behav.* 9: 339–45.

Mineka, S. (1979) "The role of fear in theories of avoidance learning, flooding, and extinction," *Psychol. Bull.* 86: 985–1010.

Modaresi, H. A. (1975) "One-way characteristic performance of rats under two-way signalled avoidance conditions," *Learn. Motiv.* 6: 484–97.

Moen, A. N. (1973) *Wildlife Ecology*, San Francisco: W. H. Freeman.

Moise, S. L. (1970) "Short-term retention in *Maccaca speciosa* following interpolated activity during matching from sample," *J. Comp. Physiol. Psychol.* 73: 506–14.

Moltz, H. (1960) "Imprinting: empirical bases and theoretical significance," *Psychol. Bull.* 57: 291–314.

— (1963) "Imprinting: an epigenetic approach," *Psychol. Rev.* 70: 123–38.

Moltz, H. and Stettner, L. J. (1961) "The influence of patterned-light deprivation on the critical period for imprinting," *J. Comp. Physiol. Psychol.* 54: 279–83.

Moon, L. E. and Harlow, H. F. (1955) "Analysis of oddity learning by rhesus monkeys," *J. Comp. Physiol. Psychol.* 48: 188–94.

Moore, B. R. (1973) "The role of directed Pavlovian reactions in simple instrumental learning in the pigeon," in R. A. Hinde and J. Stevenson-Hinde (eds) *Constraints on Learning*, New York: Academic Press.

Moore, J. W. (1979) "Brain processes and conditioning," in A. Dickinson and R. A. Boakes (eds) *Mechanisms of Learning and Motivation*, Chichester: John Wiley, 111–42.

Morgan, C. L. (1984) *An Introduction to Comparative Psychology*, London: Scott.

Morgan, M. J. (1974) "Resistance to satiation," *Anim. Behav.* 22: 449–66.

— (1979) "Motivational processes," in A. Dickinson and R. A. Boakes (eds) *Mechanisms of Learning and Motivation*, Chichester: John Wiley, 171–201.

Morgan, M. J., Fitch, M. D., Holman, J. G., and Lea, S. E. G. (1976) "Pigeons learn the concept of an 'A'," *Percept.* 5: 57–66.

Morgan, M. J. and Nicholas, D. J. (1979) "Discrimination between reinforced action patterns in the rat," *Learn. Motiv.* 10: 1–22.

Morrell, G. M. and Turner, J. R. G. (1970) "Experiments in mimicry: I. The response of wild birds to artificial prey," *Behav.* 36: 116–30.

Morris, R. C. (1976) "Behavioral contrast and autoshaping," *Q. J. Exp. Psychol.* 28: 661–6.

Morris, R. G. M. (1981) "Spatial location does not require the presence of local cues," *Learn. Motiv.* 12: 239–60.

Morrison, G. R. and Collyer, R. (1974) "Taste-mediated conditioned aversion to an exteroceptive stimulus following LiCl poisoning," *J. Comp. Physiol. Psychol.* 86: 51–5.

Morse, W. H. (1966) "Intermittent reinforcement," in W. K. Honig (ed.) *Operant Behavior: Areas of Research and Application*, New York: Appleton-Century-Crofts, 52–108.

Mowrer, O. H. (1939) "A stimulus–response analysis of anxiety and its role as a reinforcing agent," *Psychol. Rev.* 46: 553–65.

—— (1947) "On the dual nature of learning: a reinterpretation of 'conditioning' and 'problem-solving'," *Harvard Educ. Rev.* 17: 102–48.

—— (1960) *Learning Theory and Behavior*, New York: Wiley.

Mpitsos, G. J., Collins, S., and McClellan, A. D. (1978) "Learning: a model system for physiological studies," *Science* 199: 497–502.

Murdoch, W. W. and Oaten, A. (1975) "Predation and population stability," *Adv. Ecol. Res.* 9: 1–131.

Murphey, R. M. (1967) "Instrumental conditioning of the fruit fly, *Drosophila melanogaster*," *Anim. Behav.* 15: 153–61.

—— (1969) "Spatial discrimination performance of *Drosophila melanogaster*: some controlled and uncontrolled correlates," *Anim. Behav.* 17: 43–56.

—— (1973) "Spatial discrimination performance of *Drosophila melanogaster*: test-retest assessments and a reinterpretation," *Anim. Behav.* 21: 687–92.

Murton, R. K. (1971) "The significance of a specific search image in the feeding behaviour of the wood-pigeon," *Behav.* 40: 10–42.

Murton, R. K., Isaacson, A. J., and Westwood, N. J. (1963) "The feeding ecology of the woodpigeon," *Br. Birds* 56: 345–75.

Myer, J. S. and White, R. T. (1965) "Aggressive motivation in the rat," *Anim. Behav.* 13: 430–3.

Nairne, J. S. and Rescorla, R. A. (1981) "Second-order conditioning with diffuse auditory reinforcers in the pigeon," *Learn. Motiv.* 12: 65–91.

Nelson, W., Scheving, L., and Halberg, F. (1975) "Circadian rhythms in mice fed a single daily meal at different stages of lighting regimen," *J. Nutrition* 105: 171–84.

Neuringer, A. and Schneider, B. A. (1968) "Separating the effects of interreinforcement time and number of interreinforcement responses," *J. Exp. Anal. Behav.* 11: 661–7.

Neuringer, A. J. (1967) "Effects of reinforcement magnitude on choice and rate of responding," *J. Exp. Anal. Behav.* 10: 417–24.

Nevin, J. A. (1979) "Overall matching versus momentary maximizing: Nevin (1969) revisited," *J. Exp. Psychol.: Anim. Behav. Processes* 5: 300–6.

Nevin, J. A. and Berryman, R. (1963) "A note on chaining and temporal discrimination," *J. Exp. Anal. Behav.* 6: 109–13.

Nice, M. M. and Ter Pelwyk, J. (1941) "Enemy recognition by the song sparrow," *Auk* 58: 195–214.

Nicolaides, S. (1977) "Sensory-neuro-endocrine reflexes and their anticipatory and optimizing role on metabolism," in M. R. Kare and O. Maller (eds) *The Chemical Senses and Nutrition*, New York: Academic Press, 123–43.

Northcutt, R. G. and Heath, J. E. (1971) "Performance of caimans in a T-maze," *Copeia* 557–60.

—— (1973) "T-maze behavior of the tuatara (*Sphenodon punctatus*)," *Copeia* 617–20.

Nottebohm, F. (1970) "Ontogeny of bird song," *Science* 167: 950–6.

—— (1980) "Brain pathways for vocal learning in birds: a review of the first ten years," *Prog. Psychobiol. Physiol. Psychol.* 9: 85–124.

—— (1981) "A brain for all seasons: cyclical anatomical changes in song control nuclei in the canary brain," *Science* 214: 1368–70.

Nottebohm, F., Kasparian, S., and Pandazis, C. (1981) "Brain space for a learned task," *Brain Res.* 213: 99–109.

Nottebohm, F., Manning, E., and Nottebohm, M. E. (1976) "Left hypoglossal dominance in the control of canary and white-crowned sparrow song," *J. Comp. Physiol.* 108: 171–92.

Nottebohm, F., Stokes, T. M., and Leonard, C. M. (1976) "Central control of song in the canary, *Serinus canarius*," *J. Comp. Neurol.* 165: 457–86.

Oakley, D. A. (1979a) "Neocortex and learning," *Trends Neurosci.* 2: 149–52.

—— (1979b) "Learning with food reward and shock avoidance in neodecorticate rats," *Exp. Neurol.* 63: 627–42.

—— (1979c) "Cerebral cortex and adaptive behavior," in D. A. Oakley and H. C. Plotkin (eds) *Brain, Behaviour and Evolution*, London: Methuen, 154–88.

—— (1980) "Improved instrumental learning in neodecorticate rats," *Physiol. Behav.* 24: 357–66.

—— (1983) "Learning capacity outside neocortex in animals and man: implications for therapy after brain-injury," in G. C. L. Davey (ed.) *Animal Models of Human Behavior*, Chichester: John Wiley, 247–66.

Oakley, D. A. and Russell, I. S. (1972) "Neocortical lesions and Pavlovian conditioning," *Physiol. Behav.* 8: 915–26.

—— (1974) "Differential and reversal conditioning in partially neodecorticate rabbits," *Physiol. Behav.* 13: 221–30.

—— (1975) "Role of cortex in Pavlovian discrimination learning," *Physiol. Behav.* 15: 315–21.

—— (1976) "Subcortical nature of Pavlovian differentiation in the rabbit," *Physiol. Behav.* 17: 947–54.

—— (1978) "Manipulandum identification in operant behavior in neodecorticate rabbits," *Physiol. Behav.* 21: 943–50.

Oakley, D. A., Eames, L. C., Jacobs, J. L., Davey, G. C. L., and Cleland, G. G. (1981) "Signal-centered action patterns in rats without neocortex in a Pavlovian conditioning situation," *Physiol. Psychol.* 9: 135–44.

Oaten, A. (1977) "Optimal foraging in patches: a case for stochasticity," *Theor. Pop. Biol.* 12: 263–85.

Odling-Smee, F. J. (1983) "Multiple levels in evolution: an approach to the nature–nurture issue via 'applied epistemology'," in G. C. L. Davey (ed.) *Animal Models of Human Behavior*, Chichester: John Wiley, 135–58.

Öhman, A. (1979) "Instructional control of autonomic respondents: fear relevance as a critical factor," in N. Birbaumer and H. D. Kimmel (eds) *Biofeedback and Self-Regulation*, New York: Erlbaum, 149–65.

Öhman, A., Eriksson, A., and Olofsson, C. (1975) "One-trial learning and superior resistance to extinction of autonomic responses conditioned to potentially phobic stimuli," *J. Comp. Physiol. Psychol.* 88: 619–27.

Öhman, A., Fredrikson, M., and Hugdahl, K. (1978) "Orienting and defensive responding in the electrodermal system: palmar-dorsal differences and recovery rate during conditioning to potentially phobic stimuli," *Psychophysiol.* 15: 93–101.

Öhman, A., Fredrikson, M., Hugdahl, K., and Rimmo, P-A. (1976) "The premise of equipotentiality in human classical conditioning: conditioned electrodermal responses to potentially phobic stimuli," *J. Exp. Psychol.* 105: 313–37.

Olton, D. S. (1978) "Characteristics of spatial memory," in S. H. Hulse, H. Fowler, and W. K. Honig (eds) *Cognitive Processes in Animal Behavior*, Hillsdale, NJ: Erlbaum.

Olton, D. S., Collinson, C., and Werz, M. A. (1977) "Spatial memory and radial arm maze performance of rats," *Learn. Motiv.* 8: 289–314.

Olton, D. S. and Isaacson, R. L. (1968) "Importance of spatial location in active avoidance tasks," *J. Comp. Physiol. Psychol.* 65: 535–9.

Olton, D. S. and Samuelson, R. J. (1976) "Remembrance of places passed: spatial memory in rats," *J. Exp. Psychol.: Anim. Behav. Processes* 2: 97–116.

Olton, D. S. and Schlosberg, P. (1978) "Food searching strategies in young rats: win-shift predominates over win-stay," *J. Comp. Physiol. Psychol.* 92: 609–18.

Orlando, R. and Bijou, S. W. (1960) "Single and multuple schedules of reinforcement in developmentally retarded children," *J. Exp. Anal. Behav.* 3: 339–48.

Osborne, S. R. (1977) "The free loading (contrafreeloading) phenomenon: a review and analysis," *Anim. Learn. Behav.* 5: 221–35.

Otis, L. S. and Cerf, J. A. (1963) "Conditioned avoidance of learning in two fish species," *Psychol. Rep.* 12: 679–82.

Overman, W. H., McLain, C., Ormsby, G. E., and Brooks, V. (1983) "Visual recognition memory in squirrel monkeys," *Anim. Learn. Behav.* 11: 483–8.

Overmier, J. B. (1968) "Interference with avoidance behavior: failure to avoid traumatic shock," *J. Exp. Psychol.* 78: 340–43.

Overmier, J. B. and Brackbill, R. M. (1977) "On the independence of stimulus evocation of fear and fear evocation of responses," *Behav. Res. Therap.* 15: 51–6.

Overmier, J. B. and Bull, J. A. (1969) "On the independence of stimulus control of avoidance," *J. Exp. Psychol.* 79: 464–7.

Overmier, J. B., Bull, J. A., and Trapold, M. A. (1971) "Discriminative cue properties of different fears and their role in response selection in dogs," *J. Comp. Physiol. Psychol.* 76: 478–82.

Overmier, J. B. and Curnow, P. F. (1969) "Classical conditioning, pseudoconditioning and sensitization in 'normal' and forebrainless fish," *J. Comp. Physiol. Psychol.* 68: 193–8.

Overmier, J. B. and Lawry, J. A. (1979) "Pavlovian conditioning and the mediation of behaviour," in G. H. Bower (ed.) *The Psychology of Learning and Motivation*, New York: Academic Press, 1–55.

Overmier, J. B. and Payne, R. J. (1971) "Facilitation of instrumental avoidance learning by prior appetitive Pavlovian conditioning to the cue," *Acta Neurobiol. Exp.* 31: 341–9.

Overmier, J. B. and Schwarzkopf, K. H. (1974) "Summation of food and shock based responding," *Learn. Motiv.* 5: 42–52.

Overmier, J. B. and Starkman, N. (1974) "Transfer of control of avoidance in normal and forebrainless goldfish," *Physiol. & Behav.* 12: 605–8.

Palmerino, C. C., Rusiniak, K. W., and Garcia, J. (1980) "Flavor–illness aversions, the peculiar roles of odor and taste in memory for poison," *Science* 208: 753–5.

Panksepp, J., Toates, F. M., and Oatley, K. (1972) "Extinction induced drinking in hungry rats," *Anim. Behav.* 20: 493–8.

Parrish, J. (1967) "Classical discrimination conditioning of heart rate and bar press suppression in the rat," *Psychon. Sci.* 9: 267–8.

Paton, J. A., Manogue, K. R., and Nottebohm, F. (1981) "Bilateral organization of the vocal control pathway in the budgerigar, *Melopsittacus undulatus*," *J. Neurosci.* 1: 1276–88.

Patten, R. L. and Rudy, J. W. (1967) "The Sheffield omission training procedure applied to the conditioning of the licking response in rats," *Psychon. Sci.* 8: 463–4.

Patterson, F. G. (1978) "The gestures of a gorilla: language acquisition in another pongid," *Brain Lang.* 5: 56–71.

Pavlov, I. P. (1927) *Conditioned Reflexes*, Oxford: Oxford University Press.
(1928) *Lectures on Conditioned Reflexes*, translated by W. H. Grant, New York: International Publishers.
(1932) "The reply of a physiologist to psychologists," *Psychol. Rev.* 39: 91–127.
(1934) "An attempt at a physiological interpretation of obsessional neurosis and paranoia," *J. Ment. Sci.* 80: 187–97.

Payne, R. B. (1981) "Song learning and social interaction in indigo buntings," *Anim. Behav.* 29: 688–97.

Pear, J. J., Moody, J. E., and Persinger, M. A. (1972) "Lever attacking by rats during free-operant avoidance," *J. Exp. Anal. Behav.* 18: 517–23.

Pearce, J. M. and Hall, G. (1979) "Overshadowing of instrumental conditioning of a lever press response by a more valid predictor of reinforcement," *J. Exp. Psychol.: Anim. Behav. Processes*.
(1980) "A model for Pavlovian learning: variations in the effectiveness of conditioned but not of unconditioned stimuli," *Psychol. Rev.* 87: 532–52.

Pearce, J. M., Nicholas, D. T., and Dickinson, A. (1981) "The potentiation effect during serial conditioning," *Q. J. Exp. Psychol.* 33B: 159–79.

Peden, B. F., Browne, M. P., and Hearst, E. (1977) "Persistent approaches to a signal for food despite food omission for approaching," *J. Exp. Psychol.: Anim. Behav. Processes* 3: 377–99.

Peele, D. B., Casey, J., and Silberberg, A. (1984) "Primacy of interresponse-time reinforcement in accounting for rate differences under variable-ratio and variable-interval schedules," *J. Exp. Psychol.: Anim. Behav. Processes* 10: 149–67.

Pepperberg, I. M. (1981) "Functional vocalizations by an African grey parrot (*Psittacus erithacus*)," *Z. Tierpsychol.* 55: 139–60.
(1983) "Cognition in the African grey parrot: preliminary evidence for auditory/vocal comprehension of the class concept," *Anim. Learn. Behav.* 11: 179–85.

Perkins, C. C. (1968) "Analysis of the concept of reinforcement," *Psychol. Rev.* 75: 155–72.

Peterson, G. B. (1975) "Response selection properties of food and brain-stimulation reinforcers in the rat," *Physiol. & Behav.* 14: 681–8.

Peterson, G. B., Ackil, J. E., Frommer, G. P., and Hearst, E. (1972) "Conditioned approach and contact toward signals for food and brain-stimulation reinforcement," *Science* 177: 1009–11.

Peterson, G. B., Wheeler, R. L., and Armstrong, G. D. (1978) "Expectancies as mediators in the differential reward of conditional discrimination performance of pigeons," *Anim. Learn. Behav.* 6: 279–85.

Pfungst, O. (1911) *Clever Hans, the Horse of Von Osten*, New York: Holt, Rinehart & Winston.

Phillips, J. and Davey, G. C. L. (1986) "Autoshaping in the hamster," unpublished manuscript.

Pierrel, R. and Sherman, J. G. (1963) "Barnabus, the rat with college training," *Brown Alumni Monthly* (Feb.).

Pietrewicz, A. T. and Kamil, A. C. (1979) "Search image formation in the blue jay (*Cyanocitta cristata*)," *Science* 204: 1332–3.

Pinckney, G. A. (1968) "Response consequences and Sidman avoidance behavior in the goldfish," *Psychon. Sci.* 12: 13–14.

Platt, S. A., Holliday, M., and Drudge, O. W. (1980) "Discrimination learning of an instrumental response in individual *Drosophila melanogaster*," *J. Exp. Psychol.: Anim. Behav. Processes* 6: 301–11.

Pliskoff, S. S. and Brown, T. G. (1976) "Matching with a trio of concurrent variable-interval schedules of reinforcement," *J. Exp. Anal. Behav.* 25: 69–73.

Plotkin, H. C. (1983) "The functions of learning and cross-species comparisons," in G. C. L. Davey (ed.) *Animal Models of Human Behavior*, Chichester: John Wiley, 117–34.

Plotkin, H. C. and Odling-Smee, F. J. (1979) "Learning, change and evolution," *Adv. Study Behav.* 10: 1–41.

—— (1982) "Learning in the context of a hierarchy of knowledge gaining processes," in H. C. Plotkin (ed.) *Essays in Evolutionary Epistemology*, Chichester: John Wiley, 443–71.

Pluthero, F. G. and Threlkeld, S. F. H. (1979) "Some aspects of maze behavior in *Drosophila melanogaster*," *Behav. Neural Biol.* 26: 254–7.

Poling, A. and Poling, T. (1978) "Automaintenance in guinea pigs: effects of feeding regimen and omission training," *J. Exp. Anal. Behav.* 30: 37–46.

Poling, A. and Thompson, T. (1977) "The effects of d-amphetamine on the automaintained key pecking of pigeons," *Psychopharmacol.* 51: 285–8.

Pomerleau, O. F. (1970) "The effects of stimuli followed by response-independent shock on shock-avoidance behavior," *J. Exp. Anal. Behav.* 14: 11–21.

Powell, R. W., Kelly, W., and Santisteban, D. (1975) "Response-independent reinforcement in the crow: failure to obtain autoshaping or positive automaintenance," *Bull. Psychon. Soc.* 6: 513–16.

Powell, R. W. and Mantor, H. (1969) "Failure to obtain one-way shuttle avoidance in the lizard, *Anolis sagrei*," *Psychol. Rec.* 19: 623–7.

Prelec, D. (1982) "Matching, maximizing, and the hyperbolic reinforcement feedback function," *Psychol. Rev.* 89: 189–230.

Premack, D. (1962) "Reversibility of the reinforcement relation," *Science* 136: 255–7.
(1965) "Reinforcement theory," in D. Levine (ed.) *Nebraska Symposium on Motivation*, vol. 13, Lincoln, Neb.: University of Nebraska Press.
(1970) "A functional analysis of language," *J. Exp. Anal. Behav.* 14: 107–25.
(1971a) "On the assessment of language competence and the chimpanzee," in A. M. Schrier and F. Stollnitz (eds) *Behavior of Nonhuman Primates*, vol. 4, New York: Academic Press.
(1971b) "Language in chimpanzees?" *Science* 172: 808–22.
(1971c) "Catching up with common sense, or two sides of a generalization: Reinforcement and punishment," in R. Glaser (ed.) *The Nature of Reinforcement*, New York: Academic Press.
Premack, D. and Woodruff, G. (1978) "Does the chimpanzee have a theory of mind?" *Behav. Brain Sci.* 4: 515–26.
Prokasy, W. F. and Kumpfer, K. A. (1969) "Conditioning, probability of reinforcement and sequential behavior in human conditioning with intermittent schedules," *Psychon. Sci.* 10: 49–50.
Prokasy, W. F. and Williams, W. C. (1979) "Information processing and the decremental effect of intermittent reinforcement schedules in human conditioning," *Bull. Psychon. Soc.* 14: 57–60.
Pröve, E. (1984) "Psychological basis of sexual imprinting in male zebra finches," in S. Ishii, B. K. Follett, and A. Chandola (eds) *Environment and Hormones*, Tokyo: Japan Scientific Societies Press.
Pubols, B. H. (1960) "Incentive magnitude, learning, and performance in animals," *Psychol. Bull.* 57: 89–115.
Pulliam, H. R. (1976) "The principle of optimal behaviour and the theory of communities" in P. P. G. Bateson and P. H. Klopfer (eds) *Perspectives in Ethology*, vol. 2, New York: Plenum Press.

Quinn, W. G. (1984) "Work in invertebrates on the mechanisms underlying learning," in P. Marler and H. S. Terrace (eds) *The Biology of Learning*, New York: Springer-Verlag, 197–246.
Quinn, W. G., Harris, W. A., and Benzer, S. (1974) "Conditioned behavior in *Drosophila melanogaster*," *Proceedings of the National Academy of Science, USA*, 71: 708.

Rachlin, H. (1969) "Autoshaping of key pecking in pigeons with negative reinforcement," *J. Exp. Anal. Behav.* 12: 521–31.
Rachlin, H. C., Battalio, R., Kagel, J., and Green, L. (1981) "Maximization theory in behavioral psychology," *Behav. Brain Sci.* 4: 371–417.
Rachlin, H., Green, L., Kagel, J. H., and Battalio, R. C. (1976) "Economic demand theory and psychological studies of choice," in G. W. Bower (ed.) *The Psychology of Learning and Motivation*, vol. 10, New York: Academic Press, 129–54.
Rachlin, H. and Hineline, P. N. (1967) "Training and maintenance of key-pecking in the pigeon by negative reinforcement," *Science* 157: 954–5.
Rackham, D. W. (1971) "Conditioning of the pigeon's courtship and aggressive display," Unpublished thesis, Dalhousie University.
Rakover, S. S. (1979) "Fish (*Tilapia aurea*), as rats, learn shuttle better than lever-bumping (press) avoidance tasks: a suggestion for functionally similar universal reactions to a conditioned fear-arousing stimulus," *American Journal of Psychology* 92: 489–95.

Randich, A. (1981) "The US pre-exposure phenomenon in the conditioned suppression paradigm: a role for conditioned situational stimuli," *Learn. Motiv.* 12: 321–41.

Randich, A. and Lolordo, V. M. (1979) "Associative and nonassociative theories of the UCS pre-exposure phenomenon: implications for Pavlovian conditioning," *Psychol. Bull.* 86: 523–48.

Rashotte, M. E., Griffin, R. W., and Sisk, C. L. (1977) "Second-order conditioning of the pigeon's keypeck," *Anim. Learn. Behav.* 5: 25–38.

Razran, G. (1955) "Conditioning and perception," *Psychol. Rev.* 62: 83–95.

(1971) *Mind in Evolution: an East–West Synthesis of Learned Behavior and Cognition*, Boston: Houghton Mifflin.

Reberg, D. and Black, A. H. (1969) "Compound testing of individually conditioned stimuli as an index of excitatory and inhibitory properties," *Psychon. Sci.* 17: 30–1.

Reberg, D., Innis, N. K., Mann, B., and Eizenga, C. (1978) "'Superstitious' behavior resulting from periodic response-independent presentations of food or water," *Anim. Behav.* 26: 506–19.

Reberg, D., Mann, B., and Innis, N. K. (1977) "Superstitious behavior for food and water in the rat," *Physiol. Behav.* 19: 803–6.

Reisbick, S. H. (1973) "Development of food preferences in newborn guinea pigs," *J. Comp. Physiol. Psychol.* 85: 427–42.

Reiss, S. and Wagner, A. R. (1972) "A CS habituation effect produces a 'latent inhibition effect' but no active 'conditioned inhibition'," *Learn. Motiv.* 3: 327–45.

Rensch, B. (1959) *Evolution Above the Species Level*, New York: Columbia University Press.

Rescorla, R. A. (1967a) "Inhibition of delay in Pavlovian fear conditioning," *J. Comp. Physiol. Psychol.* 64: 114–20.

(1967b) "Pavlovian conditioning and its proper control procedures," *Psychol. Rev.* 74: 71–80.

(1968) "Pavlovian conditioned fear in Sidman avoidance learning," *J. Comp. Physiol. Psychol.* 65: 55–60.

(1969) "Pavlovian conditioned inhibition," *Psychol. Bull.* 72: 77–94.

(1973) "Effect of US habituation following conditioning," *J. Comp. Physiol. Psychol.* 82: 137–43.

(1974) "Effect of inflation on the unconditioned stimulus value following conditioning," *J. Comp. Physiol. Psychol.* 86: 101–6.

(1975) "Pavlovian excitatory and inhibitory conditioning," in W. K. Estes (ed.) *Handbook of Learning and Cognitive Processes*, vol. 2, Hillsdale, NJ: Erlbaum.

(1979) "Conditioned inhibition and extinction," in A. Dickinson and R. A. Boakes (eds) *Mechanisms of Learning and Motivation*, Chichester: John Wiley, 83–110.

(1980a) *Pavlovian Second-order Conditioning*, Hillsdale, NJ: Erlbaum.

(1980b) "Simultaneous and successive associations in sensory preconditioning," *J. Exp. Psychol.: Anim. Behav. Processes* 6: 207–16.

(1981) "Simultaneous associations," in P. Harzem and M. D. Zeiler (eds) *Predictability, Correlation, and Contiguity*, Chichester: John Wiley.

(1984) "Associations between Pavlovian CSs and context," *J. Exp. Psychol.: Anim. Behav. Processes* 10: 195–204.

Rescorla, R. A. and Colwill, R. M. (1983) "Within-compound associations in unblocking," *J. Exp. Psychol.: Anim. Behav. Processes* 9: 390–400.

Rescorla, R. A. and Cunningham, C. L. (1978) "Within-compound flavor associations," *J. Exp. Psychol.: Anim. Behav. Processes* 4: 267–75.

Rescorla, R. A. and Durlach, P. J. (1981) "Within-event learning in Pavlovian conditions," in N. E. Spear and R. R. Miller (ed) *Information Processing in Animals: Memory Mechanisms*, Hillsdale, NJ: Erlbaum, 81–111.

Rescorla, R. A. and Freberg, L. (1978) "The extinction of within-compound flavor associations," *Learn. Motiv.* 9: 411–27.

Rescorla, R. A. and Furrow, D R. (1977) "Stimulus similarity as a determinant of Pavlovian conditioning," *J. Exp. Psychol.: Anim. Behav. Processes* 3: 203–15.

Rescorla, R. A. and Gillan, D. J. (1980) "An analysis of the facilitative effect of similarity on second-order conditioning," *J. Exp. Psychol.: Anim. Behav. Processes* 6: 339–51.

Rescorla, R. A. and Holland, P. C. (1976) "Some behavioral approaches to the study of learning," in M. R. Rosenzweig and E. L. Bennett (eds) *Neural Mechanisms of Learning and Memory*, Cambridge, Mass.: MIT Press.

Rescorla, R. A. and Lolordo, V. M. (1965) "Inhibition of avoidance behavior," *J. Comp. Physiol. Psychol.* 59: 406–12.

Rescorla, R. A. and Solomon, R. L. (1967) "Two-process learning theory: relationships between Pavlovian conditioning and instrumental learning," *Psychol. Rev.* 74: 151–82.

Rescorla, R. A. and Wagner, A. R. (1972) "A theory of Pavlovian conditioning: variations in the effectiveness of reinforcement and nonreinforcement," in A. H. Black and W. F. Prokasy (eds) *Classical Conditioning II: Current Research and Theory*, New York: Appleton-Century-Crofts.

Revusky, S. (1971) "The role of interference in association over a delay," in W. K. Honig and P. H. R. James (eds) *Animal Memory*, New York: Academic Press, 155–213.

(1974) "Retention of a learned increase in the preference for a flavored solution," *Behav. Biol.* 11: 121–25.

(1977) "Learning as a general process with an emphasis on data from feeding experiments," in N. W. Milgram, L. Kranes, and T. M. Alloway (eds) *Food Aversion Learning*, New York: Plenum Press, 1–51.

(1985) "The general process approach to animal learning," in T. D. Johnston and A. T. Pietrewicz (eds) *Issues in the Ecological Study of Learning*, Hillsdale, NJ: Erlbaum, 401–32.

Revusky, S. H. and Garcia, J. (1970) "Learned associations over long delays," in G. H. Bower and J. T. Spence (eds) *The Psychology of Learning and Motivation*, vol. 4, New York: Academic Press.

Reynierse, J. H. (1966) "Excessive drinking in rats as a function of number of meals," *Canadian Journal of Psychology* 20: 82–6.

Reynolds, G. S. (1961a) "Behavioral contrast," *J. Exp. Anal. Behav.* 4: 57–71.

(1961b) "Attention in the pigeon," *J. Exp. Anal. Behav.* 4: 203–8.

(1966) "Discrimination and emission of temporal intervals by pigeons," *J. Exp. Anal. Behav.* 9: 65–8.

Reynolds, G. S., Catania, A. C., and Skinner, B. F. (1963) "Conditioned and unconditioned aggression in pigeons," *J. Exp. Anal. Behav.* 6: 73–4.

Ricci, J. A. (1973) "Keypecking under response-independent food presentation after long simple and compound stimuli," *J. Exp. Anal. Behav.* 19: 509–16.

Richards, R. W. and Rilling, M. (1972) "Aversive aspects of a fixed-interval schedule of food reinforcement," *J. Exp. Anal. Behav.* 17: 405–11.

Richardson, W. K. and Loughead, T. E. (1974a) "The effect of physical restraint on behavior under the differential-reinforcement-of-low-rate schedule," *J. Exp. Anal. Behav.* 21: 455–62.

(1974b) "Behavior under large values of the differential-reinforcement-of-low-rate schedule," *J. Exp. Anal. Behav.* 22: 121–9.

Richter, C. P. (1950) "Taste and solubility of toxic compounds in poisoning of rats and man," *J. Comp. Physiol. Psychol.* 43: 358–74.

Riess, D. (1971) "Shuttleboxes, Skinner boxes and Sidman avoidance in rats: acquisition and terminal performance as a function of response topography," *Psychon. Sci.* 25: 283–5.

Riley, A. L., Wetherington, C. L., Delamater, A. R., Peele, D., and Dacanay, R. J. (1985) "The effects of variations in the interpellet interval on wheel running in the rat," *Anim. Learn. Behav.* 13: 201–6.

Rilling, M. (1967) "Number of responses as a stimulus in fixed-interval and fixed-ratio schedules," *J. Comp. Physiol. Psychol.* 63: 60–5.

Rizley, R. C. and Rescorla, R. A. (1972) "Associations in second-order conditioning and sensory preconditioning," *J. Comp. Physiol. Psychol.* 81: 1–11.

Roberts, S. and Church, R. M. (1978) "Control of an internal clock," *J. Exp. Psychol.: Anim. Behav. Processes* 4: 318–37.

Roberts, W. A. (1972) "Spatial separation and visual differentiation of cues of factors influencing short-term memory in the rat," *J. Comp. Physiol. Psychol.* 78: 284–91.

(1974) "Spaced repetition facilitates short-term retention in the rat," *J. Comp. Physiol. Psychol.* 86: 164–71.

(1984) "Some issues in animal spatial memory," in H. L. Roitblat, T. G. Bever, and H. S. Terrace (eds) *Animal Cognition*, Hillsdale, NJ: Erlbaum.

Roberts, W. A. and Grant, D S. (1976) "Studies of short-term memory in the pigeon using the delayed matching to sample procedure," in D. L. Medin, W. A. Roberts, and R. T. Davis (eds) *Processes of Animal Memory*, Hillsdale, NJ: Erlbaum.

(1978) "An analysis of light-induced retroactive inhibition in pigeon short-term memory," *J. Exp. Psychol.: Anim. Behav. Processes* 4: 219–36.

Roitblat, H. L. (1984) "Representations in pigeon working memory," in H. L. Roitblat, T. G. Bever, and H. S. Terrace (eds) *Animal Cognition*, Hillsdale, NJ: Erlbaum, 79–97.

Roitblat, H. L., Tham, W., and Gollub, L. (1982) "Performance of *Betta splendens* in a radial arm maze," *Anim. Learn. Behav.* 10: 108–14.

Roper, T. J. (1973) "Nesting material as a reinforcer in female mice," *Anim. Behav.* 21: 733–40.

(1975) "Nest material and food as reinforcers for fixed-ratio responding in mice," *Learn. Motiv.* 6: 327–43.

(1981) "What is meant by the term 'schedule-induced', and how general is schedule induction?" *Anim. Learn. Behav.* 9: 433–40.

Roper, T. J., Edwards, L., and Crossland, G. (1983) "Factors affecting schedule-induced wood-chewing in rats: percentage and rate of reinforcement, and operant requirement," *Anim. Learn. Behav.* 11: 35–43.

Roper, T. J. and Wistow, R. (1986) "Aposematic colouration and avoidance learning in chicks," *Q. J. Exp. Psychol.* 38B: 141–9.

Ross, D. M. (1965) "The behavior of sessile coelenterates in relation to some conditioning experiments," *Anim. Behav.* 13: 43–57.

Ross, L. E., Ferreira, M. C. and Ross, S. M. (1974) "Backward masking of conditioned stimuli: effects of differential and single-cue classical conditioning performance," *J. Exp. Psychol.* 103: 603–13.

Ross, L. E. and Hartman, T. F. (1965) "Human eyelid conditioning: the recent experimental literature," *Genet. Psychol. Monogr.* 71: 177–220.

Rovainen, C. M. (1979) "Neurobiology of lampreys," *Physiol. Rev.* 59: 1007–77.

Rowell, C. H. F. (1961) "Displacement grooming in the chaffinch," *Anim. Behav.* 9: 38–63.

Royama, T. (1970) "Factors governing the hunting behavior and selection of food by the great tit (*Parus major L.*)," *J. Anim. Ecol.* 39: 619–68.
–44.

Rozin, P. (1967) "Specific aversions as a component of specific hungers," *J. Comp. Physiol. Psychol.* 64: 237–42.

(1969) "Adaptive food sampling patterns in vitamin-deficient rats," *J. Comp. Physiol. Psychol.* 69: 126–32.

Rozin, P., Gruss, L., and Berk, G. (1979) "Reversal of innate aversions: attempts to induce a preference for chilli peppers in rats," *J. Comp. Physiol. Psychol.* 13: 1001–14.

Rozin, P. and Kalat, J. W. (1971) "Specific hungers and poison avoidance as adaptive specializations of learning," *Psychol. Rev.* 78: 459–86.

Rozin, P. and Mayer, J. (1961) "Thermal reinforcement and thermoregulatory behavior in the goldfish, *Carassius auratus*," *Science* 134: 942–3.

Rudolph, R. L. and Van Houten, R. (1977) "Auditory stimulus control in pigeons: Jenkins and Harrison (1960) revisited," *J. Exp. Anal. Behav.* 27: 327–30.

Rumbaugh, D. M. and Gill, T. V. (1976) "Language and the acquisition of language-type skills by a chimpanzee (Pan)," *Annals of the New York Academy of Science* 270: 90–123.

Rumbaugh, D. M., Gill, T., and Von Glaserfeld, E. C. (1973) "Reading and sentence completion by a chimpanzee (Pan)," *Science* 182: 731–3.

Rumbaugh, D. M., Gill, T. V., Von Glaserfeld, E., Warner, H., and Pisani, P. (1975) "Conversations with a chimpanzee in a computer-controlled environment," *Biol. Psychiat.* 10: 627–41.

Rusiniak, K., Hankins, W., Garcia, J., and Brett, L. (1979) "Flavor-illness aversions: potentiation of odor by taste in rats," *Behav. Neural Biol.* 25: 1–17.

Russell, I. S. (1966) "Animal learning and memory," in D. Richter (ed.) *Aspects of Learning and Memory*, London: Heinemann.

Russell, P. A. (1979) "Fear-evoking stimuli," in W. Sluckin (ed.) *Fear in Animals and Man*, New York: Van Nostrand Reinhold, 86–124.

Ryle, G. (1951) "Thinking and language," *Proc. Aristotel. Soc. Suppl.* 25: 65–82.

Sadler, E. W. (1968) "A within-and-between-subject comparison of partial reinforcement in classical salivary conditioning," *J. Comp. Physiol. Psychol.* 66: 695–8.

Sahley, C. L. (1984) "Behavior theory and invertebrate learning," in P. Marler and

H. S. Terrace (eds) *The Biology of Learning*, New York: Springer-Verlag, 181–96.

Sahley, C. L., Gelperin, A., and Rudy, J. W. (1981) "One-trial associative learning in a terrestrial mollusc," *Proceedings of the National Academy of Science, USA*, 78: 640–2.

Sahley, C. L., Rudy, J. W., and Gelperin, A. (1981) "Analysis of associtive learning in a terrestrial mollusc. I. Higher-order conditioning, blocking, and a US–pre-exposure effect," *J. Comp. Physiol. Psychol.* 144: 1–8.

Salzen, E. A. and Meyer, C. C. (1967) "Imprinting: reversal of a preference established during the critical period," *Nature* 215: 785–6.
(1968) "Reversibility of imprinting," *J. Comp. Physiol. Psychol.* 66: 269–75.

Savage-Rumbaugh, E. S., Pate, J. L., Lawson, J., Smith, S. T., and Rosenbaum, S. (1983) "Can chimpanzees make a statement?" *J. Exp. Psychol.: General* 112: 457–92.

Savage-Rumbaugh, E. S., Sevcik, R. A., Rumbaugh, D. M., and Rubert, E. (1985) "The capacity of animals to acquire language: do species differences have anything to say to us?" *Phil. Trans. R. Soc. Lond.* 308: 177–85.

Scaife, M. (1976a) "The response to eye-like shapes by birds, I: The effect of context: a predator and a strange bird," *Anim. Behav.* 24: 195–9.
(1976b) "The response to eye-like shapes by birds, II: The importance of startings pairedness and shape," *Anim. Behav.* 24: 200–6.

Scarr, S. and Salapatek, P. (1970) "Patterns of fear development during infancy," *Merrill Palmer Q.* 16: 53–90.

Scheuer, C. (1969) "Resistance to extinction of the CER as a function of shock-reinforcement training schedules," *Psychon. Sci.* 17: 181–2.

Schiff, W. (1965) "Perception of impending collision: a study of visually directed avoidant behavior," *Psychol. Monogr.* 79.

Schiff, W., Caviness, J. A., and Gibson, J. J. (1962) "Persistent fear responses in rhesus monkeys to the optical stimulus of 'looming'," *Science* 136: 982–3.

Schiller, P. H. (1952) "Innate constituents of complex responses in primates," *Psychol. Rev.* 59: 177–91.

Schleidt, W. M. (1985) "Learning and the description of the environment," in T. D. Johnston and A. T. Pietrewicz (eds) *Issues in the Ecological Study of Learning*, Hillsdale, NJ: Erlbaum, 305–25.

Schlosberg, H. (1936) "Conditioned responses in the white rat: II. Conditioned responses based upon shock to the foreleg," *J. Genet. Psychol.* 49: 107–38.

Schneider, B. A. (1969) "A two-state analysis of fixed-interval responding in the pigeon," *J. Exp. Anal. Behav.* 12: 677–87.

Schneiderman, N., Fuenets, I., and Gormezano, I. (1962) "Acquisition and extinction of the classically conditioned eyelid response in the albino rabbit," *Science* 136: 650–2.

Schrier, A. M. (1966) "Transfer by macaque monkeys between learning-set and repeated-reversal," *Percept. Mot. Skills* 23: 787–92.

Schull, J. (1979) "A conditioned opponent theory of Pavlovian conditioning," in G. W. Bower (ed.) *The Psychology of Learning and Motivation*, vol. 13, New York: Academic Press.

Schuster, C. R. and Woods, J. H. (1966) "Schedule-induced polydipsia in the monkey," *Psychol. Rep.* 19: 823–8.

Schwartz, B. (1977a) "Studies of operant and reflexive key pecks in the pigeon," *J. Exp. Anal. Behav.* 27: 301–13.

(1977b) "Two types of pigeon key pecking: suppression of long but not of short-duration key pecks by duration-dependent shock," *J. Exp. Anal. Behav.* 27: 393–8.

Schwartz, B. and Coulter, G. (1973) "A failure to transfer control of keypecking from food reinforcement to escape from the avoidance of shock," *Bull. Psychon. Soc.* 1: 307–9.

Schwartz, B. and Gamzu, E. (1977) "Pavlovian control of operant behavior," in W. K. Honig and J. E. R. Staddon (eds) *Handbook of Operant Behavior*, Englewood Cliffs, NJ: Prentice-Hall.

Schwartz, B. and Williams, D. R. (1971) "Discrete-trials spaced responding in the pigeon: the dependence of efficient performance on the availability of a stimulus for collateral pecking," *J. Exp. Anal. Behav.* 16: 155–60.

(1972a) "The role of the response-reinforcer contingency in negative auto-maintenance," *J. Exp. Anal. Behav.* 21: 351–7.

(1972b) "Two different kinds of key peck in the pigeon: some properties of responses maintained by negative and positive response -reinforcer contingencies," *J. Exp. Anal. Behav.* 18: 201–16.

Scobie, S. R. (1972) "Integration of an aversive Pavlovian conditioned stimulus with aversively and appetitively motivated operants in rats," *J. Comp. Physiol. Psychol.* 79: 171–88.

(1973) "The response-shock interval and conditioned suppression of avoidance in rats," *Anim. Learn. Behav.* 1: 17–20.

Segal, E. F. and Holloway, S. M. (1963) "Timing behavior in rats with water drinking as a mediator," *Science* 140: 888–9.

Seligman, M. E. P. (1970) "On the generality of the laws of learning," *Psychol. Rev.* 77: 406–18.

Seligman, M. E. P. and Hager, J. L. (1972) *Biological Boundaries of Learning*, Englewood Cliffs, NJ: Prentice-Hall.

Sevenster, P. (1961) "A causal analysis of a displacement activity (fanning in *Gasteroteus aculeatus L.*)," *Behav. Suppl.* 9: 1–170.

(1968) "Motivation and learning in sticklebacks," in D. Ingle (ed.) *The Central Nervous System and Fish Behavior*, Chicago: University of Chicago Press, 233–45.

Shanab, M. E. and Peterson, J. L. (1969) "Polydipsia in the pigeon," *Psychon. Sci.* 15: 51–2.

Sheffield, F. D. (1965) "Relation between classical conditioning and instrumental learning," in W. F. Prokasy (ed.) *Classical Conditioning*, New York: Appleton-Century-Crofts, 302–22.

(1966) "New evidence for the drive-reduction theory of reinforcement," in R. N. Haber (ed.) *Current Research in Motivation*, New York: Holt, Rinehart & Winston.

Sheffield, F. D. and Campbell, B. A. (1954) "The role of experience in the 'spontaneous' activity of hungry rats," *J. Comp. Physiol. Psychol.* 47: 97–100.

Sherry, C. J. (1977) "Effects of age, sex, and varying levels of dilantin on pain-induced aggression in chickens," unpublished Ph.D. thesis, Illinois Institute of Technology.

Sherry, D. F. (1985) "Food storage by birds and mammals," *Adv. Study Behav.* 15: 153–88.

Sherry, D. F., Krebs, J. R., and Cowie, R. J. (1981) "Memory for the location of stored food in marsh tits," *Anim. Behav.* 29: 1260–6.

Shettleworth, S. J. (1972a) "Constraints on learning," *Adv. Study Behav.* 4: 1–68.
(1972b) "Stimulus relevance in the control of drinking and conditioned fear responses in domestic chicks (*Gallus gallus*)," *J. Comp. Physiol. Psychol.* 80: 175–98.
(1973) "Food reinforcement and the organization of behavior in golden hamsters," in R. A. Hinde and J. Stevenson-Hinde (eds) *Constraints on Learning*, London: Academic Press, 243–63.
(1975) "Reinforcement and the organization of behavior in golden hamsters: hunger, environment and food reinforcement," *J. Exp. Psychol.: Anim. Behav. Processes* 104: 56–87.
(1978) "Reinforcement and the organization of behavior in golden hamsters: punishment of three action patterns," *Learn. Motiv.* 9: 99–123.
(1984) "Natural history and the evolution of learning in nonhuman mammals," in P. Marler and H. S. Terrace (eds) *The Biology of Learning*, New York: Springer-Verlag, 419–33.
Shettleworth, S. J. and Krebs, J. R. (1982) "How marsh tits find their hoards: the roles of site preference and spatial memory," *J. Exp. Psychol.: Anim. Behav. Processes* 8: 354–75.
Shimoff, E., Catania, A. C., and Matthews, B. A. (1981) "Uninstructed human responding: sensitivity of low-rate performance to schedule contingencies," *J. Exp. Anal. Behav.* 36: 207–20.
Shimp, C. P. (1966) "Probabilistically reinforced choice behavior in pigeons," *J. Exp. Anal. Behav.* 9: 443–55.
(1967) "The reinforcement of short interresponse times," *J. Exp. Anal. Behav.* 10: 425–34.
(1969) "Optimum behavior in free-operant experiments," *Psychol. Rev.* 76: 97–112.
Shimp, C. P. and Moffitt, M. (1974) "Short-term memory in the pigeon: stimulus–response associations," *J. Exp. Anal. Behav.* 12: 745–57.
Siddle, D. A. T. (1983) *Orienting and Habituation: Perspectives in Human Research*, Chichester: John Wiley.
Siddle, D. A. T. and Remington, B. (1987) "Latent inhibition and human Pavlovian conditioning: research and relevance," in G. C. L. Davey (ed.) *Cognitive Processes and Pavlovian Conditioning in Humans*, Chichester: John Wiley.
Siddle, D. A. T., Remington, B., and Churchill, M. (1985) "Effects of conditioned stimulus preexposure on human electrodermal conditioning," *Biol. Psychol.* 20: 113–27.
Sidman, M. (1962) "Operant techniques," in A. J. Bachrach (ed.) *Experimental Foundations of Clinical Psychology*, New York: Basic Books, 170–210.
Sidman, M. and Fletcher, F. G. (1968) "A demonstration of autoshaping with monkeys," *J. Exp. Anal. Behav.* 11: 367–9.
Sidman, M., Herrnstein, R. J., and Conrad, D. G. (1957) "Maintenance of avoidance behavior by unavoidable shocks," *J. Comp. Physiol. Psychol.* 50: 553–7.
Sieck, M. H., Baumbach, H. D., Gordon, B. L., and Turner, J. F. (1974) "Changes in spontaneous, odor modulated and shock induced behavior patterns following discrete olfactory system lesions," *Physiol. Behav.* 13: 427–39.
Siegel, S. (1970) "Retention of latent inhibition," *Psychon. Sci.* 20: 161–2.

(1977) "Learning and psychopharmacology," in M. E. Jarvik (ed.)
Psychopharmacology in the Practice of Medicine, New York: Appleton, 61–70.
(1969) "The role of conditioning in drug tolerance and addiction," in J. D. Keehn
(ed.) *Psychopathology in Animals: Research and Clinical Implications*, New York:
Academic Press, 143–68.
Skinner, B. F. (1938) *The Behavior of Organisms*, New York:
Appleton-Century-Crofts.
(1948) "'Superstition' in the pigeon," *J. Exp. Psychol.* 38: 168–72.
(1950) "Are theories of learning necessary?" *Psychol. Rev.* 57: 193–216.
(1953) *Science and Human Behavior*, New York: Macmillan.
(1957a) "The experimental analysis of behavior," *Am. Sci.* 45: 343–71.
(1957b) *Verbal Behavior*, New York: Appleton-Century-Crofts.
(1966) "An operant analysis of problem solving," in B. Kleinmuntz (ed.) *Problem-
solving: Research, Method and Teaching*, New York: John Wiley.
Skinner, B. F. and Morse, C. W. (1958) "Fixed-interval reinforcement of running in
a wheel," *J. Exp. Anal. Behav.* 1: 371–9.
Slobodkin, L. B. (1968) "Toward a predictive theory of evolution," in R. C.
Lewontin (ed.) *Population Biology and Evolution*, Syracuse, NY: Syracuse
University Press, 187–205.
Slobodkin, L. B. and Rapoport, A. (1974) "An optimum strategy of evolution," *Q.
Rev. Biol.* 49: 181–200.
Sluckin, W. and Salzen, E. A. (1961) "Imprinting and perceptual learning," *Q. J.
Exp. Psychol.* 13: 65–77.
Smith, J. B. (1974) "Effects of response rate reinforcement frequency and the
duration of a stimulus preceding response-independent food," *J. Exp. Anal.
Behav.* 21: 215–21.
Smith, J. B. and Clark, F. C. (1974) "Intercurrent and reinforced behavior under
multiple spaced-responding schedules," *J. Exp. Anal. Behav.* 21: 445–54.
Smith, J. C. and Roll, D. L. (1967) "Trace conditioning with X-rays as an aversive
stimulus," *Psychon. Sci.* 9: 11–12.
Smith, J. N. M. (1974a) "The food searching behavior of two European thrushes. I.
Description and analysis of search paths," *Behav.* 48: 276–302.
(1974b) "The food searching behavior of two European thrushes. II. The
adaptiveness of the search patterns," *Behav.* 49: 1–61.
Smith, J. N. M. and Sweatman, H. P. A. (1974) "Food searching behavior of titmice
in patchy environments," *Ecol.* 55: 1216–32.
Smith, L. T. (1973) "*Pan troglodytes:* usurper or companion?" *Bio. Psychol. Bull.* 3: 30–41.
Smith, O. A., McFarland, W. L., and Taylor, E. (1961) "Performance in a shock-
avoidance conditioning situation interpreted as pseudoconditioning," *J. Comp.
Physiol. Psychol.* 54: 154–7.
Smith, R. F. (1967) "Behavioral events other than key striking which are counted as
responses during pigeon pecking," Doctoral dissertation, Indiana University.
Solomon, R. L. and Corbit, J. D. (1974) "An opponent-process theory of
motivation: I. The temporal dynamics of affect," *Psychol. Rev.* 81: 119–45.
Solomon, R. L. and Turner, L. H. (1962) "Discriminative classical conditioning in
dogs paralysed by curare can later control discriminative avoidance responses in
the normal state," *Psychol. Rev.* 69: 202–19.
Soltysik, S. and Jaworska, K. (1962) "Studies on the aversive classical conditioning.

2. On the reinforcing role of shock in the classical leg flexion conditioning," *Acta Biol. Exp.* 22: 181–91.

Spatz, H. C., Emanns, A., and Reichert, H. (1974) "Associative learning of *Drosophila melanogaster*," *Nature* 248: 359–61.

Spear, N. E. and Kucharski, D. (1984) "Ontogenetic differences in the processing of multi-element stimuli," in H. L. Roitblat, T. G. Bever, and H. S. Terrace (eds) *Animal Cognition*, Hillsdale, NJ: Erlbaum, 545–67.

Spence, K. W. (1937) "Experimental studies of learning and the higher mental processes in infra-human primates," *Psychol. Bull.* 34: 806–50.
(1951) "Theoretical interpretations of learning," in C. P. Stone (ed.) *Comparative Psychology*, Englewood Cliffs, NJ: Prentice-Hall, 239–91.
(1956) *Behavior Theory and Conditioning*, New Haven, CT: Yale University Press.

Spence, K. W. and Goldstein, H. (1961) "Eyelid conditioning performance as a function of emotion-producing instructions," *J. Exp. Psychol.* 62: 291–4.

Spetch, M. L., Wilkie, D. M., and Pinel, J. P. J. (1981) "Backward conditioning: a re-evaluation of the empirical evidence," *Psychol. Bull.* 89: 163–75.

Spooner, A. and Kellogg, W. N. (1947) "The backward conditioning curve," *American Journal of Psychology* 60: 321–34.

retarded persons," in N. Ellis (ed.) *International Review of Research in Mental Retardation*, New York: Academic Press, 132–68.

Squier, L. H. (1969) "Autoshaping key responses with fish," *Psychon. Sci.* 17: 177–8.

Staddon, J. E. R. (1965) "Some properties of spaced responding in pigeons," *J. Exp. Anal. Behav.* 8: 19–28.
(1977) "Schedule-induced behavior," in W. K. Honig and J. E. R. Staddon (eds) *Handbook of Operant Behavior*, Englewood Cliffs, NJ: Prentice-Hall.
(1979) "Operant behavior as adaptation to constraint," *J. Exp. Psychol.: General* 108: 48–67.
(1980) "Optimality analyses of operant behavior and their relation to optimal foraging," in J. E. R. Staddon (ed.) *Limits to Action*, New York: Academic Press.
(1983) *Adaptive Behavior and Learning*, Cambridge: Cambridge University Press.

Staddon, J. E. R. and Ayres, S. L. (1975) "Sequential and temporal properties of behavior induced by a schedule of periodic food delivery," *Behav.* 54: 26–49.

Staddon, J. E. R. and Hinson, J. M. (1983) "Optimization: a result or a mechanism," *Science* 221: 976–7.

Staddon, J. E. R. and Simmelhag, V. L. (1971) "The 'superstition' experiment: a re-examination of its implications for the principles of adaptive behavior," *Psychol. Rev.* 78: 3–43.

Starr, M. D. and Mineka, S. (1977) "Determinants of fear over the course of avoidance learning," *Learn. Motiv.* 8: 332–50.

Stein, L. (1964) "Excessive drinking in the rat: superstition or thirst?" *J. Comp. Physiol. Psychol.* 58: 237–42.

Steinert, P., Fallon, D., and Wallace, J. (1976) "Matching to sample in goldfish (*Carassius auratus*)," *Bull. Psychon. Soc.* 8: 265.

Steiniger, F. von (1950) "Beitrage zur Soziologie und sonstigen Biologie der Wanderatte," *Z. Tierpsychol.* 7: 356–79.

Stevenson, J. B. (1969) "Song as a reinforcer," in R. A. Hinde (ed.) *Bird Vocalizations*, Cambridge: Cambridge University Press, 49–60.

Stiers, M. and Silberberg, A. (1974) "Lever-contact responses in rats:

automaintenance with and without a negative response-reinforcer dependency," *J. Exp. Anal. Behav.* 22: 497–506.

Stimbert, V. E., Schaeffer, R. W., and Grimsley, D. L. (1966) "Acquisition of an imitative response in rats," *Psychon. Sci.* 5: 339–40.

Stonebraker, T. B. and Rilling, M. (1981) "Control of delayed matching-to-sample performance using directed forgetting techniques," *Anim. Learn. Behav.* 9: 196–201.

Stricher, E. M. and Adair, E. R. (1966) "Body fluid balance, taste and postprandial factors in schedule-induced polydipsia," *J. Comp. Physiol. Psychol.* 62: 449–54.

Strong, P. N. and Hedges, M. (1966) "Comparative studies in simple oddity learning: 1. Cats, raccoons, monkeys and chimpanzees," *Psychon. Sci.* 5: 13–14.

Suboski, M. D. (1984) "Stimulus configuration and valence-enhanced pecking by neonatal chicks," *Learn. Motiv.* 15: 118–26.

Suboski, M. D. and Bartashunas, C. (1984) "Mechanisms for social transmission of pecking to neonatal chicks," *J. Exp. Psychol.: Anim. Behav. Processes*, in press.

Sullivan, L. (1979) "Long-delay learning with exteroceptive cues and exteroceptive reinforcement in rats," *Australian Journal of Psychology* 31: 21–32.

Sutherland, N. S. (1957) "Visual discrimination of orientation by octopus," *British Journal of Psychology* 48: 55–71.

Sutherland, N. S. and Mackintosh, N. J. (1971) *Mechanisms of Animal Discrimination Learning*, New York: Academic Press.

Szakmary, G. A. (1977) "A note regarding conditioned attention theory," *Bull. Psychon. Soc.* 69: 142–4.

Taukulis, H. K. and Revusky, S. (1975) "Odor as a conditioned inhibitor: applicability of the Rescorla–Wagner model to feeding behavior," *Learn. Motiv.* 6: 11–27.

Taylor, R. J. (1984) "Foraging in the eastern gray kangaroo and the wallaby," *J. Anim. Ecol.* 53: 65–74.

Tempel, B. L., Bonini, D. R., Dawson, D. R., and Quinn, W. G. (1982) "Reward learning in normal and mutant drosophila," *Proceedings of the National Academy of Science, USA*, 80: 1482–6.

Terk, M. P. and Green, L. (1980) "Taste-aversion learning in the bat, *Carollia perspicillata*," *Behav. Neural Biol.* 28: 236–42.

Terman, M. (1970) "Discrimination of auditory intensity by rats," *J. Exp. Anal. Behav.* 13: 145–62.

Terrace, H. S. (1966) "Stimulus control," in W. K. Honig (ed.) *Operant Behavior: Areas of Research and Application*, New York: Appleton-Century-Crofts, 271–344.

—— (1979) *Nim*, New York: Knopf.

Terrace, H. S., Gibbon, J., Farrell, L., and Baldock, M. D. (1975) "Temporal factors influencing the acquisition of an autoshaped key peck," *Anim. Learn. Behav.* 3: 53–62.

Terrace, H. S., Petitto, L. A., Sanders, R. J., and Bever, T. G. (1979) "Can an ape create a sentence?" *Science* 206: 891–1201.

Terry, W. S. and Wagner, A. R. (1975) "Short-term memory for 'surprising' versus 'expected' unconditioned stimuli in Pavlovian conditioning," *J. Exp. Psychol.: Anim. Behav. Processes* 1: 122–33.

Testa, T. J. (1974) "Causal relationships and the acquisition of avoidance responses," *Psychol. Rev.* 81: 491–505.

(1975) "Effects of similarity of location and temporal intensity pattern of conditioned and unconditioned stimuli on the acquisition of conditioned suppression in rats," *J. Exp. Psychol.: Anim. Behav. Processes* 1: 114–21.

Testa, T. J. and Ternes, J. W. (1977) "Specificity of conditioning mechanisms in the modification of food preferences," in L. M. Barker, M. R. Best, and M. Domjan (eds) *Learning Mechanisms in Food Selection*, Waco, Tex.: Baylor University Press.

Thach, J. S. (1965) "Comparison of social and nonsocial reinforcing stimuli," *Proc. 73rd Am. Psychol. Assoc.*

Theios, J. (1963) "Simple conditioning as two-stage all-or-none learning," *Psychol. Rev.* 70: 403–17.

Thielcke-Poltz, H. and Thielcke, G. (1960) "Akustisches lernen vershieden alter schallisolierten amseln *Turdus merula L.*, und die entwicklung erlernter motive ohne und mit kunstlichem einfluss von testosteron," *Z. Tierpsychol.* 17: 211–44.

Thomas, D. R. and Switalski, R. W. (1966) "Comparison of stimulus generalization following variable-ratio and variable-interval training," *J. Exp. Psychol.* 71: 236–40.

Thomas, E. and Wagner, A. R. (1964) "Partial reinforcement of the classically conditioned eyelid response in the rabbit," *J. Comp. Physiol. Psychol.* 58: 157–9.

Thomas, G. (1974) "The influences of encountering a food object on subsequent searching behaviour in *Gasterosteus aculeatus L.*," *Anim. Behav.* 22: 941–52.

Thomas, R. K. and Boyd, M. G. (1973) "A comparison of *Cebus albifrons* and *Saimiri sciureus* on oddity performance," *Anim. Learn. Behav.* 1: 151–3.

Thomas, R. K., Fowlkes, D., and Vickery, J. D. (1980) "Conceptual numerousness judgments by squirrel monkeys," *American Journal of Psychology* 93: 247–57.

Thompson, C. R. and Church, R. M. (1980) "An explanation of the language of a chimpanzee," *Science* 208: 313–14.

Thompson, R. and McConnell, J. (1955) "Classical conditioning in the planarian, *Dugesia dorotocephala*," *J. Comp. Physiol. Psychol.* 48: 65–8.

Thompson, R. F. and Spencer, W. A. (1966) "Habituation: a model phenomenon for the study of neuronal substrates of behavior," *Psychol. Rev.* 173: 16–43.

Thompson, T. and Bloom, W. (1966) "Aggressive behavior and extinction-induced response-rate increase," *Psychon. Sci.* 5: 335–6.

Thompson, T. and Sturm, T. (1965) "Classical conditioning of aggressive display in Siamese fighting fish," *J. Exp. Anal. Behav.* 8: 397–403.

Thorpe, W. H. (1945) "The evolutionary significance of habitat selection," *J. Anim. Ecol.* 14: 67–70.

(1963) *Learning and Instinct in Animals*, London: Methuen.

Nature, Garden City, NY: Doubleday.

Threlkeld, S. F., Bentley, L., Yeung, A., and Henriksen, K. (1976) "Enhanced competence in the negotiation of a T-maze by *Drosophila melanogaster* in response to possible food reward," *Canad. J. Zool.* 54: 896–900.

Timberlake, W. (1983a) "The functional organization of appetitive behavior: behavior systems and learning," in M. D. Zeiler and P. Harzem (eds) *Advances in Analysis of Behavior*, vol. 3: *Biological Factors in Learning*, Chichester: John Wiley.

(1983b) "Rats' responses to a moving object related to food or water: a behavior - systems analysis," *Anim. Learn. Behav.* 11: 309-20.

(1984) "Behavior regulation and learned performance: some misapprehensions and disagreements," *J. Exp. Anal. Behav.* 41: 355-75.

Timberlake, W. and Grant, D. L. (1975) "Autoshaping in rats to the presentation of another rat predicting food," *Science* 190: 690-2.

Timberlake, W. and Lucas, G. A. (1985) "The basis of superstitious behavior: chance contingency, stimulus substitution or appetitive behavior?" *J. Exp. Anal. Behav.* 44: 279-99.

Timberlake, W., Wahl, G., and King, D. (1982) "Stimulus and response contingencies in the misbehavior of rats," *J. Exp. Psychol.: Anim. Behav. Processes* 8: 62-85.

Tinbergen, N. (1951) *The Study of Instinct*, Oxford: Clarendon Press.

(1952) "'Derived' activities: their causation, biological significance, origin, and emancipation during evolution," *Q. Rev. Biol.* 27: 1-32.

(1960) "The natural control of insects in pinewoods. I. Factors influencing the intensity of predation by song birds," *Arch. Neerl. Zool.* 13: 265-343.

(1964) "The evolution of signaling devices," in W. Etkin (ed.) *Social Behavior and Organization among Vertebrates*, Chicago: University of Chicago Press, 206-30.

Tinbergen, N. and Van Iersel, J. J. A. (1947) "'Displacement reactions' in the three-spined stickleback," *Behav.* 1: 56-63.

Tolman, E. C. (1933) " Sign-Gestalt or conditioned-reflex?" *Psychol. Rev.* 40: 246-55.

(1948) "Cognitive maps in rats and men," *Psychol. Rev.* 55: 189-208.

Tomie, A. (1981) "Effect of unpredictable food on the subsequent acquisition of autoshaping: analysis of the context-blocking hypothesis," in C. M. Locurto, H. S. Terrace, and J. Gibbon (eds) *Autoshaping and Conditioning Theory*, New York: Academic Press, 181-215.

Tompkins, L., Siegel, R. W., Gailey, D. A., and Hall, J. C. (1983) "Conditioned courtship in Drosophila and its mediation by association of chemical cues," *Behav. Genet.*

Tosney, B. and Hoyle, G. (1977) "Computer-controlled learning in a simple system," *Proc. Roy. Soc. Lond.* 195: 365.

Trapold, M. A. (1970) "Are expectancies based upon different positive reinforcing events discriminably different?" *Learn. Motiv.* 1: 129-40.

Trapold, M. A., Carlson, J. G., and Myers, W. A. (1965) "The effect of noncontingent fixed- and variable-interval reinforcement upon subsequent acquisition of the fixed-interval scallop," *Psychon. Sci.* 2: 261-2.

Trapold, M. A. and Overmier, J. B. (1972) "The second learning process in instrumental learning," in A. H. Black and W. F. Prokasy (eds) *Classical Conditioning II: Current Theory and Research*, New York: Appleton-Century-Crofts.

Trillmich, F. (1976) "Learning experiments on individual recognition in budgerigars (*Melopsittacus undulatus*)," *Z. Tierpsychol.* 41: 372-95.

Turcek, F. and Kelso, L. (1968) "Ecological aspects of food transportation and storage in the Corvidae," *Comm. Behav. Biol.* 1: 277-97.

Ulrich, R. E. and Azrin, N. H. (1962) "Reflexive fighting in response to aversive stimulation," *J. Exp. Anal. Behav.* 5: 511-20.

Ulrich, R. E., Johnston, M., Richardson, J., and Wolff, P. (1963) "The operant conditioning of fighting behavior in rats," *Psychol. Rec.* 13: 465–70.

Ulrich, R. E., Wolf, P. C., and Azrin, N. H. (1964) "Shock as an elicitor of intra- and inter-species fighting behavior," *Anim. Behav.* 12: 14–15.

Van Hemel, P. E. (1972) "Aggression as a reinforcer: operant behavior in the mouse-killing rat," *J. Exp. Anal. Behav.* 17: 237–45.

Van Iersel, J. J. A. and Bol, A. C. A. (1958) "Preening of two tern species: a study on displacement activities," *Behav.* 13: 1–88.

Van Lawick-Goodall, J. (1968) "Behavior of free-living chimpanzees of the Gombe Stream area," *Anim. Behav. Monogr.* 1: 165–311.

Van Sommers, P. (1962) "Oxygen-motivated behavior in the goldfish, *Carassius auratus,*" *Science* 137: 678–9.

(1963) "Air-motivated behavior in the turtle," *J. Comp. Physiol. Psychol.* 56: 590–6.

Van Valen, L. (1973) "Two modes of evolution," *Nature* 252: 298–300.

Vander Wall, S. B. (1982) "An experimental analysis of cache recovery in Clark's Nutcracker," *Anim. Behav.* 30: 84–94.

Vardaris, R. M. and Fitzgerald, R. D. (1969) "Effects of partial reinforcement on a classically conditioned eyeblink response in dogs," *J. Comp. Physiol. Psychol.* 67: 531–4.

Vaughan, W., Jr. (1981) "Melioration, matching, and maximization," *J. Exp. Anal. Behav.* 36: 141–9.

Villarreal, J. (1967) "Schedule-induced pica," Paper presented to the Eastern Psychological Association, Boston.

Von Frisch, K. (1967) *The Dance Language and Orientation of Bees*, Cambridge, Mass.: Harvard University Press.

(1972) *Bees, Their Vision, Chemical Senses and Language*, Ithaca, NY: Cornell University Press.

(1974) "Decoding the language of the bee," *Science* 185: 663–8.

Waage, J. K. (1979) "Foraging for patchily-distributed hosts by the parasitoid, *Nemeritus canescens,*" *J. Anim. Ecol.* 48: 353–71.

Waddington, K. D. and Holden, L. R. (1979) "Optimal foraging: on flower selection by bees," *Am. Nat.* 114: 96.

Wagner, A. R. (1978) "Expectancies and the priming of STM," in S. H. Hulse, H. Fowler, and W. K. Honig (eds) *Cognitive Processes in Animal Behavior*, Hillsdale, NJ: Erlbaum.

(1981) "SOP: a model of automatic memory processing in animal behavior," in N. E. Spear and R. R. Miller (eds) *Information Processing in Animals: Memory Mechanisms*, Hillsdale, NJ: Erlbaum.

Wagner, A. R. and Larew, M. B. (1985) "Opponent processes and Pavlovian inhibition," in R. R. Miller and N. E. Spear (eds) *Information Processing in Animals: Conditioned Inhibition*, Hillsdale, NJ: Erlbaum.

Wagner, A. R. and Rescorla, R. A. (1972) "Inhibition in Pavlovian conditioning: application of a theory," in R. A. Boakes and M. S. Halliday (eds) *Inhibition and Learning*, London: Academic Press, 301–36.

Wagner, A. R., Siegel, L. S., and Fein, G. G. (1967) "Extinction of a conditioned fear as a function of percentage reinforcement," *J. Comp. Physiol. Psychol.* 63: 160–4.

Wagner, A. R., Siegel, S., Thomas, E., and Ellison, G. D. (1964) "Reinforcement history and the extinction of a classical reward response," *J. Comp. Physiol. Psychol.* 58: 354–8.

Wagner, A. R. and Terry, W. S. (1975) "Backward conditioning to a CS following an expected vs a surprising UCS," *Animal Learning and Behavior* 3: 370–4.

Wagner, H. (1982) "Flow-field variables trigger landing in flies," *Nature* 297: 147–8.

Wahlsten, D. L. and Cole, M. (1972) "Classical and avoidance training of leg flexion in the dog," in A. H. Black and W. F. Prokasy (eds) *Classical Conditioning II: Current Research and Theory*, New York: Appleton-Century-Crofts.

Wahrenberger, D. L., Antle, C. E., and Klimko, L. (1977) "Bayesian rules for the two-armed bandit," *Biometrika* 64: 172–4.

Wall, M. (1965) "Discrete-trial analysis of fixed-interval discrimination," *J. Comp. Physiol. Psychol.* 60: 70–5.

Wallace, J., Steinert, P. A., Scobie, S. R., and Spear, N. E. (1980) "Stimulus modality and short-term memory in rats," *Anim. Learn. Behav.* 8: 10–16.

Walters, E. T., Carew, T. J., and Kandel, E. R. (1981a) "Associative learning in *Aplysia californica*," *Proceedings of the National Academy of Science, USA* 76: 6675–9.

(1981b) "Associative learning in Aplysia: evidence for conditioned fear in an invertebrate," *Science* 211: 504–6.

Walther, F. R. (1969) "Flight behavior and avoidance of predators in Thomson's Gazelle (*Gazella thomsoni*)," *Behav.* 34: 184–221.

Warren, J. M. (1960) "Reversal learning by paradise fish (*Macropodus opercularis*)," *J. Comp. Physiol. Psychol.* 53: 376–8.

Washburn, S. L. and DeVore, I. (1961) "The social life of baboons," *Sci. Am.* 204: 62–71.

Wasserman, E. A. (1973) "Pavlovian conditioning with heat reinforcement produces stimulus-directed pecking in chicks," *Science* 181: 875–7.

(1981) "Response evocation in autoshaping: contributions of cognitive and comparative-evolutionary analyses to an understanding of directed action," in C. M. Locurto, H. S. Terrace, and J. Gibbon (eds) *Autoshaping and Conditioning Theory*, New York: Academic Press.

Wasserman, E. A., Franklin, S. R., and Hearst, E. (1974) "Pavlovian appetitive contingencies and approach versus withdrawal to conditioned stimuli in pigeons," *J. Comp. Physiol. Psychol.* 86: 616–27.

Wasserman, E. A., Hunter, N. B., Gutowski, K. A., and Bader, S. A. (1975) "Autoshaping chicks with heat reinforcement: the role of stimulus-reinforcer and response reinforcer relations," *J. Exp. Psychol.* 104: 158–89.

Waxman, H. M. and McCleave, J. D. (1978) "Autoshaping in the archer fish (*Toxotes chatareus*)," *Behav. Biol.* 22: 541–4.

Wearden, J. H. and Burgess, I. S. (1982) "Matching since Baum," *J. Exp. Anal. Behav.* 38: 339–48.

Weiner, H. (1962) "Some effects of response cost upon human operant behavior," *J. Exp. Anal. Behav.* 5: 201–8.

(1969) "Controlling human fixed-interval performance," *J. Exp. Anal. Behav.* 12: 349–73.

(1972) "Controlling human fixed-interval performance with fixed-ratio responding or differential reinforcement of low-rate responding in mixed schedules," *Psychon. Sci.* 26: 191–2.

Weissman, A. (1962) "Nondiscriminated avoidance behavior in a large sample of rats," *Psychol. Rep.* 10: 591–600.

Weitzman, R. A. (1967) "Positional matching in rats and fish," *J. Comp. Physiol. Psychol.* 63: 54–9.

Wells, M. J. and Young, J. Z. (1968) "Learning with delayed rewards in Octopus," *Z. Vgl. Physiol.* 61: 103–28.

Werboff, J. and Lloyd, T. (1963) "Avoidance conditioning in the guppy (*Lebistes reticulatus*)," *Psychol. Rep.* 12: 615–18.

Werner, E. E. and Hall, D. J. (1974) "Optimal foraging and size selections of prey by the bluegill sunfish (*Lepomis macrochirus*)," *Ecol.* 55: 1042–52.

(1976) "Niche shifts in sunfishes: experimental evidence and significance," *Science* 191: 404–6.

(1979) "Foraging efficiency and habitat switching in competing sunfishes," *Ecol.* 60: 256–64.

Werner, E. E. and Mittelbach, G. F. (1981) "Optimal foraging: field tests of diet choice and habitat switching," *Am. Zool.* 21: 813–29.

Werner, E. E., Mittelbach, G. G., Hall, D. J., and Gilliam, J. F. (1983) "Experimental tests of optimal habitat use in fish: the role of relative habitat profitability," *Ecol.* 64: 1525–39.

Wesley, F. (1961) "The number concept: a phylogenetic review," *Psychol. Bull.* 58: 420–8.

Westbrook, R. F. (1973) "Failure to obtain positive contrast when pigeons press a bar," *J. Exp. Anal. Behav.* 20: 499–510.

Westbrook, R. F., Clarke, J. C., and Provost, S. (1980) "Long-delay learning in the pigeon: flavor, color, and flavor-mediated color aversions," *Behav. Neural Biol.* 28: 398–407.

White, K., Juhasz, J. B., and Wilson, P. J. (1973) "Is man no more than this? Evaluative bias in interspecies comparison," *J. Hist. Behav. Sci.* 9: 203–12.

Wilcoxon, H. C., Dragoin, W. B., and Kral, P. A. (1969) "Differential conditioning to visual and gustatory cues in quail and rat: illness induced aversion," *Psychon. Sci.* 17: 52.

(1971) "Illness-induced aversions in rat and quail: relative salience of visual and gustatory cues," *Science* 171: 826–8.

Wilkie, D. A. and McDonald, A. C. (1978) "Autoshaping in the rat with electrical stimulation of the brain as the US," *Physiol. Behav.* 21: 325–8.

Wilkie, D. M., Spetch, M. L., and Chew, L. (1981) "The ring dove's short-term memory capacity for spatial information," *Anim. Behav.* 29: 639–41.

Williams, B. A. (1986) "Reinforcement, choice, and response strength," in R. C. Atkinson, R. J. Herrnstein, G. Lindzey, and R. D. Luce (eds) *Steven's Handbook of Experimental Psychology*, 2nd edn, New York: John Wiley.

Williams, D. R. (1965) "Classical conditioning and incentive motivation," in W. F. Prokasy (ed.) *Classical Conditioning: a Symposium*, New York: Appleton-Century-Crofts, 340–57.

(1981) "Biconditional behavior: conditioning without constraint," in C. M. Locurto, H. S. Terrace, and J. Gibbon (eds) *Autoshaping and Conditioning Theory*, New York: Academic Press.

Williams, D. R. and Williams, H. (1969) "Automaintenance in the pigeon: sustained pecking despite contingent nonreinforcement," *J. Exp. Anal. Behav.* 12: 511–20.

Willis, R. D. (1969) "The partial reinforcement of conditioned suppression," *J. Comp. Physiol. Psychol.* 68: 289–95.

Wilson, B. (1978) "Autoshaping in pigeons and corvids," Ph.D. thesis, University of Sussex.

Wilson, G. D. (1968) "Reversal of differential GSR conditioning by instructions," *J. Exp. Psychol.* 76: 491–3.

Wilson, M. P. and Keller, F. J. (1953) "On the selective reinforcement of spaced responses," *J. Comp. Physiol. Psychol.* 46: 190–3.

Wilson, W. A., Oscar, M., and Bitterman, M. E. (1964a) "Probability-learning in the monkey," *Q. J. Exp. Psychol.* 16: 163–5.

(1964b) "Visual probability-learning in the monkey," *Psychon. Sci.* 1: 71–2.

Wilz, K. J. (1970) "Causal and functional analysis of dorsal pricking and nest activity in the courtship of the three-spined stickleback *Gasterosteus aculeatus*," *Anim. Behav.* 18: 115–24.

Wodinsky, J., Behrend, E. R., and Bitterman, M. E. (1962) "Avoidance-conditioning in two species of fish," *Anim. Behav.* 10: 76–8.

Wodinsky, J. and Bitterman, M. E. (1953) "The solution of oddity-problems by the rat," *American Journal of Psychology* 66: 137–40.

Wolach, A. H., Breuning, S. E., Roccaforte, P., and Solhkhan, N. (1977) "Overshadowing and blocking in a goldfish (*Carassius auratus*) respiratory conditioning situation," *Psychol. Rec.* 27: 693–702.

Wolff, J. R. (1981) "Some morphogenetic aspects of the development of the central nervous system," in K. Immelmann, G. W. Barlow, M. Main, and L. Petrinovich (eds) *Behavioral Development*, New York: Cambridge University Press, 164–90.

Wolgin, D. L. (1982) "Motivation, activation, and behavioral integration," in R. L. Isaacson and N. E. Spear (eds) *The Expression of Knowledge*, New York: Plenum.

Woodard, W. T. and Bitterman, M. E. (1973) "Further experiments on probability learning in goldfish," *Anim. Learn. Behav.* 1: 25–8.

Woodruff, G. and Starr, M. D. (1978) "Autoshaping of initial feeding and drinking reactions in newly hatched chicks," *Anim. Learn. Behav.* 6: 265–72.

Woodruff, G. and Williams, D. R. (1976) "The associative relation underlying autoshaping in the pigeon," *J. Exp. Anal. Behav.* 26: 1–13.

Woods, R. A., Vasselli, J. R., and Milam, K. M. (1977) "Iron appetite and latent learning in rats," *Physiol. & Behav.* 19: 623–6.

Yarczower, M. and Hazlett, L. (1977) "Evolutionary scales and anagenesis," *Psychol. Bull.* 84: 1088–97.

Yaremko, R. M., Boice, R., and Thompson, R. W. (1969) "Classical and avoidance conditioning of the nictitating membrane in frogs (*Rana pipiens*) and toads (*Bufo americanus*)," *Psychon. Sci.* 16: 162–4.

Yeatman, F. R. and Hirsch, J. (1971) "Attempted replication of, and selective breeding for, instrumental conditioning of *Drosophila melanogaster*," *Anim. Behav.* 18: 454–62.

Yehle, A., Dauth, G., and Schneiderman, N. (1967) "Correlates of heart-rate classical conditioning in curarized rabbits," *J. Comp. Physiol. Psychol.* 64: 98–104.

Yori, J. G. (1978) "Active one-way avoidance to a heat aversive stimulus in Tegu lizards (*Tupinambus teguixen*)," *Behav. Biol.* 23: 100–6.

Zach, R. and Falls, J. B. (1976) "Ovenbird (Aves: Parulidae) hunting behavior in a patchy environment: an experimental study," *Canad. J. Zool.* 54: 1863–79.

Zahorik, D. M. (1977) "Associative and nonassociative factors in learned food preferences," in L. M. Barker, M. R. Best, and M. Domjan (eds) *Learning Mechanisms in Food Selection*, Waco, Tex.: Baylor University Press.

Zahorik, D. M. and Houpt, K. A. (1977) "The concept of nutritional wisdom: applicability of laboratory learning models to large herbivores," in L. M. Barker, M. R. Best, and M. Domjan (eds) *Learning Mechanisms in Food Selection*, Waco, Tex.: Baylor University Press.

Zahorik, D. M. and Maier, S. F. (1969) "Appetitive conditioning with recovery from thiamine deficiency as the unconditioned stimulus," *Psychon. Sci.* 17: 309–10.

Zamble, E. (1967) "Classical conditioning of excitement anticipatory to food reward," *J. Comp. Physiol. Psychol.* 63: 526–9.

(1969) "Conditioned motivation patterns in instrumental responding of rats," *J. Comp. Physiol. Psychol.* 69: 536–43.

(1973) "Augmentation of eating following a signal for feeding in rats," *Learn. Motiv.* 4: 138–47.

Zamble, E., Baxter, D. J., and Baxter, L. (1980) "Influences of conditioned incentive stimuli on water intake," *Canadian Journal of Psychology* 34: 82–5.

Zamble, E., Hadad, G. M., Mitchell, J. B., and Cutmore, T. R. H. (1985) "Pavlovian conditioning of sexual arousal: first- and second-order effects," *J. Exp. Psychol.: Anim. Behav. Processes* 11: 598–610.

Zener, K. (1937) "The significance of behavior accompanying conditioned salivary secretion for theories of the conditioned response," *American Journal of Psychology* 50: 384–403.

Zentall, T. R. and Hogan, D. E. (1975) "Concept learning in the pigeon: transfer to new matching and nonmatching stimuli," *American Journal of Psychology* 88: 233–44.

(1978) "Same/different concept learning in the pigeon: the effect of negative instances and prior adaptation to transfer stimuli," *J. Exp. Anal. Behav.* 30: 177–86.

Zentall, T. R., Hogan, D. E., and Edwards, C. A. (1984) "Cognitive factors in conditional learning by pigeons," in H. L. Roitblat, T. G. Bever, anrd H. S. Terrace (eds) *Animal Cognition*, Hillsdale, NJ: Erlbaum.

Ziriax, J. M. and Silberberg, A. (1978) "Discrimination and emission of different key-peck durations in the pigeon," *J. Exp. Psychol.: Anim. Behav. Processes* 4: 1–21.

Zuriff, G. E. (1969) "Collateral responding during differential reinforcement of low rates," *J. Exp. Anal. Behav.* 12: 971–6.

Name index

Ackerman, P.T. 179
Ackil, J.E. 151
Adair, E.R. 85
Adams, C.D. 215, 216
Adams, D.K. 260
Alberts, J.R. 164
Alcock, J. 90
Alcock, N. 191
Alek, M. 123, 174
Alkon, D.L. 36, 38
Allen, J. 173
Allison, J. 227, 228, 230
Alloy, L.B. 52, 106
Amiro, T.W. 35, 41
Amsel, A. 216
Anderson, D.C. 174
Anger, D. 102
Anisman, H. 166, 225
Annable, A. 105
Annau, Z. 27
Antle, C.E. 243
Appignanesi, A.A. 175
Applewhite, P. 36
Armstrong, E.A. 90
Armstrong, G.D. 220
Armstrong, S. 232
Aronson, R.B. 244
Arulampalam, T. 52, 120
Ashmole, N.P. 20
Astratian, E.A. 220, 221
Atnip, G.W. 48, 104, 143, 209
Ayres, J.J.B. 218
Ayres, S.L. 227
Azrin, N.H. 86, 87, 89, 102, 168, 205, 223

Badar, S.A. 28, 44, 49, 141, 146, 153, 164
Badia, P. 180

Baer, D.M. 106
Baer, P.E. 51
Baerends, G.P. 156, 157, 193
Baerends-Van Roon, J. 193
Bagshaw, M. 109
Baker, A.G. 33, 174
Baker, P.A. 33
Balaz, M.A. 123, 180
Balda, R.P. 300
Baldock, M.D. 45
Ball, W. 165
Balsam, P. 31
Barash, D.P. 233
Barnes, R.A. 31, 173
Barnett, S.A. 151, 152, 157, 204
Baron, A. 108
Barrera, F.J. 31, 46, 47, 49, 143, 146, 149, 153, 154, 174, 205
Barrett, B.H. 106
Bartashunas, C. 194
Basmann, R. 230
Bateson, P.P.G. 259, 262, 263, 264
Battalio, R.C. 81, 230, 243
Baum, M. 210
Baum, W.M. 79
Baumbach, H.D. 166
Baumgardner, D.J. 283
Baxter, D.J. 177, 213, 214
Baxter, L. 177
Bayliss, J.R. 267
Beasty, A. 109
Beaton, R. 184
Bedford, J. 102
Behrend, E.R. 96, 284, 289
Bellingham, W.P. 47, 184, 187
Belovsky, G.E. 233, 242
Beninger, R.J. 104, 208

Species index

388

Subject index